The New Deal and the West

Handling thirty-foot steel penstock pipe by cableway for placement in the upper Nevada header tunnel of Boulder Dam. (B. D. Glaha photo, U.S. Bureau of Reclamation)

The New Deal and the West

Richard Lowitt

UNIVERSITY OF OKLAHOMA PRESS
NORMAN AND LONDON

Books by Richard Lowitt
George W. Norris: The Making of a Progressive, 1861–1912
(Syracuse, 1963; Westport, Conn., 1980)
George W. Norris: The Persistence of a Progressive, 1913–1933
(Champaign, 1971)
George W. Norris: The Triumph of a Progressive, 1933–1944
(Champaign, 1978)
America in Despression and War (St. Louis, 1979)
The New Deal and the West (Champaign, 1984; Norman, 1993)

Library of Congress Cataloging-in-Publication Data

Lowitt, Richard, 1922–
The New Deal and the West / Richard Lowitt.
p.   cm.
Originally published: Bloomington : Indiana University Press, c1984.
Originally published in series: The West in the twentieth century.
Includes bibliographical references and index.
ISBN 0-8061-2557-8
1. West (U.S.)—Economic conditions.   2. West (U.S.)—Economic
policy.   3. United States—Economic policy—1933–1945.   4. New
Deal, 1933–1939—West (U.S.)   I. Title.
HC107.A17L68   1993
338.978′009′043—dc20   93-15538
                                                                       CIP

The paper in this book meets the guidelines for permanence and
durability of the Committee on Production Guidelines for Book
Longevity of the Council on Library Resources, Inc.

1   2   3   4   5   6   7   8   9   10

For Ben Procter
who helped show me the way West
and for Robert E. Burke
who assumed I could find my own way

Contents

Illustrations

Preface to Paperback Edition

When *The New Deal and the West* was published in 1984, I, like many historians, was not yet fully cognizant of the environmental movement as it affected the writing of American history. Reflecting almost a decade later, I doubt that I would have devoted more attention had I known more. The main focus of *The New Deal and the West* was the impact of federal programs on a region devastated by drought, dust, and the Great Depression. Government, instead of being the enemy portrayed today by historians on both the right and the left, was (despite setbacks and mistakes) the salvation of the West in the 1930s. Rather than look at what came later and then blame failures and mistakes on the New Deal, one gets a better perspective by examining the West prior to the New Deal and then noting changes that occurred during a national emergency as grave as World War I. The role of the New Deal in "modernizing" the West, bringing it into the main currents of American life, then becomes more comprehensible.

By emphasizing problems and concerns largely unique to the West, as explained in the Introduction, I examined programs and policies more national in focus and did not seek a state-by-state approach. Rather I viewed the West as a series of subregions—the Great Plains, the Interior Basin, the Rocky Mountain West (what I called "Ickes' Inland Empire"), the Northwest, and California and the Southwest—and sought to examine New Deal programs within this context, giving some recognition to contradictory policies and internal conflicts among departments and agencies. I also examined silver, petroleum, water, and lumber, the plight of Indians, and other western concerns that involved New Deal administrators. I did not examine to any meaningful extent urban areas, a deficiency remedied in part by William H. Mullins in *The Depression and the Urban West Coast* (Indiana University Press, 1991). I did read John A. Adams's *Damming the Colorado: The Rise of the Lower Colorado River Authority, 1933–1939* (Texas A&M University Press, 1990) in manuscript form but—my manuscript being in press at the time—could not incorporate a discussion of this important subject or the significant role of Lyndon Johnson.

On the whole I remain satisfied with this volume and am pleased that the University of Oklahoma Press agreed to publish a paperback edition. Their doing so provided me with an opportunity to tidy the manuscript by clearing mistakes grammatical and otherwise. And I must note my delight in John Drayton, editor-in-chief at the Press, who with insight, understanding, and subtle humor encouraged my effort in securing a paperback edition.

RICHARD LOWITT

Norman, Oklahoma

Preface to the First Edition

Several years ago when Martin Ridge asked me to prepare this study as part of a series on the Twentieth Century West, I responded with alacrity. Little did I realize what lay ahead for me. I first explained that I had to finish my biography of George W. Norris. As soon as this project was completed, I would then attack the New Deal in the West. And we both agreed that my work on the biography of Senator Norris, especially his career during the New Deal, the focus of the last volume, would give me a head start on the new project. It did, and it did not. Researching Norris's career gave me an insight and understanding into the issues and concerns affecting his Nebraska constituents during the decade of the 1930s. But was the West during the New Deal years merely Nebraska writ large? Was the West a vast region with common problems and were its people and its politics similar in general to those with which I was familiar in the Cornhusker State? And how does one define the West in the years of Franklin D. Roosevelt's New Deal?

Obviously I had much to learn; and after floundering for too many months I recognized that general research into the history of western states would not suffice and that a more formal and rigid structure was necessary because an examination of individual states would be an interminable process. Granted it would yield much valuable information about state and local developments as well as about the New Deal, but such a volume could not possibly fit within the scope of the series as outlined by the general editor.

First, I had to decide upon a definition of the West. This was not difficult because I made an arbitrary decision. The West I would examine would follow the more or less traditional twentieth-century boundaries and include all the states west of the first tier of states bordering the Mississippi River on the east. Equally easy was my decision to abandon a state-by-state approach for one that would examine New Deal agencies and programs as they affected the West. This was further refined to those agencies and programs that centered more or less exclusively on the West: namely programs and policies of the United States Department of Agriculture and the Department of the Interior. Other agencies and their activities would not be ignored, and the focus of the study would concentrate on the federal impact in the West during the New Deal years.

These decisions necessitated further definition of regions within the West. Since programs of the Department of Agriculture predominated in the Great Plains states and those of the Department of the Interior in the mountain and Great Basin states (what I call Ickes's Inland Empire), there remained the difficult problem of finding a meaningful way to examine the impact of the New Deal on the Pacific slope. It was after I was well along with drafting the early chapters that, after sorting and contemplating the mound of material I had accumulated on the Pacific slope states, I discerned a way of handling these states. The Pacific Northwest, more so than any other part of the country with the possible exception of the Tennessee Valley, represented the planned promised land where the New Deal helped transform the vision of regional planners and others into reality. This decision left me with the problem of California. The obvious answer, which I was reluctant to accept at the outset because it seemed too apparent, was that California, following Carey McWilliams, was the Great Exception. But the more I probed, the more I recognized the validity of McWilliams's thesis. California *was* different, partly in magnitude and diversity but also in the nature of its concerns and problems during the New Deal years.

My approach to the New Deal in the West then fell naturally into place. Readers should keep my approach in mind and not expect, for example, a full discussion, say, of labor unrest in California, of WPA projects in Idaho, of party politics in Colorado, of the Tri-County project in Nebraska. Labor unions, WPA projects, politics, and water projects will all be discussed—some in considerable detail—along with many other topics, all with the purpose of illustrating the impact of the New Deal in the West.

A further problem, one which I quickly resolved, was how to define the New Deal years. This problem, of course, was defined for me by the President himself who, with the onset of war in Europe in September 1939, more and more directed his attention and that of his administration to international affairs and defense preparations. Domestic considerations would yield to more pressing foreign relations. The scope of this volume is on the years 1932 through 1940, from the campaign and election of Franklin D. Roosevelt in 1932 roughly to the cancellation of his proposed trip to the West in the early fall of 1940 and his third-term campaign.

A volume such as this one could not have been written without the support and assistance of numerous individuals. At the outset it quickly dawned upon me, as already suggested, that I was entering *terra incognita*. To be sure, some scholars have probed aspects of the history of the twentieth-century West. There are some monographs and several biographies, but, like my study of George W. Norris, they examine state history and not the history of the region in an overall way. There are, too, several monographs that examine regional themes such as petroleum policy and the development of the Colorado River, but to the best of my knowledge there is only one text that examines the American West in the twentieth century. And its distinguished author, Gerald D. Nash, would be among the first to admit that much about the West in the twentieth century remains to be researched by serious scholars. For the past few years, chiefly at meetings of the Western History Association, we have held long, pleasant—and for me, at least—stimulating and fruitful conversations.

Another scholar who has stimulated my interest and expanded my horizon of understanding about the twentieth-century West is Gene M. Gressley. The depth and range of his knowledge continues to amaze and impress me. Moreover, Gressley has always taken time out from his busy schedule to answer my requests for information and to forward reprints of his exciting articles. And, like Gerald Nash, he is among the most delightful of dining companions because the conversation is always pleasant, provocative, and laced with a keen sense of humor.

Linda J. Lear, a former student, is another person who assisted me. She greatly facilitated both my research and understanding of the petroleum industry and the way Harold L. Ickes coped with its problems early in the New Deal. Ickes is a key figure in this volume. My research convinced me that only a careful, full-scale, scholarly biography, such as Professor Lear has underway, can do justice to the significant role of Ickes in the West and elsewhere during his lengthy tenure as Secretary of the Interior.

Libraries and librarians, as would be expected, have been of inestimable assistance. First and foremost are David Wigdor and the late Fred Coker and his staff in the Manuscript Division of the Library of Congress. Wigdor, as Chief of the Recent Manuscripts Section, and Coker and his associates in the Reading Room (now located in sumptuous quarters in Madison Building) continue in the footsteps of their distinguished predecessors in making the Manuscript Division one of the most pleasant and now comfortable places for scholars to work.

And the same can be said for William I. Emerson, Director, and Frances Seeber and the staff in the Reading Room of the Franklin D. Roosevelt Library at Hyde Park. They went out of their way to be of assistance. Frances Seeber extended help beyond the borders of the library.

The library at Iowa State University, since my arrival in the late 1970s, continues to surprise me with the richness of its collections. It has one of the better collections of government documents and periodicals in the country. It possesses virtually every publication, and they are almost endless, of the United States Department of Agriculture. Consequently, aside from trips to the repositories mentioned above, I was able to conduct most of my research on my home campus, facilitated by research grants. Vice President Daniel J. Zaffarano and

Dean Norman Jacobsen provided mini-grants through the Research Council that allowed me to extensively photocopy items in the university collections, to travel to both Hyde Park and Washington, and to have items copied from collections in the Franklin D. Roosevelt Library and the Manuscript Division of the Library of Congress.

I am particularly fortunate in having colleagues whose research interests parallel or relate to mine. George McJimsey shared with me some of his research notes on Harry L. Hopkins, whose biography he is now preparing. Both Richard Kirkendall and Richard Kottman responded graciously to my queries for information on topics and issues where their breadth and depth of knowledge exceeds mine. Members of the Vigilante Group within the history department gave a paper expressing some of my ideas a thorough critical examination and helped sharpen my focus on some of them.

Other friends too numerous to mention have been equally helpful. The following, however, merit a special note of thanks. Robert E. Burke of the University of Washington responded in writing to my queries and assisted my understanding of the Central Valley Project by sending me a set of documents pertaining to the project. So too did Rodman Paul, emeritus of the California Institute of Technology. He forwarded a Social Science Working Paper examining a controversy affecting this project that was presented on his campus. Darlis Miller of New Mexico State University graciously responded to my queries and photocopied articles from journals the Iowa State University Library does not possess in a complete file. And David Hamilton, a graduate student at the University of Iowa, enhanced many a summer break from our scholarly chores with stimulating conversation about our respective and related research and writing.

The manuscript was typed primarily by two patient typists, experts at deciphering my all-but-incomprehensible scrawl: Dorothy Ann Wallize and Audrey Burton. Virginia D. Ollis, a most effective copy editor, made suggestions which helped turn the manuscript into a better book; and I am indebted to Mary Jane Seaburg for her preparation of the comprehensive index. Finally, I need to express my thanks and appreciation to Carole Kennedy, whose masterful day-by-day running of the department makes it possible for me to pursue scholarly endeavors and at the same time function effectively as chairman.

The New Deal and the West

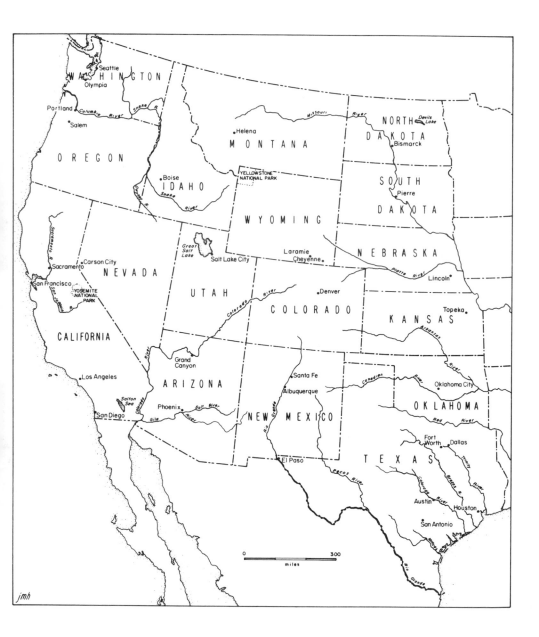

Chapter 1

1932: The West
and FDR

FRANKLIN DELANO ROOSEVELT on January 23, 1932, authorized the Democratic Central Committee of North Dakota to enter his name in their preferential party primary and thereby formally launched his campaign for the presidency. It officially began in the West, and his campaign strategy placed heavy reliance on this region. Roosevelt gained the nomination only after he was assured of the support of western delegations, and he made a big trip to the Pacific coast after receiving his party's nomination. Western politicians of both parties endorsed him, and several played instrumental roles at varying stages of the campaign. As a result of these endeavors, Roosevelt learned much about the West, its people, and their problems. He made several promises during the campaign indicating his concern about issues affecting the West, and he selected several prominent westerners for key places in his administration after his resounding victory. He carried every Western state.

Before formally launching his campaign by authorizing his party's leaders in North Dakota to enter his name in the primary, Roosevelt had been sounding western sentiment. Indeed, he regarded western support as essential to his presidential ambitions. In the summer of 1931 his "political drummer," James A. Farley, armed "with a Rand-McNally map of the United States, a flock of train schedules, and the latest available list of Democratic National Committee members and state chairmen," set off on a journey to the Pacific coast to sound out sentiment on behalf of his chief. On a hot July afternoon in a diner in Aberdeen, South Dakota, Farley heard stated most forcefully what he was to hear again and again on his trip. William W. Howes, the national committeeman, plumped his fist on the table and growled, "Farley, I'm damned tired of backing losers. In my opinion, Roosevelt can sweep the country, and I'm going to support him."[1]

In Montana and Washington support was particularly strong for Farley's chief, but in California he ran into a problem that would have to be finally overcome before Roosevelt could secure his party's nomination; namely, California politicians were inclined to endorse the former secretary of the treasury and son-in-law of Woodrow Wilson, William Gibbs McAdoo, as a favorite-son candidate. A similar situation arose in Texas where the Speaker of the House of Representatives, John Nance Garner, received the endorsement of his state's delegation. But Farley did not visit Texas on this trip and would learn of this development at a later date. Everywhere in his talks with state, county, and local political leaders in the West, Farley tried to discourage this favorite-son tactic, though he recognized it as an important political bargaining chip. Nevertheless, he returned from this trip convinced that "Democratic leaders in the Middle West and Far West were turning to the New York executive because they felt he had the political appeal which a candidate must have to be successful."[2]

By the fall of 1931, several western senators, including Burton K. Wheeler of Montana and Clarence C. Dill of Washington, had already announced their support of Roosevelt's candidacy. Earlier, in March, at a conference of progressives in Washington, Republican Senator George W. Norris of Nebraska proclaimed that "another Roosevelt in the White House" was needed to help restore prosperity and dignity to the depression-ridden nation. Thus even before the campaign year of 1932 started, there was considerable western support for Roosevelt. His January 23, 1932, letter to the chairman of the North Dakota Democratic Central Committee was necessary to make official a slate of delegates committed to Roosevelt in the primary.

As the political pace quickened in 1932, Governor William H. Murray of Oklahoma and Speaker Garner joined the several candidates seeking the Democratic nomination. Garner had the support of publisher William Randolph Hearst, a power base in the Texas delegation, and close ties with McAdoo, who endorsed his candidacy in February. And Garner won the California primary, thereby assuring him the initial support of the California delegation to the Democratic National Convention scheduled to meet in Chicago in June. At the convention it took four ballots to secure the nomination for Roosevelt. Western delegates played a key role in his victory.[3]

Thomas J. Walsh, senior United States senator from Montana, who upon the insistence of Senators Dill, Wheeler and others became the choice of the Roosevelt leaders, was approved by the delegates as permanent chairman of the convention by a close vote, 626 to 528. Arthur F. Mullen of Nebraska, who was convinced "the Roosevelt boom was spreading like prairie fire through the West," served as the floor manager for the Roosevelt forces, while Joseph C. O'Mahoney of Wyoming was one of the Roosevelt leaders serving on the Resolutions Committee responsible for the party platform. The committee was chaired by former Senator Gilbert M. Hitchcock of Nebraska, also a Roosevelt supporter. In addition, Farley selected J. Bruce Kremer of Montana as the Roosevelt forces' candidate for chairman of the Rules Committee.

As the convention got underway, Roosevelt leaders constantly wooed William Gibbs McAdoo with the hope of winning over California's 44 delegates, ostensibly pledged to Garner. William Randolph Hearst, whose California papers had played a role in the election of the delegates, was a bitter enemy of both Alfred E. Smith and Newton D. Baker, the leading contenders with Roosevelt for the nomination. Farley had numerous Roosevelt allies who knew Hearst contact him to use his influence in getting the California delegates to switch support. Farley himself phoned Hearst, who quickly condemned the effort to nominate Baker. But he remained noncommittal on the crucial question of supporting Roosevelt.[4]

It was in Washington on the Monday night of the convention week that an understanding was reached that won Roosevelt the nomination. The suggestion, hatched by Senators Harry Hawes of Missouri and Key Pittman of Nevada, quickly won the candidate's approval when related to him by phone. It called for a Roosevelt-Garner ticket. If approved it would win the California and Texas delegations, adding 90 votes to the Roosevelt camp. Farley, quickly informed of this decision, had to implement it by seeking out Congressman Sam Rayburn, Garner's campaign manager and the key man in the Texas delegation. And in Washington Hawes and others, including his long-time House colleague and poker-playing buddy, Edgar Howard of Nebraska, urged Garner to accept the vice-presidency, something he was most reluctant to do.[5]

Farley had to use all of his persuasive powers on Rayburn and others in urging a Roosevelt-Garner ticket. At the outset, Rayburn was noncommittal. He recognized that Roosevelt was the leading contender, and he did not wish for a long and bitter convention. But both Texas and California, he assured Farley, would be for Garner as long as he had a chance of winning the nomination. By Thursday of the convention week Rayburn told Farley that sometime after the third ballot, if it was clear that Garner could not get the nomination, he would then seek to switch the delegation to Roosevelt.[6]

After the third ballot, though Roosevelt was far in the lead, he still did not have the necessary two-thirds vote required for the nomination. Neither Texas nor California had wavered in their support for Speaker Garner. Farley realized that if a notable shift for Roosevelt did not occur on the fourth ballot, he would start to lose votes and Baker would benefit. Farley, therefore, sought out Sam Rayburn and made it clear that the Texas delegation was necessary if Roosevelt were to gain the nomination. Rayburn got the message, and Farley felt confident that Texas would shift on the next ballot. And Rayburn, once he received Garner's approval to release the Texas delegation, asked McAdoo to likewise release the California delegation. "Thus," as Farley later wrote, "Garner broke the deadlock and ensured Roosevelt's nomination."[7]

William Randolph Hearst also played a role in encouraging Garner to support Roosevelt. He wired George Rothwell Brown, one of his Washington correspondents and the author of a Garner campaign biography, to tell the Speaker that "nothing can now save the country but for him to throw his votes to Governor Roosevelt." Garner agreed and several hours later phoned Rayburn in Chicago to switch his delegates to Roosevelt.[8]

Rayburn, however, had a difficult time with the Texas delegation, many members of which had been selected after bitter battles over opponents favorable to Roosevelt. They were devoted to Garner and did not want to switch. After a tumultuous meeting and a very close vote, 54 to 51, the Texas delegation agreed to support Roosevelt. On the convention floor their task was made easier when McAdoo, before the roll call got underway, went to the platform and announced that the California delegation was switching to the governor of New York. The California caucus was as tumultuous as that of the Texas delegates. No agreement was reached, and it was not clear if Roosevelt could have gained a majority. Reluctantly, after much argument, an arrangement was agreed upon whereby a select committee of three delegates would confer with McAdoo and determine whom the delegation would support. On the fourth ballot McAdoo revealed their choice to the convention when he cast the delegation's 44 votes for the New York governor.[9]

That did it. Roosevelt won the nomination with the help of the West on the fourth ballot. And for vice president, though other westerners were mentioned: Senator Dill, Governor George H. Dern of Utah, Senator Wheeler—all early and devoted Roosevelt supporters—the entire strength of the Roosevelt organization was thrown behind the candidacy of John Nance Garner who was nominated by acclamation on the first ballot.

The West had played a prominent role in securing the nomination for Franklin Delano Roosevelt. In the campaign that followed, the candidate would reciprocate, tour the West, and make pledges and promises that the New Deal would try to fulfill. On his famous western tour Roosevelt delivered several important speeches with western problems and issues directly in mind, got a firsthand impression of the devastating impact of the depression throughout the region, and above all met the people: politicians, public figures, townfolk, and farmers of all kinds, enough of whom endorsed his candidacy so that he carried every western state in November.

Farmers and the plight of agriculture in the breadbasket of America were much in the candidate's thoughts as he launched his western trip. On September 14 in Topeka, Kansas, Roosevelt delivered one of his notable campaign addresses, heavily influenced in its earliest drafts by the ideas of M. L. Wilson, a professor at Montana State College. Among other things he called for equality for agriculture, planting trees on marginal lands as part of better land-use planning, and favorable refinancing of farm mortgages to reduce the possibility of foreclosure. Most important, Roosevelt assured rural America that he endorsed the view that farmers should be able to achieve price equality with industry through a self-liquidating, decentralized program that would curb production and otherwise cope with the dilemma of the surplus.

Three days later at Salt Lake City in the Mormon Tabernacle, Roosevelt delivered a lengthy but noncontroversial address in which he praised the efforts of Mormons in developing and reclaiming their seemingly barren lands. Roosevelt said, "If we can change the conditions of nature that made a place a desert, we ought to have faith in the possibility of changing the economic conditions sufficiently to bring the producer and the consumer more closely together for the benefit of each." Western producers, farmers, ranchers, miners, lumbermen, and others, once the New Deal got underway, would look forward to policies and programs designed to improve their economic conditions as they were brought into closer harmony with consumer interests. Roosevelt concluded his address saying, "That is the road to economic safety"and asking his audience "to choose that road."

His next address, this one devoted to the tariff, was in Seattle. But the speech that promised much for the West was delivered on September 21 in Portland where, in discussing public utilities and the development of hydroelectric power, Roosevelt called for "a national yardstick to prevent extortion against the public and to encourage the wider use of that servant of the people—electric power." While he did not call for public power, he strongly endorsed rigorous regulation and said that communities, if not satisfied with private services or rates, should have the right to construct and operate their own power plants. And, most important, he pledged that "the national hydroelectric power resources belonging to the people of the United States, or the several states, shall remain forever in their possession."

From this point on in his western tour Roosevelt donned a progressive mantle. In San Francisco at the Commonwealth Club on September 23, 1932, he forcefully proclaimed that "new conditions impose new requirements upon government and those who conduct government." In dramatic terms the candidate, speaking to a western audience, proclaimed that "our task is not discovery or exploitation of natural resources, or necessarily producing more goods." Rather, he asserted, "It is the soberer, less dramatic business of administering resources and plants already in hand, of seeking to reestablish foreign markets for our surplus production, of meeting the problem of under-consumption, of adjusting production to consumption, of distributing wealth and production more equitably, of adapting existing economic organizations to the service of the people. The day of the enlightened administration has come."[10]

Progressive Republicans in the West, following especially the addresses in Portland and San Francisco, more and more endorsed Roosevelt's candidacy. On the return trip from the coast, Roosevelt's train stopped in McCook, Nebraska, to allow the candidate to pay tribute to the outstanding progressive Republican in the nation, Nebraska's venerable senior senator, George W. Norris. More than 20,000 people at the county fairgrounds heard Roosevelt in welcoming Norris's support say in a remarkable tribute, "I honor myself in honoring you."

After this meeting Norris himself took to the campaign trail in support of Roosevelt, ending his speechmaking on the Saturday before election in Los Angeles. Once California's outstanding progressive Republican senator, Hiram W. Johnson, endorsed Roosevelt, Norris believed the Golden State was safely in the New York governor's column. Moreover, after the election James A. Farley and others promptly recognized the role Norris and other western progressives of both parties had played in Roosevelt's victory: Senators Burton K. Wheeler, Hiram Johnson, Edward P. Costigan, Bronson Cutting, and others.

Theodore Roosevelt, the Progressive Party candidate in 1912, carried only three states in the West: Washington, California, and South Dakota. Twenty years later his distant relative carried every western state and many western voters believed him to be in the progressive tradition. Senator Key Pittman of Nevada, who joined the campaign train at Salt Lake City, was amazed at the enthusiasm of the crowds. He wrote, "Practically all the people at small places and for hundreds of miles around such places come to the meetings. They come as those seeking salvation. They were in distress and despair and were looking for hope and encouragement. They left knowing that happy days will soon be here."[11]

Roosevelt himself thanked Senator Thomas J. Walsh of Montana for all that he did during the campaign. Among other things, Walsh and Key Pittman helped Raymond Moley draft a key speech the candidate delivered moderating considerably the party's traditional tariff-for-revenue-purposes-only position.[12] In addition, Roosevelt invited Walsh to join his cabinet as attorney general. Walsh, unfortunately, died while enroute to Washington for the inauguration.

Progressive Republican Senators Hiram Johnson of California and Bronson Cutting of New Mexico declined to be considered as secretary of the interior. Arthur Mullen of Nebraska was briefly considered for attorney general after the death of Senator Walsh, but George H. Dern, the governor of Utah, was the only person from the West to fill a post in the Cabinet. Dern was sworn in as secretary of war. Westerners, of course, filled numerous important posts throughout the government, thanks in part to Frank C. Walker of Montana, party treasurer in the recent campaign, and an adviser on lesser appointments. All would play a role in insuring the fact that the New Deal would develop a western focus. Campaigning in the West, Roosevelt appealed to liberal and progressive sentiments, and many western supporters expected the New Deal to meet their problems in the same spirit. However, there were powerful entrenched interest groups in the West, such as silver and other mining interests, who also supported Roosevelt and expected prime consideration for their concerns from the New Deal. Roosevelt appealed to these groups, too, asserting in Salt Lake City, for example, that silver must be recognized as a monetary metal.[13] Yet the fact remains that Roosevelt won the nomination in large part because western politicians and convention delegates considered him more progressive than Newton Baker and other rivals for the nomination. And in his campaign Roosevelt sought to broaden his progressive appeal to western voters. The New Deal would have to take these diverse forces into account.

Chapter 2

The State of The West: 1933-1934

"WHAT I WANT YOU TO DO," Harry Hopkins told Lorena Hickok in July 1933, "is to go out around the country and look this thing over. I don't want statistics from you. I don't want the social worker angle. I just want your own reaction as an ordinary citizen."[1]

The "thing" Hopkins referred to was the relief program, the Federal Emergency Relief Administration (FERA), he headed designed to assist the victims of the Great Depression. In this capacity, Hopkins, provided with congressional authorization totaling half a billion dollars, had to deal with more people than any other New Deal agency. Lorena Hickok was hired to provide him with information, other than what he would receive through official channels, by talking with people on all social levels, those on relief and those who were not. Hopkins wanted Hickok, a trained newspaperwoman, to tell him what she saw and heard without pulling her punches. He wanted the plain unvarnished truth as she saw it.

Throughout 1933 and 1934 Lorena Hickok traveled the length and breadth of the United States reporting to her chief and when he was away to his top associates. She visited every western state with the exception of Oklahoma and those in the Northwest: Idaho, Montana, Oregon, and Washington. Her letters present an excellent picture of conditions prevailing in the West as the New Deal was getting underway. Indeed, the FERA, as she noted, was "the spearhead of the whole New Deal" and its activities were in the forefront of the public mind. Certainly in the early days of the New Deal, FERA dealt with more people, owing to the economic collapse, than any other branch or agency of government—and it dealt with them directly. So desperate were many Americans, so devoid of hope and opportunity, that relief instead of being a last resort now seemed to be the first thing they thought of. And Hickok complained, "Sometimes I feel that we are in the unfortunate position of an army battalion that gets too far ahead of the rest of the line in an advance and finds itself in the line of fire of its own guns as well as those of the enemy."[2]

If anything, Hickok served as the pointer or lead person, sending out vital information so that the headquarters command could, if necessary, regroup its forces and act more intelligently with the resources at its disposal in coping with the crisis situation. She first entered the West in October 1933, driving into North Dakota from Minnesota. She commented about the devastation inflicted upon people "standing bleakly alone in the center of a vast tawny prairie land." She wrote of formerly well-to-do farmers who were "hailed out," their crops destroyed, and who were now applying for relief. They were land-poor, unable to care for their livestock because the land was "so bare that the winds pick up the topsoil and blow it about like sand." Their livestock and their land in most instances was "mortgaged up to the very limit," and all were "a way behind on their taxes." After a succession of poor crops, wheat in North Dakota in 1932 brought about 30 cents a bushel, while it cost a farmer about 77 cents a bushel to raise it. And in 1933 there was no crop at all. Applications for relief continually carried the simple statement, "Hailed out. No crop at all." And what Hickok saw in North Dakota reinforced the validity of that statement.[3]

In human terms it meant that people lacked clothing, owning no more than the apparel they wore, which in most instances did not provide adequate protection from heavy winds. Women and children, she learned both from observation and investigations, were worse off then the men. Women worst of all! They could stay inside and keep warm. But families would make every effort to provide work clothes for the men and shoes for the children so that they could trudge their way to school.

Bad as conditions were for farmers, the plight of their livestock was "pitiable." The only feed available was roughage, "and damned little of that." Some farmers were feeding Russian thistle, cut while it was still green, to their horses and cattle. Russian thistle, Hickok explained to Hopkins, "is a thistle plant with shallow roots that dries up in the fall and is blown across the prairies like rolls of barbed wire." If animals were fed the dried plant, she surmised it would be much the same as if they had eaten barbed wire.[4]

While relief officials, usually state or county employees distributing federal and state monies, were doing their very best under the most difficult of conditions, the counties were unable to provide any assistance. Their financial resources were exhausted and few, if any, banks were willing to take their tax warrants. In North Dakota Hickok learned that in many counties, because of bureaucratic "red tape" and inadequate personnel, no farm loans had been granted as of November

1933. Told also that the "farm holiday spirit" of criticism and defiance was rife in several counties, she visited a farmer "supposed to be a chronic kicker." She found him doing the family washing, a widower with eight children "puttering around a dilapidated old washing machine," too overwhelmed to do much kicking, almost resigned to the "utter hopelessness" of his situation. With wheat selling in North Dakota for 70 cents a bushel and farmers saying it costs 77 cents a bushel to raise, Hickok could understand the farmer's resignation. Another farmer told her that in order to make a living "we've got to get 7 cents a pound for hogs, 9 cents a pound for beef, and $1 a bushel for wheat."[5]

Everywhere in her travels, Hickok talked with people: wheat farmers, cattlemen, bankers, county judges, employees of New Deal agencies trying to assist desperate people. And in North Dakota, she concluded, a majority of the farmers, including ranchers, were actually bankrupt. Those whose wheat crops were ruined by hail, drought, or grasshoppers were destitute; those who had a crop, along with the livestock men, were not getting paid enough for their products to carry them through the winter. She heard numerous tales from cattlemen of minimum returns on the sale of their livestock. In Williston, the secretary of the Farmers' Loan Association on November 1 received his first loan check since the agency was organized during the first hundred days of the New Deal. Similar situations existed elsewhere, but as Hickok continued her travels through the West, she was able to report that bottlenecks were being broken and that federal funds were beginning to flow more freely. She also witnessed in her journeying similar instances to one she reported from North Dakota: when an applicant responded to a query as to how he was "fixed for the winter in food and clothes" for his family, he wiped the tears away with the back of his hand.[6]

Conditions in North Dakota were about as bad as any in the United States at that time and Bottineau County, on the Canadian border, was one of the most badly hit counties in the state. Conditions, made worse by a blizzard, created a desperate need for things to help keep people warm: bedding, fuel, and clothing. Moreover, many officials whom Hickok met were inclined to think that there was something wrong with a person who could not make a living in North Dakota. While state and Red Cross officials dallied, the people of Bottineau County, who had not been able to raise a decent crop for "something like four years," suffered. Hickok noted:

> Their houses had gone to ruins. No repairs for years. Their furniture, dishes, cooking utensils—no replacements in years. No bed linen, and quilts and blankets all gone. A year ago their clothing was in rags. This year they hardly have rags.

Translated into human terms, Hickok commented about two children "in what was once a house" running about "without a stitch on save some ragged overalls." Their feet, she noted, were "purple with cold." Their mother, bare-legged except for some ragged sneakers, was going to have another baby in January in a decrepit homestead that contained but one bed, "a filthy, ragged mattress, some dirty pillows," and a few old rags serving as blankets. Hickok reported having heard "of women having babies in bed with only coats thrown over them." When she visited this family the temperature recorded 5 degrees above zero and the following day a blizzard howled across the area from the northwest.

In Bottineau County 800 families were on relief with new applications coming in at the rate of 12 to 25 a day. Some families, though eligible, could not get relief until further funds arrived in the county office. But of more immediate importance than money in Bottineau County was clothing, blankets, fuel, and food. "We haven't had a scrap of meat in our house for six months," a man on relief told a case supervisor. What disturbed Hickok almost as much as the conditions she viewed in North Dakota was the lack of realization on the part of many state officials as to just how bad conditions were in their state.[7]

In all, Hickok spent a week in North Dakota, traveling more than 2,000 miles across its wide open spaces. It was her introduction to the West. And although unrest in North Dakota had not erupted into farm strikes or "any sort of rebellion," Hickok reported that those farmers who had some sort of a crop were usually "more rebellious" than those who had not. She noted that A. C. Townley was back in the state, going about with Governor William Langer and Senator Lynn Frazier criticizing the President and seeking "at $16 a head" to revive the Non-Partisan League. Meetings were occurring all over the state with "Communists, the Farm Holiday crowd, Farmers' Union" and others all on the hustings criticizing the New Deal for its lack of action or for its unwanted interference. When she left the state, all this talk had not generated any policial action. When it did, not too long afterward, she was reporting on conditions elsewhere in the West. But North Dakota was a seminal state in her western travels. It provided a yardstick by which to judge and compare conditions she found elsewhere. Only once or twice did she encounter conditions as bleak and as desperate as those she viewed in Bottineau County in November 1933. Nowhere did she see or learn anything that exceeded what she found in North Dakota, though South Dakota came close.[8]

In South Dakota, she spoke to Farm Holiday leaders, reasonable men who really did not believe in striking by keeping their produce off the market, but who viewed it as a last desperate measure to attract attention and "cooperation between the government and the farmers."

Businessmen in some towns agreed to lend moral support to the strike. She noted too that Communists were active and that many farmers were aware of their activities but had little confidence in them. Nor did many of the people she spoke to in the state have much confidence in Milo Reno, the leader of the Farm Holiday movement. The same could be said for Henry A. Wallace and other top agricultural officials. Unless missionary work on behalf of federal farm programs was quickly started, and by officials who were willing to travel and talk with farmers at county courthouses and in relief offices, Communists and "the Farm Holiday and the Farmers' Union people" would make headway because they were doing just that. Already farmers had stopped foreclosure sales, taking guns from sheriff's deputies and beating them. And, as elsewhere, there was confusion, ineptitude, and no flexibility in the way relief and other programs were administered.[9]

In general, conditions in South Dakota duplicated what Hickok had seen in North Dakota. This generalization applied particularly to the need for clothing and fuel, though in the eastern part of the state farmers were burning "buffalo chips" and "cutting rushes in the beds of dried up lakes for fuel." Conditions were not as severe only because "the needs are being met much more intelligently, skillfully and adequately" than in North Dakota, though Hickok felt the destitution was "much, much worse." She suspected politics was involved in the relief program on the upper echelons, but greater concern during the time she was in the state was evinced with the establishment of a livestock feeding program to allow that industry to survive the winter. What impressed her most was the fact that people were scared; some families lived 30 miles from a railroad depot and the prospect of being without fuel, forage for livestock, or adequate food and shelter during a severe winter was not pleasant to contemplate. Others were frightened about the possibility of drought because "the whole damned state apparently is drying up and blowing away." Indeed, she had seen some farmers who "looked like frightened children." They were mortgaged to the hilt, heavily in debt, afraid of losing their farms and, not understanding the "the federal loan setup very well," they did not want to borrow any more money. Though they could not feed their cattle, they were unwilling to reduce their herds to qualify for federal assistance. They allowed them to shift for themselves until they died from malnutrition.[10]

Mobridge, which had been a thriving community and a terminal on the Milwaukee Railroad when Hickok was growing up in that vicinity, was now a virtual ghost town "with the west wind howling down its wide, empty streets" and its depleted population staying indoors with little to do. Improved technology allowed for longer hauls and thus fewer terminal facilities. The Milwaukee had reduced its facilities in Mobridge, thereby helping the community go to seed. And what Hickok saw in this town was duplicated for varying reasons in other towns she visited, some of which she had lived in as a child. But nowhere in South Dakota did she see children going without shoes and stockings, and she made it a point whenever possible "to stop in at county schools and look them over."[11]

She dubbed the Dakotas "the 'Siberia' of the United States":

> miles and miles of flat brown country. Snowdrifts here and there, Russian thistles rolling across the road. Unpainted buildings all going to seed. Hardly a strawstack or a haystack for miles. Now and then a shabby little town spread out around two or three gaunt, ugly grain elevators. What a country — to keep out of?[12]

In letters to Eleanor Roosevelt she commented about traveling through "the *real* grasshopper area," viewing miles and miles of what appeared to be ploughed fields. Grasshoppers "simply cleaned them off—right down to the earth, even eating the roots" and leaving great bare, black patches on the landscape. Bark on trees had been eaten and women were afraid to hang the family washing because grasshoppers had eaten clothes off the lines. In addition, she knew that Mrs. Roosevelt would be interested in the woman, part Indian, in charge of relief work in one of the counties, who had "the same slant on life that you have" and who knew livestock "as well as any man." While farmers were eligible for relief work, she told Hickok there were probably not a half dozen teams of horses fit to work. Horses were dying from starvation, "right in the barnyards" and in harness on road jobs. The one thing Hickok had not seen or experienced "in the way of desolation, discomfort and misery"—namely, a dust storm—she experienced before she left South Dakota for a few days of rest and relaxation in Minneapolis. Hoping to drive through it, she felt as if she "were being whirled off into space in a vast, impenetrable land of brown dust." She turned back, unable to see a foot ahead of the car by the time it got back to town. Though the street lights were on, at noon "the sun wasn't even a light spot in the sky." It was so dark and the dust so thick that she couldn't see across the street. To Hickok "it seemed like the end of the world."[13]

By the time she was in Nebraska, in mid-November, the Federal Emergency Relief Administration had been supplemented by the Civil Works Administration (CWA). In Lincoln she had her first view of a public works project underway, aside from highway repair jobs. It was a sewer project. Both Hickok and most of the people she spoke to in Lincoln greeted the CWA approach and the various projects getting started with enthusiasm. It was far superior to providing relief money. But most of the talk she heard early in her Nebraska visit pertained to the Farm Holiday movement which, Hickok thought, had abated considerably with the arrival of wheat allotment checks and the efficient functioning of the Farm Credit Administration branch in Omaha. Moreover, Nebraska had a moratorium law that eased the financial pressures on farmers. Also in Nebraska, unlike the Dakotas, she found considerably less hostility to Secretary of Agriculture Henry A. Wallace, which she thought was due partly to the press. In the Dakotas all influential newspapers were Republican, whereas in Nebraska there were two strong "Roosevelt Democrat papers," one or the other reaching more than half the farm homes in the state and doing a lot of "missionary work" for New Deal farm and relief programs. This was not available in the Dakotas.[14]

Nebraska too experienced drought and grasshopper inundations. Hickok was concerned that owing to vast distances—one county covered 9,500 square miles—officials in Lincoln would not be able to adequately serve people in need of relief in the more sparsely settled western counties. However, she noted that Nebraska had a "lively, aggressive" Public Works Board which already had toured the state, county by county, and mapped out a statewide public works program calling for multipurpose irrigation projects.[15]

In Omaha, attending the state convention of the Farmers' Union at the shabby old Castle Hotel, she showed that Hamlin Garland's tales of depression-ridden farmers in the late nineteenth century were of more than literary and historical interest. She wrote the following passages which could have come directly from a story in *Main Travelled Roads:*

> A great big, smoky, dirty lobby, with worn, sagging leather sofas and chairs, paintings of naked ladies on the walls, cigar ashes all over the floor, untidy bellhops in worn, soiled uniforms.
> The place filled with the delegates. Cowboys in high-heeled boots, overalls, and big hats wandering about, nervous and shy. "Dirt farmers," ill at ease in "store clothes" and unaccustomed white collars. Fresh haircuts, leaving strips of white above the leathery tan on the backs of necks. Farm wives in four or five-year-old styles, staring curiously about. . . . And mixing among them, slapping backs, shaking hands, the leaders. Townmen. Perfectly at ease. Accustomed to being in cities and in hotels. Flattering them. "Bucking them up."[16]

Delegates and speakers, while in disagreement among themselves, were nearly united in their criticism of Henry Wallace and New Deal farm programs. Milo Reno; William Langer; Charles W. Bryan, governor of Nebraska and brother of William Jennings Bryan; John Simpson; and William Lemke took the lead in denouncing the treatment rural Americans were getting from their government. Having panned "Mr. Hoover and Mr. Hyde," they now found "Mr. Wallace a convenient target."[17]

In Nebraska, as elsewhere, she viewed projects and programs

undertaken by various New Deal agencies. Here, however, she noted for the first time the conflict between men and machinery: whether the idea in road-building, for example, was to put as many men to work as possible, or whether to construct roads as quickly and as efficiently as possible by utilizing modern equipment and machinery. This conflict was most evident in Public Works Administration projects. Hickok observed that they usually took much longer than CWA projects to gain final approval primarily because Harold L. Ickes in his capacity as Public Works Administrator personally reviewed most of them to make sure that taxpayers' monies would not be wasted. And in Nebraska Hickok again was aware of Communist agitation among the unemployed. She also recognized that, though many people were involved in their demonstrations, few were actually Communists. Most were dissatisfied and unemployed.[18]

Indian relief came to her attention for the first time in Nebraska. In the Cornhusker State funds were provided by the state relief committee and dispensed by the Indian agent. While there were many complaints against the agent's handling of the money, almost all, Hickok was told, were unjustified. In Thurston County, Indians who in the previous winter had received mackinaws from the Red Cross sold them for liquor, and Hickok learned of one Indian who "sold his wife's shoes for whiskey while she was sick." She was also told of a recent incident involving an Indian who tried to kidnap and rape a village postmistress. Moreover, agitators were trying to organize Indian dissatisfactions, and Hickok one evening felt the "shivers up and down" her back as she listened to the beating of drums and fierce yells from an Indian stumpdance, a protest "against the way relief is being handled here."[19]

From Nebraska Lorena Hickok journeyed eastward, not returning to the West until the following spring when she went to Texas. Because of vicious fighting there, she quickly became more discouraged than at any time since she started working for Hopkins. "Texas," she wrote, "is a God awful mess" owing to "the big political fight in Austin" where "Ma and Pa" Ferguson were replacing all possible officials with their own supporters. And when she arrived in Houston, her first lengthy stop since leaving New Orleans, she found that relief funds in the city were exhausted and all involved with the program were disgusted. Though politics, ineptitude, greed, confusion, and the like were evident elsewhere in Texas, she noted the only industry that had completely collapsed in Houston was the building industry. The other principal industry, the manufacture of oil drilling machinery, "was going right along." However, it was not expanding and was unable to take on more untrained men; "in the meantime the Houston relief load is 12,500 families with applications coming in at the rate of 1,100 a week."[20]

A week later writing from San Antonio, she began to appreciate "what an empire is this state of Texas!" She already had driven "some 700 miles" in the state and planned to drive at least 1,000 more before leaving Texas. Its diversity impressed her: East Texas oil fields where "more than a third of the gasoline made in the United States or maybe it's the World" could be produced and refined; vastly different and interesting cities; "some of the loveliest, wooded landscape you ever saw" and "some of the most uninteresting flat prairie I ever saw;" "oil, lumber, cotton, wheat, rice, beef, truck, fruit, and, out West of San Antonio, goats! No kidding." Because of an upswing in the goat business, "furnishing mohair to the automobile manufacturers," conditions in San Antonio began to improve slightly. And San Angelo, in the heart of the goat and sheep country, was "sitting on top of the world." Hickok also was interested in the "great big needlework industry" staffed by Mexican-American labor. The Chamber of Commerce claimed San Antonio as the "largest center in the country for the making of baby clothes."[21]

Impressed though she was with the great diversity of Texas, Hickok was no more cheerful than she was at the outset of her journey through Texas. The state did not seem to be badly off. East Texas, the most thickly populated part, was much better off than West Texas where El Paso was experiencing hard times. It had several bank failures and its industries were tied up with silver and copper mining, which "'just isn't being done' these days." However, except for the total collapse of the building industry, conditions were not nearly as bad as what she had witnessed elsewhere. Though she heard about droughts in the "northern half of the Panhandle," she found that in San Antonio "things aren't so bad." PWA construction on military property was going "a long way toward supporting" the city. Yet nowhere did she encounter much optimism. Texans were concerned whether the President could keep control and whether the New Deal could continue to address their manifold problems in a beneficial way without arousing a lot more "jealousy and local politics."[22]

Because of political feuding in Austin, Hickok found "the relief business in Texas . . . in pretty much of a mess" with those on relief, especially in the urban centers, "on terribly reduced rations for some time" and more interested in jobs than in being continued on relief rolls. This was particularly true of white clients, most of whom had "middleclass backgrounds." It was not the case, Hickok noted, with black and Hispanic clients with whom "relief is just too popular for anything."[23]

It was in Texas that Hickok stressed a situation that she had observed with regard to blacks in the South and which she would note again with Spanish Americans elsewhere in the Southwest. In Texas it applied to both groups, though as she went further west in the state the latter group predominated. The situation was that for blacks and Spanish Americans relief—however inadequate it might have been for whites, "especially white collar people"—did not involve any lowering of living standards at all; in fact, "it made possible in many, many cases, a BETTER standard of living." In El Paso, a Hispanic social worker told her, "All the Mexicans on relief here are perfectly happy. They've got more to eat, they're living better than they ever have in their lives before." And they were "apparently coming on relief just as fast they can get on."[24]

Hickok first wrote about this situation when she was in San Antonio. She thought it prejudicial against white families who could not subsist, paying rent and feeding themselves "on less than $35 a month," while $20 and $35 a month for "the average low class Mexican family . . . would be beyond their wildest dreams of affluence." Since about half the case load in San Antonio was Spanish American and more of them than whites were applying for assistance each week, it was clear to Hickok that "we are forcing white people, especially white collar people, who are very apt to give us trouble, down to Mexican and Negro standards of living."[25] In Texas, Hickok concluded, "Mexican and Negro farm labor won't work for the prevailing wages if they can get on relief." They came to town in hordes—at least that was the case in San Antonio, a base for migratory farm labor—to get on relief rolls. By caring for all the needy families in San Antonio, about 10,000 of them, Hickok said the government would be removing them from the migratory labor force "at the expense of white people, with higher standards of living, who are actually unable to get work." And the longer such white people were out of jobs, the harder it would be for whites over 35 years of age to get their jobs back or to compete for new positions.[26]

Hickok's letter to Hopkins from San Antonio concluded, "You'll probably think I'm getting to be a hardhearted old Bourbon." She was worried, "plenty worried" because, for example, in Jefferson County where both Beaumont and Port Arthur were located, the relief administrator was turning away "just as many Negroes as he can." He claimed he was forced into this stance "because of the mental attitude of the whites," adding, "We've been threatened with riots here." Hickok sympathized with his dilemma and asked Hopkins, "Now what the Hell are we going to DO with these people?"

The irony was that in Texas, while the economy was improving in many areas and conditions were better than in most other parts of the nation, the relief situation was probably in worse shape than anywhere else in the country. Hickok could only conclude that in Texas "we're in this relief business for a long, long time." Yet she was also prescient enough to see that a long-term, "carefully planned public works program" without a means test, with an adequate budget and with the ability to pay workers in cash, no "grocery orders" and no "relief clothes," might provide an answer enabling people who worked "to pay rents, live decently, have enough to eat, [and to] be clothed."[27]

From El Paso, Hickok entered New Mexico, where most of the population was located in the Rio Grande valley, centering around Albuquerque. Like Texas, distances were great and roads were poor. Though New Mexico comprised 78 million acres, only 2 million irrigated acres were capable of producing crops. The remaining 76 million acres were mountain and desert country worth, Hickok was told, about $1 an acre with as much of it as possible being used for grazing. On at least half of this acreage, 100 acres was needed to sustain one steer or three or four sheep. On the best lands, the ratio was 20 acres to the steer or three or four sheep. Hickok also learned that veterans and unsuccessful farmers, "practically all on relief," coming from Oklahoma, Arkansas, and Texas were homesteading in New Mexico. Their chances were "pretty damned slim," because to make a living raising cattle or sheep a lot more land than the homesteaders were acquiring was necessary. And by plowing grazing land they were only further ruining the land "such as it is."[28]

Unlike Texas, 60 percent of New Mexico's 425,000 people were Hispanic, the large majority of whom, Hickok reported, were descendants "of Indians and the Spanish conquerors." She was fascinated to learn that all state business was conducted in two languages and that Spanish-speakers were actively interested in politics. But, unfortunately, they were poor helpless people who had lost control of the land and never had exerted any control over what little industry existed. They served mainly as laborers, sheepherders, small farmers and were generally unable to earn a living or adequately care for what land and livestock they had. Between 75 and 80 percent of the families on relief were Spanish Americans with the majority living in rural areas. Since living standards were low, unlike Texas, relief needs for the majority group in the population were meager. And there were no serious problems, except that of educating clients to better agricultural practices and moving them on to better land, which, for a fortunate few, was becoming available with the completion of the government-supported Rio Grande conservancy project.[29]

However, for unemployed "Anglos" the situation was even more grim than that of their compatriots in Texas. Industry in New Mexico, Hickok said, "just ain't." The Sante Fe railroad, the largest private employer in the state in 1929 employed 7,500 men; in 1933 it employed 3,200 and many of these were working on reduced schedules. Similar data was available for almost all of the mining companies, "coal and copper, silver, lead, zinc, etc.," which had cut production and were employing fewer men. Basically in New Mexico and throughout the Southwest it was "the same old story" involving "two classes of people": whites "with white standards of living, for whom relief . . . is anything but adequate." With limited opportunities these people were growing more and more restive. And then there were the Spanish Americans, or Hispanics. For these people, as well as for blacks east of the Mississippi River, relief was both adequate and attractive. Though some were able to get work, the wages were so low that they were better off on relief. Since these two groups dominated relief rolls, Hickok complained that "we are compelled to force the white man's standard of living down to that of the Mexicans and Negroes."[30]

Moreover, "Anglo" employers, "particularly farmers and housewives," were annoyed because of difficulty hiring help at the ridiculously low wages they offered. In some urban areas, Hickok heard (but did not quite believe) that whites, desperate for work, were preventing Spanish Americans from applying for the few poorly paid jobs available. On the other hand, she was distressed that ranchers in New Mexico, offering $7 a month for sheepherders who could secure $8 to $10 a month on relief, were unwilling to raise their wage offers.[31]

In Arizona she encountered another problem which created a furor. The minimum wage rate was 50 cents an hour. It was quickly accepted by relief workers because it was "the hourly rate on public works in the state of Arizona." However, because of politics and patronage, the prevailing wage was much lower. Few workers on highways and public works received 50 cents an hour, "and damned few" Spanish Americans were included in that group. With CWA projects paying this wage, Spanish Americans had an opportunity to earn more and to live better than ever before. Hickok doubted "if the Relief administration is financially in a position to battle low wage scales all over the South and Southwest." And in Arizona she openly wondered if discrimination, "two standards of relief," might not be an answer, though she was sure "the idea will sound horrible in Washington."[32]

In Tucson she found the idea projected into reality. "They were doing it before Federal money came in"; relief officials divided their case loads into four groups: Spanish Americans, Indians, refugees from Old Mexico, and white families. Each group received a different maximum monthly wage rate. In Tucson there was a commissary where, as a work project, vegetables were raised and milk was purchased wholesale and then sold to relief families at half the retail price. What she saw in Tucson led Hickok to wonder "if we shouldn't give these state and local committees a little more latitude, a little more discretionary power." She knew, of course, that organized labor and other pressure groups would oppose bending wage scales. But she said, "Our job is to feed people and clothe them and shelter them, with as little damage to their morale as possible." By raising a family's income, while the breadwinners were on relief, beyond what it had been or what it had any immediate chance of becoming, "we are damaging the morale of that family," Hickok said. Similarly, if a relief family's standard was markedly lowered, morale would be impaired and some members could become rebels or radicals.[33]

Near Phoenix, Hickok visited a camp for transient families and was impressed with what she saw: "Good housing. Clothing. Medical care. Adequate relief." Though this was the first camp she commented upon, she had been looking at transient camps and shelters funded by Hopkins's agencies in her travels. Those in Arizona were the best she had seen, but the great weakness in the program was that it was not stopping transiency and possibly encouraged it by offering traveling unemployed people shelter, food, and clothing. Once it began to get hot, the transient camp at Flagstaff, "up in the mountains where it's cool," reported a 300 percent increase in registrations. For some unemployed it was possible to winter in the South and summer in the mountains. But Hickok reflected, "Perhaps it's just as well. . . . We'd have to support them somewhere."[34] She could come to this conclusion because most of what she viewed in Arizona impressed her. This included hospitals for ill and needy unemployed transients and others, in addition to transient camps and the relief program. Hickok liked the various administrators she met because most showed imagination in coping with their assignments and were not unduly pessimistic about the future.[35]

The big question in Arizona was when and to what extent would the mines reopen or return to full production. If they opened to any extent, some of the 25,000 to 26,000 heads of families on relief would be going back to work, but when Hickok left Arizona to return to Washington in May 1934, nobody knew when that was going to happen. Until they reopened, Arizona would not enjoy an economic revival because, aside from mining, there was not much "to look to." Stock raising and farming offered no hope because of low beef prices and also because of drought, which was making water scarce and more expensive.[36]

PWA, which in Texas was beginning to provide jobs and help resolve some of the problems affecting relief and unemployment, had not yet made much headway in Arizona and New Mexico. In Albuquerque, for example, where over 1,000 families were on relief only 23 men were working on a PWA job. In all of New Mexico, Hickok said, there were only 78 men employed by that agency. In Arizona early in May the situation was not comparable to that of New Mexico. No unemployed men from Arizona were being employed for the construction of Boulder Dam, though several projects in the state were scheduled to get underway "sometime within the next three months." PWA money, she was told, was going into Indian reservations. Enough work was offered to the Navajos so that, Hickok was told, they were quitting rug weaving.[37]

In Arizona and New Mexico she realized that agriculture could not exist without water. People engaged in "dry farming" could not make a living in the Southwest. Furthermore, Hickok was convinced that most parts of these states would have "to come under the urban classification" because the unemployed in and around mining camps could not be rehabilitated on nearby acreage. "No water." Moreover, Hickok doubted their capability for farming and thought that work-relief, available only to the urban unemployed, provided a more sensible solution, since in New Mexico and Arizona "you can't rehabilitate rural families on little plots of acreage land."[38]

Hickok left Arizona for Washington, D.C. to report in person to Hopkins and for some much-needed rest. Nothing she had seen in the Southwest could compare to what she had seen in the Dakotas, but the racial-ethnic dilemma of the relief program, a poignant and ironic example of Alexis de Tocqueville's view about the leveling effects of American democracy, was dramatically self-evident throughout the Southwest. A glimpse of an answer to this dilemma—of blacks and Spanish Americans preferring relief to working under conditions tantamount to peonage while middle-class whites on relief found it difficult to hold onto their standard of living—was suggested in Texas where PWA programs put some of the unemployed back to work on jobs in accord with their abilities. Later the Works Progress Administration in conjunction with PWA would help resolve this situation through its flexible wage scales. But as the New Deal was getting underway this dilemma accelerated racial and ethnic tensions in the Southwest and seemed almost insoluble.

Several weeks later Hickok was in Denver reporting on drought conditions in northeastern Colorado. So bad were conditions that some farmers in the drought area, trying to plow their fields, broke their blades on rocks. "Apparently most of the topsoil had blown away, and they were down to bed rock!" And cattle seeking bites of dry buffalo grass "between clumps of Russian thistle" came up with "mostly sand." Though rain would help the livestock situation tremendously, it would not benefit the wheat crop. It was too late for that. A government wheat inspector reported that in one of the drought counties only 300 bushels were anticipated from 2,560 acres of land.[39]

Though conditions in Colorado could not equal what she saw in North and South Dakota the previous autumn, this was the fifth year of drought in large areas of eastern Colorado and neighboring states. Hickok learned that several farmers "in the last few months" had gone insane. Applications for relief were increasing; everybody was broke and 85 percent of the cattle were mortgaged. Land values had dropped to less than a dollar an acre and mortgage holders refused to foreclose. Hickok reported, "They don't even bother to have tax sales. The land isn't worth it." It was a variation of the same old story throughout the plains states. Farmers plowed up range country and for a few years had "phenomenal wheat crops." Then with the Hoover years came drought and now many farmers and most New Deal administrators quickly concluded "that this land had better be turned back to grazing."[40]

What Hickok saw in Colorado "sold" her on the Agricultural Adjustment Administration; "wheat allotment checks represented the only income many of these farmers got last year." She saw the program as "another form of relief—paying them for cutting production when they didn't produce anything at all." It was providing relief out of the coffers of the processor and the pockets of the consumer and Hickok's query was "Well, why not?" Certainly the program was popular with farmers and small town merchants, but in Colorado at least "the capitalist group—sugar barons, both city and small town"—were not so favorably disposed. In turn Hickok was not favorably disposed to the "one big complicated mess" that was the sugar beet industry.[41]

Again she found peonage and exploitation; "Negroes and poor whites in the cotton fields, and in the beet fields Mexicans" brought there chiefly by the sugar companies who gouged both the farmer and his workers. While other industries were having difficulties, the Great Western Sugar Company was paying "good fat dividends." In 1933, besides paying handsome dividends, "it set aside in some sort of holding company $8,000,000 or $9,000,000, presumably to avoid having to pay income tax on it." At the same time it could not afford to pay the grower more than $4.50 a ton for his beets, which meant that the Spanish American family stooping in the fields to raise "those damned beets" got "less than $100 per family for their labor and some of these haven't been paid yet." The Great Western Sugar Company had "no responsibility whatever toward anyone—farmer or labor," paying the farmer what price it saw fit for his crop and helping to organize the Mountain States Beet Growers Marketing Association, apparently existing "only to 'yes' the Sugar Companies." The association, for example, put out contracts, supposedly prepared by the Great Western Sugar Company, for "Mexican" labor to sign.[42]

The farmer did the same for his Hispanic fieldhands, many of whom did not get paid in 1933. But the farmer's lot was much better than that of his fieldhands. He paid the company for his seed and then paid off his loan at the bank, which would not lend him money unless he agreed to raise a cash crop, sugar beets. The turnover among sugar beet farmers was so great, Hickok reported, that "Japanese are about the only farmers who can raise sugar beets and make a living." Coming first as laborers, some Japanese were now farmers "hiring Mexican and even white labor to work in the fields!"[43]

Spanish American families in many areas of Colorado dominated the relief rolls, though by the time Hickok visited in the spring of 1934, the rolls had been considerably reduced. Many families went back to the beet fields to live on credit during the summer and had little prospect of having enough to carry them through the winter. Many had not been paid for their previous year's labor. In Colorado, unlike elsewhere in the Southwest, most Spanish American fieldhands, rather than stay on the relief rolls, were willing to work under peonage conditions, thereby allowing more desperate families to remain on the rolls. One factor prompting Spanish American labor to return to the fields was the naive hope that the Department of Agriculture might set a minimum wage for farm workers.[44]

To make a living, child labor was an absolute necessity for Hispanic families in the beet fields of Colorado. And "one of the most pathetic things" Hickok observed in her travels was "the anxiety of some of the Mexican fathers and mothers that their children should be educated." The lot of these children was poor health, illiteracy, and early aging. The Great Western Sugar Company, "an industry that in 1933 had $78,000,000 in assets and no debts," was built with cheap labor as a base, while public agencies carried "most of the beet labor in Colorado on relief through the winter" of 1933–34.[45]

Elsewhere in Colorado Hickok found what she considered a similar theme; namely, "subsidizing John D. Rockefeller" by providing "federal relief funds" for the families of men employed by the Colorado Fuel and Iron Company. Until the practice was stopped workers for this company were also getting supplementary relief funds "in the form of dispensing orders for food and clothing, to be cashed at the company store!" In Pueblo the relief committee was dominated by company officials who worked out these supplementary arrangements so that workers in debt to the company could pay off their obligations, continue working and not become completely destitute. When Hickok left Colorado in late June the Colorado Relief Administration was still providing federal funds for supplementary relief to over 400 families of men employed by the Colorado Fuel and Iron Corporation. She reported that similar practices were evident in the coal mines, some of which were owned by the Colorado Fuel and Iron Corporation.[46]

Hickok's insight into the terrible dilemma Hopkins and other officials faced was evident when she queried, "But what are you going to do? Let the families go hungry? And suppose, unable to live on what they are earning, they all quit and come on relief?" She believed that some employers were taking advantage of relief by paying their workers less than a living wage and hoping that supplementary relief would

make up the difference. Her suspicions were confirmed through conversation with officials of the Colorado Fuel and Iron Corporation, one
of whom, speaking of a mining camp in Wyoming, boasted "when we
get through, we'll notify the relief administration, and they will take all
the families on relief."[47]

On leaving Denver by train for Los Angeles, Hickok noted that
there was very little snow on the mountains, thereby seriously curtailing the flow of water in the streams and rivers on both sides of the
Great Divide. Croplands dependent on irrigation were experiencing
drought conditions, adding to the relief burden in Colorado as people
dependent on irrigation for their livelihood required assistance. But the
heaviest call for relief in the state, of course, came from the Denver
area where the case load was about 15,000 families.[48]

By the end of June Hickok was reporting about "what has been
described as 'the blackest spot in the United States' from the relief
angle." But on the basis of two days of viewing the situation in Los
Angeles, she thought conditions were improving. Incompetents and
politicians were being eliminated from the administration of relief programs. The case load totaled 110,985 and Hickok hoped the county
could assume some of that burden. The trouble was that "there are too
many people in Los Angeles for the amount of employment that its
industries, even under the most favorable circumstances, can provide." If some of the unemployed could be moved out of Los Angeles,
the situation would be meliorated. Subsistence homesteads for migrant
farm laborers and their families in the San Joaquin and Imperial Valleys and a pueblo town for Spanish Americans where they could make
native wares for tourists were two of the projects proposed for reducing the number of unemployed in Los Angeles.[49]

Hickok was especially impressed with the transient camps for boys
that she visited. In Colorado she was "a bit uncomfortable at the spec-
tacle of those kids mixing with the older men," many of whom were
derelicts with a "bitter, hopeless slant on life." The atmosphere in the
California camps, populated by boys from 14 to 21, all of whom had
been riding freight trains, was markedly different. It approached that of
a summer camp or private school with the boys acquiring "a sort of
alma mater feeling after they leave!" The camps were self-governing
with "an excellent educational program," including "everything from
mathematics and languages to aviation and work on Diesel engines."
The boys seemed busy, happy, and interested. Hickok thought they
had been "caught in time to prevent their becoming professional
tramps." Some of the older boys supplemented the work of the Civilian
Conservation Corps in a nearby national forest, while the younger boys
helped construct a gymnasium. These camps providing good physical
surroundings, good supervision, and good work projects were "the

best" that Hickok had seen. The transient program could keep adults "off the road for a little while," but in these two California camps, Hickok exclaimed, "we're making honest-to-God citizens out of those kids!"[50]

From Los Angeles Hickok embarked on a three-day trip into the desert and returned with confused and not-too-cheerful impressions consisting "of heat, depression, bitterness, more heat, terrible poverty, confusion, heat again, and a passionate longing for some sort of orderly plan for procedure." All of this because she had not seen an irrigated district in California where farmers were making a living. They had to pay a private company for water and then again had "to pay a power company to distribute it." Few farmers could afford Diesel engines to pump their underground water. Since most farmers in the irrigated districts were also burdened with debts, "everything they've got is mortgaged, including their water rights!" Hickok could not see how they were ever going to get out of debt and earn a living without government assistance in easing their debt burden and forcing a reduction in the cost of water and its distribution. In San Bernardino County, half the size of New England, 38 percent of the population was on relief and most of the rest were trying to get there.[51]

Hickok quickly gained a poor impression of the California Emergency Relief Administration because it was very slow in starting available programs to assist desperate people and also because it dumped the burden of repaying emergency bond issues upon the counties, many of which were bankrupt, and not upon the state. California, she concluded, was "a mess" wallowing in the mire of political chicanery. After these observations Hickok decided a vacation was in order and she did not return to the Golden State until August, refreshed and ready to continue her investigative reporting.[52]

She spent almost a week in San Francisco discussing the tense labor situation, which in the eyes of the press and the American Legion, had degenerated into "red-baiting" and ridding the state of Communists. Hickok thought that these campaigns were also designed to fight the New Deal and the President, against whom most publishers in the state were very bitter. Also involved in these campaigns were the Chamber of Commerce and most Republican candidates. All attacked the New Deal, reserving special venom for Mrs. Roosevelt, Henry Wallace, Frances Perkins, and Rexford G. Tugwell. They hoped through those tactics "to plant in the minds of the conservative, middle class of Californians the idea that all those about the President in Washington are Communist sympathizers, if not actually Communists." In the Imperial Valley, she added, even the President was "supposed to be a Communist!"[53]

On the other hand, liberals and labor people in the Bay area were also becoming critical of the New Deal because they believed the National Recovery Administration brought with it "a promise of government support for a closed shop." As a result union membership, "particularly the long shoremen and the seamen" markedly increased as the members sought control of the hiring halls. But most of their leaders, Hickok reported, were "none too anxious for a strike" to gain this control. "And here's where your Communists come into the picture." They endorsed union control of hiring halls and gained a following, though most of the men who went on strike earlier in the year were not Communists. While the strike was not successful, "this fellow [Harry] Bridges who led the strike" had not lost his following and would be heard from again.[54]

In the meantime everyone Hickok met in the Bay area thought that Upton Sinclair would win the Democratic nomination for governor but that he would be defeated in November by "Old Man [Frank F.] Merriam." This would occur because Sinclair would be labeled as a Communist and the middle class (those afraid of Communists) would vote for Merriam despite the fact that, for the first time in the state's history, registration indicated a Democratic majority in California.[55]

Hickok devoted more space to discussing the political climate in California, as viewed from the Bay area, than in any other western state she visited. To be sure, 1934 was a critical year in the history of San Francisco and California and Hickok kept her superiors in Washington informed of developments. But she also noted that business conditions in San Francisco were not as bad as in most cities, though most of the city's businessmen and bankers would have had her believe otherwise. A notable exception was Amadeo P. Giannini, a strong "Roosevelt booster." However, the all-encompassing issue in San Francisco when Hickok was there could be summed up in the term "red baiting."[56]

From San Francisco Hickok went to the San Joaquin Valley where she spent several days and was delighted to find the valley "more peaceful than any other spot I'd visited in the state." Business seemed to be "better there than elsewhere in the state" though the big growers, "under the AAA cooperative marketing agreements," appeared to be benefiting more "than the little fellows." She noted no serious labor problems and there was "less of the red-baiting stuff." In Fresno, previously pointed out to her as "one of the worst spot in California," she found relief well organized and business "fairly good." Wages were improving. Fruit pickers received 25 cents an hour compared to 17 cents in 1933 and cotton growers, she was told, would pay a dollar a hundred pounds compared to 80 cents in 1933. In Fresno she also met the head of the Unemployed Citizen's Council, which had about 5,000 members. He had formed the organization into a "a political club to wield over the heads of the county supervisors" and in doing so had helped reorganize "the relief setup in the county" and launch a work program.[57]

From Fresno Hickok next went to Bakersfield in the southern part of the San Joaquin Valley. Here too things were peaceful; fruit picking was well underway though cotton picking had not yet started. Of grave concern to pickers during the season was adequate housing. Hickok was impressed with the model village on the ranch of Allan Hoover, son of the former President. It was infinitely superior to the tent colonies or cardboard shacks, all without adequate sanitation, provided for many workers. Others lived along the ditch banks in the irrigated sections, drinking ditch water. Sickness was rampant and these workers "were fertile territory for the Communists." Thus far, Hickok said, "young Hoover" was the only grower to provide good housing rent free for his seasonal workers.[58]

The housing of seasonal workers was a serious problem throughout the great valleys of California. Conditions did not differ from those Hickok commented upon on the outskirts of Bakersfield. Local health departments were worried, but as yet no epidemics had been reported. Though some officials tried to do something about these colonies, local opposition, Hickok said, "is terrific." If conditions were meliorated, more people would be attracted to the vicinity, adding to the local tax burden and these people then might establish residence and become voters.[59]

In the Sacramento Valley Hickok remarked that conditions were not as good as in the San Joaquin Valley primarily because the "relief situation is awful." Chiseling, politics, low relief standards, all of this was "damned depressing" to Hickok. Whereas fruit canners in Stockton used to give their surplus to the poor, now they sold it to the government and let what remained rot on the ground. By the time she left California, Hickok concluded it was "the damndest mess" because of inept and corrupt handling of relief by county and state officials.[60]

After California, Nevada was "a nice, quiet, simple place." She observed that once she got away "from the relief staff, relief committees, politicians, and big ranches," the people she met along the road at garages and gas stations, in restaurants and stores, did not feel as hopeless as others suggested they were. Though cattlemen complained that their stocks would be reduced "by starvation and government purchasing" by 50 percent before winter, though some sections had experienced drought for over a decade, though the price situation for ranchers was bad, nevertheless conditions were better than during the previous year and the people Hickok spoke to were optimistic that they would improve further. She was impressed too that there were areas in Nevada where there was no unemployment at all. Virginia City was enjoying a mild boom owing to advanced technology that allowed the reworking of old mines. The same was true for Silver City "and one or two other places." And in Las Vegas and Boulder City there were almost 5,000 men at work "on the dam and allied projects."[61]

Though ranchers and others in Nevada complained about drought, there was nothing Hickok saw that could be "mentioned in the same breath" with what she saw in the Dakotas at the outset of her western travels. There was vegetation "right there on the desert that the stock can eat" now that development projects had made water available for them to drink. And as the water development program expanded, further feeding places would become available throughout Nevada. In the interim, Hickok said the government would have to provide feed, especially after the cattle and sheep came down from the mountain ranges during the winter months. And the government would continue to purchase "the poorer stuff," livestock that was not sold to the packing houses.[62]

Around Elko, the heart of the sheep and cattle country, some relief was obtained by herding over 20,000 sheep to Idaho for the winter months. The government was expected to purchase about 50,000 sheep, and there was hay enough to provide for 20,000 of them through the winter, leaving, Hickok said, "some 270,000 sheep with no place to go this winter for food."[63]

The cattle situation was better and ranchers, after government purchases, thought they would be able to get through the winter with the hay that was available. The trouble came about because of extreme drought in the southern part of Nevada making it impossible for livestock to forage there during the winter months. Cattle from this part of Nevada purchased by the government were in such poor condition that their carcasses yielded almost no fat. But what distressed Hickok most about the situation in Nevada was the general selfishness of too many ranchers who demanded that wells to be dug on government property be located on range within their "squatter rights so as to attract cattle belonging to another owner on to range that the rancher regards as his own."[64]

Salt Lake City was Hickok's destination after leaving Elko, Nevada. She reported on "political meddling" in relief activities and on the functioning of other federal programs. She also commented on the persistence of polygamy, despite the fact that the Mormon church frowned on the practice. There were polygamists among relief clients, and Hickok was surprised to learn that in the instances brought to her attention the wives got along amicably, that one was a schoolteacher and that the "community husband" had two years of college and "gave his occupation as promoter."[65]

She also reported on her meeting with "the Mormon dignitaries" who sat "in three big, deep, soft chairs, in a dim and luxuriously furnished office in the Church Office Building." Heber Grant, Anthony W. Ivins and J. Reuben Clark were all critical, if not of the New Deal, then of the government in Washington. One insisted that the relief program encouraged people to default on their mortgages and interest payments so that they could "get government relief." Another defended the relief program stating "if we didn't give them relief, they'd come and take it." And she was given a message for the President, "Tell him to rid this country of these aliens." Hickok concluded her account of this visit with the comment, "I don't think the New Deal can count on much understanding or support from the Latter Day Saints of Utah!"[66]

But she did meet New Dealers in Utah. One was Joseph Cannon, editor of the *Desert News,* who published editorials "advocating the Administration's banking and stock exchange policies while the leaders of the church, all tied up with business, were howling with pain." Yet Heber Grant, while complaining to Cannon about these editorials, did not fire him or indicate that no further ones should appear. However, as a result of extended conversations primarily with journalists and relief workers in Salt Lake City, Hickok concluded that "the New Deal has become something of an old story." People expected more of it by way of establishing "a feeling of security." To accomplish it, many expected the President "to go to the Left," and most were willing to go along because they thought him more moderate than some radical leaders. The newly emerged American Liberty League disturbed them because they thought this type of opposition would hamper the President in furthering the New Deal.[67]

Hickok next visited Wyoming, where she resumed her practice of touring a state and examining work relief and other federal programs. Most relief projects in the West got started later than elsewhere in the country, but everywhere Hickok went she found people, except for the difficult situation in the Southwest, preferring jobs to relief of any kind. The attitude, she noted in Wyoming with its widely scattered population, was one of patience, "a rather terrible sort of patience" one that gave people "no hope for the future" and "no feeling of security" as they realized they apparently were not going "to get their jobs back in private industry." As in the East Texas oil fields, so too in Wyoming, the big oil refineries near Casper were not interested in hiring or rehiring any man over 35 years of age.[68]

But when she shifted focus from people to projects, Hickok found general approval in Wyoming. Those having to do with drought relief and water conservation were applauded. But there was a feeling on the part of the public that too many airports were being constructed in Wyoming. Enough canning projects were underway so that every family on relief would be assured of "somewhere between 15 and 20 pounds of beef a month for the next year." And she reported on a tannery project that would utilize the hides of thousands of head of sheep condemned and shot "right on the range."[69]

In Wyoming plans were underway to bring children from drought-stricken farm families into towns for the winter months and into schools. They would be housed in dormitories near the schools. The program would be financed from drought relief funds and it fitted into a broader rural rehabilitation plan involving the removal of families from dry farming land, "where they can't make a living," to areas "reclaimed by government operations."[70]

As she proceeded further east and reached the high plains Hickok reflected that "this drought business gets worse. . . ." Sage brush was "scantier and lower to the ground" in western Wyoming than in Nevada. And it got worse as she drove across Wyoming. Grasshoppers and drought plagued the state in the summer of 1934. And for the first time since leaving the Dakotas she saw stacks of Russian thistle put up for winter feed. Though the grasshoppers did not destroy the corn crop, the sun had burned out all crops in the state. Cattle were rarely to be seen and what cattle there were usually had been foraging in the mountains. Most of them were being purchased by the government as there would not be "a damned thing" available for them to eat during the winter. They could not be driven because there were "no waterholes at all." Most cattlemen, Hickok said, were "deeply appreciative" of what the government was doing to help. All were hoping for a hard winter with plenty of snow as the only thing that would save them. If it came, the cost of human relief in Wyoming and elsewhere would "mount terrifically." Hickok said the people were short of almost everything: cash, clothing, bedding, necessities of all kinds were either nonexistent or "worn out."[71]

In such a situation most people in Wyoming supported the President, did not take "the 'dictatorship' stuff" seriously, and thought moves to the Left were necessary. Some thought socialism was inevitable. Partisanship, she reported, was almost nonexistent in the state as most people believed the President was doing his best "to pull us out of this thing."[72]

Kansas was the last state Lorena Hickok reported on in her western travels for Harry Hopkins at the outset of the New Deal. Driving into Kansas from Colorado, she expected the worst, hearing "the government—especially AAA—blamed for everything from the drought and fifty days of a temperature above 100° to the farmer's hangnails." Instead she found general support for the farm program and an optimistic outlook despite "miles and miles of burnt brown pastures" and "fields of scant, ragged wheat stubble with pathetically little piles of straw."

Here too Russian thistle was being used for stock feed, selling in western Kansas "from $6 to $8 a ton." And everywhere, terribly thin cattle.[73]

Yet in Topeka at the state fair, Hickok reported that judging by the exhibits, "you wouldn't have known there had been a drought in Kansas at all!" The fair gave one the idea that Kansas was a garden spot, although Hickok was ready to "swear" that she had traveled for two days in the state without seeing a haystack and further noted that wells in northeastern Kansas that had not gone dry since the 1870s did so in the summer of 1934. The contrast between the general prosperity evident at the fair in Topeka and in the shops in Kansas City, with what she had seen in her travels throughout the week she spent in Kansas, added up to what Hickok called "the surprise of my life."[74]

Where was all the money coming from? Hickok felt most farmers and businessmen were buying on credit and had overextended themselves. In the southwestern part of the state farmers were planting winter wheat expecting to turn their cattle into the fields to eat it as it came up, thereby holding on for another year. In one county in this area, out of 1,800 families, 1,036 were on relief and others were applying. Nothing was growing there save for "a few fields of badly stunted cane, planted for forage." Stunted cane developed prussic acid in its stalks and leaves, cattle getting hold of it would walk "four or five steps and drop dead."[75]

But as she reached Salina in central Kansas the country began to get green. There was no evidence of crops but there had been some rain and farmers were planting winter wheat. And by the time she reached the rolling country just outside of Kansas City, Hickok said "you might have thought you were in New England." Though contrasts abounded in Kansas, she saw little evidence in the fields that crops were available for harvesting.[76]

Kansas farmers, like most of those Hickok had spoken to in recent weeks, had been critical at the outset of New Deal programs. Now, however, they were supportive. Kansas farmers, particularly those in the southwestern counties, had been through hard times before. Most felt that if they could hold on to their cattle, they could survive another year of drought because cattle could provide a cash reserve. But, as in Wyoming, Hickok was concerned that in some sections of Kansas relief clients during the winter months would have grave need for clothing and bedding. In one county a case worker told Hickok that more than 50 percent of her people already had such needs. Nevertheless, most people in Kansas were optimistic and it was this optimism, Hickok perceptively noted, that was going to make it difficult "to launch any sort of rural rehabilitation program out here." Most drought victims still believed that conditions next year would be better; patience, fortitude, a little rain, and a job of sorts to tide them over was all that was necessary.[77]

All in all, Kansas was "an interesting state." She concluded her report by noting that "even the Republican candidate for Governor, running for reelection, is a sort of New Dealer." Reading an account of one of Alfred M. Landon's speeches, Hickok "thought it was the Democrat talking!" She remarked that the Democratic candidate would have "a tough time of it" because Landon had grabbed all his campaign material. Her concluding comment was "well—that's Kansas."[78]

From Kansas City Lorena Hickok left for Washington and brought her western travels for Harry Hopkins to a close. She did not tour four states in the Northwest: Oregon, Washington, Idaho and Montana and consequently did not comment upon depression conditions in the most heavily forested areas of the West. Otherwise, in her travels she managed to discuss in one way or another almost every theme important to the West: oil, water, cattle, wheat, sugar beets, irrigation, ethnic diversity, sheep, urban and rural conditions, migratory labor, Mormons, mining, drought and dust as they affected various topographical areas. Her fascinating letters serve to delineate conditions as the New Deal was getting under way.

Chapter 3

Great Plains: Lowering Expectations

FRANKLIN DELANO ROOSEVELT first indicated while governor of New York State the approach the New Deal would take to problems and issues affecting the West in the 1930s. In the introduction to the first volume of his public papers and addresses published in 1938 and titled *The Genesis of the New Deal,* Roosevelt said that "many of the objectives and policies of my administration as President had their origin during my term as Governor of New York."[1] Certainly this was the case with agricultural programs operative by 1938 on the Great Plains. While Governor Roosevelt called for extension of electric service to rural areas in New York, no real accomplishments were made anywhere in the nation until after the Rural Electrification Administration (REA) was established on May 11, 1935, during the latter portion of his first term, when a concern for social justice predominated over the implementation of efficient administrative and managerial reforms. The REA affected the West in the 1930s less than other parts of the country, despite notable public power expansion in the region. However, in the broader aspects of the agricultural problem, on basic questions pertaining to land use, Roosevelt's views expressed during his years in Albany carried over to federal programs and policies affecting the Great Plains.

Governor Roosevelt understood that agricultural overproduction, stimulated in good part during World War I, encouraged the tilling of millions of acres unsuitable for agriculture or the raising of crops unsuited to the soil on which they were being raised. He also recognized that climate as well as soil affected agriculture, and he called for accumulating data on how better to use or adapt lands devoted to agriculture. Land policy to Roosevelt meant that rural land "should be used only for that purpose for which it is best fitted and out of which the greatest economic return can be derived." Submarginal lands ought to be withdrawn from agriculture and utilized after careful study for other purposes. Moreover, the state should purchase some of these lands and devote them to more suitable purposes such as reforestation, a program Roosevelt favored for New York State. Henry Wallace and New Dealers in and out of the Department of Agriculture agreed with the premise that there were "Acres Fit and Unfit," the title of Roosevelt's 1931 speech before the Conference of Governors; they attempted to translate Roosevelt's views into reality on the Great Plains in the 1930s by calling for curtailing rather than increasing areas devoted to crop production.[2]

Lowering expectations with regard to agriculture on the Great Plains was a theme that became evident to New Dealers by 1934 when the region experienced by far the most severe drought in the history of American agriculture. The Agricultural Adjustment Administration (AAA) in a massive program purchased livestock—cattle, sheep and goats—and either shipped them to better watered areas further east or had them slaughtered and the meat canned and distributed through the Federal Emergency Relief Administration and the Federal Surplus Relief Corporation. By mid-October, about 7 million head of cattle had been purchased out of special funds provided by Congress for this purpose and for drought relief. The alternative was to let cattle die; pasture, forage, grain, and adequate water in many places were lacking. Crop production fell to incredibly low levels. Corn production in Kansas, for example, as of October 1, 1934, was less than 10.5 million bushels. For 1927–31 average production had been 137.7 million bushels. To assist these drought-stricken farmers, the Farm Credit Administration through a specially allocated fund of $100 million extended emergency feed loans without security, thereby enabling some farmers to keep their remaining cattle through the winter months. In 1934 almost the only income many Great Plains farmers received was from the government—for selling their cattle which otherwise would have perished, for restricting their production, and, if need be, for relief assistance.[3]

To add to the misery of drought on the Great Plains, in the late spring of 1934, hot winds lifted tremendous clouds of dust from the sun-baked soil. People living between the Mississippi River and the Atlantic Ocean witnessed for the first time ever in the heavens a tremendous cloud out of the West so dense and so extensive that it darkened the skies on the eastern seaboard, half a continent away. Jay N. Darling, chief of the Bureau of Biological Survey, happened to be in New York City on the day that the great dust storm from the plains rolled over the city. "The sun," he recalled, "was not visible through its murky depths. The lights in the office buildings and on the streets were turned on and gave the appearance of twilight." Darling viewed this phenomenon in the company of an archeologist friend who had done research in the Gobi Desert and who remarked, "Isn't it astonishing that in America it should take just one generation to reduce its prolific nature to a condition like the Gobi Desert, which was a million years in the making."[4]

This dust storm and others throughout the "dirty thirties" denuded the top soil of vast areas on the Great Plains devoted to wheat and less so to corn. More so than the drought, the dust storms called national attention to what was occuring on the Great Plains. Secretary of Agriculture Henry A. Wallace said that the drought might be the end of a long cycle of subnormal rainfall and that it would be followed, as in ancient Egypt, by a cycle of above-normal rainfall. Future planning would be necessary to provide "an ever-normal granary" by accumulating a surplus during the fat years to provide for the lean years. In addition, the combination of drought and dust storms served to uproot thousands of families on the Great Plains. Many sought their future along Route 66 leading to the Golden State of California; others saw the Northwest as the land of opportunity. But the phenomenon of uprooted people was a national one, though the plight of refugees from the plains states received national attention.[5]

It was estimated that the May 11, 1934, dust storm moved 300 million tons of fertile soil off the Great Plains. With the fertility of the soil seriously impaired by prolonged drought, many farmers no longer worked their land. In 1936 in 45 counties of five states in the southern Great Plains, nearly 20 percent of the total cropland was lying idle and one out of every four farm dwellings, numbering more than 25,000, had been vacated. Abandoned lands became a menace to the remaining farm families because nothing was done to check or prevent wind erosion.[6]

Motion picture newsreels pictured for audiences in other parts of the country just how bad the situation really was: stunted cornstalks that crumbled into dust when touched, emaciated cattle with almost every bone protruding, and ponds and rivers utterly dry. Government officials provided hordes of figures to indicate how severe the damage was. The greatest desolation centers were the in the northern plains states—the Dakotas, eastern Montana, and large sections of Wyoming—though the states of the southern plains, where conditions were almost as critical, received more public attention. In mid-August 1934, Lawrence Westbrook, assistant to Harry L. Hopkins, Federal Relief Administrator, estimated the total loss caused by the drought at $5 billion and added that between 300,000 and 400,000 families already had been ruined by the devastation, a large percentage of whom had no prospect of making a living out of their land in the future. Westbrook also made the point, common to almost all New Dealers when they discussed conditions on the Great Plains, that much of the land never had been good for farming and that thousands, if they were to have any future at all, would have to abandon their homes and seek a livelihood elsewhere.[7]

Initially, the immediate response of the New Deal was to cope with the vast emergency by providing federal funds for relief assistance. Some families, particularly those of tenants and farm laborers who were unable to benefit directly from AAA crop-reduction checks, faced the prospect of no cash income. In addition, Secretary Wallace and others had to assure the American people that, despite drought conditions on the Great Plains, there would be plenty of food available to keep all Americans in the best of health. Employees in the Department of Agriculture, the Farm Credit Administration, and the FERA meanwhile were grappling with the crisis situation on the Great Plains. A Drought Relief Service was created in the department to expedite assistance, but all bureaus were involved in one way or another. The problem by the fall of 1934 was not one of food shortages but rather one of bringing afflicted farm families through the winter and leaving them equipped with seed and livestock to carry on in the spring. On a broader scale they had to see to it that farm and city families whose purchasing power had been wiped out did not starve.[8]

To add to the woes of farmers on the northern plains, a grasshopper infestation was expected in 1934. Congress in March 1934 appropriated more than $2 million to distribute poison bran. Throughout the spring the bait was sent to farmers with the assistance of the Extension Service. But the drought dried the poison so quickly that few hoppers were killed before the bait became unattractive. Moreover, given the already devastating conditions, many farmers quickly lost interest. Grasshoppers were welcome to what drought and dust had not already destroyed.[9]

While some farmers gave up, the Department of Agriculture continued its manifold efforts. A team of experts from Washington traveled to the fringes of the Gobi Desert in search of drought-resistant grasses. The Forest Service cooperated with other organizations in plans for reforestation and erosion control on marginal agricultural lands. And the plan for a huge shelter belt of trees reaching from the Canadian border into northern Texas was launched with much fanfare in 1934 through an executive order alloting $10 million from the General Relief Fund. It was developed by the Forest Service and carried out with the assistance of men employed in the Civilian Conservation Corps.[10] In addition, the Farm Credit Administration (though not part of the Department of Agriculture) in a six-week period in the summer of 1934 disbursed more than 60,000 feed and forage loans thereby helping farmers in the most severe drought areas to preserve foundation herds of livestock. It enabled them, if need be, to ship suitable breeding animals to pasture and to pay rent for such lands during the drought period. While most of these early projects and programs focused on immediate emergency relief action, many were filled with possibilities for the future.

"In general, it may be said that those farmers and ranchmen who survived the disaster best were in the habit of conducting their affairs with the aid of what has been learned through scientific study and experiment," observed Minnie Fisher Cunningham, Texas extension editor. She mentioned several farm wives in the drought-stricken plains portions of the Lone Star State who canned large quantities of fruits and vegetables from their gardens, where they had utilized every means to conserve moisture. Subsoil irrigation with homemade concrete tiles provided a cheap and successful way to irrigate garden patches where water was scarce. Once this became evident, workers on Civil Works Administration and other relief projects constructed tiles for similar gardens. In Scurry County, Texas, for example, 4,000 tiles were made and put down. Good seed also justified itself under the testing it received in 1934, while trench silos helped some Texas farmers save feed and compensate for pasture shortages. Terracing, nearly 7 million acres in 1934, helped save some Texas lands by bringing its owners greater returns than surrounding acres unable to conserve every possible bit of moisture. Extension agents encouraged these and similar practices elsewhere in the plains states. Farmers in Pembina County in North Dakota, following suggestions by H. Earl Hodgson, agricultural adjustment agent, harvested a drought-hit crop in 1934 that was 70 percent of normal. Many New Deal programs merely elaborated on the approach of Extension Service and other agricultural agents in effectively relating to farmers in the drought emergency.[11]

Emergency practices launched in 1934 continued through 1935 and 1936. The drought and the dust storms during these years culminated in the worst drought and possibly the worst ecological disaster in American history. By the end of 1936 the Drought Relief Committee in the Department of Agriculture had designated 1,194 counties as "emergency drought counties." While all of these counties were not located on the Great Plains, every county in the tier of states extending from Oklahoma to North Dakota was included; only Nebraska had two or three counties not so designated. Though the names of the federal agencies operative in 1934 changed, the programs being encouraged were similar. Forage and cover crops, along with practices for controlling erosion, were encouraged. Railroads assisted farmers by reducing freight rates in emergency-designated drought counties. The government continued to purchase cattle in distressed areas where feed was insufficient. Thousands of farmers were given temporary emergency work by the Works Progress Administration (WPA) and assistance by the Resettlement Administration. In some counties on the Great Plains, anywhere from 80 to 90 percent of the farm families had to apply for relief at one time or another. Usually it was from one-fifth to one-third of all farm families. Agents of the Extension Service spearheaded many of these relief activities by bringing the farmer into contact with particular agencies, helping him to cull his cattle while maintaining a good foundation herd for better times, procuring emergency pasture and forage seed, and helping dig emergency trench silos to get the most feed value out of drought-damaged corn. The newly organized Soil Conservation Service provided skilled technical assistance to farmers in establishing workable soil and water conservation procedures. Practices such as these continued unabated until conditions on the Great Plains started to improve markedly late in the decade.

Erosion, involving the disappearance of topsoil chiefly by the action of wind—and less so by water—was a particular problem on the Great Plains. Restoring the sod that held the soil before it was plowed was the New Deal approach encouraged by agents and bureaus in the Department of Agriculture. The Soil Conservation Service advised and assisted Great Plains farmers in adopting a rain conservation program through contour plowing and through plowing up earthen ridges with gaps so that rain might accumulate in them for distribution as needed. In areas to be set aside for grazing, time was necessary for grass roots to gain a foothold.

Another proposed cure for wind erosion, already briefly noted, was the shelterbelt project for planting trees in strips running north and south from Texas to the Dakotas, the width of the belts and their distances apart depending upon local climate and soil conditions. While Congress was reluctant to appropriate funds directly for the project, the Forest Service was able to use WPA and CCC labor to further the project. By 1940 over 2,500 miles of shelterbelt strips had been planted with nearly 45 million trees on 6,500 farms. Moreover, the idea of farm windbreaks found favor with Congress; in 1937 it approved the Farm Forestry Act whereby the government provided trees to farmers to develop their own shelterbelt system.

Wind erosion on the Great Plains, which was responsible for the creation of the Dust Bowl, was caused in large part by faulty farming techniques and by overgrazing, as New Dealers both in and out of government proclaimed. But the worst problems were caused by planting wheat on marginal lands that should have been kept for grazing. The New Deal solution to this problem was double-edged: restoring the abused soil and regulating the use of grazing lands.

Given the conditions of the drought, dust storms, and repeated crop failures, their inevitable legacy was a burden of heavy mortgages, unpaid feed and seed loans, mounting tax delinquencies, forced sales, and increasing tenancy. All contributed to the economic insecurity of Great Plains farmers. On the northern and central Great Plains during the dry years, anywhere from two-fifths to three-fourths of the cash receipts of farmers came from federal funds in the form of production control (AAA) payments, emergency livestock purchases, or relief grants. Many farmers also obtained crop and seed loans from the government. Others secured temporary jobs on WPA, Public Works Administration (PWA) projects, or with other federal agencies, constructing farm-to-market roads or dams of various kinds, to cite but two examples. And the Resettlement Administration in 1936 provided for a year's moratorium on all of its loans to individuals in the officially designated drought counties.

Aside from the Texas and Oklahoma panhandles, and a few neighboring counties in Kansas, Colorado, and New Mexico where severe wind erosion aggravated the drought situation and where farmers were in serious straits prior to the dirty thirties, the situation on the southern Great Plains was less serious—thanks to more precipitation, normally mild winters, and a longer growing season. However, small farms throughout the Great Plains, heavy indebtedness, nonresident land ownership, and increasing tenancy intensified the need for agricultural readjustments. The New Deal approach to rehabilitating these farmers involved increasing the size of some farms, reorganizing operating units by retiring some land from crops, increasing pasture acreage, rebuilding livestock herds, repairing buildings, and either repairing or replacing farm machinery. But the emphasis was always on retiring crop lands and increasing pasturage.[12]

To further this process the Resettlement Administration, besides making loans and grants to distressed farmers in the drought area, also developed land-use adjustment projects. The projects in North and South Dakota, Montana, Nebraska, and Wyoming by mid-August 1936 involved the purchase of about 4 million acres of land considered unsuitable for farming at a cost of almost $14 million. Most of this land was scheduled for conversion into controlled grazing ranges once grasses built a natural cover for the soil, making it less prone to destructive wind erosion. Besides adding to the public domain, the agency through its loans and grants also encouraged some farmers to expand the size of their units, thereby facilitating the shift from grain cultivation to raising livestock fodder and utilizing larger acreages for pasture. The AAA also encouraged this shift by paying farmers in the drought area for diverting acreage from soil-depleting crops to grass and other soil-enriching vegetation and to feed and forage crops for livestock.[13]

At the outset Roosevelt's approach to the emergency situation on the Great Plains, like his approach to the depression crisis in general, stressed relief and recovery more than reform. In his June 9, 1934, message to Congress calling for additional funds to carry on drought relief, among other things he requested $50 million for emergency acquisition of submarginal farms and assistance in relocating destitute farm families. And it is clear from his further remarks that meeting the emergency dominated his thinking. On his trip across the northern plains, the best he could say in his extemporaneous remarks at Devils Lake, North Dakota, on August 7, 1934, was "I hope to goodness it is going to rain, good and plenty." To meet the problem of wind erosion he was able to inform Governor Alfred M. Landon of Kansas in 1935 that "a project involving strip-listing and cross-plowing had been developed by the Department of Agriculture" and was being put into effect in the plains states.[14]

At a press conference on July 17, 1936, while discussing relief problems caused by the drought, the President protested that "nobody ever had any idea in their sane senses of depopulating the country." On wheat lands the water table, he noted, was dropping about eight inches a year with the result that "the water runs off and the surface blows away." But if grass could regain a foothold, "acreage will be used more and more for cattle" and the population on the plains would adjust to the new economy. At this press conference Roosevelt also said, "We are working on a plan to avoid a continuation of what we have been going through now for the last three or four years." Having already spent around $300 million, unless the economy of the Great Plains was changed or "unless the cycles change," the government would have to continue spending millions through its emergency programs. Circumstances had made it obvious to Roosevelt that relief activities were not sufficient. Reform was now dominant in the President's thoughts.

Shortly thereafter Roosevelt asked Morris L. Cooke, chief of the Rural Electrification Administration (REA), to chair a Great Plains Drought Area Committee. While requesting the committee to recommend "practicable measures for remedying the conditions" which brought widespread losses and acute distress to so many inhabitants of the Great Plains, the President also suggested the approach the committee would take when he explained that perhaps "practices brought from the more humid part of the country are not most suitable under the prevailing natural conditions." A distinguished group of government officials was asked to serve with Cooke and to meet with the President.[15]

Cooke was not totally unaware of the problems facing the region. Early in the New Deal Roosevelt had asked him to chair a Mississippi Valley Committee. While this committee was engaged in its research on May 11, 1934, a massive dust storm swept across the Dakotas, on into Nebraska, Kansas, and parts of the Southwest. The Soil Conservation Service estimated that this storm swept about 300 million tons of topsoil off the Great Plains. When it was all over, fence posts along with bushes and hedges in many areas were all but covered. Windmills seemed to be standing on stubby legs. Drifts of topsoil rivaled those of snow during severe blizzards. Cooke and his committee, pondering this disaster, sought long-range solutions rather than immediate palliatives to insure that, if possible, such disasters would not occur in the future.[16]

Though its charge covered more than a study of the rivers crossing the Great Plains, the Mississippi Valley Committee report underscored the dimensions of the problem, discussed erosion, and its social implications. The report stressed the fact that erosion in the upper valleys could only mean serious flooding as rivers emptied into the mighty Mississippi. Dust was only one side of the problem; water—either an abundance of it or a lack of it—was the other side of the problem, especially so on the Great Plains. Massive programs to deal with flood control, soil erosion, forest coverings, and power installations were among the items covered in the final report submitted on October 1, 1934, to Harold L. Ickes, administrator of the Federal Emergency Administration of Public Works (PWA). The report in effect was a plea for planning the use and control of water as a basic function in national life, recognizing at the same time that relevant problems of the land and of the people inhabiting it also had to be taken into consideration. Though nothing immediately came from this report, Cooke had become acutely aware of the problems overwhelming people on the Great Plains and thus was an ideal choice to chair the Great Plains Drought Area Committee.[17]

While the Drought Committee was at work, Henry A. Wallace wrote the President about his concern that a considerable section of the Great Plains could become a "semi-desert" if "a real change in climate" was under way. He suggested that the role of the federal government should be one of helping in shifting to "appropriate types of grazing and [to an] agriculture with emphasis on the right kind of drought-resisting plants." Harry Hopkins, appointed by Roosevelt to the Great Plains Drought Area Committee, was convinced that the only permanent solution lay in turning the farmlands into pasture and resettling the farmers.[18]

Meanwhile, as part of his reelection campaign, the President decided to secure at firsthand all the information he could about the drought area. He invited the governors, including his Republican opponent in the campaign—Alfred M. Landon—and other officials of states in the drought area to meet with him in Des Moines on September 1 to discuss the situation. This was the largest and most important of the drought conferences Roosevelt held on this campaign trip. At several stops he left the train and ventured into the country to view various water conservation projects and to chat with drought- and dust-stricken farmers.[19]

At Bismarck, North Dakota, on August 27, 1936, with the President in attendance, a preliminary report of the Great Plains Drought Area Committee was presented, focusing on the "long-term problem of readjustment and reorganization." The report noted that since January 1, 1933, federal agencies had spent in the "Great Plains regions on works related to conservation of physical assets, about $140,000,000, not including grants, loans and relief disbursements amounting to approximately $355,000,000." To stabilize the region's economy, to curb "the shock of inevitable droughts," to conserve both land and water, to eliminate dependence on "public grants and subsidies," to restore both the income and the credit of individuals as well as of local and state governments, and, finally, to consider "how great a population, and in what areas, the Great Plains can support," these were the grandiose goals of the committee as it propounded the official New Deal gospel for the Great Plains during the 1930s.

The basic premise of this gospel was succinctly stated: "The basic cause of the present Great Plains situation is our attempt to impose upon the region a system of agriculture to which the Plains are not adapted or to bring into a semi-arid region methods which are suitable, on the whole, only for a humid region." From this premise flowed a critique of "highly speculative" wheat farming which involved continual plowing of the soil, thereby exposing it "to the destructive forces of sun and wind." The report speculated that 80 percent of the soil of the Great Plains was already in some stage of erosion "and as much as 15 percent may already have been injured seriously and permanently." To remedy the damage "caused by a mistaken homesteading policy, by the stimulation of wartime demands which led to overcropping and overgrazing, and by encouragement of a system of agriculture which could not be both permanent and prosperous," the federal government, which was thus indicted as being partially responsible for prevailing conditions, had to play a role in meliorating the situation. There then followed a series of suggestions designed to "arrest the wastage of soil by erosion" and to provide for the "efficient use of the water resources of the region."

The suggestions, the heart of the New Deal gospel for the Great Plains, called for taking "certain sub-marginal lands permanently out of commercial production" and carefully studying other lands to determine how best they could be utilized. On lands devoted to agriculture and grazing a potpourri of soil-conserving practices were recommended: regrassing, contour plowing and furrowing, terracing, listing, strip-cropping, water spreading, and the planting of trees. Water conservation practices of all kinds, including "some readjustment of water rights," were called for to achieve the central premise of never allowing water "needlessly to go to waste."

In addition, government on all levels should cooperate and continue to acquire lands "too seriously injured to warrant restoration by private enterprise." Some of these lands eventually could be leased or optioned under supervision to individuals or local associations. All of the suggestions made by the Great Plains Drought Area Committee were designed in one way or another to stabilize the population drift throughout the region by sustaining a regional agriculture that could "support a family in independence and comfort." This meant that in many areas holdings would have to be larger than the traditional 160 or more acres provided in the various Homestead Acts; in other areas, the committee noted that "farmers are attempting cultivation of too much land;" the report also concluded "there would seem to be justification for the use of the public credit to enable competent tenants to purchase and operate their own farms."[20]

Following his drought inspection trip, Roosevelt brought the message to the American people in the first "Fireside Chat" of 1936, delivered on September 6. Proclaiming that "we are going to conserve soil, conserve water, conserve life," the President commented on what he had seen in the drought states, on what federal and local authorities were doing to provide relief, and on what remained to be done "to defend the people of this country against the effect of future droughts." His words carried dramatic impact as he said, "I shall never forget the fields of wheat so blasted by heat that they cannot be harvested. I shall never forget field after field of corn, stunted, earless, stripped of leaves, for what the sun left the grasshoppers took. I saw brown pasture that would not keep a cow on fifty acres." Roosevelt, however, could not linger in his remarks on devastation and despair. In the midst of a campaign for reelection, and as Chief Executive, he had to accentuate the positive by noting the role and the responsibilities of the federal government.

Work relief for members of farm families through the oncoming winter months was an absolute necessity, especially on projects aimed at alleviating future drought conditions, such as construction of ponds or small reservoirs "to supply water for stock and to lift the level of the underground water to protect wells from going dry." Spending for water conservation projects, Roosevelt insisted, was not waste; but "it would spell future waste if we did not spend for such things now." He also stressed the point that "no simple panacea can be applied to the drought problem in the whole of the drought area." Planning depended on local conditions in which different variables, such as annual rainfall, soil characteristics, altitude, and topography, had to be considered. Though he did not discuss details, Roosevelt mentioned the Great Plains Drought Area Committee and its preliminary recommendations, indicating that successful cooperation already was occurring with governors and state planning boards.[21]

Thus in his Fireside Chat, Roosevelt brought the gospel concerning the Great Plains in dramatic outline form to the American people. It remained to be formalized, cast in an official statement. Eleven days later, Roosevelt asked Morris L. Cooke, chairman of the Great Plains Drought Area Committee, to chair a special committee to report back to him no later than the first day of the new year "on a long-term program for the efficient utilization of the resources of the Great Plains area," amplifying in effect the recommendation Cooke's committee presented previously to him at Bismarck. A group of informed bureaucrats was invited to serve with Cooke and shortly thereafter the President asked the National Resources Committee to bring together materials and recommendations assembled in the course of its work pertaining to the Great Plains. In addition, he asked the National Resources Committee "to secure the advice and recommendations" of the concerned state planning boards. All of this data would be available to Cooke's committee.[22]

While Roosevelt campaigned for reelection, Cooke and his committee considered their assignment and by year's end had drafted its report, harmoniously and without fundamental disagreements necessitating compromises in its conclusions. The committee in its 194-page report recommended action on five specific fronts: intensively surveying the land and other resources of the region; acquiring range lands for controlled sale or lease; encouraging family-size farms large enough "to provide a secure and adequate living"; encouraging small-size irrigation systems and other measures of water development and conservation; and, lastly, establishing a coordinating agency to cooperate with all groups concerned with "the future of the Great Plains," the phrase placed on the title page of the report.

While the committee recommended federal action, it could only suggest activities that might be acceptable to state, local, and private groups in a concerted effort to achieve a unified and cooperative program. It recommended, for example, that states codify laws pertaining to land and water use and conservation, that they encourage and supervise grazing associations, seek to control erosion and develop more coherent administrative practices with regard to land use and taxation. In addition, Cooke's committee also suggested a broad-gauged educational campaign to acquaint local officials and other individuals with "proven principles of land and water conservation." And finally, in presenting the report, Cooke told the President, "that to be wholly successful the program must be initiated by the Federal Government and without unnecessary delay."[23]

In presenting the Great Plains Drought Area Committee report to Congress, Roosevelt succinctly stated, "The problem is one of arresting the decline of agricultural economy not adapted to the climatic conditions because of lack of information and understanding at the time of settlement, and of readjusting the economy in the light of later experience and of scientific information now available." Following Cooke's suggestions, Roosevelt said the program "must be cooperative," involving action by individuals and government agencies at all levels. The New Deal gospel regarding the Great Plains now had its bible in the report titled *The Future of the Great Plains*. Congress and the states in the region had to translate it into a policy, and thereafter a specific program had to be formulated and put into execution with all deliberate speed.[24]

The report itself attracted widespread public attention. It indicated that, owing to depression and drought on the Great Plains, a social order as well as America's earlier agrarian ideal of a self-sustained yeoman farmer was in the process of disintegration. It noted too that a new and more cooperative social order, one that could counter both soil erosion and its counterpart of human erosion, was required. The entire drought problem was set forth vividly, simply, and with constant recognition of the important roles that individual habits, established institutions, and vital social and economic forces played. As a human and cultural problem, it was being presented to a large number of people in a remarkable documentary film initially prepared to educate employees of the Resettlement Administration and cooperating agencies to the problems facing them.

Pare Lorentz's classic film, *The Plow that Broke the Plains* (with a musical score by Virgil Thomson) by the summer of 1936 had received critical acclaim and national attention. The situation on the Great Plains and the New Deal gospel about the conditions prevailing there, as well as the concern for cooperative conservation practices, was dramatically presented to a large movie-going audience. At least two successful Democratic House candidates, one from Texas and the other from South Dakota, used the film in their campaigns. And Senator Alva Adams of Colorado said the film was a remarkable presentation "of the unplanned cooperation of land-hungry men, war, drought and wind in the destruction of grass lands in the West." New Deal doctrine regarding the region was more succinctly related by Pare Lorentz, who overheard two women sitting in front of him when *The Plow that Broke the Plains* was shown in a leading Broadway theater. One woman turned to the other and remarked, "They never should have plowed them plains."[25]

The Plow that Broke the Plains could very well be considered as the cinematic version of *The Future of the Great Plains*. Lorentz, who spent seven weeks on the plains preparing the film, as film scholar Richard Dyer MacCann observed, "was interested in human problems, in the bitter results of human mistakes, in the vast drama of the impact of the elements on human beings." These themes were also of primary concern to the authors of the report of the Great Plains Committee. Speaking of the film, Lorentz said "Our heroine is the grass, our villain the sun and wind, our players the actual farmers living in the plains country."[26] Though the film brought the problem of the Great Plains to a large audience, though it presented New Deal gospel regarding the area, and though it attracted congressional attention both pro and con, it was unable to play a role in assisting the translation of that gospel into legislation.

Congress never fully responded to the program of readjustment and development presented in *The Future of the Great Plains,* though segments of it were implemented by various agencies with little federal funding. Implementation of the New Deal aroused increasing congressional ire once the President presented his plan for the reorganization of the judicial branch of the government on February 5, 1937, five days before he urged Congress to adopt the program for the future of the Great Plains.[27] The tumultuous controversy generated by his court-packing proposal put the New Deal on the defensive. Relatively few of its domestic legislative suggestions would henceforth be accepted by Congress. Tensions within the Democratic party came to the forefront and destroyed the effective working relationship between 1600 Pennsylvania Avenue and Capitol Hill. And in 1938 the Republicans added notably to their congressional strength, further impairing the effectiveness of the New Deal. Moreover by 1938 the gospel enunciated in *The Future of the Great Plains* was being fractured as drought, "black blizzards", and hard times abated with a shift in the weather cycle and a return of adequate rainfall. Abundant crops and the threat of war promising overseas markets meant better times for farmers and others on the Great Plains. The gospel in many instances was abandoned as the Dust Bowl once again gave way to fields of golden winter wheat. To be sure, not all of the suggestions and doings of the New Deal were jettisoned. The problems that riveted American attention in the dirty thirties would return to haunt residents of the region in the postwar period. *The Future of the Great Plains* retains a freshness that will only become antiquated when the American people and their representatives are ready to fully translate the recommendations suggested in the report into legislative reality.

Farmers watering stock thinned by drought, near Belfield, North Dakota, July 1936. (Library of Congress)

A belt of cottonwoods, planted in rows twenty feet apart, in Foard County, Texas, in 1936. (FDR Library)

WPA Federal Arts Project, Melrose, New Mexico. (FDR Library)

The CCC felling a beetle-infested tree in California's Lassen National Forest. (FDR Library)

Camp Council meeting at FSA camp, Tulare County, California, May 1939.
(FDR Library)

Entrance to California's Kern County migrant camp, November 1936.
(FDR Library)

U.S. forest ranger issues grazing permits to Spanish American ranchers, Chacon, Mora County, New Mexico, January 1943. (Library of Congress)

Lange-Siphon—the world's longest—carries water five miles to Dead Ox Flat, Malheur County, Oregon, October 1939. (Library of Congress)

All American Canal reclamation project, California. (Library of Congress)

Irrigation of a citrus grove, Yuma Valley, Arizona. (FDR Library)

The Bonneville Dam, Columbia River, July 1939. This aerial view looks northeast and shows the approach channel and navigation lock, the powerhouse, Bradford Island, the spillway dam, and the Washington shore. (FDR Library)

Upstream view of the Grand Coulee Dam, Columbia Basin reclamation project, Washington state. (FDR Library)

Chapter 4

Great Plains: Fragmented Reform

PERSONAL ACCOUNTS OF experiences on the Great Plains during the dirty thirties are numerous. Inhabitants of the region, journalists, and others have extensively commented about conditions: the blazing sun, the black blizzards, starving cattle, brown fields, the desperate people seeking to hang on for another season or pulling up stakes and moving on—walking or in a laden-down jalopy. Between 1935 and 1937 approximately 235,000 persons left their farms for opportunities elsewhere. While outward migration has received much attention, not so well known are the efforts of the New Dealers, chiefly field personnel, who in administering various programs among the people, sought to advise and aid them in coping with their plight. These lesser officials tried to implement programs devised in Washington to meet the crisis on the Great Plains. Various agencies of the state and federal government, while continuing relief efforts, carried out programs seeking the reconstruction of Great Plains agriculture during Roosevelt's second administration.

To begin, the problem first had to be defined. The Government Printing Office turned out an incredible number of publications devoted to doing just this and then explaining what had been, was being, and would be done. For example, *Areas of Intense Distress 1930–1936* was the first of a series of monographs prepared by members of the Division of Social Research of the Works Progress Administration, examining economic and social conditions in the drought area of the Great Plains states. The study depicted the cumulative effects of the drought in 803 counties and defined two centers of acute distress: one on the northern plains, extending to the Canadian border; the other on the southern or high plains. It concluded that in more than one-third of the counties, federal assistance granted from 1930 to 1936 amounted to $476 for an average family of four.[1]

Other reports of the Division of Social Research probed conditions in the areas of acute distress. By presenting vast amounts of data pertaining to farm income, crop yields, farm acreage, irrigated lands, federal aid from wheat and hog contracts, and from relief agencies, conclusions were reached that reinforced the New Deal gospel pertaining to the Great Plains. Throughout the intense drought areas the size of the farms in most instances provided inadequate support for most families. The impact of government cattle purchases and emergency relief grants was carefully determined and presented in many of these reports. So too was data on land ownership with breakdowns between resident and nonresident owners, number of tenants, ethnicity and mobility, along with statistics pertaining to mortgages and tax delinquency. Besides presenting profiles of prevailing conditions in large numbers of distress counties, the authors of these reports made recommendations as to the chief rehabilitation measures they deemed necessary: the advance of working capital to farmers with exhausted credit, replacing machinery and livestock in extreme instances, reducing over time the number of small farms, returning eroded acreage to grass, encouraging strip farming, and increasing the number of livestock.[2]

Literally hundreds of reports covering one or the other of the 803 counties included in *Areas of Intense Distress 1930–1936* were appearing by the summer of 1936. Their findings supported the New Deal gospel and certainly convinced their compilers and many readers of the necessity of reform and change from past practices necessitating a lowering of expectations, increased assistance, and greater cooperation among federal, state, and local agencies. From the outset, the New Deal was coping on a piecemeal basis with different agencies or bureaus providing different services. To be sure, most of the federal programs giving assistance on the Great Plains centered either in the Department of Agriculture or in one or another of the agencies or programs handled by the "Minister of Relief," Harry Hopkins. For example, by 1937 the Works Progress Administration, utilizing relief labor, was engaged in an extensive water conservation program in states subject to drought. Numerous small dams were constructed and wells were drilled where favorable conditions existed. Also through the Department of Agriculture small dams were constructed or aid was granted to farmers for constructing them. In Montana, to cite another example, the Resettlement Administration built hundreds of small earthen dams to furnish stock water on publicly owned rangelands, thereby providing work for thousands of needy people. Throughout the Great Plains in 1937 the Resettlement Administration was conducting a program of locating limited supplies of groundwater and seeking to coordinate the use of available supplies with other natural resources of the region.[3]

Though Roosevelt's preoccupation with *The Future of the Great Plains* declined markedly after the report was presented to Congress, he never lost interest in "the need for preservation of the soil and water resources of the Great Plains, and the general lines of action required to bring about their effective use." He never lost faith in the necessity of federal and state agencies cooperating to seek better procedures and national policies to promote the rehabilitation of the area. After the Great Plains Committee prepared its report, Roosevelt relied on the National Resources Committee for information and assistance on problems pertaining to the region.[4]

Serious drought conditions asserted themselves again during the summer of 1939 in parts of the Great Plains. Roosevelt's actions indicate the fragmented response which continued to be the New Deal's approach to the situation on the Great Plains. Late in July he directed the secretary of agriculture, the secretary of the interior, the Works Progress Administration, and the director of the Civilian Conservation Corps to prepare for an emergency under authority previously granted these agencies by Congress. In the Department of Agriculture, the Agricultural Adjustment Administration had the authority under such circumstances to provide funds for reseeding croplands where weather had destroyed previous seedings. The Farm Security Administration could provide assistance in the form of loans or grants, while the Federal Surplus Commodities Corporation was authorized to purchase surplus foods for distribution to needy families. The Farm Security Administration, to curtail wheat production, required that land have a moisture penetration in the soil at seeding time to a depth of at least two feet before a loan would be made. The Works Progress Administration could give special consideration to projects in drought-stricken areas and the Civilian Conservation Corps was prepared to expand its enrollment quotas in judging the relief needs of these areas. In addition, Roosevelt conferred with members of Congress and officials of the Department of Agriculture "about the extent of drought damage, the availability of feed supplies and measures which seemed more appropriate in alleviating distress as a result of the drought."[5]

Fortunately the October crop report of the Agricultural Marketing Service indicated that there would not be extensive crop damage on the Great Plains and no shortage of feed supplies. But the President's response indicates immediate concern for alleviating possible distress, while revealing that efforts to meliorate conditions through cooperative conservation of land and water resources were no longer central considerations. The challenge of the drought after 1937 prompted only fragmented responses. Different officials, bureaus, agencies, and departments of government still talked about and engaged in meaningful conservation practices, but a consistent, concerted, cooperative effort was not to be. With the return of more favorable weather conditions and the onset of war in Europe, the emphasis of government officials focused more and more on ways and means of increasing food production throughout the Great Plains states. Discussions about returning eroded and exhausted lands to grass and the adoption of a land policy designed to curb continued destruction of the land were now seldom heard.

Nevertheless, the New Deal eased the situation and some of its efforts while providing relief also effected reform. The Department of Agriculture, more so than any other department of government, was familiar with conditions on the plains and several of its programs did more than provide for relief. Secretary Henry A. Wallace, in calling for an "Ever Normal Granary"—a supply of grain kept perpetually at a stated level to be drawn on in time of need comparable to the way a water reservoir functions—recognized that, if put into operation, drought-stricken farmers and their families could "call upon the centralizing power of government to help them in their collective efforts." Through its various bureaus and divisions, its vast personnel, and its equally vast number of publications, the department during Wallace's tenure encouraged the use of every known means to keep the topsoil capable of holding water in place. It also worked to discourage the raising of cultivated crops on land where there was little probability of enough moisture to mature them and to encourage the reversion of these lands to pasture. In addition, Wallace and his associates called for better farm management, recognizing that individual ownership of Great Plains lands was initimately involved with social needs and concerns that affected the overall general welfare.

While nature made the role of the New Dealers, their policies, and their programs throughout the plains possible, it continued throughout the decade to pose new challenges. To add to the burdens that placed over five million people (about 17 percent of the farming population) at the mercy of the scorching sun, the rainless clouds, the blown dust, and the dry wind thereby involving them with the worst, most destructive, and costliest drought in the nation's history, a new menace threatened in the spring of 1937. Billions upon billions of grasshoppers, capable of destroying thousands of square miles of growing crops, were hatching in the West. On April 6 Secretary Wallace broadcast a warning to farmers throughout the plains and prairie states about the greatest grasshopper menace "in modern times." While the menace was not as severe as threatened, because the summer of '37 was not as dry and warm as previous summers and thereby did not provide the ideal climate for "young hoppers to mature into full-grown, voracious destroyers," plans were made for coping with this crisis. States made appropriations for a "poison bran barrage" to kill the insect invaders, and Congress authorized the spending of $2 million. If a potential grasshopper invasion was not enough to concern agricultural officials, there was also a battle against the Mormon cricket, with poison as its principal weapon, in many parts of the West led by experts from the Bureau of Entomology with local and WPA help.[6]

The most effective work of the Department of Agriculture on the Great Plains was performed in coping with soil erosion. The parched soil throughout the region became an easy prey to wind and water, and black blizzards were the result. Soil erosion occurs not because of impoverished soil but from a lack of vegetation that once held the soil together. Once the topsoil was blown away, there was no way it could be replaced. The Soil Conservation Service, under the direction of a dynamic chief, Hugh Hammond Bennett, estimated in the summer of 1936 that 9 million acres had been irretrievably ruined by erosion and that 50 million additional acres were so seriously affected that there was little chance of their survival. Moreover, about 200,000 acres were annually being eroded and the direct loss of all of this erosion was estimated at about $400 million annually. To be sure, not all of the erosion occurred on the Great Plains, but a good portion, possibly half, did. And the Soil Erosion Service devoted much attention to the Great Plains.[7]

It had good reason to do so. Lands laid bare by plows to grow wheat during World War I, by the 1930s were almost literally surrendering topsoil to every breeze. Throughout the region people and animals had difficulty breathing when the hot winds blew. Housewives taped windows to keep windblown soil from entering their houses. They did not succeed because the soil was sifted so fine by the wind. People got lost in these storms; trains, struggling through, were always several hours late. At times the wind whipped the topsoil into great drifts which settled over hundreds of miles. Minor streams disappeared and major ones, such as the Red River along the eastern boundary of the Dakotas, became hardly more than a creek. Noon was like night; visibility was diminished, and if the dust became mixed with moisture, a plaster would attach itself to buildings, cars, streets, and people unfortunate enough to be caught in one of these black blizzards.

The brunt of these storms fell on western Kansas, eastern Colorado, western Oklahoma, the Texas panhandle, and parts of New Mexico. This area soon became known as the Dust Bowl, but dust swirled over the entire area of the Great Plains. Dust pneumonia accompanied these storms and scores of women and children were sent out of the most seriously afflicted areas. Livestock, like humans, had trouble breathing and crops, including trees, were destroyed. Secretary Wallace reckoned it would take about a decade to establish an effective program of rehabilitation involving grass and other cover crops, tree belts, small reservoirs, and terraces. The Soil Conservation Service played a dominant role in this rehabilitation.

Many residents of the region gave up before these efforts could have an impact. Others, wheat farmers and ranch operators, made a determined fight to stay on their lands. All, however, experienced economic and other losses beyond calculation. Lawrence Svobida, a Kansas wheat farmer, wrote a graphic account of his seven-year battle against "an empire of dust." He finally acknowledged defeat. With his financial resources exhausted and his health impaired, he left his farm in western Kansas and joined the exodus of those leaving the Great Plains "in despair, haunted by famine and disease, yet fearful of a future without hope."[8]

Rehabilitation was launched officially when Congress responded to one of the recommendations of the Great Plains Committee with the passage of the Water Facilities Act in August 1937. The Act appropriated $5 million for the construction and maintenance of facilities for water storage and placed a limit of $50,000 to be spent on any one project. Congressional appropriations, however, were sufficient for only a fraction of the requests for credit and technical assistance to farmers in the development of water resources too small to fall within the scope of other public agencies.[9] It was the Soil Conservation Service that provided the technical or engineering assistance for this program.

Soil conservation as an effective public program began with the New Deal. First functioning in the Department of the Interior as the Soil Erosion Service, Congress in 1935 provided for soil conservation work on a permanent basis and established the Soil Conservation Service as the agency to conduct the program. It was transferred to the Department of Agriculture but the agency remained under the aegis of the dynamic Hugh Hammond Bennett. Though national in its scope, much attention was given to the problems of the Great Plains where, as elsewhere, labor provided either by the Civilian Conservation Corps or the Works Progress Administration assisted the Soil Conservation Service in programs for the newly established soil conservation districts. These districts, units of local government created first in 1937 under state law, allowed farmers to work together on common problems with members or agents of the Soil Conservation Service.[10]

Once the agency started functioning on the Great Plains, research on ways and means of controlling wind and water erosion was conducted on a larger scale than in the past; demonstration projects were launched; actual land conservation measures and programs were undertaken; individual farmers and ranchers received financial and technical assistance; others received loans or gifts of seed, supplies, and equipment to assist in conservation work on their farms or ranches. Meanwhile, the Soil Conservation Service also developed land-use plans for a district as well as for individual farms and ranches.

Most of the financial support for the soil conservation districts was provided by the federal government primarily through the Soil Conservation Service.[11]

The New Deal gospel was brought directly to Great Plains residents by Hugh Hammond Bennett's disciples. They showed farmers and ranchers how to replant damaged land with buffalo grass and other hardy varieties. They extolled the virtues of sorghum as a robust, drought-resistant crop and showed farmers how to cut it high on the stalk leaving a stubble to shield the land from wind. A 1934 survey conducted under Bennett's direction (when he headed the Soil Erosion Service) indicated that wind erosion affected a total area of 322 million acres with 35 million of them essentially destroyed, chiefly on the Great Plains from North Dakota down through southwestern Texas and eastern New Mexico. Bennett by 1938 now had a chance to help in translating aspects of the gospel, those emphasizing land more so than water utilization, into reality.[12]

Earlier, as chief of the Soil Erosion Service operating with funds allocated from the Public Works Administration, Bennett began actual fieldwork controlling soil erosion on representative areas scattered throughout the nation, half of which were located in the West. But only two programs were located on the Great Plains, one in Oklahoma, the other in Texas. Here techniques and approaches later extensively recommended by the Soil Conservation Services were first utilized. Steep erosive slopes were taken out of cultivation and planted to grasses or other thick-growing crops. Strip cropping, terracing, and rotation were practiced and other control measures were employed. The cooperation of farmers, ranchers, and local residents was encouraged in the first attempt in the nation's history to establish a comprehensive, large-scale program to curb soil erosion and provide flood control. A wide array of expertise involving agronomists, range specialists, soil experts, engineers, and economists was brought into play on these selected projects. Primarily they were aimed at saving areas rather than reclaiming hopelessly worn-out, gullied land. The program was preventive, to forestall soil erosion from building a new public domain, "an empire," as Bennett said, "of worn-out land, land stripped of its rich surface soil down to poor subsoil and land gullied beyond the possibility of practical reclamation."[13]

The first wind erosion control project in the country was set up in August 1934 at Dalhart, Texas, widely known as the "Capital of the Dust Bowl" before the Soil Conservation Service was established. The project included 28,765 acres of which 23,841 acres had been damaged by moderate-to-serious wind erosion. With the project established, the entire acreage was still subject to blowing. By the end of 1937, thanks to soil and moisture conservation practices employed during the previous three years, it was estimated that only 3,740 acres remained subject to wind erosion. These results were obtained with a rainfall never exceeding twelve inches during this three-year period.[14]

The keys to the success of the soil conservation districts, as Bennett learned from his previous experience, were research, education, and cooperation. The fund of technical knowledge on which the districts could draw was provided by both state and federal agencies, by state universities and field employees of the United States Department of Agriculture. Civilian Conservation Corps workers aided by WPA funds and workers were also available to provide labor necessary for particular projects, such as water-impounding dams. Farmers and ranchers then had to be convinced that they could put this information to practical use on their lands. Finally, there had to develop among farmers, ranchers, and others in the district, a common understanding and agreement with the program and its purpose. In this way the Soil Conservation Service sought not only the stabilization of land severely damaged by wind erosion but the restoration of much of this land to profitable agricultural uses as well. In many instances this meant the substitution of a crop better adapted than wheat to the emergency conditions. By the end of the 1930s the Soil Conservation Districts on the Great Plains had launched a beginning of the program of readjustment and development recommended to Congress in *The Future of the Great Plains*.[15]

So effective was the work of the Soil Conservation Service that, when the internal structure of the Department of Agriculture was reorganized in October 1938, Secretary Henry A. Wallace added further responsibilities, including a number of action programs, to those already being conducted by Hugh Hammond Bennett and his associates. In addition to its program of administering soil erosion control, the Soil Conservation Service assumed responsibility for the purchase and development of submarginal land under Title II of the Bankhead-Jones Farm Tenancy Act of 1937;[16] the treatment of land for flood control under the Flood Control Act of 1936, which recognized that soil conservation and flood control were just two phases of the same problem and that the entire watershed had to be considered when examining remediable flood-control programs; the development of farm and range water facilities under the Water Facilities Act of 1937; farm forestry under the 1937 Cooperative Farm Forestry Act; and the drainage and irrigation work formerly handled by the Bureau of Agricultural Engineering. Taken together it appeared that the Soil Conservation Service under Bennett's direction at the end of 1938 was in a position to fulfill the recommendations of the program of readjustment and development called for in *The Future of the Great Plains*.

The suggestion, however, was illusory because Bennett's concerns were national in scope, affecting all physical land-use programs involving operations by the government on farm lands. While Bennett understood the necessity of intensive cooperation with services and agencies in the various states, he could never focus enough attention and funds on the Great Plains to insure that, as the New Deal waned, the program would be anything more than a fragmented reform though, certainly, the land-use program that was outlined for a better rural life was meaningful for the Great Plains.

The Future of the Great Plains by the end of the New Deal was translated through various pieces of legislation and numerous programs, largely centered in the United States Department of Agriculture, into a reality that paid attention to the critical situation prevailing on the plains in a piecemeal, haphazard way. Along with a shift in the weather cycle, it did much to meliorate conditions. By 1940 the war in Europe focused attention on increased production of wheat and beef, and the Great Plains again became the breadbasket of the nation and of the world. As the experiences of the 1930s receded in memory, the programs and policies of government on all levels, while not unmindful of conservation, emphasized the necessity of expanding production.[17]

What New Deal programs on the Great Plains could not take into account in implementing its land-use programs was that in some areas—the state of Oklahoma, for example—the majority of the farmers were tenants who sought a new farm every year. Although the New Deal helped publicize ways and means of conserving the soil, the knowledge and available assistance did not necessarily reach the soil-depleting operations conducted by tenants working farms and ranches. There was some conflict for farmers and ranchers who were other than owner-operators between the best practices for a stable or balanced agriculture and those possibly providing maximum returns. While this conflict was not insuperable, it called for extended cooperation between landlords and tenants and additional efforts to encourage both to take advantage of the New Deal programs and services available to help them improve their situation.[18]

New Dealers saw their programs in operation on the Great Plains, particularly soil conservation, as furthering economic democracy and in accord with the vision of Henry A. Wallace, who said, "We must invent, build and put to work new social machinery." And this machinery—be it in a soil conservation district, rural electric cooperative, a county agricultural control association, or any of the numerous groups set up under the multitude of New Deal programs—through democratic methods, provided that farmers, ranchers, and others by banding together and cooperating could cope with common problems. Hugh Hammond Bennett was the continuing champion of the cause of soil conservation. With his increased responsibilities after 1938 as chief of the Soil Conservation Service, he became the spokesman for a broader democratic ethic based on cooperation, conservation, and a growing sense of community predicated upon a broad-gauged program of land readjustment and development.

The Great Plains benefited both from the vision and the program of the New Dealers. But neither was approached in a way to bring about basic economic changes. This meant that the conditions and practices fostering erosion and drought would not disappear. Indeed they would return in later decades. Nevertheless, the New Deal, as it affected the Great Plains, provided a vision of *New Frontiers,* the title of a 1934 volume by Henry A. Wallace, suggesting solutions that went beyond relief, calling for extensive modifications in institutional factors affecting land tenure as well as land use. The New Deal on the Great Plains, in short, provided a base and a heritage of fragmented reforms that others, if they cared to consider what had occurred during the dirty thirties, could examine and build upon.[19]

Though the New Deal efforts were fragmented, work of great significance was done. Moreover, the Department of Agriculture tried to coordinate its varied programs for the Great Plains by dividing the area into two separate regions: the northern Great Plains with head-quarters in Denver and the southern Great Plains with headquarters in Amarillo. Advisory committees assisted the regional directors in their efforts to coordinate programs. In one sense these efforts were too little and too late; in another they suggested the piecemeal approach to the critical problems and issues affecting the Great Plains in the 1930s. But all the efforts of the New Deal, aside from the initial immediate one of providing relief, recognized that the Great Plains presented the problem of building an economy decidedly different from that established in any other agricultural area of the nation. John Wesley Powell, famed explorer and director of the U.S. Geological Survey, had recognized this when he addressed the North Dakota Constitutional Convention in 1899. Powell told the delegates that "in the western portion all dependence on rain will ultimately bring disaster to the people" and that "years will come of abundance and years will come of disaster, and between the two the people will be prosperous and unprosperous. . . ." While Powell was noting the necessity for irrigation, New Dealers accepted his basic premise that federal land policies needed revision because it was generally understood that 160 acres of land in the humid regions was roughly equivalent in productivity to about 2,500 acres of semiarid lands, thereby necessitating modifications for the Great Plains.

As national attention shifted to international relations and the threat of American involvement in war, New Dealers believed that progress had been made in solving the problems of the Great Plains. By the end of 1940 acreage subject to blowing in the Dust Bowl area of the southern plains was less than four million acres. In 1934 and 1935, 50 million acres were subject to blowing.[20] Sorghum and Sudan grass were now planted by many farmers and the stubble of these and other grasses and crops was left on the land; contour-furrowing was practiced; acreage was left fallow; demonstration areas were increasing and agricultural programs of all kinds were encouraging a conservation ethic designed not only to save soil but to promote a better life, one in which the farmer played a role in program making and had the benefit of a greater volume of technical help than he had had in the past. Copious rainfall also increased optimism that the worst was over and that New Deal cooperative programs could be rated by and large as successful. But by 1942 Great Plains farmers and ranchers, though conservation-oriented, were again producing wheat for the United States and its allies at war. A beginning had been made but with the war and the waning of the New Deal, the query also was voiced as to whether the historic cycle of boom and bust, of feast and famine, of adequate rainfall and drought would begin anew.[21]

Chapter 5

Sharing Land Usage

THE LAND BETWEEN THE mountains, the Great Basin between the Rocky Mountains and the Sierra Nevada range, was the territory primarily of the Department of the Interior. Its policies and its programs, especially those related to public lands and natural resources, predominated. It had to share some responsibility with the Forest Service and the bureau concerned with wildlife, both housed in the Department of Agriculture. Secretary of the Interior Harold Ickes was not too happy about sharing anything and waged a mighty but unsuccessful effort to establish a Department of Conservation, which would have made him supreme in this territory. Ultimately, late in the New Deal, responsibility for wildlife was transferred to Ickes's domain. Much to Henry Wallace's chagrin, Ickes also gained responsibility for the management of grazing lands, which penetrated the western reaches of the Great Plains and predominated throughout the Great Basin and mountain areas where most of the remaining public domain was located. If Henry A. Wallace, the Department of Agriculture, Franklin Roosevelt, and numerous others viewed the Great Plains in terms of lowering expectations to save the soil, Harold Ickes and his allies viewed his domain largely in terms of expanding horizons chiefly through the development of water facilities, especially hydroelectric power, and enhanced production. Nevertheless, Wallace and Ickes both spoke in terms that stressed balance, scientific management, conservation, and cooperation with state and local agencies. And in dealing with the public lands comprising the open range, the views of Ickes and Wallace and their respective departments were not far apart.

In the 1930s the greater part of the western two-fifths of the United States was used primarily as grazing land, including the western half of North Dakota, veering down to include parts of western Kansas, and shifting slightly to the east to encompass more than half of Texas. Farming was practiced on about four percent of these lands. The total area defined as grazing land was about 975 million acres, slightly more than a third of which was federally owned. The federal lands were located in the western part of the range region, largely to the west of a line extending from eastern Montana down through the center of New Mexico, primarily within the Interior domain of Harold Ickes.

In dealing with the western public range lands, the theme prevalent on the Great Plains, that of lowering expectations, continued to prevail. It is encapsulated in the title of the best book on the subject, *The Closing of the Public Domain,*[1] and concisely stated by Henry Wallace in transmitting to the president of the United States Senate an important report prepared in 1936 by the Forest Service titled *The Western Range.*[2] Noting that the western range was a great but neglected natural resource, Wallace called for measures "that will stop depletion and restore and thereafter maintain the resource in perpetuity, while at the same time permitting its use." He was undeviating in his views. Noting the same problem on the Great Plains, he also called for the return to public ownership of lands so devastated or impaired that private owners could "hold them only at a loss." The difficulty arose when the secretary of agriculture in his April 28, 1936, letter of transmittal called for placing the grazing districts and the public domain under the aegis of his department, "since the administration of the range resource and its use is agriculture." Ickes saw the problem in terms of the conservation of natural resources, a subject well within the scope of the Department of the Interior. Congress, however, thought it had resolved the problem previously when in June 1934 it approved the Taylor Grazing Act, providing a *modus vivendi* between the two secretaries which Ickes did not wish to disturb.[3]

The purpose of the act was "to stop injury to the public grazing lands by preventing overgrazing and soil deterioration, to provide for orderly use, improvement and development, to stabilize the livestock industry dependent upon the public range, and for other purposes." Roosevelt called the act "a great forward step in the interests of conservation." The measure, providing the base to achieve these goals, authorized the secretary of the interior to create grazing districts from suitable portions of the public domain to a total of no more than 80 million acres. In accord with New Deal policy, before a grazing district could be created, local hearings were held and the stockmen were to have a voice in the administration of their district. Essentially, the grazing associations that were created rested upon a private contract between members to manage a given area, centralize the leasing of lands, work out plans for range improvement, and develop rules and procedures for distributing grazing privileges.

What is more significant about the Taylor Grazing Act is the fact that it reversed the previous land policy of providing open use to all comers to one of restricted use and management. On November 26,

1934, all vacant, unreserved, and unappropriated public lands were withdrawn from all forms of entry. Though public lands included in grazing districts were withdrawn from entry and settlement, by a Presidential proclamation on February 9, 1935, prospectors and others could develop and use mineral and timber resources on these lands. Grazing, however, was regulated under a permit system comparable to that in use on the national forests. Preference in granting these permits—which were not transferable but were revokable and renewable at the end of ten years—was given to stockmen and other landowners within or near the proposed grazing district. However, the number of livestock permitted to graze in a district would be specified by the secretary of the interior and a reasonable charge, again a reversal of the open-range tradition, was to be levied for grazing within established districts. Stockmen benefited despite the fees, because the carrying capacity of the range would be decreased; overcrowding would disappear. In addition, one-fourth of the fee money would be used for range improvement within the district where it was collected. And one-half of the fees collected would go to the state for distribution to the county or counties wherein the grazing district was located.[4] Moreover, decisions of administrative officers in charge of grazing districts might be challenged by local boards specifically established by the law.

If a rancher or stockman wished to make improvements, such as fences, wells, reservoirs, sheds, cattleguards, stock driveways, truck trails, or canals on the range during the tenure of his ten-year permit, he could apply for permission to do so and subsequent users would pay a reasonable price for the right to use these improvements. To consolidate scattered sections of public lands, the secretary of the interior was allowed to accept title to any private or publicly owned lands within the exterior boundaries of a grazing district in exchange for other public lands within the state or vicinity of the grazing district. The law also added to Ickes's domain by granting the secretary of the interior jurisdiction over national forest lands principally valuable for grazing.[5] And it prescribed terms for the leasing or sale of isolated tracts of the public domain to owners of contiguous lands. Finally the law called for cooperation with local and state agencies, as well as other departments of government, concerned with range administration and wildlife protection. It was enacted with the understanding that practically no funds would be required for its administration.

Though there was grumbling on the part of some stockmen and others, the Taylor Grazing Act was favorably received throughout the West. A Division of Grazing Control, headed by F. R. Carpenter, was set up in the Department of the Interior charged with supervising the creation of grazing districts and allocating permits for range use. Once its work got under way it became evident that more stockmen sought grazing permits than 80 million acres, the total acreage provided in the law, would accommodate. To correct this and other apparent weaknesses a series of amendments to the act were approved by Congress in 1935 but vetoed by the President upon the advice of both the secretary of agriculture and the secretary of the interior on the ground that some of the proposed changes gave too much authority to the states, reduced that of the Department of the Interior in supervising the law, and favored the large operator. But all agreed that the proposed 142-million-acre limit was acceptable. Indeed Ickes recommended that there be no acreage restriction. In a September 11, 1935, statement he indicated that the legal division of the Department of the Interior held that jurisdiction over grazing on the entire public domain could be assumed under the Presidential Proclamation of February 9, 1935, which closed the public domain by withdrawing all public land from entry. In June, 1936, the act was successfully amended to increase the 80-million-acre limit to 142 million acres, permitting an additional 62 million acres to be included within grazing districts.[6]

By 1940 nine grazing regions[7] were functioning under the supervision of the director of grazing and an undersecretary in charge of grazing. There were numerous districts within each region and advisory boards within each district provided for some home rule. Periodically members of the advisory boards met with Ickes and other officials in Washington to discuss questions of administration and problems affecting stockmen. Tensions arose as advisory boards sought greater voice in the management of the grazing districts and an amendment to the act was proposed in 1939 along these lines. Cooperation was arranged in some instances with the CCC, the Soil Conservation Service, and other agencies in facilitating range rehabilitation and livestock improvement.

By the end of the New Deal over 11 million head of cattle, sheep, horses, and goats grazed on federal range lands. And Harold Ickes, true to his progressive principles, made every effort to insure fair use of the range, to prevent discrimination in favor of large operators, and to insure "that all questions of doubt must be resolved in favor of the little fellow." His chief concern—and this was at the core of the tension with the stockmen—was that the administration of publicly owned grazing lands be regarded primarily as a problem of conservation. "When this is fully realized," Ickes said, "it will do more than save the livestock range; it will bring a new element of harmony into the conservation program in America."[8]

On May 10, 1940, Harold Ickes presented Colorado Congressman Edward T. Taylor, sponsor of the Taylor Grazing Act, a unique gold-plated hammer with a silver inscription symbolic of the millions of staples, thousands of posts, and miles of fences erected on the federal range by CCC forces under the supervision of the Grazing Service of the Department of the Interior. In addition to the CCC, faculty from agricultural colleges worked with Grazing Service officials and stockmen in setting up range stations to improve both range and livestock management. Representatives from other agencies, such as the Soil Conservation Service, the Biological Survey, foresters both federal and state, also cooperated since much of the range was located in forested areas. It was estimated that altogether the range area in national forests, federal ranges, and other federal reservations in the western states beyond the Great Plains amounted to approximately one-fifth of the United States, making Ickes's domain larger than that of many nations. His role, unlike that of other rulers, was to develop a program, a combination of administrative and advisory work, leading to a unified effort by western stockmen and the Grazing Service to rehabilitate and improve the range areas and thereby help stabilize the economy of the Great Basin. Since the problem of range management involved a balanced relationship between private and public lands and devising plans to utilize all lands compatible with the available resources and the economic structure of the area, cooperation with and among the 20,000 users of the federal range was essential. Ickes could not administer his domain as an imperial potentate. Community and regional welfare was of immediate concern in the development of range restoration and use patterns, and local leaders and stockmen had a voice in these matters. On July 15, 1940, at Denver, for example, eighteen stockmen, all members of district advisory boards, came as delegates to discuss and draft with the director of grazing and his staff revisions or amendments to the federal range code. They brought to these deliberations the practical and businesslike advice of experienced stockmen.[9]

Range livestock moved from valley in winter to mountain in summer, part of the time on their owners' lands and part of the time within the grazing district. They moved with developing forage, with threatening snows, and with completed use of various areas. District graziers working with individual stockmen and advisory boards developed range-management programs seeking to improve range conditions, to avoid trespassing, and to utilize available equipment. They also maintained an up-to-date inventory of range resources, including one of vegetation, to aid in more effective range management and in locating stock-watering places, many of which were built by the CCC on federal range areas. The goal was a planned economy to replace the previous lack of meaningful land-use methods. They hoped to achieve a stable livestock industry through most beneficial use of western range areas based on public lands. This was to be accomplished through local participation establishing home-rule on the range.

By the end of the New Deal these goals, while not fully achieved, were recognized and accepted by all parties with the result that during the war period livestock production could be increased without destroying segments of the western range. Forage on public lands within grazing districts, thanks to range regulation and management, would expand during the war years. Considerable improvements of a permanent nature made during the New Deal proved to be peacetime investments that served wartime needs for increased production of meat, wool, and leather. Some federally owned land within grazing districts was withdrawn and granted temporarily to the Army and Navy, all without seriously impairing either the livestock industry or orderly range use. And, equally important, throughout the New Deal stockmen themselves were among the staunchest supporters of orderly range use and conservation. Congressman Edward T. Taylor, who died on September 3, 1941, was largely responsible for bringing the stockmen and the federal government together in efforts to rehabilitate the range. He lived, as he said, to see "less conflict, less selfishness on the range and the mistakes of the past being put to right."[10]

Like other New Deal programs throughout the West, the administrators of the Taylor Grazing Act were concerned with promoting conservation. At the same time they sought to raise prices for producers through cooperation between stockmen and local and state government, meanwhile stressing decentralized administration, education, or propaganda about the program and its purposes. The Taylor Grazing Act and its administration, again like other New Deal programs in the West, was facilitated by the emergency situation and it underwent modifications or adjustments throughout its first decade as a result of careful studies, criticisms, and experience. Moreover, it should be noted that though the larger part of the western range was in private ownership (although in one or two western states public ownership ran as high as 50 percent), the economics of western livestock production, more so than any other type of agricultural production, rested "upon public land policy and management."

Criticisms of the Taylor Grazing Act focused upon two related premises. First, it lacked, either in the law or in its administration, any means of enforcement or penalties for violation. Second, it tended to favor the larger operators, the more established stockmen within the grazing districts. Nevertheless, despite criticism, Ickes throughout the New Deal did his best to follow the intent of the law in providing for the protection, orderly use, and regulation of the public range lands through the establishment of grazing districts. And as an old Bull Mooser who fervently supported Theodore Roosevelt's views on conservation, he maintained a vigilant concern for conservation of natural resources and an open hostility to monopolistic control over them, favoring instead wise use by small developers and homesteaders.[11]

Ickes thought he would function more effectively if Roosevelt could

couple the passage of the Taylor bill with the transfer of the Forest
Service from the Department of Agriculture to the Department of the
Interior. But Wallace, who thought the final version of the Taylor
Grazing Act was not a strong conservation measure, objected, and
Ickes had to share part of his domain with the Department of Agriculture though the Forest Service came under Ickes's aegis whenever its
lands were included in or became part of a grazing district. If Ickes had
to share with Wallace part of his interior domain, so too did cattle and
sheepmen. They buried many of their differences and cooperated in
efforts to abolish unfair range practices and to conserve natural resources. Cattle and sheepmen also served together on advisory boards
and in local associations, seeking greater autonomy in the administration of the law by helping to make decisions necessary to bring livestock usage in line with appraised range productivity.[12]

Privately owned range lands also experienced depletion and the
programs launched under the Taylor Grazing Act did not necessarily
apply to those lands. The range conservation program of the Agricultural Adjustment Administration was aimed at restoring these lands.
Continual grazing prevented adequate storage of food materials in the
root systems of range forage plants. Effective range maintenance
called for having part of each year's growth ungrazed. The approach of
the New Deal was to convey to stockmen using both public and private
range lands the view that full productivity of the land could be achieved
only be grazing or pasturing less than the maximum of previous years.
This approach called for a reversal in the usual outlook of most stockmen who continually over-utilized the range in an effort to maintain or
expand production.

Prior to the adoption of the Taylor Grazing Act, whatever supervision of the public range existed was done by the Forest Service of the
Department of Agriculture as part of its managing national forest reserves. The Forest Service was assigned the task of seeing that the
maximum number of cattle and sheep were grazed on these lands with
the least possible injury to vegetation. Many of the practices and procedures developed and utilized by the Forest Service were followed
and expanded during the New Deal by the Grazing Service in pursuing
its responsibilities. But the Forest Service was dealing with choice
lands; the majority of land falling under Ickes's purview consisted of
leftover lands rejected as unfit for human settlement. While the Forest
Service was seeking sustained yields and orderly management of its
lands, the Grazing Service in the 1930s attempted for the first time to
achieve a semblance of order on the western range. Both services
stimulated, encouraged, and persuaded stockmen to adopt intelligent
conservation practices. Stockmen through their advisory boards had a
voice in formulating and questioning decisions of the Grazing Service

district supervisors; with regard to decisions by Forest Rangers during the New Deal years they had no redress. Responsible stockmen, some of whom were trying to resolve their own problems, were pleased, but there always remained some skeptics who were dubious about the restraints federal agencies were seeking to impose upon a hitherto largely unrestrained industry.[13]

The enactment of the Taylor Grazing Act, while marking a profound change in the attitude toward the use of western range lands, also marked the end of an age. With its enactment, distinguished author and critic Wallace Stegner has written, "a historical process was complete; not only was the public domain virtually closed to settlement, but the remaining public land was assumed to be continuing federal property, income producing property to be managed according to principles of wise use for the benefit of the nation."[14]

In 1933, Ickes had observed "We have reached the end of the pioneering period of go ahead and take. We are in an age of planning for the best of everything for all."[15] In the West conservation was the approach of the New Deal and to Ickes this meant scientific management of the public domain. In November 1934, as already noted, the President withdrew from entry all public lands in the West until they had been classified. Thereafter they again would be available for entry and from 1935 to the end of the decade entries ran in excess of 100,000 acres per year. These lands, unlike public lands available for entry prior to 1935, were classified in accordance with their potentialities.[16]

Here, too, Ickes had to share the job with the Department of Agriculture and other agencies interested in better land use and conservation throughout the interior basin. At the outset of the New Deal, the Rural Rehabilitation and Land Programs of the Federal Emergency Relief Administration started the program. This assignment was soon transferred to agencies within the Department of Agriculture, which under Henry A. Wallace was calling for a national land-use program. M. L. Wilson, while still at Montana State College, published an article calling for such a program with most of the responsibility located in the Department of Agriculture.[17] And for the remainder of the decade Wallace challenged Ickes for sovereignty in what Ickes considered his domain. The work of agencies within both departments that functioned in the West indicated in one way or another the interdependence of land uses and the manner in which the profitable use of one resource was dependent upon the proper management of another. For example, the improvement and management of upland watersheds affected— besides irrigation—forest and range lands (largely in government ownership), Indian lands, recreation opportunities, and the balance of wildlife. Capital values, income, the number of farm families, and the extent of grazing and timber operations were related to the improvement and management of western upland watersheds. Divided authority did not preclude cooperation, but along with the rivalry between departments went tensions that at times made cooperation difficult, despite the fact that the USDA directed most of its attention to working with farmers, ranchers, and others in conserving and improving privately owned lands. The Department of the Interior dealt only with public lands. But one point pertaining to both public and privately owned lands is clear: namely, after 1935 land-use planning gave validity to the term "New Public Domain" as throughout the West both county commissioners and individual owners optioned and sold lands under various programs to different government agencies which sought in one way or another to consolidate parcels and centralize control to promote better land use.[18]

The problem early in the New Deal was that too many agencies were dealing with the land problem more or less on an independent basis. Some of the early agencies were: Agricultural Adjustment Administration, Resettlement Administration, National Resources Board, Subsistence Homestead Division, Soil Conservation Service, Extension Service, Forest Service, Taylor Grazing Administration, Biological Survey, National Park Service, Indian Service, State Land Boards, State Planning Boards, State Agricultural Colleges and Universities. Gradually both consolidation and cooperation occurred. But in the interior basin, where Ickes was responsible for developing meaningful land-use patterns on the public domain, the greatest threat to his hegemony was provided by the Forest Service, located in the Department of Agriculture. It controlled millions of acres of national forests and provided an everlasting reminder that in any adjustment in the use of water or the regulation of public lands, the Forest Service would have to be considered. Throughout his tenure as secretary of the interior, Ickes sought the transfer of the Forest Service to his department, which he proposed to transform into a Department of Conservation.

In examining the role of the Forest Service in the West during the New Deal, it should be stated at the outset that about four-fifths of the available commercial timber land was in private ownership, that the rate of drain on the forests was estimated to be double the rate of growth, and for saw timber about five times the growth rate. Private owners, engaged "in a mad competitive race" that frequently meant "more loss than profit," could not focus meaningfully on the concerns of the Forest Service for the public welfare. While forests supplied fuel and timber for farmers and materials for industry, they were an important element of beauty in the landscape providing a habitat for game and opportunities for outdoor recreation. They also served to prevent erosion and floods and were an important source of local revenue. The

Forest Service sought to manage its forests so as to provide these benefits permanently. It also concluded that it was too much to expect private owners to do these things at personal loss. But efforts to reduce taxation on private forest lands, to share the cost of fire protection, to provide cheap nursery stock, and similar measures had not noticeably improved methods of forest management in private forests. The Forest Service estimated early in the New Deal, much to Ickes's chagrin, "that there are some 224 million acres now in private ownership that sooner or later will have to be brought under public management."[19]

In a sense the national forests, containing about 175 million acres of forest and range lands, formed the roof of the West, serving as a giant cistern for the water supply of the region. Usually these lands were physically unsuited to agriculture because they were either at too high an elevation, too dry, too rocky, or too steep. "From National Forest Land," President Franklin Roosevelt said, "comes domestic water for more than 6,000,000 people." The water also offered prospects for irrigation undertakings and for the development of hydroelectric power. Under supervision the forests also provided timber for lumbermen, grazing areas for stockmen, and recreational opportunities for campers, hunters, and fishermen. But principally, as journalist Richard L. Neuberger wrote, "The National Forests are the storehouse of the West," conserving the resources of water and power on which the West depended for survival and which migrants needed for a new start in life. As of October 1934, there were 162,009,145 acres of national forests, 133,490,204 acres of which were in the West.[20]

In the 1930s less than 30 percent of American forests were publicly owned; they contained only one-fifth of the commercial timber, usually the least accessible and of the poorest quality. The national forests were adequately protected against fire, while almost half of the private lands were not. More than 380 million acres of privately owned lands were without forest management of any kind, whereas less than 15 million acres of publicly owned lands, chiefly state and local, were in a similar situation. These approximate figures indicate what New Dealers and others interested in conservation quickly concluded; namely, that what private owners did with their privately owned forest lands, as in the case of grazing lands, could be of grave concern to many others besides the owners.

Three great industries of the West in the 1930s—farming, livestock production, and lumbering—were based on renewable resources: soil, forage, and trees. New Deal programs and policies managed these elements with the intent of both conserving the resources and advancing the industries. Like some farm and range lands in the 1930s, private forest lands reverted to public ownership due to tax delinquency and other factors. For example, in portions of the Douglas fir region in four counties of western Oregon and western Washington, 51,700 acres had reverted to public ownership in 1932. In 1941, the figure had increased to 342,500 acres. Both wise management and stable ownership were necessary concomitants for permanent timber production and the Forest Service, through the example of its management, hoped to provide a basis for more permanent production of private forest lands bearing marketable timber.[21]

With labor provided by the CCC and the WPA, national forests in the inter-mountain area and elsewhere benefited from a multitude of improvements that affected the entire public domain and the constituencies dependent upon these lands: check drains to control water runoff and curb erosion, the planting of additional millions of trees, new roads and trails through the forests as well as the construction of camping and fishing grounds, and the development of fish ponds and hatcheries. In addition, fire hazards were removed and lookout towers, telephone lines, firebreaks, and other facilities were built; timber stands were thinned and strenuous efforts at disease and insect control were undertaken. Income generated by the sale of timber products, logging permits, grazing fees, hunting and fishing privileges, and by renting cabins and camps for recreational use helped maintain these facilities when development work in the forests was concluded.

Forests, when managed to provide community support because of their economic, conservation, and recreational contributions, were considered to be under "sustained yield forest management." This form of management, furnishing various services from the forests, was also called "timber farming" and was the approach of the Forest Service as it strove to relate to the economic and social welfare of the West. But in the 1930s it lost its dominant position to Harold Ickes and the Grazing Service, which invaded its territory and sought similar or very closely related goals. Throughout the West in the 1930s the Forest Service was on the defensive against the marauding efforts of agencies under the hegemony of Harold Ickes.

In addition, with the decade's decrease in the demand for forest products used in industry, the multipurpose goals involved in sustained-yield management would be more difficult to maintain. Through the CCC and the WPA the national forests provided employment for thousands of young men whose endeavors assured a measure of community stability. They improved the productive capacity of the forests by constructing roads, trails, and firebreaks; by eliminating accumulations of slash and other hazards; by destroying breeding places of harmful insects; by maintaining proper grass cover to bring about, along with timber cover, infiltration of water into the soil; by removing diseased trees and seeding areas of denuded land; and by improving other areas through selective cutting and thinning. In addition they developed recreational facilities and helped to check erosion. To achieve its goals of both improved utilization and conservation the Forest Service sought cooperation with private owners, public regulation of all forest lands, and continued extension of public ownership and management. F. A. Silcox, chief of the Forest Service, estimated in 1939 that the national forests, chiefly in the West, annually provided a living for almost a million people and recreation for about 30 million. They also returned to counties, through the states, more than a million dollars each year in lieu of taxes.[22]

In 1936 the four states of Oregon, Washington, Idaho, and Montana contained over 93 million acres of forest land, about 55 percent of the available timber supply of the nation. These four states supplied more than one-third of the forest products requirements of the United States, thereby giving the Forest Service and the Soil Conservation Service anxiety about land-use practices on these lands and stimulating great efforts to encourage better management of privately owned forest lands through cooperation, exhortation, and the example of administration and research occurring in adjacent national forests. Of the 147 national forests in 1936 with an aggregate net area of more than 165 million acres (slightly larger than the entire state of Texas), about 96 percent was located in the West and Alaska. In 1936 the national forests alone provided an estimated stand of 552 billion feet of marketable timber, insuring the fact that the Forest Service, thanks to increased allocation from various federal agencies, was better able to conduct its programs than private operators. Net allocations of WPA funds through June 30, 1936, totaled over $26 million. Aside from maintaining and improving the national forests, a portion of these funds allowed the Forest Service to continue its operations on the shelterbelt project, launched in 1934, of tree planting to conserve both soil and moisture and to protect homesteads and crops from the drying effects of hot summers and cold winters on the Great Plains.[23]

Throughout the New Deal additions to national forests in the West were made under various emergency and relief programs and by Executive Order. Purchase of these areas and the subsequent improvement and protection work done on them provided for large-scale employment. By these means and through allotments of funds under various emergency relief designations, the Forest Service, besides improving its properties, employed thousands of unemployed men in outdoor jobs that were noncompetitive with private industry. Prior to 1933 federal acquisition of forest lands had totaled less than 550,000 acres in any one year. Within a twelve-month period in 1933–34, more than 4 million acres were acquired or placed under contract sale to the federal government. And from 1933 to 1941, over 12.5 million acres of forest land had been approved for purchase at a cost of more than $54 million.

During the New Deal, however, most of this acquired forest land was confined to territory east of the Rocky Mountains.[24]

The Farm Forestry Act of May 18, 1937, authorized a program of farm forestry and opened the way for continuation of tree planting in the plains area under the direction and technical supervision of the Forest Service. Earlier, the Fulmer Act of August 29, 1935, had authorized cooperation with the states for the purpose of stimulating the acquisition, development, and management of state forests and of coordinating federal and state activities in carrying out a national program of forest land management. The law provided for the purchase of lands for state forests through the use of federal funds and called for returning proceeds from such lands to the federal government until the amount equaled the cost of the land, at which time title would be turned over to the states. The Fulmer Act, more so than the Farm Forestry Act, was applicable to the inland empire of Harold Ickes. Together these laws comprised the only legislation in the 1930s involving the Forest Service, and they did not noticeably expand its dominion in the West. However, the President took an acute interest in forestry. With exhortations calling for cooperation among state authorities, the public, the forest industries and the Forest Service, he helped dramatize the dual necessity for conservation and sustained yield in American forests. And in 1938 he suggested a comprehensive congressional study of the forest land problem.[25]

Though the New Deal promoted the cause of conservation and sustained yield throughout the West, it did not convince all timber men of the validity or efficacy of its plea. Pursuant to Roosevelt's March 1938 message to Congress, a joint committee on forestry investigated the condition, ownership, and management of forest lands. Three of its eight hearings were held in the West. Its report presented in March 1941 took the position that the states should administer and enforce the regulation of forests with the federal government merely approving the standards and providing financial support. Indicative of the conservative reaction against the New Deal, the report did not explicitly and directly call for the acquisition of new tracts to safeguard the public interest, though it recognized "that private forest lands constitute the Nation's most critical and important forest land-use problem."[26]

Congress in the late 1930s, however, was unable to prevent the National Forest Reservation Commission, created in 1911 under the Weeks Act, from considering proposals for the purchase of forest lands. During the New Deal, beginning in 1935, some funds allocated for presidential use went for forest land acquisition. In the fiscal year ending June 30, 1936, a total of $45,900,000 was available for this purpose. On June 30, 1941, the total expenditure was $65,969,439.98. The bulk of these purchases were in the West. Most of the western lands purchased were either cut-over lands or lands damaged by over-grazing and erosion. But mature timber stands, including virgin red-wood timber lands, were also secured.[27]

While New Dealers were critical of private timber operators, western timber men, ever conscious of the depressed timber markets, decried the sale of national forest timber as unfair competition. Aware of the validity of this charge the Forest Service consciously held back its timber and tried to limit its sales to noncompetitive areas. This was notably the case in Oregon when a fire in the Tillamook region devastated a virgin stand of 11 billion feet and the Forest Service, to encourage liquidation of salvageable material, followed a curtailment policy. By the late 1930s the economic situation in the industry began to revive with increased commercial demand. No longer was the Forest Service viewed as a competitor. As production increased so too did cooperation. In 1941 the western producing area accounted for almost one-half of the total lumber production of the United States. Yet in the same year a prominent conservationist wrote: "Today the most urgent problem in the whole field of conservation is that of stopping destructive timbering and instituting forest practices that permanently sustain the forest and, with it, local industries and local communities."[28]

Both the Forest Service and the Grazing Service pursued a multipurpose approach. This view, widely accepted by New Dealers, became a major goal of many programs and agencies in the West, utilizing various resources and integrating their management for either enhancing production or rendering better service. The ultimate objective was to make these resources—land, soil, forest, forage, water, wildlife—a social and economic benefit. Not to do so merely invited continued waste and depletion. The reconciliation of various uses was the task of administrators. To the extent that the Forest and Grazing Services engaged in planning, to that extent they were concerned with the future use of land resources to meet the needs of an expanding population throughout the region. In the 1930s both services were critical of the private sector. Both graziers and rangers understood that the function and use of land was no longer a problem of the individual owner. A multipurpose approach, they insisted, necessitated that land use be elevated from personal whim to the importance of a public utility. Complex usage demanded competent management to achieve continuous yield within the maximum capacity of the soil to produce forest products, range cover, and crops. They disagreed only as to who should supervise forage management and grazing on forested public lands.

While calling for cooperation, both agencies recognized that private development had destroyed much good western land and that only through careful management could the national domain, both private and public, be restored to significant production. Cooperation gave state and local groups a role to play in the functioning of these agencies. Since grazing districts included lands in national forests, cooperation was called for with other agencies: CCC, SCS, AAA, and numerous bureaus within the Department of Interior and Department of Agriculture. Though tensions existed between these departments and between their secretaries, infighting did not disrupt the inland empire.

The Taylor Grazing Act gave the President unqualified authority to transfer national forest lands primarily suitable for grazing from Agriculture to Interior for inclusion in grazing districts. About 30 million acres were of this character. The political power of the Forest Service was based far more on its influence with stockmen's associations, through the favors it could grant or withhold in utilizing its lands, than on the support it received from the less numerous and not so well-organized lumbermen. Though the transfer action would not be subject to review by Congress, Roosevelt did not choose to exercise this authority. By not exercising it, he kept tensions between his feuding cabinet members at a high level of intensity and allowed the Forest Service to sacrifice, if necessary, timber and watershed values to strengthen its influence with stockmen.[29]

Ickes, hoping to re-create his department into a Department of Conservation, stated that the Department of Interior was organized primarily to take charge of government-owned land, while the Department of Agriculture was organized primarily to look after the needs of private landowners. Following this logic he insisted that the Forest Service belonged to his department, that its acquisition was necessary to create a Department of Conservation. But feuding in Washington did not lead to open hostilities in the West where the enormous national forest lands continually served to remind Harold Ickes that his hegemony over the inland empire was not complete. Agencies and bureaus within the Departments of Interior and Agriculture continued to cooperate to better fulfill their responsibilities in managing and conserving western lands, while at the same time seeking a further extension of public ownership to add to their respective western empires.[30]

Wallace and Ickes competed for the attention of a President whose previous experience made him better informed on the wise use of natural resources than most of his predecessors. Roosevelt had long practiced forestry on his estate at Hyde Park and had firsthand knowledge of economic and technical problems involved in the management of productive lands. In "Who's Who in America," he listed his occupation as "tree-grower." As President his interest and enthusiasm led him to consider multiple-use conservation of natural resources as an important part of all germane New Deal policies and programs. He kept abreast of them and was concerned about their functioning in the West. It was his vision, understanding, and sympathy that made possible the Civilian Conservation Corps to assist in this work.

Another way he did this was through the appointment on July 20, 1933, of a National Planning Board to aid Harold Ickes (as Administrator of Public Works) in preparing "comprehensive and coordinated plans for regional areas" and to engage in research pertaining to "the distribution and trends of population, land uses, industry, housing and natural resources." The Administrator of Public Works was required by the National Industrial Recovery Act to prepare "a comprehensive program of public works" and the board would help him do so. Though its title changed throughout the decade to the National Resources Board (1934) to the National Resources Committee (1935) to the National Resources Planning Board (1939), both Roosevelt and Ickes maintained a keen interest in its work and in its numerous reports dealing with natural resources and the broad subjects of regional and national planning. The concerns of the President and Ickes insured consideration of western themes and problems by the board. But it is difficult to pinpoint or cite any specific laws pertaining to the West that can be traced directly to its influence. Nevertheless the work of the board was influential in defining programs and influencing policies pertaining to water, other resources, and land use in the West. Ickes's chairmanship of the board assured the fact that their reports would be in accord with the statement in a December 31, 1934, report that "the natural resources of America are the heritage of the whole nation and should be conserved and utilized for the benefit of all of our people." Roosevelt insisted that "men and nature must work hand in hand" and in January 1935 called the reports then available "an inventory of our national assets and the problems relating to them."[31]

An indication of the impact in the West of the work done by this group is evident in a November 1935 report submitted to Ickes by the chairman of the advisory committee to the National Resources Committee. Under the heading of "Progress and Work Done" the following was listed, among several examples, of implemented recommendations made by the board: "Over 10 million acres of submarginal farm land are under operation for use as wildlife refuges, parks and Indian reservations. The forest acquisition program has been approved, involving about 3 million acres in addition." The Water Resources Committee of the board had undertaken at the request of local or federal organizations preliminary studies in the drainage basins of the Central Valley in California and of the Red River of the North, Upper Rio Grande, Columbia, Colorado, and the Grand-Neosho in Oklahoma. Moreover, consultants and staff were assigned to various state and regional planning commissions, including the significant Pacific Northwest Regional

Planning Commission. Roosevelt, himself, took a direct interest in the work of the committee expressing, for example, in 1936 an interest in "opening up certain sections of Idaho into which no wagon or automobile trail now exists" and requesting in 1940 "a progress report on land management and water use in the Gila River Basin in Arizona and New Mexico."[32]

In short, the board under its various titles was of inestimable value to the New Deal in coordinating plans and proposals of different agencies, in conducting surveys and preparing reports for consideration by various agencies, and in providing personnel to assist groups in developing their own plans for the conservation and development of available resources. The fact that Harold Ickes chaired these various planning boards assured that his domain would not be ignored in the plans and proposals the board recommended. Studies indicating the need for large-scale planning most often involved projects for developing inland waters, for developing and controlling ground waters and drainage systems, for utilizing existing lakes and ponds, and for reducing pollution and controlling runoff water to check erosion. These studies, as far as the West was concerned, almost exclusively involved the Bureau of Reclamation.

It was the work of this agency in the inland empire that made Ickes the key figure in the West throughout the New Deal years. On the Great Plains he conceded sovereignty to Henry Wallace and the Department of Agriculture. Ickes's sovereignty was reinforced because the Department of the Interior also was concerned with national parks, game refuges, Indian reservations, mineral policy, and other matters that were dominant once one left the plains. His empire also extended to the Pacific Coast, but the interior basin was its heartland. Unified programs for the development of water and land resources, through the Bureau of Reclamation, were responsible for Ickes's influence. And through his control of PWA funding, he was able to compensate for the indignity of sharing large portions of his domain by penetrating the bastion of the Department of Agriculture on the Great Plains.

Chapter 6

Water Creates
an Empire

HAROLD ICKES, THROUGH the Bureau of Reclamation, firmly established his hegemony over the Great Basin states. Along with the Grazing Service, the Bureau of Reclamation made Ickes the dominant figure and the Department of the Interior the dominant presence in the Inland Empire. Other agencies within the department further consolidated its presence. But the work of the Bureau of Reclamation left visible monuments confirming the fact that, from the Rockies to the Sierras and in some areas directly to the Pacific Coast, Harold Ickes was the public official whose words and directives, as administered through the various bureaus and agencies comprising the Department of the Interior, permanently left their mark throughout the length and breadth of the Inland Empire during the New Deal. He was able to accomplish so much because, as administrator of Public Works Administration, he saw to it that ample funding went to proposals and projects located in the Inland Empire, thereby providing the labor force and the additional equipment necessary for their implementation. The PWA in the 1934 fiscal year, for example, granted the Bureau of Reclamation a construction allotment totaling more than $103 million, a sum equivalent to about half the amount spent on bureau projects from 1902 to 1933.

There were many aspects of water use in the West: erosion control, water supply for rural areas and urban centers, drainage, flood control, generation of electricity, irrigation, recreation, wildlife conservation, and forest development. The Bureau of Reclamation had to consider all these things as it pondered new or reviewed existing projects, some of which were recommended in the 1937 report of the Water Resources Committee of the National Resources Committee studying drainage basin problems and programs. During the New Deal the bureau carefully considered these multiple aspects, though its primary mission focused on the irrigation of arid lands. Twenty-six projects under construction by the Bureau of Reclamation, involving expenditures of

$335,480,000, were recommended for immediate consideration and completion by the Water Resources Committee.[1]

With the approval of the Federal Reclamation Act in 1902, the Bureau of Reclamation became the principal agency concerned with irrigation in the West. And as the years went by the developments undertaken by the agency became increasingly complex, presenting difficult engineering problems and necessitating more expensive projects. By the 1930s they almost universally required utilization of water previously flowing unimpeded to the sea and called for the control of entire river systems. One such project (authorized during the last months of the Coolidge Administration), calling for the construction of a dam in Black Canyon on the Colorado River, was completed early in the New Deal.[2]

Boulder Dam, as it was called throughout the New Deal, was the first major federal project based on multipurpose objectives. It cost about $114 million. The services it rendered justified the effort and the expenditure in the eyes of its promoters. It regulated the erratic Colorado River for the control of floods and provided water for irrigators in the Imperial Valley and for downstream towns and cities. Los Angeles and neighboring cities constructed a 259-mile aquaduct costing $220 million to provide water for their increasing populations. Hydroelectric power generated at the dam would help repay the cost of construction, and Lake Mead, created by the construction of the dam, became the world's largest artificial lake, an impressive new recreation area. Before Pearl Harbor and the nation's entrance into World War II, power generated at Boulder Dam was providing electricity for people in Los Angeles and in southern Arizona; irrigation water was helping to make the Imperial Irrigation District, covering over 500,000 acres, one of the most productive in the world. And it was estimated that new acreage would be opened to irrigation, about 1.5 million acres, roughly "half as much as all the new land opened up to date by all government irrigation projects, totaling twenty-nine."[3]

Boulder Dam was the first of several New Deal multipurpose projects in the West that provided jobs for thousands of "construction stiffs," tough itinerant workers who, working three shifts, helped complete the project ahead of schedule. More than fifty workers lost their lives in constructing Boulder Dam, chiefly from falling rocks. They worked for a group of western contractors, calling themselves the Six Companies. In turn they were under the direct supervision of the Bureau of Reclamation in whose Denver office the design of all features of the dam was prepared. While the Six Companies bore all the construction costs, they did not purchase the raw materials utilized in construction or any of the operating machinery of the dam. They did construct Boulder City, a community to house about 5,000 workers, their families, and others involved with the project. *Fortune* magazine estimated that the Six Companies stood to "turn a profit estimated at $7,000,000 and upward for all their work," while the total cost of the dam, not to exceed the $165 million authorized in the Boulder Canyon Project Act, would be repaid in fifty years by profits from power and water sales. The dam would be one of the highest in the world, about the height of a fifty-story building, and the powerhouse, containing the largest generators and turbines yet installed, would produce at least four times as much electricity as Niagara Falls. Every operation in its construction required calculations in millions. Millions of cubic yards of rock had to be removed; millions of tons of gravel and sand had to be dug, processed, and transported; millions of cubic feet of concrete were poured. All were part of the construction of a magnificent dam on an isolated site surrounded by towering cliffs on either side of an unpredictable river.[4]

Out of 1934 PWA funds, Ickes allotted $38 million for Boulder Dam thereby furthering the completion of the project almost two years ahead of contract requirements. Storage of water behind the dam commenced on February 1, 1935. On September 30 the President dedicated the dam, calling the transformation wrought in the canyon "a twentieth-century marvel." Roosevelt's remarks stressed not only the physical achievement in controlling the river, in translating its unused waters "into a great national possession," but also the cooperation necessary to achieve the conservation, regulation, and equitable division and use of the waters, "which will insure to the millions of people who now dwell in this basin, and the millions of others who will come to dwell here in future generations, a just, safe and permanent system of water rights."[5]

In February 1939, Ickes visited Boulder Dam for the first time since it was dedicated. The reservoir now was filled; there were over 500 feet of water just above the dam and Lake Mead extended about 115 miles up the canyon. Electricity had been produced since September 1936 when the President pressed a key in Washington that started the first generator. Ickes saw how the water level was being lowered in anticipation of spring flooding in the Colorado River. At this time, Ickes (and soon thereafter the President) was engaged in combat with Senator Key Pittman, who had introduced a bill calling for a Nevada state park on the shore of Lake Mead created out of federal lands. Ickes believed that "gamblers and saloonkeepers" in nearby Las Vegas, seeking to enlarge their activities through contact with the increasing horde of tourists, were behind the measure. But the President vetoed the measure when it passed the Congress in August on the premise that granting more than 8,000 acres of federally owned land to Nevada for a state park would create an unfortunate precedent jeopardizing important federal reservations, including national parks and forests.

Pittman worked hard to get his bill through Congress, and he did not easily accept Roosevelt's veto. In correspondence he suggested to the President the error of his ways. Roosevelt, to assuage Pittman, asked the senator to introduce a measure establishing the Boulder Dam National Recreational Area with the provision that prospecting, mining, and grazing could be conducted in this area under already established federal guidelines, thereby providing the people of Nevada with profitable opportunities in this reserved area. Pittman at this point conceded defeat by ceasing the correspondence.[6]

Electricity to be generated at Boulder Dam had been contracted for in 1930 with the Metropolitan Water District of Southern California, the City of Los Angeles, and the Southern California Edison Company. Consequently, in September 1936, when energy was first generated, the powerhouse was operated by the City of Los Angeles and the Southern California Edison Company. The City of Los Angeles operated units generating electricity for itself, for other municipalities, for the states of Nevada and Arizona, and for the Metropolitan Water District of Southern California. The Southern California Edison Company operated units generating for itself and for other utility companies. While the powerhouse and equipment belonged to the federal government, the contractors were responsible for its maintenance.

By the end of the decade with Boulder Dam fully functioning, it was evident, as Harold Ickes had announced at its dedication in 1935, that "another milestone has been passed in the history of the West." By regulating the flow of "a great and dangerous river" in the service of millions of people in the Southwest, the security and the future of the people of southern California, Nevada, and Arizona was enhanced by insuring adequate water supplies for their farms and cities and tremendous amounts of cheap power for use in increasing their necessities and comforts while also developing their industries. In 1937, for example, two years after water storage behind Boulder Dam began, the silt load on the Colorado River at Yuma, Arizona, had been reduced from about 96,000 acre-feet to about 8,500 with large savings to irrigators in southern California, Arizona, and Mexico.[7] In brief, as Ickes understood, Boulder Dam had helped consolidate his imperial domain by fulfilling on a tremendous scale the new multipurpose goals of the Bureau of Reclamation which, under his aegis, was now receiving great national attention. This engineering triumph would help insure further starts on new projects that Ickes could assist with generous grants of Public Works Administration funds.

One hundred and fifty-five miles below Boulder Dam, Parker Dam was authorized in 1935 to be constructed by the Bureau of Reclamation. It was financed not by PWA but by the Metropolitan Water District of Southern California, whose bonds were purchased by the Reconstruction Finance Corporation, a federal lending agency. Parker Dam was designed primarily to store water for the district, but it also helped in flood control and irrigation. In 1939 Secretary Ickes announced an agreement with the Salt River Valley Water Users' Association and the Central Arizona Light and Power Company by which power would be supplied to central Arizona, once the powerhouse at Parker Dam was completed and a transmission line from the dam to Phoenix was constructed. Half the power generated at Parker Dam would belong to the Bureau of Reclamation, which could also dispose of the other half until such time as it was needed by the Metropolitan Water District. A transmission line was quickly constructed by the Metropolitan Water District from Boulder to Parker Dam and this line was initially used, until the Parker power plant was completed, to supply power to central Arizona users in the vicinity of Phoenix.[8]

Representatives of other Colorado River states protested assistance to Arizona projects because that state was not a signatory to the 1922 Colorado River Compact allocating the waters of the river for irrigation and other purposes. The signatories from the Upper Basin States—Colorado, New Mexico, Utah, and Wyoming—also protested the extensive assistance received by southern California from the Boulder and Parker Dam projects. Nevada joined in these protests. These states resented the undue amounts of water that went to the Imperial Valley where, after being utilized for irrigation and power purposes, remaining waters were discharged into the Colorado River close to the Mexican border.[9]

Still Nevada, in particular, while unable to utilize much of the power generated or the water stored behind Boulder Dam, did not want California users to receive favorable rates for the large quantities of water and electricity they secured from this project. Discrimination in favor of California could preclude Nevada at some future time from developing an industrial or agricultural base of its own. In June 1940, owing to the efforts of Senator Key Pittman, Congress approved the Boulder Dam Adjustment Act insuring Nevada against any discrimination in the matter of power rates and awarding both Arizona and Nevada an annual sum of $300,000 from surplus power revenues for fifty years, at which time the federal treasury should have been reimbursed for the cost of the project.[10]

The completion of Boulder Dam, by providing flood protection for the Imperial Valley and by regulating the river so that upstream development could occur without seriously encroaching on waters needed below the dam, resolved pressing problems in portions of the

Inland Empire and adjacent areas. It made water available in arid areas so that ranchers could graze their animals on a broader range before moving them into forested areas. It also allowed for irrigation by 1939 of over 2.5 million acres for agricultural production, about equally divided between individuals (mainly in Wyoming, Colorado, and Utah) and large enterprises, principally in Arizona and California.[11]

The headwaters of the Colorado River are located in the Rocky Mountains high above surrounding areas of fertile lands, which are inadequately watered from limited local supplies. The source was some distance from expanding urban areas on or near the eastern slope that were reaching out for needed water. Several small or moderate diversions had been built prior to the New Deal. A major project to divert water to drought-stricken and dust-ravaged eastern slope areas was launched but it was not completed until late in the 1950s.

The Colorado-Big Thompson Project, calling for the diversion of 300,000 acre-feet annually with the aid of a 13-mile tunnel and extensive reservoirs, was approved by Congress in 1937. Construction started in 1938 with PWA funding under the supervision of the Bureau of Reclamation. This undertaking, completed in the 1950s, was one of the largest irrigation projects in the West. Included in it was a network of water collections, including supply canals, on the western slope, five major dams, a tunnel named after Senator Alva B. Adams that went under the continental divide, five power plants, plus storage reservoirs on the eastern slope. Its purpose was to provide irrigation water for about 615,000 acres of parched lands in eastern Colorado and an abundance of electricity for the several markets in the vicinity of the project. Water sales and power charges would meet most of the costs. Property owners in the conservancy district that was created to work out arrangements with the federal government would repay the balance. The Colorado-Big Thompson Project represented the greatest construction program thus far undertaken by the Bureau of Reclamation. It also marked a significant change from previous projects. By providing supplemental water to existing farmlands and not reclaiming an arid or desert area, by exempting water users from the 160-acre limitation clause in the 1902 Reclamation Act, and by allocating close to half the cost of the project to power sales, the Bureau of Reclamation began a process that would lead to extensive controversy in the West in the years following the New Deal.[12]

Elsewhere major projects in or bordering Ickes's Inland Empire included the construction of the Fort Peck Dam designed to harness the Missouri River, and the Casper-Alcova project which had as its purpose the use of the North Platte River for developing the region's agricultural possibilities and making available its mineral resources. The Corps of Engineers in 1933 called for the construction of Fort Peck Dam as an aid to navigation by means of regulating channel flows. But several senators from Missouri Basin states favored constructing the reservoir as a public works project. Construction got under way in the spring of 1934 and was boosted several months later when Ickes granted $25 million of PWA funds to help make the dam a multipurpose one furthering irrigation and flood control as well as navigation. In all, PWA allocated more than $49 million for the construction of the Fort Peck Dam, which it was estimated would cost $108 million. President Roosevelt, speaking at the dam site on August 6, 1934, noted the multipurpose dimensions of the project and said it would provide irrigation water for 84,000 acres of land. The Corps of Engineers, in charge of construction, made no specific provision for generating hydroelectric power. Congress remedied this deficiency with the Fort Peck Act of 1938. It provided for surplus power to be delivered to the Bureau of Reclamation for distribution. Initially regarded as a project to support Missouri River navigation, Fort Peck Dam, substantially completed by 1939, was functioning as a multipurpose project closely coordinated with the Bureau of Reclamation. It also helped extend Ickes's domain eastward into the Great Plains territory of the Department of Agriculture. Tensions between the Bureau of Reclamation and the Corps of Engineers throughout the Missouri Basin were exacerbated by the late 1930s as the two agencies suggested differing approaches to stream development. The Corps of Engineers focused its planning almost exclusively on navigation with incidental attention to flood control. The Bureau of Reclamation strongly endorsed multipurpose development with heaviest emphasis on irrigation and the generation of electricity, sale of which would ease the repayment burden of the settlers using the waters for irrigation.[13]

Fort Peck Dam, a great earth-filled barrier across the Missouri River in eastern Montana, is one of the largest structures of its kind in the world. It stretches across the Missouri from bluff to bluff, a distance of 3.68 miles and is about a half mile wide at its base. The lake formed behind the dam would extend about 180 miles. When the President first visited the dam site in August 1934, more than 7,000 men were at work and the town of Fort Peck was being constructed to house personnel and others involved with this project. Besides residences, municipal buildings and various shops were constructed by the Corps of Engineers along with a power line extending to Great Falls, 228 miles to the west, to provide electricity for construction purposes.[14]

Ickes through the PWA also played an important role in launching another major project that would extend the boundaries of his Inland Empire further into the Great Plains by making the North Platte River yield more water for irrigation and power for electricity in eastern Wyoming and western Nebraska. An earth and rock-fill dam in Alcova Canyon would provide irrigation water converting about 66,000 acres of desolate range area heretofore dotted sparsely with isolated sheep ranches to cropland for alfalfa, sugar beets, potatoes, and feed grains. More than 1,000 farms, it was estimated in 1933, could be carved from range lands covered with sage brush, cactus, and bunch grass. At the end of 1933, following a PWA allocation of $22.7 million, work was about to get under way. The development consisted of two major engineering projects under the supervision of the Bureau of Reclamation. The Alcova diversion dam was to provide water for irrigation; further upstream the Seminoe Dam would be used for power development and water storage. Water for the Alcova Dam would be diverted through a 106-mile canal, passing through Emigrant Gap Ridge by tunnel, to a project area about six miles north of Casper. Since the North Platte River in sum would be irrigating over a million acres of land along its course through Colorado, Wyoming, and Nebraska, the Seminoe Dam in Granite Canyon would provide additional storage of the surplus flow during the nonirrigation season. Its location above the Pathfinder Reservoir, an earlier Bureau of Reclamation project, made power development highly favorable without the waste of any water for irrigation.[15]

All did not go well with this project because of an extended and long-standing dispute over water rights between Wyoming and Nebraska water users. In October 1934, Ickes announced that further expenditures would cease until the water-rights controversy could be resolved. Finally, in February 1935, the President approved a modified project which reduced the acreage to be irrigated from 66,000 to 35,000 acres, thereby temporarily resolving the dispute among water users' groups in Nebraska and Wyoming. The controversy over the allocation of waters, also involving groups in Colorado, was not resolved until 1945. But in 1937, with the approval of the Department of the Interior's appropriation bill, the Casper-Alcova project was renamed the Kendrick project, honoring the Wyoming senator, John B. Kendrick (1857–1933), who from 1928 to 1933 conducted an active campaign to have the project approved. In 1937 all the major features of the project were under construction and the project as a whole was about 35 percent complete. In 1940 the first unit of the Kendrick project was finished; however, operation was delayed for several years owing to lack of water pending the completion of other units.[16]

Ickes and the Bureau of Reclamation over-extended themselves with this project, which never met the expectations of the bureau chief, Elwood Mead, or those of John B. Kendrick. Conflicts between and among water users in the three states through which the North Platte River flowed delayed the project and Ickes's penetration into the Great Plains dominion of the Department of Agriculture. It also did not reflect favorably upon the bureau, which appeared overly eager to construct projects that ran counter to the interests of powerful local groups and whose feasibility was questionable. Casper-Alcova-

Kendrick was the first project where such questions arose. None, however, came prominently to the forefront during the New Deal. Ickes
and the Bureau of Reclamation, armed with PWA funds, continued to
play a prominent and largely unchallenged role during the New Deal
years throughout the Inland Empire and elsewhere in the West.

It also should be noted that other federal agencies, as well as various state groups, initiated or expanded existing projects. For example,
the Resettlement Administration in 1936 and 1937 purchased additional
tracts, later leased and sold to selected operators, on the Milk River
and Sun River Reclamation projects in Montana. The Farm Security
Administration helped launch irrigation projects on the Great Plains. In
Nebraska and Texas PWA funds were used to construct notable multipurpose projects on the Platte and Colorado Rivers respectively. In
July 1938, when a flood occurred on the Colorado River in Texas, only
one of a series of dams was completed; the Buchanan Dam, designed
primarily for power and to help pay for the rest of the project, nevertheless helped reduce one of the largest floods ever recorded on this
Texas river. With the completion of the Marshall Ford Dam in 1941,
further downstream, the main flood control dam in the project, the
menace of floods virtually disappeared.[17]

A Bureau of Reclamation project proposed for the Ogden River in
Utah to augment the water supply of lands subject to severe drought
got under way in September 1934. The Pine View Dam project in
Ogden Canyon was intended to provide supplementary water to about
17,250 acres and to irrigate fully an additional 4,500 acres, while also
providing storage water for the city of Ogden. Funded by the PWA,
Bureau of Reclamation engineers designed the dam, and some of the
initial labor for it was provided by the Civilian Conservation Corps.
Construction was largely done by private firms under competitive bidding. The dam and related pipelines, conduits, and canals were completed in June 1937, in time for farmers to receive its waters during the
irrigation season. This project, to which an additional canal and
pipeline were added in 1941, posed difficult engineering problems
which, successfully mastered, greatly facilitated the ensuing growth
and prosperity of northern Utah. It was one of the rare single-purpose
projects constructed during the New Deal.[18]

The work of Ickes and the Bureau of Reclamation met largely with
approval as they sought, through studies and investigations developed
in the bureau's expanding Denver office where the chief engineer was
headquartered, to provide additional water resources for the West in
general and the Inland Empire in particular. Throughout the New Deal
years average annual expenditures of the agency totaled $52 million;
prior to 1933 the figure was $8.9 million. With numerous new projects
getting under way, bureau engineers in accord with New Deal gospel
stressed the multipurpose approach and combined hydroelectric power

with water for irrigation in their planning. They reviewed reports from the National Resources Planning Board as they also considered flood control, drainage, and recreation in their major projects. Ickes further assisted with PWA funding, and labor in some instances was provided by the CCC and the WPA. Congress also assisted with an amendment to the 1938 Department of the Interior appropriation bill donating half of the revenue derived from naval petroleum reserves to the depleted Reclamation Fund and allowing repayment for projects financed by emergency and general funds to go to the Reclamation Fund, thereby providing the bureau with monies to continue its work after federal largesse abated. In 1939 a fundamental piece of legislation, the Reclamation Project Act, clarified and improved the procedure for construction of projects under authority of the Reclamation Act of 1902, principally by setting a ten-year development period before repayments were to begin and by charging portions of reservoir costs to other purposes (flood control and navigation, for example) where appropriate. And the Wheeler-Case Act, enacted also in 1939, established the principle that the cost of available relief labor (WPA or CCC) used in the construction of irrigation projects could be charged as reimbursable only insofar as the settlers were capable of making repayments. These two laws enabled financing to be extended to many projects which could not qualify for 100 percent reimbursement under terms of the 1902 Reclamation Act.[19]

By 1937 the Bureau of Reclamation was engaged in its largest construction program with seventy-two contracts totaling $87.8 million in force, which when completed would expand storage capacity in reservoirs to 56.6 million acre-feet. Increased agricultural production would provide numerous other benefits throughout the Inland Empire, such as stabilizing local communities, improving transportation facilities, and assisting western cities by providing power and domestic water supplies. Though the massive multipurpose projects with their giant dams and spectacular engineering feats received the most attention, they did not form the whole of the agency's work. Small earthen dams by the dozens were constructed by the Bureau of Reclamation during the 1930s to catch and store flood waters from smaller streams in an effort to help stabilize intermountain and other areas of the West characterized by hurried agricultural settlement, overgrazing, plowing up of range lands, and a high degree of speculative farming which had resulted in repeated failures. Where stability existed, such as in counties with flourishing Bureau of Reclamation projects, population increased during the 1930s. Such was the case with the Riverton Project in Fremont County, Wyoming, where the population increased nearly 60 percent. In eastern Oregon, the population of Malheur County, site of the Vale and Owyhee projects, increased more than 75 percent.[20]

Federal Reclamation in its normal activities sought to anchor farm families by irrigating areas that were unsuitable for dry farming, thereby helping to support an increased number of inhabitants in the vicinity and stabilizing the surrounding region. Another related purpose was to replenish or supplement depleted water supplies for established irrigated areas and also to provide new agricultural opportunities by irrigating dry, undeveloped lands where farm families, migrants from drought and dust, could become self-sustaining. While the work of the Bureau of Reclamation through its massive projects and its more normal activities was helping to stabilize areas throughout the West, it should be noted that, aside from the six Great Plains states, the Works Progress Administration and its predecessors expended from 1933 to 1941 more than $1.75 billion in the West. In the six Great Plains states the sum totaled more than a billion dollars, for a combined figure of almost $3 billion. In the first forty years of its existence, from 1902 to 1942, the Bureau of Reclamation received from all sources about half of this amount. While the agency benefited enormously during the New Deal, it also faced increased competition.[21]

The Water Facilities Act of August 28, 1937, according to Harold Ickes, created another Bureau of Reclamation in the Department of Agriculture and challenged his hegemony. Ickes sought to have this measure modified in 1939 to bring its functions directly into the Bureau of Reclamation. While he did not fully succeed, the measure that resulted called for greater cooperation between the Bureau of Reclamation, the Department of Agriculture, the Works Progress Administration, and the Civilian Conservation Corps—with the National Resources Planning Board serving as coordinator. But, most important for Ickes, it authorized him as secretary of the interior to undertake these projects. By 1941 these groups by and large under the supervision of the Bureau of Reclamation were involved with twelve projects in eight western states aimed at readjusting about 2,500 families, enabling them to live on irrigated lands, and providing for the stabilization of the surrounding areas. By the end of the New Deal, thanks to congressional enactments, Ickes's position as the key figure in the Inland Empire was even more secure and the Bureau of Reclamation was the agency that assured his supremacy. So powerful was its impact that the annual meeting of the Western Farm Economics Association held in Salt Lake City in June 1941 devoted a panel discussion to "Control of Development in New Reclamation Projects."[22]

This academic discussion was prompted by the great increase in reclamation projects under construction in the late 1930s. Economists and others were beginning to question the wisdom and objectives of the projects. Basically there were two types. One, the more traditional type, was designed to rescue developed irrigation communities through rehabilitation and through provision of adequate, regulated stored water supplies. The other, more common during the New Deal, was designed to expand the agricultural base of the arid and semiarid states by watering new lands, thereby creating new opportunities for distressed farm families. In the Inland Empire these projects, aside from those already mentioned, chiefly included the Pine River Project in Colorado, the Boise-Payette Division in Idaho, the Upper Snake River Storage in Idaho-Wyoming, the Buffalo Rapids Project in Montana, the Gila Project in Arizona, the Tucumcari Project in New Mexico, the Deschutes Project in Oregon, the Provo River Project in Utah, the Roza Division of the Yakima Project in Washington, and the Kendrick and Shoshone-Hart Mountain Projects in Wyoming. Labor for most of these projects came from Emergency Relief Administraton funds, estimated for 1937 at about $64.5 million. WPA labor, directly involving about 20,000 people, constructed canals, canal structures, and canal linings. WPA labor also helped construct tunnels, dams, and spillways to store water primarily for irrigation.

In 1939 Senators D. Worth Clark of Idaho and Joseph C. O'Mahoney of Wyoming sought an appropriation to grant the Bureau of Reclamation the sum of $83.5 million to be used on various projects, half of which were already under construction, encompassing about 2.5 million acres, and the other half to irrigate about 500,000 acres "either authorized or ready to go." The great attraction of these projects was that they would be self-liquidating; all the money advanced would ultimately be repaid. In 1939 Senator Clark said "the record of repayments, over a long period of years, is 97.7 percent." The Reclamation Fund, from which monies for new projects was to come according to the 1902 enabling act, could not sustain the stepped-up program these senators proposed. In all instances federal funds were advanced on the security of repayment contracts with the beneficiaries of the projects and in some instances by power contracts, where the power was developed as incidental to the irrigation works. In 1939 out of about $400 million of federal funds expended since 1902, $50 to $60 million had been repaid. At this time the Bureau of Reclamation had construction contracts amounting to approximately $102 million in operation, indicating the stepped-up role of the agency under Ickes's tenure as Secretary of the Interior.[23]

Among the crops raised on these projects were specialty items, fruits and vegetables, not in conflict with crop control programs in agricultural commodities that were supervised by the Department of Agriculture. Official statistics of this department indicated that about half of all the crops grown on western irrigated lands were fed to livestock in the form of hay and feed. Of the remaining half, non-competitive crops—those not adding to the agricultural surplus—predominated. Sugar beets, for example, were raised only on irrigated lands and were not considered a surplus commodity.

An important factor in attracting congressional support for new projects was the claim that they stabilized families on the land. In 1939 it was estimated that "something over 300,000 farm families" were moving about in the West. Many came from devastated areas in the Great Plains and were seeking an opportunity to establish themselves again as farm families. To critics who questioned the vast expenses of new projects, western supporters responded that they would be self-liquidating, that they would justify themselves in strengthening and stabilizing particular communities, and that experience extending over thirty years indicated close to the full return of monies expended to the federal treasury. In brief, as their friends and supporters insisted, the Bureau of Reclamation was a fundamental agency of public welfare "in broadening the base of the country's food supply, in strengthening and supporting its industry, in extending the opportunity for establishing self-supporting homes, in enlarging and building up the Nation's transportation system. . . ."[24]

Fundamental as it was, the future of the Bureau of Reclamation and the integrity of reclamation policy were dependent upon repayment by those who benefited directly from federal construction of their projects. The repayment schedule, laid down in the Reclamation Act of 1902, was altered in intervening years. But the principle remained unchanged and was the main pillar of support for the federal policy of constructing irrigation projects throughout the arid regions with funds collected from western sources. To launch this program a revolving fund was created with receipts from land sales in the public domain; the water users then would return to it the cost of their projects so that the money might be used again. By and large, though Congress had written off certain noncollectible charges, federal reclamation projects had a creditable repayment record until the Great Depression. Congress in 1930 granted a moratorium on construction repayments and then extended it to cover five years during which time the Reclamation Fund was severely depleted by moratoria and by diminishing returns from the sale of public lands and other monies allocated to the fund.

In 1936 Congress again came to the aid of western water users by granting a moratorium on 50 percent of the construction charges due that year and called for a commission to investigate and determine the ability of the various projects to meet their repayment charges. As the three-man commission began its work at the close of 1936, a total of 3,038,187 acres were included in reclamation projects. These acres were divided into 46,462 irrigated farms with a population of 205,055. They also supported 244 towns with a population of 635,208. At the end of 1936 the Bureau of Reclamation had 19 dams under construction. These projects employed thousands of men and utilized large quantities of machinery, steel, cement, and other products that helped stimulate the economy in the West and elsewhere. By September 1939, total contracts for labor, materials, and machinery amounted to $130 million.[25]

In 1938 Congress took two steps to increase the Reclamation Fund. One was to make available to the fund a portion of the receipts collected as royalties on oil from the naval reserves. The other directed that construction money received from Public Works and Emergency Relief funds, and by most appropriations direct from the Treasury, would be siphoned into the Reclamation Fund. This legislation by replenishing the Reclamation Fund assured Ickes and the Bureau of Reclamation that projects under way would be completed on schedule and that new ones could be contemplated. What remained to be considered was an effective repayment schedule that would end the moratorium imposed earlier by Congress. The commission, considering a more feasible and practicable repayment plan, made suggestions that were incorporated into the important 1939 modification of the Reclamation Act. This law resolved an acute problem for western water users by introducing flexibility into the contracts, allowing lesser payments in poor years and higher ones in good years, thus assuring Ickes that water would continue to be made available to strengthen the Inland Empire despite the fact that in 1940 Congress appropriated starting funds for only one new project, the San Luis Valley Project in Colorado.[26]

By 1940 one-fifth of the entire installed hydroelectric capacity in the West was generated at 23 plants operating on Bureau of Reclamation projects. In addition, with the 15 power plants still under construction, the total capacity of power plants on Bureau of Reclamation projects would almost equal the entire western hydroelectic development of 4,461,618 kilowatts reported for November 1939. Power generated at these projects would be sold wholesale with preference given to municipalities and other public or nonprofit agencies.

At the same time the Bureau by 1940 had built 138 storage and diversion dams on irrigation projects and had 15 more under construction. It had also constructed more than 20,000 miles of canals, ditches, and drains; 4,600 miles of telephone lines; 13,000 bridges; and almost 200,000 other irrigation structures. These dams, canals, and other structures irrigated fully 6 million acres of arid land, supporting approximately one million people whose homes, farms, villages, and towns represented a stabilizing investment in an unstable region. Annual crop production was valued at more than $100 million, and the annual market for nationwide business created through these projects was estimated in 1940 at double this figure. After 1940 appropriations began to accelerate markedly as defense needs, especially rising demands for additional electrical energy, came to the forefront of congressional attention. New projects were launched, and Ickes stressed how Bureau of Reclamation projects could provide additional power for western airplane and ship construction, while advancing mining and additional manufacturing activities through the use of latent power resources abounding in the West.[27]

Despite these impressive figures, irrigation affected only about 3 percent of the arid lands of the West, an amount insufficient to supply all the needs of the population of the region. In the United States as a whole the area farmed and cropped averaged about 8.1 acres per capita in the late 1930s, while in the reclamation states, those west of the hundredth meridian, the average was 3.7 acres per capita. Irrigated areas provided pasture and forage and produced alfalfa hay for live-stock, along with vegetables, grain crops, special fruits, potatoes, and some cotton. Vegetables and fruit were processed, when necessary, in the region where they were produced. As specialty crops they found a nationwide market, but agricultural and industrial products of other sections of the country commanded the bulk of the income of reclamation farmers and of most consumers and producers in the West. The Bureau of Reclamation took special care to note that irrigated crops did not add to the surplus of basic foodstuffs and did not impede the administration's oft-repeated goal of reducing agricultural output. Nor were irrigated crops in competition with eastern crops. Most of the food and feed produced on reclamation projects was consumed locally. And only one irrigation crop, sugar beets, merited special attention from Congress during the New Deal.[28]

Western reclamation producers competed very remotely with corn-hog farmers in Iowa or Illinois. And irrigation farmers, seeking to expand their production of sugar beets and vegetables, were distressed that Corn Belt congressmen feared their competition, particularly since they constituted a steady market for mid-western foodstuffs and manu-factured goods. All taxpayers derived benefits from western reclama-tion projects and Congress, accepting this premise, responded during the New Deal by furthering reclamation agriculture through increased subsidization for sugar beets, a cash crop in a nonsurplus industry.

Neither beet nor cane sugar were included under the stabilization and subsidy provisions of the 1933 Agricultural Adjustment Act. In 1934 Texas Congressman Marvin Jones and Senator Edward P. Costi-gan of Colorado sponsored a measure which, by using the proceeds of a processing tax, granted a bounty to domestic sugar beet and cane farmers to limit production, thereby providing relief to depressed irri-gation farmers who continually had to cope and compete with tariff preferences favoring sugar imported from Cuba, Puerto Rico, Hawaii, and the Philippine Islands. The average return to domestic beet sugar producers fell from $7.14 per ton of beets in 1930 to $5.13 in 1933. This measure in effect brought beet sugar within the framework of the Agricultural Adjustment Act. With its enactment in May 1934, the large sugar surplus declined drastically, and the income of domestic growers improved. By 1936 sugar beet growers were receiving an average return, including benefit payments, of $6.05 per ton.[29]

When the Supreme Court in 1936 declared the 1933 agricultural legislation with its processing tax provision unconstitutional, the plight of western beet sugar producers became precarious once again, especially so as various Bureau of Reclamation projects were making new lands available to irrigation farmers. Other provisons of the Jones-Costigan Act, those affecting quotas for imported cane sugar, expired at the end of 1937 making new legislation imperative. New legislation introduced in 1937 affected domestic beet sugar producers who relied heavily on migratory workers to harvest their crops. It called for minimum wage payments and the virtual elimination of child labor as a condition for receiving price support. In brief, payments to family-sized operations were at a higher rate than those applicable to larger units. Funds for these payments, which averaged out to about $19.42 an acre for a yield of 10.9 tons of beets per acre and a recovery of 297 pounds of sugar per ton of beets, would come from an excise tax levied on quota-imported raw sugar. Producers of sugar beets were allocated marketing quotas designed to curb excessive or surplus production and to redistribute income more equitably among growers, processors, and labor. In 1937, 1938, and 1939, sugar beet crops averaged $6.76 per ton. And as a result of the minimum wage provision, child labor was being eliminated. The average wage for the 1940 beet crop was 6.4 percent higher than for the 1937 crop.[30]

In September 1939 the President by proclamation suspended all marketing limitations on sugar as a way of curbing excessive speculation and rapidly rising consumer prices following the outbreak of war in Europe. The suspension of quotas meant the removal of almost all restrictions on domestic sugar production thereby allowing irrigation farmers to temporarily increase their acreage and improve their financial position. Excess production quickly stabilized prices to consumers and at the end of 1939, before the September suspension could markedly benefit western beet sugar producers, Roosevelt in another proclamation terminated the suspension of the marketing quotas provision of the 1937 Sugar Act. Nevertheless, by 1940 domestic producers were receiving incomes, including benefit payments, at approximately the parity level and were expanding production. Wages and working conditions for field hands had been improved and child labor greatly reduced. Despite efforts of beet sugar producers to achieve larger marketing quotas, Congress on October 15, 1940, continued the Sugar Act of 1937 beyond its expiration date of December 31, 1940. Ickes believed that failure to expand marketing quotas hurt the President in the West on Election Day and later claimed that "a gentleman's agreement" between the President and "some of the beet sugar Senators" had been made over his "vigorous protest."[31]

The Secretary of Agriculture under the 1937 Sugar Act was authorized to set minimum wage rates for workers engaged in the production of the crop and to ascertain that child labor was not utilized. These provisions helped bring to public attention conditions among laborers, largely Mexican-Americans, in the western beet fields. Their labor was characterized by extremely low annual incomes secured from intermittent periods of intensive work by whole families and by a scarcity of supplementary work during the off season, making sugar beet workers largely dependent upon public relief during the winter months. In Colorado, the leading producer in the nation, sugar beets were a cash crop raised on irrigated areas by farmers under contract with the Great Western Sugar Refining Corporation. So great were the labor requirements of beet raising that hand labor on most of the acreage was performed by contract workers despite the small average acreage per grower. The work was arduous, much of it done in a stooping posture, and carried with it a low social status in addition to low wage rates and poor living conditions. The industry utilized more labor than any other major agricultural product grown on commensurate acreage in the United States.[32]

Western sugar beet production was located largely in irrigated valleys whose waters were provided by Bureau of Reclamation projects. The growers, continually seeking to expand their production beyond the limits assigned by law, were beginning to make headway late in the New Deal with their argument that an increasingly substantial portion of the nation's sugar requirements should be grown on western irrigated lands to protect the United States against loss of supply in time of war. Since sugar beet producers were served by an established industry for converting beets into sugar, every gain made by the farmers in expanding domestic production and lowering import quotas gave further protection to the large corporate organizations that controlled beet sugar refining.[33]

Setting acreage quotas also created problems. Calling for reduced acreage in some areas and increasing it in others, brought forth charges that the Department of Agriculture through its decisions could make or ruin many irrigation farmers. Moreover, farmers on newly irrigated lands found it difficult to get their acreage included under the payment provisions of the sugar acts. In late 1934 a furious controversy arose in Idaho when 12,000 acres of that state's sugar beet production controlled by the Amalgamated Sugar Company of Ogden, Utah, was proposed for transfer to a California irrigation district with the claim that the company had the consent of administration officials to do so. Secretary Wallace and the Department of Agriculture won no friends throughout the Inland Empire when a department representative testified at a congressional hearing early in the New Deal (before the enactment of the Jones-Costigan bill), that the beet sugar industry was an inefficient industry and ought not to be maintained any longer than necessary. While the Idaho controversy turned out to be based on misunderstanding, enough suspicion was generated to allow Senator William E. Borah and several Idaho editors and irrigation spokesmen to continue voicing their suspicions about unfair competition and unsympathetic Department of Agriculture officials. About 80,000 farmers of the irrigated West depended for a large portion of their cash income, during the New Deal, upon the federal government, which through tariffs and Bureau of Reclamation projects helped promote the related refining complex and migratory labor situation in the beet fields.[34]

For the small farmers in the Inland Empire and along its borders, the Bureau of Reclamation through its numerous projects provided the basis for their homes, their livelihood, and their future hopes. Marshall N. Dana, president of the National Reclamation Association in 1935, reviewing his tenure as president of the organization, concluded his remarks by stating what all New Dealers, most conservationists, and inhabitants of the West considered a truism: "Without reclamation western progress stops." Organized in December 1932 at a meeting of the Western Governors' Conference in Salt Lake City, the National Reclamation Association throughout the New Deal served as a powerful pressure group cooperating with the Bureau of Reclamation in urging desirable legislation and the speedy completion of projects to create what another association president called "a new West—a bountiful dwelling place—using the natural resources of a pioneer empire."[35]

In 1939 with the entrance of Oklahoma and Kansas into the association, 17 western states now were included in the National Reclamation Association, extending its influence from the Missouri River to the Pacific Ocean. Also in 1939 a tristate alliance was created for Texas, Oklahoma, and New Mexico with the purpose of securing assistance from the Bureau of Reclamation for building small dams and reservoirs to conserve water and control floods in the dust bowl area. At this time, irrigation farmers, like most New Deal officials, were discussing reclamation as a factor in the program for national defense.

However, by the end of the New Deal, much had been accomplished in the Inland Empire and throughout the West. About 20 million acres were irrigated and these lands provided almost all the opportunities for close settlement in rural areas beyond the hundredth meridian. In 1940 John C. Page, Commissioner of the Bureau of Reclamation, believed his agency was "approximately at the halfway point in the development of the West by irrigation. . . ." But, more important, conservation was no longer a slogan; it was a national policy applicable, as thus far noted, to both the Great Plains and the Inland Empire. Harold Ickes perhaps best expressed what the New Deal meant for the West when he said in a 1939 address, "At long last, after years of exuberant squandering our people are insisting that our public lands, our forests, our water, our soil, our metals and minerals, our wildlife, and our natural recreational assets be used without waste." But when applied to metals and minerals in the West during the New Deal, Ickes's statement was not valid.[36]

Chapter 7

Privileged Producers

DEFEAT, THE ONE SERIOUS blow the New Deal ethic of conservation experienced in the West, occurred in the realm of minerals policy. Oilmen, silver producers, and their political allies and supporters in the ranks of big business forced New Dealers to modify their views so that producer policies prevailed in the West and provided a serious setback to the programs Ickes hoped to supervise. Not that he did not try. Oil policy over which he had a say would be bitterly contested and Ickes conceded only when the President yielded to massive pressures from the oil-producing states. And in the formulation of silver policy, Ickes had no voice. Pressure applied by inflationists and silver state senators led the New Dealers to accept legislation that bailed out silver mine operators by subsidizing production of their not-so-precious metal.

In both industries, as the New Deal got underway, the basic problem was one of overproduction. Oil and silver were a glut on the market. Producers in both industries were faced with bankruptcy. Yet efforts to curb overproduction meant that marginal operators both in oil and silver would go under. Better to have the government, if possible, subsidize the industry. Or, if that did not work, keep federal supervision to a bare minimum and let the states, where the larger operators would have a greater voice, oversee or regulate production in the operators' interest without concern for conservation and future needs. Oilmen and mine owners were able to accomplish what lumbermen, ranchers, wheat producers, and others were unable to achieve: they forced the New Dealers to accept many of the premises of their largest and most powerful producers. The enemy, as Harold Ickes viewed them, had gained a foothold in his Inland Empire. What he considered unsound policies in the Inland Empire proved by 1936 to be good politics for the Roosevelt administration.[1]

Of the two minerals, the situation regarding oil was more immediate and precarious. The problem, overproduction, was not new. It had been endemic since the late 1920s. It was accentuated in October 1930 when Joiner Test Number 3 was spudded and started producing, according to some estimates, about 10,000 barrels a day. All hell broke loose in East Texas when an oil field, roughly twice the size of Manhattan Island, attracted hordes of people seeking their fortunes, constructing a forest of derricks around the discovery well, and in other ways participating in the boom. It was a small man's field, attractive to independent operators because it was relatively close to tidewater and because the field was relatively shallow, could be drilled inexpensively, and yielded large quantities of high grade crude. As of March 1931 a dozen wells a day were being completed. By December 1932 there were 9,072 producing wells in the field. Overproduction led to over expansion of refining capacity and this in turn accentuated declining prices in a drastically depressed national economy. The field, about 50 miles long and from 3.5 to 10 miles wide, contained about 130,000 acres of productive territory. Soon at least two-thirds of the flowing oil wells in Texas were located in this field. By 1937 about 15 percent of the national oil output, nearly as much as the aggregate production from all the wells in Louisiana, Kansas, and New Mexico, ranking fourth, fifth and sixth in output, emanated from East Texas.

By March 1933, when Ickes took office, the plight of the industry was most precarious. The price of crude paid to producers in many areas was less than the cost of production. State regulatory machinery had all but collapsed as smaller operators, ignoring proration quotas, produced and refined "hot oil" to avoid bankruptcy and remain in business. The major integrated companies and the larger independent producers called for a more effective crackdown on hot oil, while the smaller producers clamored for vigorous antitrust enforcement and divestment of pipelines from the integrated corporations. Almost everyone involved with the industry by 1933 turned to the federal government because, aside from the largest integrated companies, all were unable to produce profitably. In addition, state officials, unable to exercise their regulatory authority, wanted federal assistance to help regulate and secure all available revenue from the industry in their states. In short, as Ickes noted in 1936, "the vast oil industry was in a deplorable state when this administration took over the Federal Government." Moreover, he added, "the recognized leaders flocked to Washington to beg the administration to do something, anything, to save the industry from chaos and possible collapse."[2]

By May 1933, East Texas oil was selling for four cents a barrel. Ickes by this time was convinced that a strong federal administrator was necessary to cope with overproduction and bootlegging. Though it was not in the form he wanted, Ickes became that administrator in July, a month after the President signed the National Industrial Recovery Act. Ickes became the Petroleum Administrator, head of the Petroleum Administration Board, charged under Section 9 with regulating pipelines, seeking their divestiture from petroleum holding companies, and curbing the interstate shipment of hot oil. In addition, the Petro-

102 • THE NEW DEAL AND THE WEST

leum Code adopted in December 1933 provided for minimum prices and allocation of allowed domestic production among states, reservoirs, and wells based on Bureau of Mines demand forecasts, among other provisions. Thus Ickes, who also had to approve all plans for the development of new pools, gained enough authority to make a mighty effort to bring some stability to a demoralized industry engaged in what he considered the "criminal waste of an irreplaceable natural resource."

In 1932 the Supreme Court reversed lower courts and approved state prorating laws. It became the job of the Petroleum Administration Board under Ickes to see that production was kept in line with the state quotas and to curb interstate shipment of hot oil in violation of these quotas, which were formulated after estimating the daily production of crude necessary to balance the demand for petroleum products. But prorating, a device to maximize profits for large established producers, was at best incidental and secondary to conservation. Nevertheless, Ickes worked hard in trying to stabilize the chaotic oil industry. During the period the code was operative the amount of production exceeded by an average of less than 5 percent the amount determined necessary to meet market demands for petroleum products.[3]

The Petroleum Advisory Board continued its regulatory activities, despite the fact that the Petroleum Code of the NRA was invalidated in May 1935 by the Supreme Court, because Congress in February had approved the Connally Act continuing federal authority to curb interstate shipment of hot oil. Its structure was formally institutionalized in the Petroleum Conservation Division created in April 1936 and housed in the Department of the Interior. As a result by the end of the decade hot oil, primarily from the East Texas oil field, was no longer a serious factor and voluntary restriction of production through an Interstate Oil Compact, involving Texas, Oklahoma, Colorado, Kansas, New Mexico, and Illinois, further stabilized the industry.

The situation in the far West, involving the petroleum industry in California, Arizona, Nevada, Oregon, and western Washington, was somewhat different but the results were the same. A Pacific Coast Petroleum Agency was created and refiners' agreements were concluded under the aegis of the National Industrial Recovery Act that permitted restraint of competition in the California fields and refineries and in the above-mentioned states where California petroleum was marketed. The agreements also were devised to keep hot oil from Texas and other mid-continent fields from being marketed in this region. Curbing chaotic marketing conditions on the Pacific Coast was their goal. The agreements, in preventing the waste of oil and in keeping the industry reasonably stabilized, made the situation on the Pacific Coast far more placid than elsewhere in the West.

With the demise of the federal law, the cartel arrangement continued on an informal basis. Basically it involved prorating the markets chiefly among the major California producers, their subsidiaries, and independent producers and refiners. This cartel was the first agreement in the petroleum industry to concede a differential to independents in an attempt to permit them to stabilize their position as well. In short, the Pacific Coast arrangement sought the end of ruinous marketing competition by eliminating the incentives for it and by curbing the production of crude oil as well.

Stabilizing this marketing structure was the chief goal of the Pacific Coast Petroleum Agency and of the refiners' agreements approved by Ickes as administrator of the Petroleum Code. The agreements continued more informally after 1935 following an initial period in which prices dropped markedly and prorationing broke down. Self-government by the oil industry in the far West functioned with less official support than elsewhere, but stabilization was the goal sought by all sectors of the industry. In addition, the Pacific Coast arrangements involved refiners and dealers to a greater degree than other agreements. They were equally concerned with crude conservation and market stabilization. State authority played a lesser role than elsewhere in the West, and Kettleman Hills in California, discovered in 1928, during the New Deal years was the best managed and least wasteful major oil field in the nation.[4]

At a meeting of the American Petroleum Institute in Dallas in November 1934, Ickes argued for federal control of the industry, saying that it should be treated as a public utility subject to federal supervision and regulation. Though his suggestion was turned down by the Institute's Board of Directors, the vote was surprisingly close, possibly because its members were aware of rising congressional support for regulation of the industry either through a federal agency or through an agreement of oil-producing states.[5] The Interstate Oil Compact, which was ratified by all of the leading oil producing states (except California), on July 10, 1935, received congressional approval despite opposition from Ickes and those members advocating federal controls. The President on August 27, 1935, signed the joint resolution endorsing the compact.[6]

Earlier in the year Roosevelt had signed the Connally Act, a temporary measure which was renewed for another two years in 1937, to check interstate movement of hot oil. Though these various measures helped meliorate conditions within the industry, they were not to Ickes's liking. He favored stricter controls in the interests of conservation and the American public. The accepted solutions to the problems of the industry, he was fully aware, were crafted along lines favorable to the major integrated petroleum companies and the large independent pro-

ducers. They did not represent or reflect New Deal policies or programs in operation elsewhere in the West. While the President
accepted these solutions as politically viable, Ickes was distressed by
them—even though in his role as Petroleum Administrator and as Secretary of the Interior he was able to establish a semblance of federal
control in such a way as to raise prices and improve conditions within
the industry.

Ickes's disillusionment with the solution to the problems of the
petroleum industry was based on his "interesting experiences" at the
outset of his tenure, when he became fully aware of "the results of
unchecked and ruthless exploitation" within the industry. At that time
state conservation laws were openly flouted and hundreds of thousands
of barrels of bootlegged oil were flooding already depressed markets
throughout the country. Ickes said "one rugged individualist was steal-
ing the oil of a brother rugged individualist," taking away markets by
selling below cost and thereby compounding the crisis situation the
New Deal and the American people faced in the spring of 1933.

Because of recent discoveries and conditions within the industry,
new wells were being brought into production at a time when vast
amounts of crude oil were already being produced. Instead of leaving it
in the ground, oil was wastefully produced and then stored at great
expense in tanks, through fear "that some fellow rugged individualist
would get away some dark night with oil that was not his." With most
banks in 1933 unwilling or unable to extend credit, and with some
already calling loans, oil men of all persuasions came to Washington
and asked that the government "take over the industry and run it,"
confessing in effect "that the situation was beyond control and that
only the strong hand of government could save it." Ickes listened in
amazement to their pleading and was astounded at their "willingness to
entrust the destinies of a great enterprise to a government official who
was without scientific knowledge with respect to oil as a product, or
special acquaintance with oil as a business." And the oil men were not
alone. The *Dallas Morning News* called proposed federal control of
petroleum production "a life-preserver tossed out to an industry
drowning in a sea of oil." State authorities agreed that the situation was
beyond their control. They too requested federal supervision.[7]

In his capacity as Petroleum Administrator, Ickes, despite his initial
lack of knowledge or possibly because of it, was pleased with the
restoration of a measure of stability as the price of oil soared toward a
dollar a barrel, from a low of four cents a barrel for crude oil in the East
Texas field in 1933, with no significant price increase at the pump for
customers.[8] Ickes preferred that the federal government take the lead
in formulating policies and programs seeking to balance production of
crude oil with customer demand for petroleum products. As Petroleum

Administrator he did just this, allocating quotas among the states, which in turn set production amounts among the fields and wells within their jurisdiction. In this way hot oil, oil produced in excess of production quotas, was brought under some control and the NRA petroleum code, though beset with legal challenges, sought through a national purchasing and marketing agreement to stabilize refinery and retail prices and to provide some protection to independent refineries and distributors.[9]

The best that can be said about New Deal policy is that it curbed the production, refining, and interstate shipment of hot oil and brought a measure of coherence to the East Texas oil field. By the end of 1934 Ickes had set up a Tender Board in this field. No oil could be shipped without a clearance certificate with the result that several refineries processing hot oil closed and a semblance of stability was imposed on the field and the industry.

With the demise of the NRA, Ickes's role in the oil industry, as confirmed by the Connally Act and the Interstate Compact, would be confined largely to curbing the bootlegging of hot oil. The industry would once again regulate itself, mostly in the interest of the major integrated companies and the larger independents. Government would assist by seeking to eliminate oil produced in excess of the quotas the compact states determined. The Connally Act, in short, embodied no independent policy with respect to the production of oil. It merely assisted the states or state agencies in the enforcement of their own laws and regulations. It in no way encroached on their authority. Rather it provided that those who disobeyed would be denied the privilege of interstate oil shipment.

Ickes was not happy in his new role, and he complained bitterly as he and the New Deal lost control over an important segment of western economic activity. He understood that prorationing was not a conservation measure. Its purpose was to stabilize output and thereby control prices. In no way would the Interstate Oil Compact prevent or curb physical waste in petroleum production. To Ickes in 1935 it was still a matter of central control or chaos, and conservation, he believed, could be achieved only through central control.

A meaningful conservation program, Ickes knew, would have to consider the geological unit. Unified operation of an oil pool would guarantee efficient utilization and minimum costs. Geologic factors special to the pool should determine the number and placement of wells and not the arrangement of leaseholds. Moreover, unit operation would necessitate stricter controls so that wise management could be assured and the interests of consumers adequately protected. Unless a pool was treated as a unit, no operator could afford to curtail or cease production awaiting a better price because, since oil is migratory, a competitor on a neighboring or nearby tract could siphon off all the available oil. To stabilize the industry effectively, Ickes knew that both conservation and control were necessary.[10]

Prorationing was a product of economic distress, a measure of desperation though its proponents proclaimed it was created in the name of conservation. At best it could serve as a method of bringing oil production under effective control, of bringing output into harmony with consumption. Just prior to the New Deal, the failure of prorationing had led the governors of Oklahoma and Texas to call out the state militia and thereby force a temporary but complete shutdown of the newly discovered Oklahoma City and East Texas pools. Under Ickes's supervision these conditions would be eliminated and the allowable quotas of the Interstate Oil Compact would be enforced under federal supervision. Ickes would be helping to attain the goal desired by the leaders of the industry, that of stabilization, of maintaining production quotas in harmony with or slightly below consumption levels.[11] What previously would have been regarded as collusive action among oil producers was now being sanctioned by state agencies and federal authority and was regarded (with Ickes as a notable exception) as an act of economic statesmanship. The goals of output restrictions, price advance, and profit increase—laudable goals in themselves—were to be achieved at the expense of conservation and waste elimination. Petroleum policies then differed fundamentally from other New Deal policies affecting natural resource use in the West. Private interests, aside from mineral policies, were not being pursued by New Deal agencies and administrators at the expense of the public welfare elsewhere in the West. Moreover—and herein resides the irony of the petroleum policy pursued during the New Deal—stabilization could never be effective as long as overcapacity or overproduction was a dominant characteristic of the industry, as long as market demand in a depressed economy lagged. About 31,000 new wells were drilled in 1937, the year Congress renewed the Connally Act. The situation permanently changed only at the end of the New Deal. War in Europe enhanced demand and from that time forward supply would usually lag behind market needs.

Certainly Ickes had reason to be worried. The largest known oil reserves at the end of the decade were those of Texas, California, Oklahoma, Louisiana, and New Mexico. If the rate of output continued at the 1939 level, petroleum reserves would last, according to the most optimistic industry figures, at best another fifteen years. New discoveries and improved technology would bring changes in the estimates but Ickes knew that, with the outbreak of war in Europe and an improving economy in the United States, petroleum reserves had to be increased at a faster rate than the steady growth in demand, lest the

situation become precarious and possibly endanger the national interest in a world engulfed by war.[12] Because of little concern for conservation, the situation in the western oil states had shifted from coping with
overproduction and seeking stability in a chaotic industry to worrying
about adequate reserves and future needs. During the New Deal years
Ickes failed in his quest to convince other New Dealers, including the
President, legislators, state officials, and significant segments of the
population in the West and elsewhere, that oil and the entire industrial
and commercial apparatus associated with its production was clearly
charged with a public interest and required broad supervision and regulation that extended beyond quota allocations, price fixing, and licens-
ing to curb bootleg shipments. New Deal programs from the Petroleum
Code to the Connally Act and the Interstate Compact came only to the
threshold of the new deal in oil that Ickes desired.

Ickes, of course, was not entirely alone in his concerns. Others
tried and failed as well. Senator Elmer Thomas of Oklahoma did not go
as far as Ickes. He was interested in establishing some sort of planning
in an industry unable to do so by itself and to provide oil-producing
states with valid estimates upon which to base their deliberations. In
1935 he introduced a measure calling for an "impartial board" authorized to determine the amount actually required to supply petroleum demands at home and abroad and to "justly and equitably"
allocate quotas to the oil-producing states. Thomas wished to prevent
exploitation of oil resources through a minimum of federal regulation,
while at the same time offering oil states absolute control of production
within their boundaries and a guaranteed share of national production.
Thomas's approach was similar to other oil measures considered in the
1930s. It was in accord with the views of major producers in the western oil states, and it was eventually accepted in legislation and agreements. But it was not conservation as Ickes viewed it, though he
supported the measure introduced by Senator Thomas as a necessary
first step.[13]

The New Deal at its best played a role in providing stability by
assisting leading producers and the oil states in their efforts to balance
production with market demands. By 1939, for example, major producers owned an estimated 80 percent of the wells and proved acreage
in the East Texas oil field, recognized as the largest in the world. At the
outset of the New Deal they owned less than 20 percent. The major
producers played the leading role, along with their supporters and
spokesmen in Washington and in their states, in achieving stability.
The President, though sympathetic to Ickes's broader vision, was willing to accept stability as the price necessary to maintain political support in the leading oil-producing states. The oil frontier ended in the
1930s and was succeeded by efficient business management concerned

with production, refining, and marketing—in short, with their own self-interest, and in no way with conservation and a broader public or national interest. Ickes, nurtured on the conservationist ethic as propounded by Theodore Roosevelt, believed the government had as broad a role to play in this industry as it was playing elsewhere in the West.

Ickes was educated to some of the realities of the oil business by three young lawyers sent to East Texas. Charles Fahy, J. Howard Marshall, and Norman Meyers established themselves first at the Blackstone Hotel in Tyler, Texas, and set out to devise ways and means of assisting Ickes as Petroleum Administrator in curbing the bootlegging of hot oil. They engaged in litigation, secured restraining orders, and learned much about the oil business as practiced in East Texas and elsewhere in the West. At Marshall's suggestion the Federal Tender Board was established. Its creation brought the trio back to Tyler in October 1934, to help inaugurate a system to certify that oil leaving Texas was legally produced. It was a simple system, but instead of the government proving the oil was "hot," the situation was reversed and the shipper had to certify it was not. And the legal code backed up the system. If convicted an offender could be fined, imprisoned, or both. Investigators from the Department of the Interior, though terribly short-handed and receiving little or no help from Texas officials, pursued the work with honesty and efficiency. As a result, hot oil shipments from East Texas were reduced considerably.[14]

But litigation challenging the constitutionality of Section 9-C of the National Industrial Recovery Act, the provision authorizing the federal government to prohibit the transportation of hot oil in interstate and foreign commerce, was accepted by the Supreme Court in January 1935 by a vote of 8 to 1. The court held that the Federal Tender Board's operations comprised an improper delegation of legislative power to the executive branch. The President, the decision stated, had put 9-C into effect by proclamation without a proper fact-finding effort ascertaining that there was illegal oil. In short, granting authority to the executive branch to forbid interstate transportation of hot oil was held invalid.[15]

The Supreme Court decision was handed down on January 7. On February 16, 1935, President Roosevelt signed the so-called Connally "Hot Oil" Act into law reinstituting with statutory standing the system of the Federal Tender Board. The law was drafted by Norman Meyers and J. Howard Marshall for Senator Thomas Connally. It gave the government the specific authority in a manner acceptable to the courts to confiscate hot oil and thereby assisted in staving off cuts in the price of crude oil. Before the Supreme Court acted, Ickes in January 1934 cancelled the price-fixing provision of the Petroleum Code and meanwhile sought to gather information on the costs of producing crude petroleum and of available supplies. With the demise of the National Industrial Recovery Act and of price fixing in general, Ickes was left with a marginal role as a collector of reliable data on the petroleum industry.[16] His image among oil men had changed. At the outset of the New Deal the vast majority of the industry were singing his praises. By 1935 they were criticizing him, and the activities of federal oil officials in the West were meeting with increasing opposition.

The Interstate Compact to Conserve Oil and Gas, also approved in 1935, confirmed Ickes's marginal role. Though he disagreed, its proponents insisted the compact would regularize the industry without regenerating it and at the same time would assure conservation without destroying competition. While Ickes and the New Deal encouraged conservation and helped manage the public lands, as far as petroleum policy was concerned Ickes and the New Deal were confined at best to a role calling for cooperation and encouragement. Ickes, of course, recognized that effective conservation in these circumstances was a consummation devoutly to be wished, that preventing waste was less of a concern to the major producers than controlling prices and adjusting production to demand. And by 1935 in the closing months of the National Industrial Recovery Act, Ickes fully understood—though he was unable to convince the President and other leaders of the New Deal—that partial regulation of the industry was impossible, that it should be treated as a public utility subject to federal regulation. His popularity among oil men waned quickly as the major companies and others were now most firm in their belief that no regulation beyond control of production by state agencies and the prohibition by federal authority of the transportation in interstate commerce of hot oil was necessary.

The hearings chaired by Maryland Representative William P. Cole, Jr., in 1934 allowed Ickes, through the Solicitor of the Department of the Interior, Nathan Margold, to endorse a measure enhancing federal control of the petroleum industry. Though Margold's measure was never actually introduced in Congress, it aroused apprehension throughout the industry. Under the Margold bill, with Ickes as the final arbiter, federal agencies in the Department of the Interior would fix well quotas and prohibit interstate shipments in excess of the quotas. They would regulate the construction of wholesale and retail outlets and, in addition, would fix prices of all petroleum products. If the federal government could prorate production down to individual wellheads and if it could fix the price of petroleum and its products as well, then Ickes believed that conservation in the national interest could be secured, as it was elsewhere in his Inland Empire, with other natural resources. National authority then would consider national needs in the national interest. Since every natural resource, none being infinite, could be mined to exhaustion, Ickes believed it a sound principle of government to utilize every resource to the greatest extent possible and this called for a permanent oil conservation policy on the part of the federal government. New Deal oil legislation, on the other hand, fitted in with the recovery program that Ickes and a handful of other New Dealers considered as but temporary expedients.[17]

Ickes had to be satisfied with prescribing contracts and production principles in the Inland Empire only in the area of his original jurisdiction: namely, on public lands and Indian properties. But, much as he disliked the reality, his views on petroleum policy did not prevail and, after 1935, would not seriously concern western oil men who were now able to attempt stabilization of their industry as they saw fit with the assistance of the federal government. Neither the majority of the American public, who were virtually dependent upon oil, nor the needs of national defense were central to the solution of the dilemma of overproduction during the New Deal years.[18] As Ickes stated in 1934 when testifying before a Senate subcommittee, "The very abundance of our present supply is perhaps responsible to a large extent for our apparent condonation of inexcusable waste and explains, but does not justify, our failure to be more seriously concerned about the critical condition that must inevitably arise when our depleted fields will no longer meet our ever increasing demands and we must turn to foreign nations for the satisfaction of our requirements."[19]

Conservation in the oil industry, however the term was defined, meant limitation of competition. By 1935 it was clear that in the West the parameters of both conservation and competition would be decided in ways favorable to the major producers. Through the Federal Tender Board, through estimates supplied by the Bureau of Mines to the various oil-producing states, and through other assistance provided by bureaus in the Department of the Interior, the New Deal assisted in this process. California was the only major western oil state without a proration law. It was not a partner in the Interstate Oil Compact. In its stead, however, was a voluntary plan administered by a committee of oil producers. This committee, using monthly data provided by the Bureau of Mines, arrived at a quota that was then prorated among the various California oil producers in rough proportion to their potential production, a process designed primarily to provide price stabilization similar to the one used by the western states participating in the Interstate Oil Compact.

Stabilization, which had a formal structure by the end of 1935, represented the solution arrived at during the New Deal owing to the breakdown of the competitive system. It was not Ickes's solution, but it was one that he was required to accept and help administer. His role had changed markedly from the heady days of 1933 when all groups in the industry called for federal intervention and Ickes became Petroleum Administrator. Shortly thereafter groups within the industry, the major companies and the leading independents, began to change their minds and to take the lead in clamoring for self-government. And by early 1935 they were successful.

Ickes was convinced early in his relations with the industry that no meaningful plan of nationalization and conservation could be effectuated without doing away with a basic premise accepted by most oil men: namely, the law of capture, which Ickes said was "actually a lethal law of destruction." It meant that whoever got the oil out first owned it. Since the surface owner legally held a right of access to an oil pool, for the right to be meaningful it had to be used—and used quickly, lest someone else drain the pool. Thus allocation on the basis of well potential resulted in drainage from adjoining leases on an inequitable basis. Inequities fostered by the law of capture literally forced some producers to run hot oil in self-protection. During the first three months of 1934, for example, the Bureau of Mines estimated the daily average production of illegal oil at 149,000 barrels. Control of production thus could never be truly achieved until this method of production was no longer perpetuated. A Federal Tender Board, Interstate Compacts, and other methods, while helpful, could not fully curb the shipment of hot oil. Ickes understood that the federal government was in the impossible position of endorsing allowables between leases that were both inequitable and wasteful. Without equity among leaseholders within a state and within a pool, it was impossible to maintain equity in the allocations between the states. Sensible development focusing on conservation called for treating a pool as a unit, an approach antithetical to the law of capture by substituting an equitable pooling of interests so that each landholder received the volume or the value of the recoverable oil or gas beneath his land for the competitive individualistic right of access to a common reservoir. And as long as the law of capture prevailed, Ickes knew that unitization and meaningful oil conservation would be impossible.[20]

Ickes became increasingly adamant in his views because he was convinced that, without limited reserves of an irreplaceable resource essential to the well-being of the citizenry and indispensable to national defense and with the United States utilizing them faster than the rest of the world, there would be an oil shortage in the United States long before there would be one elsewhere in the world. Other nagging concerns could then be realized: forced dependence upon more costly substitute fuels or paying a higher price for foreign oil as soon as domestic production failed to meet the national need. It was these views, uttered usually at the outset of his remarks when testifying before congressional committees, that led Ickes to regard the petroleum situation in the West as one of crucial national interest. Unfortunately, his concern for conservation was not seriously considered in the quest for stabilization.

Conservation, which the New Deal was achieving throughout the West with its programs affecting other industries, was never achieved in the petroleum industry. Neither was it achieved in another important mining industry in the West: silver. In both instances the large producers determined the policy that the New Deal accepted. In the case of silver, Secretary of the Treasury Henry Morgenthau, Jr., accepted reality far more easily than Harold Ickes.

There was a basic difference between oil and silver, let alone other natural resources. Silver stayed in the ground until removed; oil departed as soon as a well was opened through which it could escape. In both instances, however, basic determinants of the policies remained within the jurisdiction of either the states or the mine operators. The federal government in the case of oil would enforce state determinations; in the case of silver it would fund quotas but would not seek to hinder mine operators who produced beyond them. Ickes merely helped sustain state authority; Morgenthau subsidized silver production which, like oil, was largely a western industry. Ninety-five percent of American silver production was concentrated in seven western states containing about three percent of the country's population.

As Secretary of the Treasury, Henry Morgenthau, Jr. (like Ickes), would reluctantly bow under presidential prodding to the wishes of powerful producers, the silver mine operators, and their equally powerful spokesmen in the Congress, senators such as Key Pittman of Nevada, Elbert Thomas of Utah, and Burton K. Wheeler of Montana. Silver policy, of course, had broad national and international ramifications affecting monetary policy and diplomacy. But unlike oil, depression prices for silver were the culmination of a downward trend stretching back into the late nineteenth century. In addition, silver differs from most commodities because its supply is not limited by the amount produced in any year. Since it is not consumed in any ordinary sense, its use could go on indefinitely. Its market consisted of three parts: use in the arts and industry, use as coinage, and use in the Orient, especially India and China, where silver in any form was a symbol of social position rather than an article of trade. Of the leading producing nations in the 1930s, the United States ranked first, with Mexico next, Canada third, and Peru fourth. With the advent of the Great Depression the demand for silver in all of its forms steadily declined and the situation became acute as several European nations and Mexico debased their coinage by reducing the silver content of coins. With demand shrinking, the mining of silver was adversely affected. Moreover the market was glutted as Russia and Indochina, for example, joined India, which had been at it since 1926, in melting and selling some of their silver currency in 1932, thereby further depressing silver prices.[21]

Early in 1933 Senator Wheeler argued before the House Committee on Coinage for free silver at a 16 to 1 ratio with gold. In January 1933 silver stood at 83 to 1 in the open market and was selling at 25 cents an ounce. By April it was selling at 37 cents an ounce boosted by increasing talk about free silver; it stood at 54 to 1 in the open market. Free silver (favored by Wheeler), by reducing the purchasing power of the dollar to its silver content, would have sparked inflation and increased the output of western mines thereby restoring prosperity to a long-depressed industry. Most of the congressional delegations from the western silver-producing states, fearing the political hazards of such a measure, endorsed proposals to peg the price of silver or to have the government purchase varying quantities at favorable prices to achieve the same goal. The legislative problem was to agree on a measure that could secure congressional and presidential approval and restore production of silver, which was concentrated in seven Rocky Mountain states and whose senators carried great weight in that august body.

During the presidential campaign Roosevelt had promised to "do something for silver," and the question early in the New Deal was how that pledge would be redeemed. Since silver was often found and mined in conjunction with zinc, lead, and copper, any subsidy or support it received would help provide a margin of profit for operators whose properties contained several metals. Silver proponents found allies among other western congressional delegations, many of whose members favored some degree of inflation to alleviate the pressures on their agrarian constituents. Something was done for silver when the Thomas Amendment to the Agricultural Adjustment Act was approved in April 1933. It gave the President authority in several ways to remonetize silver and to use it in the payment of war debts. It recognized silver as a basic legal tender for all debts, public and private. To the extent that Roosevelt exercised this authority, the New Deal would restore a measure of prosperity to the mountain states in particular and to hard-pressed farmers in general by giving the dollar less purchasing power and thereby helping to raise commodity prices.[22]

Roosevelt made sparing use of the Thomas Amendment late in 1933 and early in 1934. In the first instance, as a means of implementing the London Silver Agreement, newly mined silver would be purchased over a four-year period at 64.5 cents an ounce, about 20 cents an ounce above the prevailing market price, providing producers with a moderate subsidy. In the second instance, in an effort to raise prices, he decreased the gold content of the dollar. But in neither instance did the

President appease the clamor for increased subsidization and enhanced commodity prices emanating from the western regions of the country.

Senator Key Pittman of Nevada, a champion of silver, was responsible for the London Silver Agreement that helped to boost the price of silver and bring cheer to silver producers in the western states. Pittman encouraged representatives of the chief silver-holding nations not to dump their large hoards on the world market. And India, China, and Spain signed a four-year pact agreeing not to do so. The governments of the leading silver-producing countries agreed to do the same, as well as to take from the market 35 million ounces each year for use as silver or currency reserves. Pittman won for western silver producers an impressive victory at the London Economic Conference.[23]

His victory, as well as the amendment sponsored by Senator Elmer Thomas of Oklahoma, indicated the dimensions of the silver issue during the New Deal. Besides being a western concern, it was also a factor in international relations and an important domestic economic issue affecting the content of the dollar and the flow of prices. These accomplishments also indicated divergent opinions among the members of the "Silver Bloc" in the Senate and elsewhere. Burton K. Wheeler, for example, championed the old Bryan stance of free silver. Former Senator Charles S. Thomas of Colorado and Senator William E. Borah of Idaho agreed with him. Along with others, they were highly critical of Key Pittman, who refused to accept bimetallism but favored instead optional or limited use of silver as a currency base. These differences among silver proponents continued throughout the New Deal. Nevertheless, success crowned their efforts on behalf of western silver producers. And the increased price of silver helped stimulate production of lead, zinc, and to some extent copper, thereby helping to revive the economy of the Rocky Mountain states. But, as Senator Pittman recognized, the Silver Bloc in the Senate "made a great mistake in not having metals placed in [National Industrial] Recovery Act as primary products, so that metals could have been beneficiaries of a processing tax."[24]

By the end of 1934 the immediate resumption of silver mining, thanks to the President's proclamation calling for the purchase of newly mined silver at the fixed price of 64.5 cents per ounce, was anticipated on an extensive scale. Western mining communities now would experience a return of prosperous conditions with this incentive to expand mining operations. C. H. McIntosh, a distinguished mining lawyer, summed up the impact of Roosevelt's proclamation by calling it "a splendid Christmas present to the silver mining industry, and also, as we earnestly believe, to the country at large."[25]

Less moderate members of the Silver Bloc, led by Senators Borah and Wheeler, regarded the President's proclamation as a first step toward the complete remonitization of silver, restoring silver as primary money at an acceptable ratio. The proclamation to the more ardent silver proponents was viewed as a four-year commodity purchasing program. Their goal was to base one-fourth, 25 percent, of the nation's money on silver through bimetallism based upon the free and unlimited coinage of silver rooted in legislation and not in a presidential edict that could be modified at will. Though influential in the Senate, the champions of free silver enjoyed little influence in the House of Representatives where they were vastly outnumbered. They received additional support in March 1934 when the Western Governors Meeting in Salt Lake City urged the legislative recognition and reestablishment of silver as a primary money metal. However, moderates, like Key Pittman, though he supported all free-silver proposals, continued to believe that Roosevelt could do more for silver production in the West than the Congress.

Pressures upon the President from the Silver Bloc, western governors, and the silver producers led him to weigh political necessities more heavily than economic concerns. A compromise was reached in May 1934 between the President and the Silver Bloc which resulted in the Silver Purchase Act approved on June 19, 1934, authorizing the Secretary of the Treasury to purchase silver until it either constituted one-fourth of the monetary reserve or its price reached $1.29. Through this subsidization of western silver producers, Roosevelt could be assured of political stabilization by alleviating pressures from the Silver Bloc in particular and inflationists in general. The President, however, had some options. He could, if he wished, peg the price of silver at $1.29 and thereby halt Treasury purchases long before the metal constituted 25 percent of the money supply. The measure, in short, was a compromise which would not satisfy all the proponents of free silver.

Pittman, who sponsored the measure in the Senate, was delighted. The law, as he saw it, would add approximately 1 million ounces of silver to the currency, enough to restore prosperous conditions to the mining industry, especially as the price of silver would rise gradually to its now established parity price of $1.29 an ounce. He now considered a step toward "the opening of the mints throughout the world on the natural ratio between gold and silver." While others in government complained about a silver fiasco, silver mine operators and their allies in Congress had much to be pleased about. Executives of the western mining and smelting companies had accomplished what major petroleum producers had also achieved—namely, a government policy to suit their interests.[26]

Secretary of the Treasury Henry L. Morgenthau, Jr., in 1935 indicated how western producers were benefiting from New Deal silver programs. When he noted that "the total acquisitions of silver by the

United States during the calendar year 1934 amounted to 287,100,000 ounces, or 262,600,000 ounces more silver than we agreed in the London Agreement to withdraw." This 1934 figure, he also noted, was more silver than the Treasury acquired during the three and a half years the Sherman Silver Purchase Act of 1890 was in operation and more than was withdrawn for monetary purposes throughout the entire world during the decade of the 1920s. Senator Patrick McCarran of Nevada summed up the significance of the Silver Purchase Act shortly after leaving a White House conference by stating that the measure would be "more permanently worthwhile for silver than anything that has taken place in many years."[27]

By a series of proclamations throughout the remainder of the decade, the President decreed how many ounces of silver the United States mint could purchase and how much could be paid per ounce. On August 9, 1934, he decreed 50 cents per fine ounce. But by April 24, 1935, the price was raised from about 71 cents per ounce to about 77 cents per ounce for silver mined after that date. The point to be emphasized here is that the Treasury, for a four-year period beginning with 1934, was purchasing freshly mined silver at 64.5 cents an ounce under the terms of the proclamation of December 21, 1933, implementing the London Silver Agreement. These proclamations applied to accumulated stores of silver in bulk which in August 1934, were estimated at 150 million ounces. Members of the Silver Bloc, of course, hailed these proclamations as steps toward achieving a monetary system 25 percent of which would be based on currency backed by silver, and that these actions would help the market price of the metal rise toward the agreed-upon parity price of $1.29 an ounce.[28]

Morgenthau, however, had the option of issuing silver certificates on the basis of the market price of silver and not of the statutory parity price of $1.29. And as the Treasury issued silver certificates, it retired Federal Reserve and National Bank notes thereby preventing, much to the dismay of many members of the Silver Bloc, any significant increase in the supply of paper currency. Nevertheless, the Treasury continued to purchase silver and slowly forced up the market price of the metal. Silver producers and their congressional allies, however, would never be fully satisfied until the market price reached the prescribed parity price, a feat that was not accomplished during the New Deal. Fortunately for the Administration, members of the Silver Bloc in the Senate remained divided. Some members, such as Borah and Pittman, accepted Morgenthau's moderate policies. Others, most notably Elmer Thomas and McCarran, agitated continually for parity at $1.29. But as conditions slowly improved in the western regions, concern for pursuing the terms of the Silver Purchase Act abated. Silver supporters did not seriously complain as long as the Treasury continued to subsidize the industry under the terms of the December 1933 proclamation implementing the London Silver Agreement.[29]

This agreement, however, expired in December 1937. Key Pittman, its architect, called for its continuation and was joined in this demand by members of the Silver Bloc who were ensconced since August 1935 in a Special Committee on Silver, and by silver mine operators championed by the American Silver Producers Association, headquartered in Salt Lake City. After some discussion with Morgenthau, Roosevelt agreed to continue subsidizing the silver producers, provided the market price could be lowered to what it was when the Treasury first agreed to purchase silver in December 1933, half of the parity price, 64.5 cents an ounce.

Throughout the New Deal years the Treasury continued to purchase the output of western silver mines providing profits for producers, employment for miners, and a measure of prosperity for Rocky Mountain communities, shippers, and others associated with mining in the West. This prosperity was artificially produced by Treasury grants for silver usually at a level in advance of the world market price. And it paid handsome political dividends, even though members of the Silver Bloc in Congress disagreed among themselves about the progress the administration was making in its stabilization efforts. When Governor Edwin C. Johnson of Colorado in September 1935 learned that the President's train would be stopping in Denver, he sent a telegram to Roosevelt expressing the sentiments of people in the Rocky Mountain states, "Among other constructive achievements you have brought a complete revival of mining in this great mining state and we want to show you that we appreciate it."[30]

Key Pittman was chairman of the Special Senate Committee on Silver, whose purpose was to confer with the Secretary of the Treasury relative to the administration of the Silver Purchase Act and its commercial and economic effect both at home and abroad. With the creation of this committee, pressures on Morgenthau increased. He was besieged at times with requests to furnish the committee members with statements such as the amount of silver purchased by the Treasury with the date and amount of each purchase, from what sources the silver was purchased, the world price of silver in the leading money markets on specific dates. Besides Pittman, William H. King of Utah, Thomas of Oklahoma, Charles L. McNary of Oregon, and Borah comprised the Special Committee on Silver. In addition to supervising Treasury actions with regard to silver, its members in the fall of 1935 conducted hearings in Salt Lake City and possibly elsewhere in the West, to dissipate the premise that the operations of the Silver Act had injured trade and was otherwise disadvantageous to silver-using countries. Throughout these hearings the split in the committee, reflecting one in the entire Silver Bloc, was evident. Senator Pittman adhered to the opinion that silver price increases should be attained gradually and steadily until $1.29 was reached. The other side, represented by Elmer Thomas, insisted that the $1.29 price should be fixed speedily with silver given full weight as a basic money with gold. The goal was the same; differences among silver senators were over methods, over ways and means of reaching a common objective.[31]

To its supporters throughout the West, silver was an emotional symbol as well as an economic hope and monetary necessity. It transcended sectionalism because its proponents insisted that economic distress was due to collapsing credits precipitated by an inadequate supply of gold. The use of silver in conjunction with gold would help to sustain credit by providing metallic guarantees. Rather than store gold and silver in Treasury vaults, silver proponents wished to put these stores to work by restoring them as measuring devices of commodity wealth, reestablishing a set ratio between gold and silver that was available to individuals as well as governments. By nationalizing both gold and silver with a stabilization price of $1.29 for the white metal, government action would help restore normal consumption and provide both the individual and the government tangible guarantees with respect to money. Inflation, restricted to the utilization of precious metals, aroused few fears in the West and none among the champions of silver who agreed that silver was something more than a commodity. It was, they insisted, a monetary metal.

As a monetary metal, silver men argued, it would stimulate commodity price levels that would ultimately dissipate the need for all other price support programs. While all mining men were interested in the price of silver, its production for most of them was not a major business. It was mined in most instances in conjunction with copper, lead, and zinc. Silver was a by-product, but a by-product, westerners insisted, upon which their well-being and that of the American people rested. Bimetallism, the monetary use of silver, would stimulate economic processes. But continued purchasing of silver without soon achieving stabilization based on bimetallism would only create surpluses in the primary metals and defeat the broad objectives silver champions had in mind when they extolled its virtues. The New Deal brought them within sight of their Promised Land but never provided the fulcrum for gaining admission. Roosevelt and Morgenthau, however, convinced enough silver supporters that they were continually interested in doing something for silver by purchasing virtually the entire annual output of the industry, by not tampering with the agreed-upon domestic price no matter how the world or market price was manipulated, and by giving lip service to the concept of bimetallism and stabilization of silver at a parity price of $1.29 an ounce. New

Dealers were able to walk in tandem with western silver proponents because both groups accepted the premise that international cooperation in money and most other businesses and economic matters would come only after domestic affairs were set in order.[32]

Roosevelt's reelection in 1936 pleased silver men throughout the West. Many believed that his reelection would give silver a standing in other countries it had not previously enjoyed and that Roosevelt now would be in a commanding position to take the lead in stabilizing the world price of silver. After 1936 western silver producers and their spokesmen in Congress, like the administration, were more concerned with the international aspects of silver. The domestic side of the problem was resolved through the operations of the purchase agreements that subsidized and stabilized silver in the United States, though members of the Silver Bloc continually reminded Morgenthau of the legislative commitment to attain one-fourth of the money stock on a silver base or to achieve a parity price of $1.29 an ounce.[33]

Bliss, however, did not last very long among western silver producers. Their concern heightened during the 1937 recession when prices for copper, lead, and zinc declined to a point where, but for the value of the silver contents of these ores, it no longer paid to mine them. Many mine operators by the end of 1937 depended on the value of silver to sustain their production. If the purchase price of silver were reduced, after the expiration of the December 1933 proclamation, havoc would have resulted. Roosevelt, by renewing the terms of the 1933 proclamation with its purchase price of 64.5 cents an ounce for newly mined silver, again rescued the western mining industry and staved off critical times for western regions otherwise adversely affected by the 1937 recession. Silver producers, however, were unhappy with the renewal of the 1933 proclamation because the government receded from the prevailing price of 77.57 cents per ounce for silver, a decline of about 13 cents an ounce.[34]

Among the mining states of the Inland Empire, Idaho probably benefited the most from the government's program of purchasing newly mined domestic silver. It led the nation in the production of silver throughout the New Deal years. Within its borders were located the largest silver producer in the world, the Sunshine Mine, and the largest lead-silver property in the United States, the Bunker and Sullivan Mining and Concentrating Company. About 7,000 men were employed directly in the mining industry of Idaho and, it was estimated, about 60,000 people were indirectly dependent upon the industry because it affected employment, wages, purchases of new machinery and equipment, orders for supplies of all kinds, consumption of foodstuffs, and increased freight tonnage in Idaho. In 1936 Idaho produced 14,537,530 fine ounces of silver, the largest output recorded in the state and an increase of 42 percent over 1935. New Deal silver policy was the salvation of Idaho in the 1930s. Utah and Montana ranked next as silver-producing states and benefited, as did the other silver states, to a lesser degree from the beneficence of the New Deal. Benefit though they did, there was increasing disgruntlement owing to the presidential proclamation of December 31, 1937, which extended the London Silver Agreement for another year.[35]

With a reduced purchase price in effect during a period of recession, silver mining operations were somewhat curtailed. In Utah, for example, by December 1938, about 2,000 mine workers were unemployed and pressures mounted as members of the Silver Bloc sought a renewal of the presidential silver proclamation at a higher purchase price. Key Pittman was convinced, as were others in the mining communities, "that no more economical or practical relief measure could be adopted than to restore the price of American produced silver to 77.5 cents an ounce."[36]

The Roosevelt Administration, however, did not accept Pittman's advice. It merely extended the proclamation scheduled to expire at the end of 1938 for another six months. This action prompted Pittman, as chairman of the Senate Special Silver Committee, to hold hearings examining the impact of the reduction in the price of domestic silver from its previous high of 77.57 cents to 66.64 cents per ounce on January 1, 1938. Testimony at the hearings indicated both increasing unemployment in the western mining regions and a decline in the production of silver from 71 million ounces in 1937 to 60 million ounces in 1938. The decline in the production of silver was also reflected in the production of copper, lead, and zinc. It was Pittman's strategy to lead the Senate Silver Bloc in a fight to restore the 77.57-cent price by suggesting that sixteen senators might not be able to endorse an extension of the President's authority to devalue the gold content of the dollar. More potent, however, was the fact that Pittman, as chairman of the Senate Foreign Relations Committee, could impede the President's desire to repeal neutrality legislation.[37]

By the summer of 1939 conditions in the mining regions had deteriorated so that members of the Silver Bloc cast aside their differences and supporters of bimetallism, who, like Borah, found fixing silver prices obnoxious, endorsed price fixing. To Pittman's chagrin, Borah and the others of his persuasion in the block urged—possibly for bargaining purposes—a price of 85 or 80 cents an ounce. Though members could not agree on the price, pressure from the Silver Bloc was successful. The President by proclamation on July 1 raised the purchase price for a two-year period to 71.11 cents per ounce for newly mined silver and, in effect, ended the controversy over silver during the New Deal.[38]

Whether government purchase of silver accomplished what it was supposed to do is a moot point. What needs to be reiterated is that the Treasury purchased virtually the entire output of western silver mines during the New Deal. In 1938 this amounted to 270 million ounces. While this action did not bring prosperity to the mining regions of the West (and by the summer of 1939 the industry in some locations was in dire straits), the Treasury throughout the New Deal subsidized a western industry that otherwise would have collapsed. That it did so was a tribute to a handful of senators united in the Silver Bloc and responsive to the needs and wishes of an equally influential group of silver producers, as well as an even larger group in the West who favored free silver or bimetallism and some degree of currency inflation as a way of raising prices. The Roosevelt administration, recognizing political realities, as in the case of the oil industry, caved in, albeit reluctantly. Morgenthau, like Ickes, was a reluctant participant in an endeavor that directly benefited a few powerful companies with little consideration of broader policies and programs espoused during the New Deal. Domestic silver policy during the New Deal was largely a tribute to the formidable nuisance value of a handful of western senators ably serving their constituents. Unable to achieve bimetallism, nevertheless, they were superb salesmen seeking stabilization of a commodity for which there was little or no demand. Roosevelt, aware of this situation, would have preferred to find "more permanently useful methods of developing farming and manufacturing" in the mountain states. But by the summer of 1939, both his interests and his concerns were already dominated by foreign affairs.[39]

Chapter 8

Whither the American Indian?

WHEN HAROLD ICKES selected John Collier as Commissioner of Indian Affairs, he accelerated forces already in motion that would secure a New Deal for the American Indian. Collier deemed it both better and wiser to make Native Americans good Indians rather than poor whites. And the best way to do this was to keep them on their tribal lands while restoring tribal rights and practices. Not wishing to aid or encourage Indians to merge into the mainstream of American life, Collier, a believer in cultural pluralism, desired to assist tribal members in living according to their cultural patterns. His appointment resolved an argument that had been raging throughout the 1920s and was preceded by what one scholar called a "false dawn" during the Hoover Administration. It insured a New Deal for the American Indian, but like other aspects of the New Deal, it was seriously impaired by inadequate support and mounting hostility in Congress.[1]

At the outset of the New Deal, Indian population in the United States had reached its highest point since the nadir of the 1890s. In 1891 there were 246,834 Indians on reservations. In 1933 the population had increased to 320,454; in 1940 there were 361,816 Indians, the largest numbers being in Oklahoma, Arizona, New Mexico, and South Dakota. The Indians belonged to about 200 different tribes, spoke different languages, had different cultures, and differed widely in purity of Indian blood, wealth and property holdings, and in contact with white communities. But the Indian, like the buffalo, was no longer a vanishing species, and Collier's appointment indicated that efforts would be made toward restoring former Indian lands to tribal ownership, completely abandoning the allotment system, granting tribes further opportunities at self-government, and encouraging the revival of tribal customs, including the original language and religion of each tribe. Collier, who in the 1920s had been executive secretary of the American Indian Defense Association, told a conclave in the Black Hills there was no reason why the United States "should go on disgracing itself in

Indian matters." He said that "the President, Secretary Ickes and the Indian Bureau have determined that the time has come to stop wronging the Indians and to rewrite the cruel and stupid laws that rob them and crush their family lives." Collier repeated this message at other pow-wows and before other groups throughout the first year of his tenure.

He spoke at a time when destitution was the lot of most Indians. It was estimated in early 1934 that over 100,000 Indians were reduced to begging, unable to provide for themselves. When Collier took office there were 52 million acres of tribal lands, much of it in a deteriorated condition. About 20,000 of these acres were desert or semidesert lands. With their population increasing, Indians were experiencing a substantial shrinking through poor management of their basic resource, the land with its protective cover of vegetation. In 1887, when the Allotment Act was passed there were 135 million acres.

In addition, tribal funds had been reduced from $500 million in 1887 to $12 million in 1933 with over 90 percent of tribal income being utilized to assist in maintaining the Indian Bureau. At the same time federal funds were supporting boarding schools which took children from their parents and, in the course of providing them with an education, indubitably suppressed the tribal and social customs of the students. Indians suffered more during the Great Depression than possibly any other group in the nation.[2]

Yet, despite wide variations among the tribes, one important generalization that boded difficulty for Collier's approach should be noted. Indians could be divided into two general categories: those, chiefly in the Southwest, who lived as tribes set apart from the white communities and who were primarily full blooded, and those whose tribal organization was weak or partially destroyed, who lived in communities interspersed with whites and whose blood had intermixed, often to a considerable degree, with that of the whites. Indians in the latter category tended to seek individual responses to their needs and problems; those in the former would be more responsive to group treatment of their social and economic problems.

Collier at the outset of his tenure as Commissioner of the Office of Indian Affairs, commonly called the Indian Service, sought to put the boarding schools out of business. To do so he secured $3.6 million from the Public Works Administration, chaired by his boss, the Secretary of the Interior, to finance Indian day schools. He also stopped the sale of Indian lands, eliminated incompetent and corrupt employees, organized emergency conservation work for Indians supervised by the Civilian Conservation Corps, and insisted that all agency officials, particularly reservation and agency superintendents, respect tribal customs. And, most important, he helped draft and then champion the

Wheeler-Howard bill which Congress was considering in the spring of 1934.[3]

In adopting a policy of reducing and ultimately eliminating boarding school attendance, Collier wrought a significant change in Indian life. More and more Indian children would remain with their parents and attend local public schools or United States day schools. During the first two years of Collier's tenure, enrollment in boarding schools decreased from 22,000 to about 13,000. In 1934 alone, ten boarding schools either closed or changed to community day schools. Boarding schools that continued to operate tended to specialize in vocational training and to provide institutional care for orphans and others until a program of foster-home placement was developed or until enough community day schools were operative. In 1934 it was estimated that about 12,000 children were without school facilities.

Under the guidance of Willard Beatty, Director of Education in the Office of Indian Affairs, Indian school policy moved toward the more general use of both public and federal day schools. Beatty encouraged a richer curricular and activity program both on the reservation and in local public schools that some Indians through tuition payments attended. In the reservation schools and in some of the public schools, increasing emphasis was placed upon utilization of materials offered by the environment and adult education was stressed. In the Navajo area, for example, adult use equaled or exceeded juvenile use in the forty-five or more day schools in the reservation area which encompassed parts of Arizona and New Mexico.

During Collier's tenure the United States Public Health Service began to pay increasing attention to Indians through efforts to control epidemic diseases, to safeguard water supplies, and generally to promote public health, which was exceedingly expensive since all clinical and hospital services were provided without charge. Concentrated efforts were directed against trachoma and tuberculosis, diseases particularly affecting Indians. In the summer of 1934, to cite a specific example, an institute for nurse-aides was conducted at the Santa Fe Indian School. Twenty-five graduates were declared eligible for appointment in newly opened Navajo day-school centers. This example illustrates a point that greatly concerned Collier; namely, putting more professionally trained Indians to work in meaningful and responsible jobs affecting their own lives and community welfare.

Most Indians, however, when they could find work were employed either in agriculture or in jobs requiring little or no skill. With the inauguration of the Civilian Conservation Corps in 1933, $5,875,000 was set aside for Indian employment under the direction of the Indian Service. Road and fence building projects were undertaken, as were projects in forest conservation, erosion control, water development, telephone line construction and others. All occurred on Indian lands and helped improve conditions. In addition, selected Indians from the various CCC camps were given intensive instruction in leadership during the winter of 1934. Combined with other Indian Service programs to promote food production on some reservations through cooperative livestock associations, the more severe effects of the depression among the Indians were being mitigated by the winter of 1934.

Harry Hopkins, as Federal Emergency Relief Administrator, made every effort to assure that non-ward Indians, those living in scattered areas, be assisted by the states in receiving direct relief and work relief. His jurisdiction did not extend to Indians living on reservations or other ward Indians. In Montana, for example, this meant that the County Emergency Relief Administration officers, functioning in 56 counties, would have to consider the plight of approximately 3,000 non-ward Indians.

In November 1934 Hopkins went further and stated that because of the crisis created by the drought, State Relief Administrators should include in their programs and activities all Indians who applied for relief. Indians, wherever located, were to be governed by the same rules and regulations as any other relief applicant. In Montana the population on the seven reservations within the state was about 15,000.

A cooperative arrangement was worked out in Montana between the State Relief Administration and the seven Indian superintendents wherein the superintendents served as acting administrators for the State Relief Administration on their respective reservations assisted by a social worker and Indian aides. While the arrangement was satisfactory, restricted funds and emergency needs prompted the administrators to decide upon direct rather than work relief, thereby negating previous efforts to instill the desire to be self-supporting among the Montana reservation Indians. Relief on the basis of individual or family need was new to most Indians who previously experienced a pro rata distribution of government benefits. So too were the visits of social workers, chiefly women, who were met with distrust, partly because of the low social status of Indian women in some tribes, and partly because they generally needed to work through interpreters.

These social workers found the destitution that was the lot of most Indians in the West. Badly undernourished children were plagued by measles and whooping cough, while adults were ravaged by tuberculosis. Trachoma played havoc with both adults and children. Medical and nursing care was inadequate, all but nonexistent. And housing, largely improvised, lacked adequate furniture. It was also unsanitary and overcrowded. Finally, because they leased much of their land to sheepmen for grazing, Indians found themselves without any range; practically all the land was grazed out. Morale was at a low ebb as

Indians were unable to meet their obligations and had virtually no way to provide for themselves and their families.

In Montana the Emergency Relief Administration, handicapped as it was by limited funds, made an effort to cope with Indian destitution, while at the same time letting the Indian live his own life with a minimum of outside interference. Montana administrators also recognized that federal guidance was essential in planning by and with the Indians. In short, as Hopkins and others understood, relief was a temporary expediency for both Indians and other citizens and would have to be replaced by more meaningful long-range programs. But it should be emphasized, it was only through the expenditure of millions of dollars for relief and emergency conservation work on reservations that Indians were able to support themselves and their families at the height of the Great Depression as the New Deal was getting underway.[4]

Emergency federal funds, chiefly from the PWA, totalling more than $15 million through 1934, were used for such things as the purchase of sheep and goats from various tribes to check over-grazing and the resulting soil erosion; for construction projects of various kinds: roads, irrigation, schools, hospitals and other public buildings, sewer and water systems. In these and other projects emphasis was placed upon using Indians whenever possible both as laborers and supervisors. In addition, the Federal Surplus Relief Corporation under Harry Hopkins granted $2.5 million for the purchase of land adjacent to Indian reservations that could be utilized with proper care for grazing, forestry, and other purposes.[5]

Most important, however, were two enactments by Congress championed by Collier that institutionalized the Indian New Deal by joining federal guardianship and aid with Indian responsibility and freedom. The first, the Johnson-O'Malley Act of April 16, 1934, called for cooperation between the federal government and the states (including their subdivisions) in providing Indians with services available to other citizens in education, health, agriculture, relief, and welfare. The second, the Wheeler-Howard or Indian Reorganization Act of June 18, 1934, provided for several important changes. Among other things it stopped the allotment in severalty of tribal lands and set in motion the revestment of the Indians with lands for subsistence use, predicated on the practice of conservation on range and timber lands; it encouraged and assisted tribes to organize for purposes of self-government and economic cooperation and it supplied financial credit through tribal corporations. It also authorized a yearly appropriation of $2 million for land purchases which by June 1940 totalled 366,270 acres. Other provisions gave preference to Indian candidates for positions in the Indian Service and provided loans for Indians seeking to further their education. The act applied to all tribes, unless a tribe specifically voted to exclude itself.

By the end of the New Deal, 192 tribes or bands had voted by referendum to accept the terms of the act; 77 indicated they did not wish to be included under its provisions. Of those accepting the act by January 1940, 80 had organized with constitutions and bylaws and 57 had formed chartered corporations. In May 1936, Congress extended the appropriate terms of the act to include the natives of Alaska. However, in Oklahoma with over 100,000 Indians the situation was very different. Members of the Five Civilized Tribes—the Choctaw, Chickasaw, Cherokee, Creek, and Seminole—were among the most assimilated Indians in the West. They constituted nearly four-fifths of the Indians in the state. The other tribes, having experienced fewer contacts with whites, retained more of their original culture. All suffered severely from the impact of the Great Depression as well as from neglect and maladministration by Indian Service officials during the Hoover Administration. Yet most were not enthused about the Indian Reorganization Act since it did not particularly benefit, indeed some provisions excluded, Oklahoma Indians who could not accept the reservation concept embedded in the act. Full-bloods generally accepted Collier's ideas but the mixed-bloods and those Indians well along the road to assimilation generally were not interested in a return to tribal life, self-government, and independence. And Collier himself concluded in October 1934, after conferring in the state, that the act would have to be modified to meet the Oklahoma situation.

What was needed was legislation enabling individual Indians to secure credit for purchasing land or starting a business, legislation which at the same time provided legal safeguards from outside encroachments. This is what the Thomas-Rogers bill attempted to do, all the while protecting the more full-blooded Indians in maintaining their tribal life. "The whole plan of the bill" said Congressman Will Rogers, who in February 1935 introduced the measure, "is intended to extend to the Indian citizens [of Oklahoma] the fullest possible opportunity to work out their own economic salvation." After reconciling some opposition by amending and reintroducing the measure, Congress on June 18, 1936, approved the Thomas-Rogers Indian Welfare Bill. It extended to the 100,000 Indians of Oklahoma, about one-third of the country's total Indian population, the land and credit provisions of the Indian Reorganization Act along with comparable organization features. The law permitted the "tribeless Indians" of Oklahoma, those whose lands had been liquidated by allotment, to form corporations and to borrow from a revolving $2 million loan fund for their projects.[6]

The involvements of the Indian Service were both highly complex and complicating owing to the myriad of rules and regulations, statutes, and interdepartmental relations affecting Indian affairs. Policies and programs formulated in and administered from Washington pertaining to remote and diverse areas were both difficult and impracticable, a point Collier quickly realized. Under his leadership reorganization in the form of divesting the Office of Indian Affairs of much of its administrative control over operations in Indian jurisdictions was concluded in more than one hundred instances. Various patterns of decentralization were followed. In Kansas and Oklahoma, for example, all regional supervisors worked under the direction of one advisory officer, while in New Mexico all nineteen Pueblo tribes were consolidated in a single jurisdiction. In Arizona the six jurisdictions of the Navajo Reservation similarly were consolidated into one. In these and other jurisdictions local reservation superintendents were vested with broad authority. They were expected to supervise and work with agency staffs cooperating with tribal and other groups of Indians to develop area projects through local initiative. This approach applied, Collier claimed, to all reservations whether or not they chose to accept the Indian Reorganization Act.

The approach, called the area-project method, sought to develop Indian and Indian Service programs from local centers through continuous interaction between staff, personnel from other agencies, and the organized Indians. When a substantial and reasonably stable plan and program was agreed upon, it became the task of Collier and his associates in Washington to make, provide, or secure the necessary administrative and budgetary accommodations possible under the law. Since funds might come from different sources depending on the program involved, no particular pattern of decentralization existed. Administration within any local area was a complicated enterprise directed toward the goal of the Indians progressively assuming responsibility for their own affairs. Staff and personnel through summer institutes and other programs continually were made aware of practical and theoretical problems relating to administration and Indian life. Late in the New Deal a grant from the Rockefeller Foundation established in Albuquerque a federal field-training school to help provide this awareness for carefully selected employees seeking administrative careers in the Indian Service.

Cooperation occurred on other levels as well. At the outset of the New Deal an interdepartmental group selected by the secretaries of the interior and agriculture examined the land situation in the Indian Southwest. Its report to the Navajo Tribal Council in July 1933 led to the Soil Conservation Service launching programs on millions of acres of Indian lands. The agency's first demonstration project in the nation was started on the Navajo reservation at Mexican Springs, New Mexico.[7] These soil conservation programs in calling for severe reductions of livestock prompted tensions and controversies that made the Navajo area a battleground of Indian administration. Though the Navajos reduced their sheep and goat herds, the livestock load remained more than the carrying capacity of the range lands throughout the decade.

The Navajo tribe comprised about 45,000 pure blooded mostly non-English-speaking Indians, pre-Columbian in their religion, who occupied nearly 25,000 square miles of desert land in Arizona and New Mexico. While they were increasing in population, their flocks, chiefly sheep and goats, multiplied faster, overpopulating and overgrazing the barren range with the result that Navajo living standards were low and the soil of the reservation was being eroded and washed into the Colorado River. At the outset of the New Deal there were 1.3 million sheep and goats on Navajo lands. Changes had to be made, Collier realized, through the choice of the Navajos themselves. But difficulties arose because those Navajos who could provide leadership in coping with this crisis were the ones whose individual sacrifice would be the greatest. Wealth and social standing among the Navajos was measured in part by the size of an individual's or family's herd of sheep and goats.

At the outset of the New Deal, government agents indicated that soil erosion had totally destroyed several hundred thousand acres of the Navajo range and seriously damaged millions more. To prevent utter destruction, a program of soil conservation had to be instituted and this meant that the Navajos would have to sacrifice hundreds of thousands of sheep and goats. This was the situation that sparked the controversy and divided the tribe. It led the Tribal Council not to accept the Indian Reorganization Act and made Collier almost a hated figure among some tribal members. Since federal funds could not pay for all the needed innovations on the tribal lands, the Navajos themselves would have to resolve the situation with guidance, suggestions, and advice provided by land-use experts.

The crisis was a grave and emotional one for the Navajos who viewed goats and sheep almost as human children. That the Navajos did reduce the size of their herds, that they made an effort to conserve their range lands, and that the tribe vigorously debated these and other issues is testimony to the effectiveness of the Indian New Deal despite the fact that not enough was done and that Collier himself found few friends among the Navajos.[8]

In the Pueblo areas the situation was different. The tribes cooperated effectively and successfully in combating soil erosion. To conserve Indian lands, personnel of the Departments of the Interior and Agriculture cooperated with reservation superintendents in preparing and presenting programs for tribal consideration. In addition, the Indian Division of the Civilian Conservation Corps worked on water development, truck and fire trails in timbered areas, and other projects on reservations in the Southwest and elsewhere. In the Rio Grande area of New Mexico several agencies from the Departments of the Interior and Agriculture joined together in the interdepartmental Rio Grande Board to engage in regional planning and to promote programs that affected Indians and Mexican-Americans alike.[9]

On a tour visiting Indian reservations in 1935, Collier in a Soil Conservation Service plane flew from Albuquerque to the Wind River Mountains near Lander, Wyoming, to visit the Shoshone and Arapaho Reservation, "a potentially golden land, two and a quarter million acres, mountains and mountain lakes, vast forests, rich ranges, views of thousands of irrigated acres, inhabited by 2,200 powerful, beautiful Indians." Once there he noted the poverty, the "unimaginably bad" housing, the polluted ditch-water available only for half a year, the high sickness and death rate, none of which had as yet broken the spirit of these proud Indians, who, Collier believed, had a great future as the owners of a golden land.

That future could be assured, Collier insisted, through planning—and planning was what the New Deal could provide. With the Soil Conservation Service integrating its work with the Indian Service, planning was initiated. Forestry, extension schools, health, land adjustment—all of these were integral parts of an over-all program getting under way on the reservation. Acceptance of the Reorganization Act would end the allotment inheritance system, which was responsible, Collier believed, for thousands of irrigated acres having gone to weeds because they could not be used or rented. The collective distress of the Shoshones and Arapahos would be alleviated through programs getting started on the reservation. And what was occurring on this reservation in varying degrees was occurring on all reservations throughout the Inland Empire.[10]

In Nevada and Idaho, to cite but one more example, the Indian Service was encouraging Indians on the 289,500 acres comprising the Duck Valley Indian Reservation to become more self-supporting by raising their own livestock instead of leasing their lands, as had been their custom. Indians heretofore usually leased their grazing rights to outside stockmen. The returns from these leases plus federal funds formed their principal means of livelihood.

In promoting this change from lessors to operators, the Indian Service was also encouraging a change in attitude as well as in methods of utilizing the land. Individual initiative on the part of the Indians in raising their own livestock was assisted through conservation measures initiated by the Indian Service, such as the installation of windmills and stock ponds. A forestry program provided a dependable supply of fence posts and firewood. The construction of Wild Horse Dam, a project of the Bureau of Irrigation of the Indian Service, provided sufficient water for the irrigation of about 26,000 acres.

Tribal members by 1940 were helping to determine crops required by the reservation, considering the placement of forage species, and formulating soil management and cropping practices. They did these things and more in association with Indian Service and Soil Conservation Service officials. In most instances the latter provided only technical assistance and supervision. The Indians did the basic construction and other work. While much remained to be done, a basic shift had occurred which contributed to the development of individual initiative on the part of the Indians on the Duck Valley and other reservations.[11]

Though Collier's endeavors met with opposition from some tribes and from factions within tribes (as well as from an increasing number of Congressmen), he never abated in pursuing the Indian New Deal. He paid increasing attention to the cultural values of Indian life, and his attention was not confined to those tribes where the ancient cultures survived as language and institutional systems. His approach was to avoid discouraging any productive or disciplinary element of the old life, while at the same time endeavoring to bring to all Indians an awareness of some of the more beneficial aspects of modernity and to equip them as much as possible with modern technologies. For example, the Acoma Pueblo tribe—full-blooded, speaking an ancient language, and living according to its ancient customs—was economically assimilated into American life, while other tribes, with white blood in their veins and largely oblivious to their cultural past, were neither economically nor individually assimilated.

Collier was particularly pleased with the Indian Arts and Crafts Statute of 1935. It created an Arts and Crafts Board with wide powers of research and promotion, including the responsibility to authenticate Indian hand-made goods. It was an important step in encouraging native cultures. The statute, besides helping to foster an appreciation of beautiful and useful Indian products, at the same time made a contribution to the economic and social welfare of the Indian. Ickes estimated that "in normal times" the trade in Navajo rugs could exceed $1 million a year. In addition, the curriculum of Indian schools increasingly incorporated Indian traditions and customs, while Collier, following the beginning made during the Hoover Administration, went out of his way to assist in extending full liberty of conscience and culture to all Indians.[12]

To state the goals of the Indian New Deal can serve as a summary of what it attempted and as a standard of measuring its success. First and foremost the Indian New Deal set the premise that the Indians themselves should determine their own futures which, Collier recognized, would be diverse. At the same time it sought to provide Indians with a measure of economic assistance in developing their assets, including plans for land management and encouragement of individual enterprise in farming and grazing. While tribes would own the land as a means of preventing further land alienation, Collier envisioned its use as primarily individual. The Indian New Deal also began a process of decentralizing Indian administration and tying it into local governmental services with the aim of expanding opportunities for education and experience in administration and technical functions. In brief, it sought to achieve three great goals: economic sufficiency, cultural freedom, and civic responsibility, thereby allowing Indians as citizens "to earn decent livelihoods and lead self-respecting organized lives in harmony with their own aims and ideals, as an integral part of American life."[13]

Collier's programs and the Indian New Deal in general met with what at best could be called mixed success. On a few small reservations with closely knit and homogeneous populations, the authority granted to tribes for self-government and the management of their own affairs gave them a new vision and an initiative for progress. On the larger reservations, having widely separated population groups and diverse interests, similar advances were rarely noted.[14] Better progress was made in saving Indian range lands. Nearly four-fifths of the total Indian area experienced various conservation programs, possibly because the work was facilitated by the Indian Division of the Civilian Conservation Corps and with the cooperation of the Soil Conservation Service and other federal employees.[15] And much was achieved in protecting and reviving Indian crafts and in expanding educational opportunities for Indians of all ages. In the school year ending in June 1939, for example, 594 Indian high school graduates were assisted through appropriations from the Office of Indian Affairs in furthering their educations in institutions running the gamut from universities and colleges to trade and beauty culture schools. Furthermore, the health of Indians constantly improved with the growing availability of better facilities and services. Experiments involving the use of sulfanilamide, inaugurated in 1937 on the Rosebud Sioux Reservation in South Dakota, indicated that the eventual eradication of a dreaded scourge, trachoma, from the Indian population was now a possibility.

Yet at the end of the New Deal, despite tremendous improvements, Indians throughout the Inland Empire still faced serious problems and difficulties. By any standard most Indians were very poor and over 20 percent of their income was unearned, derived from leases, rentals and royalties from corporations, and individuals utilizing their lands. Another 20 percent of their substandard income came from relief and other emergency funds. Roughly, less than a third was obtained through their own individual operations. Indian income was insecure, and a major problem in the following decades would be to increase income and earning power so that living conditions could be improved along with further opportunities for individual economic development.

One New Deal program that proved of great value to Indians, though it was not designed with them in mind, was Social Security. In October 1939, for example, 7,063 Indians received old-age assistance, 4,125 received aid to dependent children assistance, and 550 sight-impaired Indians secured aid to the blind. Indian children also benefited from maternal and child health programs sponsored by the United States Children's Bureau. In addition, they shared in welfare services and work for crippled children, also sponsored by the Children's Bureau and administered by the states. Relatively few Indians, because of the nature of their existance, were eligible for either unemployment insurance or retirement benefits. And none of the western states, Oklahoma being the possible exception, granted Indians, though they were citizens, the right to general relief until Congress in the Emergency Relief Appropriation Act for the 1941 fiscal year included specific provisions for Indian relief and rehabilitation.

In areas where there were Indians of mixed blood, many were employed on local Works Progress Administration, Public Works Administration, and other federal projects not directly under the Indian Service. In addition, there were some WPA group projects utilizing Indians for work on their reservations. Owing to drought conditions in the Southwest, the Surplus Marketing Administration (formerly the Federal Surplus Commodities Corporation) in 1939 and 1940 made available quantities of food for distribution to the Hopi and Navajo tribes.[16]

By the end of 1939, nearly 77,000 Indians had been given employment for varying periods with the Indian Division of the Civilian Conservation Corps. For the most part these Indians worked on the land of their own reservations. Special regulations permitted Indian recruits to live in their own homes or in camps near the work projects. Recruits could earn anywhere from $30 to $42 or $45 a month depending on whether or not they lived at home. Those who lived at home or in a family camp received an additional subsistence allowance. One of the first noticeable results was an improvement in the physique and weight of recruits who, besides their own physical rehabilitation, engaged in work that improved and rehabilitated their lands.

While improving their lands, Indians received training in various skills, including safety and first aid and how to operate machines. They also received leadership training. The Indian CCC involved both production and training programs. Both proved invaluable for those Indians who went from CCC work into regular positions in the Indian Service, into private employment, and even into business for themselves. In 1933, for example, there were at best a few hundred Indian employees on the Indian Service staff. In 1940 there were 4,682, of whom eight were reservation superintendents and 261 had professional positions.[17]

One aspect of the Indian New Deal that no one considered at the time became a matter of grave concern in future decades. K. Ross Toole, an able historian and conservationist, has called attention to a 1938 Supreme Court decision holding that "Minerals and standing timber are consistent elements of the land itself" unless specifically reserved. In the same year Congress approved the Omnibus Tribal Leasing Act specifying that unallotted Indian land could be leased for mineral exploitation only with the approval of the secretary of the interior, thereby providing a means of further depriving Indians of the use and control of tribal land.[18]

In the following year the Supreme Court again decided a matter that would have ramifications of great significance. In January 1939 it reversed a lower court decision and held that when the allotments were sold, "the right to use some portion of the tribal waters essential for cultivation passed to the owners" who were then free to sell their rights to others. This decision, *United States* v. *Powers,* 305 US 527, left to a future court the resolution of the critical question of Indian water rights. It merely addressed one phase of the problem and it did so in a manner most inhospitable to the tenor of the Indian Reorganization Act.[19]

On the other hand, an aspect of the Indian New Deal that attracted a great deal of attention at the time was the use Collier made of anthropologists. While critics ranted against their employment because they, like Collier, resisted assimilationist views, others were delighted that a federal agency was willing to utilize social scientists in furthering the welfare of the Indian population by encouraging respect for traditional cultural values and artistic forms. The anthropologists recognized that educational reorganization could be related to cultural renaissance by rooting the whole system of training and preparation firmly in Indian life. In this way the Indian would enter the adult world strengthened with a rich and authentic background that would be meaningful whether or not the individual chose to remain on the reservation.

H. Scudder McKeel was director of the Applied Anthropology Unit in the Office of Indian Affairs from 1935 through 1937. In a 1944 appraisal of the Indian Reorganization Act, he anticipated the conclusions of scholars writing several decades later by noting that conditions varied widely and that Collier and his associates ran into difficulties by trying to move too rapidly and not fully taking into account tribal differences. Problems were exacerbated at times because ill-prepared personnel who did not respect cultural differences were unable to assist in reviving traditional tribal institutions as a means of achieving social and economic development. While results were mixed, the social scientists met their greatest success in those areas where cultural entity remained strongest, among the largely full-blooded tribes in the Southwest.[20]

In addition to social scientists, Indians on western reservations also met other professionals they had rarely encountered in previous contacts with white men: engineers from the Bureau of Reclamation involved with proposed irrigation projects, soil erosion experts from various government agencies, farm credit financiers, as well as advisors on the establishment of cooperatives. As a result of these contacts, which brought with them practical jobs such as road and dam building, and which focused attention on the necessity of creating markets, they also raised the question—as did the entire Indian New Deal—of the Indians' three-fold relationship to tribe, state, and nation. In many instances, owing to these contacts, hopefulness and confidence replaced distrust; at other times confusion and anger added to the distrust that was engendered by the momentum of change. But on the whole, tribal authority (the waning of which had brought disaster in personal and social life) had revived and was playing an increasingly important role in Indian life. Reservation life was more integrated with life in the state where it was situated than ever before in matters of public works, employment, public benefits, and services. By 1940, however, neither the tribe nor the individual Indian was participating in any meaningful way in national life.

But it also is clear that the Indian New Deal set the Indian on the road to such participation through fundamental shifts in policy. The allotment system came to an end and the Indian Reorganization Act assumed that tribal lands would never again be divided and sold. Beneficial use of these lands became an accepted policy basic to an overall program of rural rehabilitation. The old-time boarding schools, which helped wreck Indian culture and family life, were slowly being eliminated or transformed into training schools designed to provide students with knowledge useful for meeting problems related to their economic and social needs. Efforts were also expanded to send competent graduates of Indian secondary schools on for further education and training so that at some future time all employees on any reservation would be tribal members, in this way eliminating the bureaucratic control of Indian affairs.

Harold Ickes, the dominant figure in the overall management of the Inland Empire, derived great satisfaction from the accomplishments of the Indian New Deal. The Department of the Interior, charged with the administration of Indian affairs, was responsible for the well-being of the Indian peoples and was directed by law to conserve their lands and other natural resources. Ickes took these responsibilities seriously. His interest was keen and extensive, based on his first wife's active participation, during the years he was a prominent Chicago lawyer, in the National Indian Defense Association. Collier was executive secretary of the association. In 1935, while endorsing the Oklahoma Indian Welfare bill, Ickes proclaimed that "few achievements of the present Administration" had given him "more personal satisfaction" than the effort, "successful so far but not completed," to bring about a basic reorganization of Indian policy and of the Indian Service, to help make Indians self-supporting while at the same time extending the right of self-determination. Ickes also worked hard at getting the President to approve funding for various projects for Indians. And he was effective, noting on one occasion, "My approach touched his sense of humor and before I was through I had him laughing," and that "I had been working him right along for the Indians." In this instance Roosevelt approved projects totaling between $4 and $5 million and Ickes returned to his office "in high good humor."[21]

This tale also suggests the difficulty of the Indian New Deal in accomplishing its goals. The Indian New Deal accelerated Indian dependency upon technology, scientific know-how, tools and other artifacts and concepts of the dominant social order.[22] In addition, despite changes in the service and its personnel, the Indian Bureau was essentially government from the top down. Edicts were issued to employees; regulations were imposed on tribal members and at times employees and tribal members did not fully understand or agree with one another. Technical concepts, reflected in terms such as "carrying capacity" or "over-grazing" had no counterpart in the thought of most reservation Indians. Neither did the white man's concepts of time. Suspicion, lack of cooperation, and open hostility all too often prevailed and were not confined exclusively to the Navajos even though great efforts were made to train and to place Indians in responsible positions. This, of course, was not what Collier and Ickes intended. To counteract it they utilized the services of anthropologists and other social scientists to enhance an appreciation of the importance of integrating various programs with folkways markedly different from the prevalent American culture. They took these steps despite rumblings in Congress from western members, many of whom initially supported the Indian Reorganization Act, that the Indian New Deal in encouraging tribes to maintain their own cultural and religious life would make it impossible to Americanize the Indian. By 1937 several bills were introduced abolishing the act for particular states and Senators Burton K. Wheeler and Lynn J. Frazier introduced one repealing the act in its entirety. Wheeler was one of the prime sponsors of the Indian Reorganization Act and his name is historically associated with it.[23]

Yet, despite criticism, valid and otherwise, Indian life within the Inland Empire would never again be the same. The Indian New Deal unleashed what Adlai E. Stevenson later called "a revolution of rising expectations" among a people who in the 1930s were encouraged by Collier, Ickes, and other bureaucrats to embark on the arduous journey of finding a meaningful place for themselves in American life. Public good, as most Indians understood the term, involved the survival and triumph of the race. The Indian New Deal assisted in promoting the public good by aiding and encouraging Indians to help themselves. That so much attention was showered on fewer than 400,000 people scattered chiefly in the West, is little short of remarkable. Such encouragement, aid, and assistance as was forthcoming during the years of the Indian New Deal had never been considered seriously prior to the Hoover Administration, nor would it ever be matched or surpassed in future decades. While many Indian problems remained unresolved at the end of the New Deal, most had been attacked and brought into the realm of public discussion by Collier and his associates during the Indian New Deal.

Chapter 9

The Planned Promised Land

WHILE INTERIOR'S DOMINATION of the Inland Empire had important extensions into the Pacific coastal states, Ickes had to share hegemony there with the Department of Agriculture, which had to cope with vast problems largely pertaining to the plight of farm workers; in the Northwest there was surplus wheat as well. And in the Northwest, more so than any other part of the country (with the possible exception of the Tennessee River Valley), planning was conducted on both a regional and state level. The annual regional planning conferences enabled New Deal administrators to explain and promote their programs. Administrators of all kinds and on all levels were convinced that regionalism could serve as a framework for social planning and social action enabling the Pacific Northwest to achieve its potential as a promised land.

Agriculture was one of the two major occupations in the region and more than three-fourths of those gainfully employed depended directly or indirectly upon agriculture, including forestry, and its associated industries. At the outset of the New Deal, agriculture in the Northwest, like agriculture elsewhere, was both depressed and ineffective. Farm and rangeland, owing to misuse and erosion, were no longer fully productive. And, as elsewhere, various New Deal programs encouraged proper tillage to minimize erosion, the growing of "soil building" crops in rotation with those considered "soil exhausting," and restorative measures based upon cooperative action to remedy damage already done—all this with the help of federal funds. Soil Conservation Districts, Grazing Districts, CCC projects and the like, all furthered programs in the West that purchased marginal lands unsuited for agricultural use, encouraged the development of watershed protection measures, including the development of farm and range water supplies, and devising economical methods of draining and irrigating lands. Sustained-yield timber production was a most important goal, as vast areas of the region were forested lands.

To aid in orderly development, the Pacific Northwest Regional

Planning Commission, representing Washington, Oregon, Idaho, and western Montana, played an active role. Composed of a small group of private citizens interested in stimulating public interest in problems concerning the Northwest, the commission also included representatives of the four state planning boards. It received funding from the National Planning Board to prepare studies and reports dealing with the region's resources and the problems afflicting them.[1]

Beginning in 1934 an annual Pacific Northwest Planning Conference was held to further planning that would develop the economy of the region integrated with national interests, "including immediate relief of unemployment"; that would promote effective plans for public works projects; that would establish long-range social and economic values; and would widen human opportunities. At the annual meetings the discussions at various sessions were usually conducted on a technical level. State and local officials, university specialists, civic, professional, and business representatives discussed regional topics revolving around land, water, and mineral resources. They considered industry, commerce, transportation, utilities, welfare, education, as well as the problems afflicting communities from small towns to metropolitan districts from a regional point of view.[2]

The promoters of the Pacific Northwest Regional Planning Commission, especially its chairman, Marshall N. Dana, believed that with the full-scale functioning of the regional planning boards and with effective regional organization "we shall have a body of public sentiment and of support later on for effective use." By 1935 when Dana expressed this view, planners in the region had already prepared several resource inventories by which they intended to establish priorities of use for power, reclamation, fisheries, industry, domestic and municipal needs and recreation. Federal programs were involved in the development of several of these priorities. The cooperation of authorities in British Columbia was necessary for others. Such cooperation was generally achieved and the development of the New Deal in the Pacific Northwest was predicated upon this cooperation.

"We are undertaking, in the Pacific Northwest," Dana observed, "to bring about a sustained yield of the forests and of the fields, of the gardens and orchards, and the water; a sustained yield of game and wildlife; a sustained yield of recreation and its pleasures. Thus we seek a sustained yield of food and the means of material sustenance, all in order that we may bring about the most important objective—the sustained yield of life." This goal, Dana and other planners recognized, was dependent upon massive New Deal projects and vigorously functioning programs which needed to be integrated into the regional economy to insure the most beneficial social and economic returns from public expenditures. Though Dana's goals were not fulfilled completely during the New Deal, it was not for want of effort. Besides traditional and established federal and state agencies, a galaxy of new ones—the Soil Conservation Service, the Farm Security Administration, the AAA, the Bonneville Power Authority, WPA and PWA, the Grazing Division among other New Deal agencies, plus several newly created state boards and commissions—were all actively engaged in efforts to further planned development in the region.[3]

The Northwest, like most of the West during the 1930s, was plagued by the problem that it shipped to markets outside the region materials for which it received a relatively low return and imported items of relatively high cost. In seeking greater self-sufficiency, planners sought utilization of regional resources to better serve the regional population as well as a larger portion of the national population. While New Deal programs, particularly the multipurpose development of the Columbia River, would help in achieving a regional balance, there were several immediate problems that demanded the attention of planners in the Pacific Northwest.

One of the most pressing was population. It was estimated that 10,000 new farm families settled in Washington, Oregon, Idaho, and western Montana in 1936, refugees chiefly from the devastation afflicting the northern Great Plains states. These people had to be absorbed one way or another into the population and some of the resource inventories, plans, studies and reports presented to the state and regional planning conferences factored increased population into their conclusions. While these numerous plans did not constitute a "blue-print" for the region, they did provide a framework of desirable regional objectives, policies, and programs for the region's principal resources and for its general development and progress. Moreover, planning was facilitated through the cooperation of the regional agency with the organization and work of both state and federal agencies in the Northwest.[4]

The question of markets was one that plagued the Northwest and it was one that the New Deal tried to assist in resolving. In 1934 Eugene A. Cox, chairman of the Idaho State Planning Board, remarked that in Canada a bushel of wheat was carried 800 miles for 8 cents. In parts of the Northwest it cost 22 cents to transport a bushel of wheat about 500 miles to Portland. When the wheat reached Portland, the question of marketing it became acute. With a sparse population, about 3.5 million people scattered throughout a vast region, the grain could not be consumed within the four-state area. Though the region produced less than 10 percent of the nation's wheat crop, anywhere from one-half to two-thirds of it could not be marketed within the region. And foreign markets, let alone the national market, held out very little promise given high production and transportation costs, competition with Canadian,

Australian, and midwestern producers, declining foreign trade, and other factors. In attempting to resolve this endemic difficulty, accentuated by the Great Depression, the secretary of agriculture under authority granted to him in the Agricultural Adjustment Act, devised an export arrangement to assist grain growers in the Pacific Northwest. It involved an export subsidy, a device utilized for the first time since the colonial period of American history.[5]

Grain sales through the North Pacific Emergency Export Association in 1933–34 totaled 21.85 million bushels of which nearly three-fourths went to the Far East: Hong Kong, China, Japan, and the Philippine Islands. In all about 35 million bushels of Northwest wheat were disposed of through this arrangement which subsidized wheat at the rate of about 20 cents a bushel. Funds for this came from the processing tax on wheat. The operation of the export association accounted for about 87 percent of the net exports of wheat, including flour, during the single year it functioned. Thereafter the wheat situation in the Northwest improved without the benefit of this special arrangement. Drought and severe crop curtailment in the Great Plains helped to increase sharply wheat prices to the immediate benefit of producers in the Pacific Northwest. Wheat prices in 1934–35 were higher in the region than in the previous year when exports were subsidized. The wheat situation in the Northwest never again commanded special attention, though export subsidies were provided for in the Agriculture Act of 1938 whereby the Federal Surplus Commodity Corporation purchased surplus wheat at the prevailing market price and sold it to exporters at prices enabling them to sell it abroad. In 1938–39 the effective subsidy was about 29 cents per bushel of wheat and 22 cents per bushel equivalent for flour.[6]

A more pressing problem both to the planners and to New Deal administrators was expressed in the fact that more than 400,000 persons had entered the region since 1930, seeking new opportunities, jobs, and cheap land, only to find unemployment and a lack of good land immediately available. It was the promise of new opportunities that brought migrants, chiefly from the northern tier of states from the Mississippi River westward, with small cash reserves and their few personal belongings packed into the old family car or farm truck. They left behind them drought, dust, eroded lands, unemployment, and a horde of other depressing conditions that offered them a bleak future. They came to what many envisioned as a promised land, a land of opportunity, of pleasant climate, of adequate rainfall, and of resources of all kinds awaiting development. When most of these migrants arrived in the mid-1930s the New Deal was already in the process of developing the Northwest through various projects that would reclaim unproductive lands and provide cheap power for new factories. For those coming to the region, these developments meant jobs or a chance to farm again. Though most of the migrants in the West during the 1930s headed for California, Bonneville and Grand Coulee were words and symbols that impelled others to escape from misery and find their future in the Pacific Northwest, primarily in Oregon and Washington.[7]

But not every migrant following the new Oregon trail, the Lincoln Highway, found the promised land in the Northwest in the 1930s. A survey by the Farm Security Administration of 20,917 recent settlers indicated that 24 percent had obtained farms previously abandoned; 48 percent were endeavoring to settle on a tract of unimproved land; and only 28 percent had either obtained or were working on a going farm. Too many migrants settled in areas where submarginal lands predominated, despite efforts by the Resettlement Administration and the Pacific Northwest Regional Planning Commission to guide them to lands offering farming opportunities and away from those which did not. Others found themselves in even more dire straits. As nonresidents they were denied relief, barred from access to community services, and were not eligible to vote. Without cash or opportunity for employment, many migrants followed the crops and helped pick fruits and vegetables in the Willamette, Yakima, and Snake River valleys.[8]

A small mobile army of transient workers, numbering approximately 80,000, moved into these and other valleys during the peak of the harvesting season, a period of about four months. They lived mostly in crowded dirty shacks along ditch banks or in jungles (squatters' camps) under the most primitive of conditions. A fortunate few were provided with better facilities and services by a handful of growers: tents pitched on the growers' lands or cabins furnished with utilities. Little was done to improve the conditions of migratory labor in the Northwest until late in the New Deal. The growers, many on the verge of bankruptcy owing to uncertain markets for their crops, were unable or unwilling to provide better living conditions or higher wages. In 1939 the program of farm labor camps initiated by the Farm Security Administration spread to the Northwest with the construction of four permanent and three mobile camps, providing housing and facilities of all kinds, including a clinic, nursery, and kindergarten in the permanent camps.

The Farm Security Administration in the Northwest was the first agency in the nation to develop and utilize portable tent camps that could accommodate 200 families in valleys where the harvests were short and one-crop farming was the practice. The managers of these Farm Security Administration camps also helped workers find jobs, cooperating with the United States Employment Service by keeping a record of growers' and other employers' needs for labor. The residents in the camps had a large voice in their own governance. While the plight of migrants in the Northwest was in no way as severe or as publicized as those in California, nor were there racial or ethnic dimensions to their plight, their situation was similar. Until 1939 neither public officials nor the New Deal itself was able to meliorate and cope with the scandalous treatment, exploitation, and deprivation of migratory workers and families throughout the region. Planning in this instance had little to offer.

Nor did it have much to offer the tens of thousands already unemployed in the Northwest and the thousands more experiencing intermittent unemployment owing to the seasonal character of lumber and agriculture, the region's basic industries. Until recovery was under way in these industries, prosperity would elude the region. Nevertheless, planners and their associates were optimistic about the future of the region primarily because developments along the Columbia River would provide a power potential attractive to industry. This, however, would be a postwar development, the foundation of which was established during the New Deal. But before discussing this momentous development it will be worthwhile to examine briefly New Deal developments pertaining to forestry and other programs affecting agriculture.

The lumber industry was hit particularly hard during the Great Depression, and as a result the Northwest was devasted. Here forest industries accounted for 87 percent of the tonnage of inland water carriers and 63 percent of all freight tonnage. By 1938 in Washington and western Oregon about 18 percent employment prevailed.[9] It was this depressing situation that permitted the Forest Service to proclaim the virtues of sustained-yield production with some chance of persuading larger lumber firms that it was a sensible procedure to follow. In the Pacific Northwest, however, Harold Ickes and the Department of the Interior played the dominant role in proclaiming these virtues over the pressures for rapid cutting of timber holdings.

The O and C lands in western Oregon, comprising about 2.5 million acres of fine timberlands, reverted to the federal government in 1916 when the Supreme Court, in an action initiated when Theodore Roosevelt was President, decided that the Oregon and California Railroad and the Coos Bay Wagon Road had not fulfilled the conditions of their 1866 railroad land grant. Congress authorized the Department of the Interior in August 1937 to harvest and sell the timber on these lands on the basis of sustained yield, a variable method to insure permanent productivity including such measures as planting and reseeding cutover areas, protection from fire, disease and insects, reducing waste through more complete utilization of timber, and furthering the forest's multiple-use values by considering recreation, range, wildlife, soil conservation, and watershed protection. In addition, Congress further approved a procedure through which a major portion of the revenues from the use of these lands would be granted to the eighteen O and C counties with no restrictions as to their expenditure. Never before had counties been so favored. These lands, according to Ovid Butler, Executive Secretary of the American Forestry Association, contained "more standing timber than is in all of the Rocky Mountain States from Canada to Mexico."[10] This congressional mandate gave Ickes the opportunity to further his claim that the Department of the Interior was the leading conservation agency and should be so recognized through a Department of Conservation in charge of all conservation work engaged in by the federal government.

The Oregon and California Revested Land Grant Administration established under the 1937 statute, which, incidentally, was initially drafted in the Department of the Interior, would direct the sustained-yield management of these lands scattered in parcels of varying size in checkerboard fashion in the western third of Oregon from the Columbia River to the California border. Intermingled with these lands were other sections of both public and private lands totaling about 6 million acres. These lands in toto comprised the world's richest stand of Douglas fir, though in the southern part of Oregon about 150,000 acres covered largely with oak and chaparral were best utilized for grazing.

Prior to 1937 O and C timber was sold to the highest bidder with little regard for the goal of sustained yield because there was virtually no demand for it. By the early New Deal about 90 percent of the lumber companies in Oregon were on the verge of bankruptcy and at least one-half of the timber land in the state was tax delinquent. By 1935, however, conditions in the industry began to improve and a continuous-yield program was already in place. It involved a land classification plan and one calling for integrated management units to assure that the annual cut, plus timber lost from fire and other causes, would approximate annual timber growth. By 1938 sustained yield was at work on the O and C lands and, because of the checkerboard pattern, on the interspersed private lands as well. For all intents and purposes, Ickes now had a forestry division in the Department of the Interior through which he could extend O and C standards based on cooperative management to the lumber industry in the Northwest.[11]

At the outset under Chief Forester Walter Horning, CCC volunteers were put to work reforesting portions of unproductive O and C lands. They assisted in fire fighting and also constructed bridges and roads. While recreation, grazing, and other supplementary uses of the lands were planned, during the New Deal years the major emphasis was confined to sustained yield and protecting the O and C lands from fire and further erosion. By 1941, historian Elmo Richardson has written, "students of forest management were describing the O and C

Administration as a model in cooperation between public interests and private enterprises." And the Chief Forester of the O and C lands, noting the transformation occurring in the landscape of western Oregon said, "the rusty sheet iron smokestacks of a migrant industry engaged in hasty exploitation had been replaced by the brick and concrete chimneys of a permanent industry engaged in processing and refining." The flimsy shacks of migrant workers "had been replaced" by substantial houses of "taxpaying citizens" seen "through green woods rather than ghost towns viewed across desolate wastes of stumps and shattered logs."[12]

Another New Deal program in the Northwest also involving land-use planning got under way in 1935 and was sponsored by the Resettlement Administration. It placed special emphasis on the development of submarginal lands with a view to employ people currently on relief rolls. Of the five projects launched in 1935, two were primarily adapted to forestry, another involved a forest and recreation area, and two would find their greatest use in grazing.

One of the forest projects was located in northwestern Washington, the other along the west coast of Oregon. The forest and recreation project was situated about 25 miles east of Salem, Oregon, while the remaining two projects were in central Oregon and in southeastern Idaho. About 90 percent of the men employed were taken from the relief rolls and anywhere from 5,000 to 7,000 men found work on these projects. Besides rehabilitating submarginal lands, numerous farm families were provided with opportunities for a livelihood and a chance for a better life through these Resettlement Administration programs.[13]

Another Resettlement Administration project in the region that attracted attention was Longview Homesteads in Washington, a housing project designed to provide low-income part-time workers an opportunity to engage in small-scale subsistence gardening. The project consisted of 60 houses, all completed and occupied by the end of 1935. Located three miles west of the business district of Longview, this project was successful from the outset. The occupant families were able to improve their living standards by means of the crops they raised, thereby supplementing their regular income from industrial employment. Each family received a house, combination barn and poultry shed and a garage. Each property was landscaped as a part of the original cost. Since the project was part of a larger community, the Resettlement Administration did not have to provide educational and recreational facilities for the 60 resident families. The average cost per house was $2,915 with an average monthly rental of $14.40. At the end of the first crop year, the Longview *Daily News* on October 26, 1935, estimated that project residents averaged a return of $308 in food products consumed and an additional $247 from sale of foodstuffs. Successful from the start, Longview Homesteads showed what New Deal planners working with local officials could accomplish. By 1937 the community had been transferred to private ownership "practically at face value and a reasonable interest return during the amortization period." But, probably owing to difficulties enveloping the Resettlement Administration in the nation's capital, the Longview project was the only one of its kind in the Pacific Northwest.[14]

Though one successful housing project was launched there were no new irrigation projects completed in the Pacific Northwest. There were seven projects in the region by 1933 and in varying degrees they prospered during the New Deal, particularly the Yakima project where the Yakima Valley served as a show-window for reclamation.[15] All projects in the Northwest faced the problem of high shipping costs and of distance from the San Francisco market, where a portion of the crops and livestock raised in these irrigation districts were marketed. The further development of the Columbia River would change the agricultural outlook of the region in the years following the New Deal.

The Bureau of Reclamation had construction work under way during the decade on several established projects in the region. The total storage capacity on the Minidoka project was exceeded during the New Deal years only by the Boulder Dam project with its huge Lake Mead. Minidoka received its water from Lakes Jackson and Walcott created by three dams constructed on the Snake River prior to 1933. During the New Deal starts were made on two tributary dams to provide for further irrigation throughout the Idaho project area. Elsewhere on the Snake River, in the Payette Division of the Boise project, the main Black Canyon Canal was dedicated in 1939, making available about 26,000 acres for irrigation and providing opportunities for farmers and recent migrants to file entry claims on these newly created farm lands. By 1940 there were about 2 million irrigated acres located along the Snake River plain in Idaho and developed chiefly by the Bureau of Reclamation. By 1940 Idaho projects also produced annually about 1.5 million kilowatt-hours of electricity, more than one-third of which was transmitted out of the state.[16]

A further illustration of New Deal developments on existing projects can be observed on the Vale and Owyhee projects in eastern Oregon where additional acreage for irrigation and hence for settlement was provided.[17] Dams on the Malheur and Owyhee Rivers, tributaries of the Snake, provided the water for these projects. Both projects got under way in the 1920s, though their beginnings go back to the 1890s. The dams, however, were completed in the 1930s. During the depression years when the dams were under construction, Malheur County experienced little unemployment and little suffering from drought. First deliveries of water from the Owyhee Dam, for example, were made in 1935 with further deliveries, as diversionary canals were completed, occurring in 1938 and 1939. Between 1930 and 1938 almost 56,000 acres of new land were developed on the Owyhee project providing farm units for more than 700 settlers.[18]

Other Bureau of Reclamation projects throughout the Pacific Northwest experienced similar developments and provided opportunities for new homesteaders. None had a marked or dramatic impact in making changes in the region, though taken together within the planning context proclaimed by the Pacific Northwest Regional Planning Commission and the state commissions as well, these developments furthered the goal of meaningful land use and provided opportunities for a small segment of the migrants pouring into the region. There were, in addition, other significant developments during the New Deal in the Pacific Northwest that attracted attention both within the region, throughout the nation, and in foreign lands that dealt with some of the basic concerns of the region's planners.

One of these developments—the lesser in terms of dramatic impact and immediate significance—was the creation of Olympic National Park, one of two new parks established in the West during the New Deal years. A third park, encompassing the Big Bend country in Texas, was authorized by a 1935 Act of Congress when title to all of the lands within the area designated by the secretary of the interior became vested in the United States. It became a national park in 1943 when Texas deeded some 788,682 acres of spectacular desert and mountain scenery, lying at the southern extremity of the Big Bend of the Rio Grande, to the federal government.

In 1909 President Theodore Roosevelt set aside Mount Olympus National Monument to save the last remnants of the elk population in the nation's last frontier forest (outside of Alaska). The boundaries of the area had been reduced three times since 1909 because commercial interests, unconcerned with its savage grandeur, wished to market the Douglas fir, Sitka spruce, cedar, and hemlock trees, some 45 feet in circumference, abounding on the peninsula in a forest which it was estimated would take 500 years to reproduce. Nowhere else in North America could be found such stands of Douglas fir and Sitka spruce or such underwoods of pine, maple, and alder, or such rich mosses and almost tropical ferns. By the mid-1930s, the diminished elk herd could no longer find adequate winter range in the depleted forest, now totaling about 300,000 acres.

It was also in the mid-1930s that Representative Monrad C. Wallgren first introduced a bill to establish the Mount Olympus or Olympic National Park. When established in June 1938, it became the first national park that was entirely a wilderness area free from hotels and other commercial establishments. Covering about 634,000 acres in the northwest corner of the state of Washington, the area with its splendid forest and sharp, snow-crested mountains would thus be preserved. But it would not be established without a loud clamor, chiefly from the lumber interests which in the past had been successful in reducing the area Theodore Roosevelt set aside to preserve the elk herd. The Forest Service objected because the expanded acreage for the proposed park would be subtracted from the Olympic National Forest containing about 3 billion feet of virgin timber that the Forest Service wanted to market on a sustained-yield basis. The Washington State Planning Council raised a similar objection. Its members saw in these lands a great opportunity for conducting a large scale program of sustained-yield forest management in conjunction with adjacent tracts of state forest.[19]

In this instance the New Dealers and the National Park Service won out over the planners, the Forest Service, lumber interests, and their allies and associates, including Washington's governor, Clarence D. Martin, all of whom wished to keep the proposed park at the minimum acreage possible. Fortunately the President wanted the largest area that it was possible to get out of Congress, as did Ickes who insisted "that in the long run it will mean more for the State of Washington to have a real national park on the Olympic Peninsula than it will be to log this area, either selectively or otherwise." When approved at the end of June 1938, the measure authorized the President to add further lands to the park provided that the total acreage not exceed 898,292 acres, an increase of 264,292 acres over its original size.[20]

Once the park was established it became the task of the Forest Service and the National Park Service to soothe the tensions that had developed since Congressman Monrad Wallgren introduced his bill in 1935. An informal joint board with representatives of the Departments of Agriculture and of the Interior was suggested with the objective of working out relationships between Olympic National Park and surrounding national, state, and privately owned forest lands. Because of the inability of the two secretaries to cooperate on this matter, the joint board was never created. The objectives it sought were attended to by Ickes and the National Park Service with no objections from the Forest Service. And for the remaining years of the New Deal, when the President, Henry A. Wallace, Harold L. Ickes, and their associates devoted their attention to Olympic National Park, it was chiefly to discuss or debate proposed additions to the park area.[21]

The successful fight to establish Olympic National Park brought to the fore a sharp difference between the secretary of the interior and some regional planners in the Pacific Northwest, most notably those in Washington State.[22] Though a firm believer in sustained-yield forestry, Ickes was unalterably opposed to logging in national parks and to portions of national forests in the Cascade Mountains being set aside as recreational areas. Fortunately in this instance his views coincided with those of the Washington State Planning Council, thereby preventing further exacerbation of the differences between them. Ickes insisted that "Mount Baker, Glacier Peak, Mount Adams, Mount Saint Helens, Mount Hood, and the scenic wilderness areas of the High Cascades are national recreational resources" and could not be considered as forestry or timber-producing lands.

With reference to the Northwest, Ickes asserted his views on both sides of the conservation controversies of the New Deal. On the one hand he favored wise use and prudent management of national resources, as in the instance of the O and C lands and the development of the Columbia River Valley. On the other hand he endorsed the preservation of national and wildlife resources as indicated in the fight for creating and then expanding Olympic National Park as well as establishing recreational areas in the Cascade Mountains. This position was further reflected in various efforts to achieve wildlife and wilderness preservation in the Northwest. Ickes and the region's planners were in accord when New Deal programs and policies under his aegis focused on the developmental side of conservation. When they focused on the preservation side the planners and their business allies many opposed Ickes.

While a "New Deal" for wildlife did not focus exclusively on the Northwest, the region contained the greatest remaining wildlife resource in the United States and can serve as an example or manifestation of its functioning. The Department of Agriculture took the lead in this development, but before the New Deal was out wildlife programs became the responsibility of Harold L. Ickes, adding to his hegemony over vast areas in the west. Although the Bureau of Reclamation, the Forest Service, and other agencies operating in the Northwest affected wildlife population, only two were specifically charged with its preservation and restoration: the Bureau of Biological Survey in the Department of Agriculture and the Bureau of Fisheries in the Department of Commerce. Both were primarily engaged in research and administration of bird and game refuges and a network of fish hatcheries. During the New Deal concern for wildlife conservation resulted in increased funding and in legislation that added to and improved both refuges and hatcheries, in part with CCC workers and funds provided by Ickes through the Public Works Administration. It also led to interdepartmental cooperation and encouraged state wildlife conservation projects.[23]

The wildlife New Deal benefited enormously when Roosevelt appointed Jay N. Darling, nationally known cartoonist and conservationist, to head the Bureau of Biological Survey. Darling disbursed funds to restore and maintain water levels in depleted reservoirs on some of the older reclamation projects in order to provide continued refuge to birds and wildlife. This was a scheme that long interested the President, who encouraged these efforts and devoted some of his energies to furthering them. In a 1934 address Roosevelt asserted that more "wildlife sanctuary area has been acquired or is now being acquired than in all the preceding years of the history of our government." And as part of the limited reorganization plan approved by the Seventy-Fifth Congress in 1937, the two conservation bureaus, Fisheries from Commerce and Biological Survey from Agriculture, were merged as the Fish and Wildlife Service effective July 1, 1939, to be located in the Department of the Interior.[24]

"Ding" Darling in his brief tenure as Chief of the Biological Survey launched a major effort to further wildlife conservation. Private lands in the winter range of the elk at Jackson Hole (Wyoming) and privately owned ranches in the Hart Mountain region (Oregon), where an antelope range had been withdrawn from a grazing district, were acquired, completing two major projects Darling considered "as outstanding as any that I know of in the field of conservation of wildlife. . . ." In addition, with presidential support, he prepared guidelines for the Bureau of Reclamation to follow in regulating reservoir levels so that vegetation and nesting birds would not be destroyed. He also drafted rules that Ickes and Farrington Carpenter, chief of the Bureau of Grazing, agreed to follow dealing with the regulation of game on lands under Carpenter's jurisdiction.[25]

Another victory for wildlife scored by Darling was an agreement, worked out in the summer of 1935 before he returned to private life, to enlarge the Tule Lake Wildlife Refuge, comprising about 10,000 acres located on the Tule Lake Reclamation Project. The President complied with an Executive Order in 1936 that helped conserve waterfowl in northern California and southern Oregon. In his brief tenure, thanks to the backing of the President and general support from Secretaries Wallace and Ickes, Darling proved himself to be a formidable figure in battling for wildlife conservation.

Ira N. Gabrielson, who in 1935 succeeded Darling, stated that since 1934 upwards of $21 million had gone into the acquisition and development of refuges. At that time the Biological Survey had 254 wildlife areas comprising more than 13.5 million acres under its jurisdiction. In the West large areas had been set aside for the protection of big game such as ranges for mountain sheep in Arizona, for antelope in southern Oregon, and for deer in Montana. Restoration of soil, water, and forest resources were basic to wildlife conservation. Other New Deal agencies cooperated with the Biological Survey and after 1939 with the Fish and Wildlife Service. In addition, concern was expressed to both the Bureau of Reclamation and the Corps of Engineers, each in charge of constructing a major dam on the Columbia River, over incorporating improved fishways in their respective projects. Since the fate of wildlife was inseparably linked with problems of soil erosion, stream pollution, ground cover on watersheds, destruction of forests, and denuding of natural vegetation on grazing lands, to the extent that New Deal programs grappled with these problems, they promoted wildlife restoration and conservation.[26]

Irrigation, so vital to the development of the West, was entirely in tune with wildlife conservation. In the Boise Valley, for example, with the development of irrigation, the number of ducks and geese increased over 100 percent within 30 years. Game animals in the national forests in the Northwest increased rapidly during the New Deal years. Winter feeding remained a problem as game were forced into the high mountains, owing to the fact that most valleys and open lands in the region were settled. The problem resolved itself into one of retaining soil and water so trees, shrubs, plants, and grasses could grow. A most important and beneficial by-product of the New Deal in the West, and the Northwest in particular, was the impetus it gave to wildlife conservation and restoration.[27]

A potential threat to wildlife conservation was raised by Senator Elbert Thomas of Utah in 1937 when he wrote the President explaining, "It is my belief that prospecting and location under the United States mining laws should be permitted within the boundaries of national game preserves." Thomas requested an Executive Order reserving mining rights in such preserves because the national game preserves were created in this way. Roosevelt, citing the 1929 Migratory Bird Conservation Act, concluded that he had no such authority and suggested that Thomas's objective could be effected only through an Act of Congress. Though such a bill was introduced, no such measure was enacted during the New Deal.[28]

In developing these refuges or preserves the Biological Survey, utilizing CCC and later WPA labor, engaged in the construction of dams and dikes with spillways and other devices for controlling water levels. In addition shelters and nesting islands were built for birds. Also of importance was the construction of roads and trails, fencing and boundary markings, and other improvements to facilitate the administration of the refuges. By 1940, Montana and Oregon had more wildlife refuges and ranges than any other western state.[29] While the Departments of Agriculture and Interior and their secretaries bickered continually before the creation of the Fish and Wildlife Service in the Department of the Interior in 1939, both secretaries and their departments were concerned about wildlife preservation and conservation.

In the Pacific Northwest wildlife was abundant. Here the preservation side of the conservation movement received emphasis with the creation of the first wilderness park, Olympic National Park. The planners who were opposed to the park, nevertheless, forgave Ickes and the President for what they possibly considered a New Deal indiscretion because in this region major projects were started which all believed could achieve the planned promised land. Developing the Columbia River was an accomplishment that commanded national and international attention. The construction projects at Bonneville and Grand Coulee resulted in public works on such a grand scale that they rivaled those of the pharaohs in ancient Egypt. The pyramids were constructed to exalt the glory of individuals who held sway over the Nile basin. The dams along the Columbia were designed to achieve the promised land for the people of the Pacific Northwest.

The President gathers first-hand evidence on a drought inspection trip in Mandan, North Dakota, August 1936. (FDR Library)

The President and construction engineer F. A. Banks at the Grand Coulee Dam on the Columbia River in Washington State, October 1937. (FDR Library)

Harry L. Hopkins, administrator of FERA and WPA. (FDR Library)

Ferdinand A. Silcox, Chief of Forest Service. (National Archives)

Harry L. Hopkins at Timberline Lodge, September 1936. (FDR Library)

Harold L. Ickes, Secretary of the Interior. (FDR Library, Constant Collection)

Rexford G. Tugwell, administrator of the Resettlement Administration. (FDR Library)

Vice President Henry A. Wallace (FDR Library)

Hugh Hammond Bennett, Chief of the Soil Conservation Service. (National Archives)

John Collier, Commissioner of Indian Affairs. (National Archives)

Dr. Elwood Mead, Commissioner of Reclamation. (Library of Congress)

Edward T. Taylor, Colorado Congressman, sponsor of the Taylor Grazing Act. (National Archives)

Arno B. Cammerer, Director, National Park Service. (National Archives)

Chapter 10

The Columbia River Basin

SPEAKING AT PORTLAND on September 21, 1932, Franklin D. Roosevelt, seeking the presidency, pledged "that the next great hydroelectric development to be undertaken by the Federal government must be that on the Columbia River." This development could fulfill the vision of a planned promised land with its potential, as Roosevelt said, for "cheap manufacturing production, economy and comfort on the farm and in the household." During the New Deal two immense projects were undertaken to translate Roosevelt's promise into reality: one high on the plateau of the inland wheat plains, the other further downstream and deep in the fastness of the Cascade Mountains. With these projects the New Deal made its greatest and most lasting impact in the Northwest.

Bonneville, developed first and located close by Portland, affected Oregon more so than Washington, while Grand Coulee, located within Washington State, was developed late in the New Deal. Together they were expected to revolutionize the economic life of the entire region. Both projects, the former constructed by the Corps of Engineers and the latter by the Bureau of Reclamation, taken together provided an ideal demonstration of the feasibility of flood prevention, water storage and irrigation, the collateral development of hydroelectric power, the curbing of soil erosion, and the economic desirability of land use, all coupled with planning for community growth, extended transportation, and market development. These projects, in short, allowed planners in the Northwest to envision the region's future as a promised land. However, by the end of the New Deal planners and others throughout the region were quarrelling among themselves (as were New Dealers in the nation's capital) over the desirability of creating a Columbia Valley Authority with an organizational framework comparable to the Tennessee Valley Authority.

Improvement of the Columbia River at Bonneville, about forty miles east of Portland, got under way on September 30, 1933, with the blessing of Harold Ickes in the form of Public Works Administration Federal Project No. 28. It was formally authorized by Congress in the River and Harbor Act approved August 30, 1935. The Corps of Engineers, the construction agency, supervised the task of building a dam, a powerhouse, a ship lock, and fishways. The total cost of the project was estimated at the outset to be about $45 million. Final cost was $75 million of which PWA furnished $42 million. Besides providing abundant and cheap hydroelectric power—scheduled at the outset to be about 600,000 horsepower—the completed project extended an inland seaway 188 miles from the Pacific Ocean making the Columbia River navigable as far as the Dalles, thereby providing low-cost transportation to a wide territory. This was possible because the water stored behind the dam formed a navigable lake deep enough for ocean-going vessels. Bonneville, like Grand Coulee, is a self-liquidating project scheduled to pay off late in the decade of the 1980s that portion of its cost allocated to power production at 3.5 percent interest. The project was ready to begin operation late in the summer of 1938.[1]

At the outset and throughout the construction of the Bonneville project, concern was expressed regarding its effect on the fisheries of the Columbia River. The entire run of salmon spawning in this watershed would have to surmount the obstruction imposed by Bonneville Dam on their upstream spawning migration. The returning progeny had to reach the Pacific Ocean without injury if the communities of the lower Columbia Basin were not to be economically destroyed. The fishing industry there was worth about $6 million annually and about 20,000 people, directly or indirectly, were dependent upon it for their livelihood.

The Columbia River, moreover, was the dominant parent stream for the Chinook salmon caught by trollers in the North Pacific from Monterey, California, to Juneau, Alaska. "Hence," explained an official of the Bureau of Fisheries, "not only will the extensive canning industry of Washington and Oregon be directly affected but also every mild cured salmon packer and dealer on the Pacific Coast is concerned, every fresh salmon buyer and retailer in the country is affected, and every salmon smoker in the United States will feel the effect of the destruction of the Columbia River as a breeding ground for salmon."[2]

The Army Engineers in the planning and construction of Bonneville Dam, which was calculated to lift the level of the water above the dam to a maximum of 65 feet and create a lake 50 miles long, appreciated the importance of providing adequate fishways. Assisted by studies prepared by employees of the Bureau of Fisheries, the fishways were built and in operation before the construction of the dam itself could interfere with the free passage of fish. Never before had a major salmon run been required to hurdle an obstruction as formidable as Bonneville.

Grand Coulee would provide an even greater challenge. In November 1937 when Bonneville was nearing completion, Richard L. Neuberger wrote, "Prevalent throughout the principal salmon producing region of the world today is the almost unshakable opinion that within a few years the fighting fish with flaky flesh will be one and the same with the dodo bird—extinct." An Indian chief put it more succinctly when he told Neuberger, "White man's dams mean no more salmon."[3]

An elaborate system of traps, locks, elevators, canals, and ladders shepherded adult fish over the dam and a series of by-passes brought those of their progeny, who did not go over the spillway or through the chambers of the turbines, downstream. So successful were the Bonneville fishways that thousands of spectators flocked to the dam every spring to watch the salmon swim, jump, or flip themselves from pool to pool. Data collected at the dam through 1942 indicated that a large portion of the fingerlings that went downstream in 1938, over the spillway and through the turbines or by-passes, completed their cycle and made the arduous return journey as adults. The President, however, was deeply concerned about the increased costs incurred in providing for the safety of the salmon at Bonneville. In a 1935 memo he wrote, "All I can hope is that the salmon will approve the spillways and find them really useful, even though they cost almost as much as the dam and the electric power development."[4]

Grand Coulee was too large a dam to duplicate the methods developed at Bonneville. Elwood Mead, Commissioner of the Bureau of Reclamation, explained: "It is infeasible to provide for the passage of salmon either up or downstream over a dam the height of the proposed Grand Coulee." Instead biologists worked out a large-scale experiment relocating the fish runs which traditionally went upriver past the dam site. Techniques were devised to divert the salmon to four tributaries entering the Columbia below Grand Coulee. Completed during the war years these experiments were largely successful. By the end of the 1940s most salmon were diverted to the tributary streams and their progeny, in completing their life cycles, were returning to the tributaries instead of going upriver to the dam.[5]

Construction at Bonneville, where the river rushed between ramparts in a gorge 3,000 feet deep, was the first federal enterprise on the Columbia River. Starting with an initial Public Works Administration allotment of $20 million and supplemented by a second-year allotment of $11 million, construction of the huge dam under the direction of the Corps of Engineers was well along by the end of 1934. The contracts that had been let called for the building and maintenance of coffer dams and railroad crossings; excavation for the powerhouse, locks and foundations; construction of permanent living quarters at the site; exploratory drilling; clearing; work on experimental models and test drainage areas; and construction of the main spillway sections of the dam. Before its formal authorization in the 1935 Rivers and Harbors Act, wherein Congress allocated funds to projects supervised by the Corps of Engineers, construction of the Bonneville project, employing about 3,000 men, was well under way. Indeed the 1934 allotment was expected to bring the dam (not the entire project) close to completion.[6]

Early on it became clear that Bonneville, despite the initial desire to construct a low dam for navigation purposes, would be primarily a power project. Oregon politicians insisted and prevailed over the views of the President and Secretary Ickes who, relying on the reports of various specialists, claimed that Grand Coulee would generate more than enough power for the entire region. Mayor Joseph Carson of Portland served notice on the President that his city would not buy "a dime's worth of power" from the projected Grand Coulee plant if the Bonneville dam was constructed for navigation only. A visit by Senator Charles McNary, who took a plane to Washington and went directly to the White House, apparently turned the tide. The next day the first PWA allocation calling for a high dam was made. And in August 1934 when Ickes visited the site with the President, he noted in his diary, "The dam that is to be built here is for power and navigation."[7]

With construction well along by the end of 1934, planners in the Northwest started calling for studies and the actual funding of transmission power lines from Bonneville Dam. Oregon would be the main beneficiary of such construction. Only 31 percent of its farms were electrified in 1935. Many of the remaining 69 percent, comprising 38,000 individual farms, would be among the first to benefit from the construction of transmission lines. Moreover, availability of electricity in rural areas, the governor of Oregon believed, would stimulate development and further settlement in the Willamette Valley. Until a definite announcement about transmission lines from Bonneville was made, the governor insisted that the Oregon legislature could not properly plan a scheme of distribution, "and unless such announcement is made prior to the 1937 session of the legislature, proper and adequate use of Bonneville power in Oregon might possibly be delayed until the year 1939, or even later."[8]

To handle the distribution of power and to develop the widest possible markets for it, the Bonneville Power Administration was approved by the President in August 1937. Shortly thereafter, J. D. Ross, superintendent of Seattle City Light and a nationally known and respected proponent of public power, became the first administrator. His appointment, a responsibility of the secretary of the interior, marked the culmination of the first phase of an on-going debate among New Dealers as to how Columbia River developments were to be administered.

In turn this debate was part of a larger one involving regional development and a national power policy. The Bonneville Power Administration Act of 1937 indicated too that the controversy in the Northwest was far from over. One clause stated: "The form of administration herein established for the Bonneville Project is intended to be provisional pending the establishment of a permanent administration for Bonneville and other projects in the Columbia River Basin." However, in 1940, the President by Executive Order made BPA, headquartered in Portland, the marketing agency for the power generated by Grand Coulee. More than forty years later this provisional agency was still administering the public power program in the Pacific Northwest.[9]

Because Congress made no provision for transmission lines in its original appropriation establishing the BPA, funds for that purpose were not provided until May 1938. Thereafter, further assisted by a PWA allotment, a network of transmission lines emanating from the Bonneville Dam was soon under construction, in part assisted by WPA labor. Because of congressional negligence in the matter of transmission lines, Bonneville generators were operative long before there were transmission lines to take the electricity to various centers. Before the transmission system started, J. D. Ross and his associates devised a master plan to integrate Bonneville power with that produced by other public power systems in the Northwest into a "high capacity network" to eventually provide consumers with a perpetual source of energy at a lower cost than in any other comparable part of the nation.[10]

J. D. Ross, who effectively launched the BPA, died suddenly in March 1939. As administrator he was followed by Paul Raver and it was Raver who guided the system through its tremendous rapid expansion during the ensuing war years. But during Ross's brief tenure the BPA was already becoming the chief supplier of electric power in the Northwest. By establishing at the outset a system of uniform rates, the agency was able to provide a "yardstick" as power was distributed. Since BPA could only sell power wholesale, the ultimate cost to the consumer would depend upon how the purchasers distributed it and the manner in which the power was used. And that, Ross concluded, "is up to the people of the Northwest." In addition, as Charles McKinley noted in 1952, "private power installations have virtually ceased since the launching of Bonneville and Grand Coulee dams by the federal government and the creation of a federally owned and operated regional transmission grid, essential to private and public distribution agencies alike."[11]

As an indication of what Bonneville power could mean to the Northwest, in the summer of 1935 Charles B. Bohn, president of Bohn Aluminum and Brass Corporation of Detroit, announced in Portland that he wanted to buy all the power generated at Bonneville Dam. He promised to construct a city for at least 5,000 workers and their families, plus a dozen laboratories where chemists would assist in the production of something like 200 million pounds of aluminum a year. Bohn proposed to ship vast quantities of alumite from Utah to Bonneville for conversion to aluminum. And his was only one of the earlier and more grandiose schemes to convert the Columbia River Valley into an American Ruhr.[12]

Planners in the region had another opinion, one that the President articulated. Speaking at Bonneville on September 28, 1937, Roosevelt talked about doing "everything in our power to encourage the building up of the smaller communities of the United States" and "planning from the bottom up" through regional planning boards comparable to those operative throughout the Northwest. His visit to Bonneville allowed Roosevelt an opportunity to project its impact. "Its cost," he said, "will be returned to the people of the United States many times over in the improvement of navigation and transportation, the cheapening of electric power, and the distribution of this power to hundreds of small communities within a great radius." Roosevelt's vision and that of most of the New Deal planners for a promised land in the Pacific Northwest was broader gauged than that of Charles B. Bohn and other developers seeking to utilize Bonneville power.[13]

Federal power became a reality in the Pacific Northwest on the date Roosevelt spoke at Bonneville, September 28, 1937. After delivering his address the President pressed a button starting the two hydroelectric generators installed at the dam.

Since flood control was of minor interest and the Corps of Engineers never considered a dam for navigation alone as justifiable, Bonneville Dam was regarded as a separate unit concerned primarily with the production of hydroelectric power. But when considered as a part of a broader development on the Columbia River furthering the improvement of the Pacific Northwest, criticisms of the project, including those questioning its legality, quickly gave way to querying how the project was to be administered. No solution was forthcoming until the Bonneville Power Administration was created in August 1937. Thereafter, for the remainder of the New Deal, the chief controversy concerning Bonneville revolved around J. D. Ross's refusal to advocate a policy of differential wholesale rates. He called for a uniform or "postage stamp" rate base, rates ignoring transmission distance or consumption as factors in determining the price per kilowatt-year to wholesalers, who then retailed electricity to the public in the familiar kilowatt-hours.

Ross and those who supported this approach to rate-making in the region enunciated a social philosophy predicated on the "widest possible use." Ross's goal and that of planners in the region was to attract manufacturing industries through cheap power, thereby furnishing markets, providing jobs, and helping establish a regional equilibrium. At the very outset Ross found more demand for Bonneville power than the output of the two initial generators. He called for the installation of two more units and predicted the full utilization of all of Bonneville's kilowatt potential by the time power from Grand Coulee would become available. In short, the rate policy endorsed by Ross was in accord with the views expressed by the President in his 1937 remarks at Bonneville. And their views reflected those of the regional planners who envisioned an integrated grid system tying in all generating and transmission units and bringing cheap electricity to even the most remote parts of the region. It is believed, said one planner, that "generating stations in the Pacific Northwest, whether constructed and owned by public utilities, municipalities, states and/or the United States Government, can be operated in parallel on a permanent paying basis and likewise give highly satisfactory service for all electric-power market requirements." Prior to the war years, despite the confusion after Ross's death, the BPA operated on the premise stated in its enabling act that this federal power project "shall be operated for the benefit of the general public and particularly of domestic and rural customers."[14]

In August 1940 the President announced at a cabinet meeting that he was taking steps to coordinate "the great power resources of the Columbia River" by combining the marketing of power produced at the Bonneville and Grand Coulee Dams under one marketing agency. The transmission network under construction by the Bonneville Power Administration would carry electricity from both projects throughout the Pacific Northwest. When Roosevelt promulgated Executive Order No. 8526, his concern was focused on national defense and providing power for war industries in the region. The BPA could now count on power from Grand Coulee, shortly to be available, to help fulfill its expanding committments and to further utilize the more than 40 percent of the unharnessed water power of the United States located on the Columbia River.[15]

While hydroelectric power, electricity, was the chief purpose of the Bonneville Dam, New Deal development of the Columbia River Valley was multipurpose in its intent and goal. While navigation and concern for the salmon run were also evident at Bonneville, irrigation was not a consideration in its development. It was, however, a major factor in the development at Grand Coulee, where more than a million acres could be irrigated to provide opportunities for resettlement. At the same time it would make electric energy available for the widest possible use at the lowest possible cost. But by all odds, irrigation offered the largest potential for providing both work and settlement opportunities for immigrants and residents in the Northwest and establishing a base for balanced regional development. Grand Coulee, more so than any other project or program in the entire nation—with the notable exception of the Tennessee Valley Authority—became a symbol of the New Deal's committment to the planned promised land.

With $14 million provided by the Public Works Administration late in 1933, construction at Grand Coulee got underway. It is located approximately 235 miles northeast from Bonneville on the Columbia River and ninety-two miles by highway northwest of Spokane. Like Bonneville, it is a self-liquidating project. It was specifically authorized by Congress in 1935 to control floods, regulate the flow of the river, provide water for the reclamation of public lands, and to generate electricity "as a means of financially aiding and assisting such undertakings." By 1940, $69 million had been appropriated for Grand Coulee.[16]

The project consists of a dam 4,300 feet long at the crest and 450 feet from its foundation, capable of raising the river about 355 feet above its low water level and creating a lake 150 miles long, extending to the Canadian boundary. Called "the biggest thing on earth," the dam was completed in 1941. Neither irrigation nor power production got under way during the New Deal years. The ambitious program of creating a region of prosperous farms, capable of supporting 20,000 to 30,000 farm families, thriving towns, and small communities from a largely desert area, a planned promised land, had to be postponed and modified to meet the exigencies of war. During the New Deal years 6,000 men toiled night and day to help fulfill that promise through the construction of Grand Coulee Dam.

In 1935 Secretary Ickes transferred the building of Grand Coulee Dam from the Public Works Administration to the Bureau of Reclamation. The dam became part of the Columbia Basin project, a vast scheme of comprehensive land and water planning that was formally undertaken by the Bureau in 1939. On a less systematic basis various groups, including regional planning committees, had been engaged in similar activities for several years prior to 1939. World War II changed the situation in the valley from "waste" country to "waiting country." But during the New Deal years public imagination was awed in contemplating the potential of the biggest man-made thing on earth nestling in a canyon, a mile wide and 1,600 feet deep. Like the statistics of the dam, those pertaining to the project's potential were mind-boggling to most observers in the late 1930s. As many as 8,000 visitors in one day, and hundreds of thousands in the years prior to the war period, helped to make the dam site what one visitor called "a kibitzer's paradise."[17]

When Harold Ickes first visited the site with the President on August 4, 1934, the Reclamation Service was erecting a low dam for power purposes which he said would ultimately become a high dam for both power and irrigation. Senator Clarence C. Dill in introducing the President said that his presence signalized the real beginning of the development of the Columbia River and Roosevelt's remarks focused on the power potential of the project. Since the project was so stupendous, at Roosevelt's suggestion it was being built in sections with the low dam as the initial base. Power sales could help pay for the high dam to be constructed on it.[18]

Before Roosevelt would approve constructing a high dam creating a massive project, he wanted assurance that the government would control all of the arid land subject to irrigation. The area encompassed what Elwood Mead, Commissioner of Reclamation, called "the largest compact body of undeveloped compact land remaining in the United States and the most fertile." The President was concerned about the possibility of promoters purchasing desert, arid lands at a very low price. For the head of the Resettlement Administration, Rex Tugwell, however, this was not a major concern. He endorsed the project after visiting the dam site, located in "a broad valley between cliffs twice the height of Niagara."

Tugwell favored a high dam at Grand Coulee, despite the fact that "in years past, it would have been heresy for any one connected with the Department of Agriculture to speak kindly of a new irrigation project." Tugwell did so because of what he called "a new administration policy"; for every acre brought into cultivation by reclamation, the government had an obligation to remove from competition an equivalent area of submarginal land and "if necessary return it to the public domain, plant it to trees and grass, and allow it to recover what fertility it can." Moreover, Tugwell understood at the time of his visit in 1935 that lands in the Columbia basin could not arrive at development for at least another decade. Nevertheless, he was pleased the government could move directly to utilize a great natural resource for the common good, though, like the President, he did not want the project to become one "for the relief of land speculators."[19]

Roosevelt's concern was considered by Congress when it enacted the Columbia River Basin Anti-Speculation Act approved on May 27, 1937. This legislation was prompted by concern about speculation in Columbia Basin lands and by the desire to break up large dry-land farming operations in areas that could be irrigated. Over a million acres were involved. The act provided that acreage exceeding 80 acres per family would be considered excess land. Owners of such land would not receive water for any part of their land as long as they refused to sell excess land under an arrangement satisfactory to the secretary of the interior and at prices determined by appraisal. Moreover, the measure gave the federal government, if it desired, an option to purchase excess lands.[20]

The high dam, as projected in 1935, would have 2.6 million installed horsepower, more than Boulder Dam, more than any other dam yet constructed in the entire world, and would cost $179 million. Adding the projected cost of providing irrigation facilities ($214 million), the entire project would total $393 million. These facilities, however, would not be in place during the New Deal, since construction was not fully completed during these years. Final plans called for a 4,200-foot base with a dam 550 feet high. In such a large-scale undertaking many new engineering problems had to be solved and new construction methods utilized. The project also necessitated planning of power, land, and water resources which was well under way during the New Deal. Population distribution, however, would not occur until after World War II. But to some critics Grand Coulee involved anything but planning; it was merely part of "the old fight about who gets what."

To James Rorty, visiting the community at the dam site known as Coulee Dam, planning was nowhere evident: a ramshackle community a foot deep in mud, whose inhabitants—including 2,500 women: prostitutes, bar maids, taxi-dancers, beauty parlor operators, and housewives—were working largely in hope of profiting from land speculation. That assuredly was the goal of the six real estate agents Rorty located in the town and the powerful banks, railways, utilities, insurance, and real estate companies in the region. Rorty's views, blatantly expressed in public print, were no different from those expressed more privately by New Dealers and planners involved with developing the Columbia River Valley. With the enactment of the Columbia Basin Anti-Speculation Act and with the remarks of the President at Bonneville that year, plus the rate policies enunciated by J. D. Ross, the criticisms presented by Rorty in 1935 were less valid by the end of 1937. In the Anti-Speculation Act, Congress placed restrictions on the size of farms and provided for the recapture by the government of excessive profits in the sale of land. But since it did not provide funds for the purchase of lands to assist settlers, particularly immigrants and those who would be removed from submarginal farms to make way for the project, some New Dealers and others continued their criticisms.[21]

When Rorty visited the site in 1935 Grand Coulee, like Bonneville, had not yet received congressional authorization in the Rivers and Harbors bill. This measure, approved on August 20, authorized the construction, operation, and maintenance of the Grand Coulee Dam and necessary canals, structures, and other incidental works. It was considered the key project in planning for the comprehensive development of the Columbia River, and emphasis shifted between focusing on Grand Coulee's potential for industrial development and the possibility of turning a million acres of arid land into a diversified agricultural empire based on prosperous small farms. During the New Deal years both planners and promoters asked people to visualize the possibilities involved in harnessing the Columbia River, declared to have the highest power potential of any American river, and to view the progress made in constructing what would be the world's largest masonry structure.

Whereas at Bonneville the Corps of Engineers constructed the dam, at Grand Coulee the Bureau of Reclamation, with Frank A. Banks as construction engineer, was in charge. Construction of these projects kept before the American people the vision of a planned promised land. In the Pacific Northwest, thanks to developments on the Columbia River, there was a measure of cooperation between the federal government and state and local agencies that promised to promote a more viable economy. At that time the region diverted a goodly portion of the riches of its soil, forests, mines, and streams elsewhere to be consumed, fabricated, and coined into profits. And in turn, most of what it purchased had to be shipped in, much from east of the Mississippi River. Since in the Northwest materials were sold largely in the raw state, generating little labor income, the region was dependent upon finished products, the price of which included high freight rates and labor costs.

Developments on the Columbia River promised to keep in the Northwest some measure of the wealth which heretofore had been drained from the region. This would be done through planning and cooperation rather than, as in the past, through private exploitation of natural resources. More so than elsewhere in the West, the staggering engineering achievements were cast within a framework of concern for a more viable economy that would end the region's colonial status. The area gutted its natural resources for the benfit of consumers, merchants, processors, and manufacturers in other parts of the country; at the same time it had to import some of its foodstuffs along with much of the machinery and manufactured goods it utilized. In short, Grand Coulee would become the instrument through which the people, those long in the region and more recently attracted to it, could help plan and direct the social and economic currents of their harnessed river. The promise of a Pacific Northwest with thousands of new farms in the state of Washington and new industry throughout the region, allowed utopian visionaries, calculating planners, and even cautious skeptics to believe that Grand Coulee, "the most elaborate and expensive engineering development ever undertaken by a Government," was also a great lever of social change through which water and electric power would insure the planned promised land.[22]

Though a public enterprise, three private contractors performed the actual construction work on Grand Coulee Dam with Bureau of Reclamation engineers acting only in a supervisory capacity. Construction workers were housed in Mason City, a town created especially for this purpose. The government village, the town Rorty visited, was known as Coulee Dam. It was a temporary community and would not remain after the dam was completed. Mason City, the permanent community which Bureau of Reclamation engineers had called home since 1934, from the outset was heated by electricity. Coulee Dam initially was heated by oil furnaces and fireplaces. Mason City was a company town. Contractors operated all the facilities and charged what Richard Neuberger called "fairly high" prices. Coulee Dam was a more open, less-regulated community. A large number of the 6,000 workers on the project were young men, many from nearby colleges and universities. More than twenty employees lost their lives and rarely was there a day or night that one or more workers were not injured on the job. What these workers did in almost every respect established records, helping to make Grand Coulee the outstanding power and irrigation undertaking in the United States during the New Deal years.[23]

On December 10, 1937, Bureau of Reclamation officials at Spokane opened the bidding for contracts to complete Grand Coulee Dam in either 1941 or 1942, depending upon the rate at which Congress made needed funds available. Secretary Ickes in his remarks, delivered over a national radio network from Washington, while noting the profound influence the dam would have on the social and economic life of the Pacific Northwest, also stressed the point that "this is one of the most important conservation projects ever undertaken." And in this same month the Commissioner of Reclamation, John C. Page, called for organizing the entire project into one, but not more than two irrigation districts and cited the need for state laws necessary to comply with federal statutes to facilitate the program.

To insure that control of the irrigation area would be vested in the rural population, Page suggested that existing towns, as well as any that might develop in the vicinity of Grand Coulee Dam, be excluded from the irrigation area. In February 1939, landowners of central Washington, following Page's advice, voted overwhelmingly to form the largest irrigation district in the country, the first of two to be watered by the Grand Coulee Dam when it was completed. Harlan H. Barrows of the University of Chicago was engaged by the Bureau of Reclamation to direct the work of surveying and mapping the Columbia

Basin land below the dam. Irrigation proponents in the proposed district estimated it would take at least three additional years before canals would be in place and water available to enter the canals. The earliest year in which it was anticipated the project might deliver water to irrigation settlers was 1944. All of which indicated that the New Deal years would witness only the promise of the promised land.[24]

The President in 1939 also was concerned about the future of the promised land. He wrote to Secretary Ickes, "I believe it is time for us to plan for its use," which, as he saw it, divided itself into two parts. First, there was the matter of surplus power over and above the needs for pumping water onto basin lands. It affected the tie-in with the Bonneville Power Administration and public power groups, and it had a bearing on the site of a possible third dam in the Columbia River. Second, and equally important to Roosevelt, was the development of the Columbia Basin itself. He understood that when irrigation water became available, about 80,000 families could be placed on the land and that another 20,000 families would be engaged in servicing the needs of these settlers. As to the settlers, Roosevelt wanted to give "first chance to the 'Grapes of Wrath' families of the nation." He recognized that in successfully settling migratory families, supervision and instruction would be necessary to assist them in adjusting to intensive irrigation agriculture. In addition, the President thought a comprehensive economic survey was required so that the entire basin could be planned with the thought of making it "economically self supporting as far as possible."[25]

By 1940, at the end of the New Deal, officials in the Bureau of Reclamation were estimating that it would take a half century before the estimated 1.2 million acres of dry and largely unused land would be fully irrigated and in production, supporting an estimated increase of 500,000 people in the state of Washington. But by the time of the attack on Pearl Harbor, irrigation districts had been formed; the irrigable lands, thanks in part to the work of Harlan H. Barrows and his team of consultants, were being classified and appraised, and repayment contracts were being drafted. More than 30 agencies of federal, state, and local governments, educational institutions, civic organizations, and private businesses were involved with studies of a series of problems suggested by Barrows and his associates. These investigations represented one of the most ambitious attempts ever made to plan the development of a new reclamation area. Water for the first block of lands was anticipated in either 1943 or 1944, depending upon congressional appropriations for canal construction. Commissioner Page considered the project area comparable to a blank sheet of paper, a *tabula rasa*. The opportunity existed to sketch upon this sheet as perfect an agricultural community as could be devised, following the President's wishes that all planning take into account "that part of the new opportunities be extended to indigent but worthy farm families. . . ."[26]

On March 22, 1941, the first tangible result of the construction of Grand Coulee was achieved. It was a gala day. Two years in advance of schedule, turbines at the dam generated power which was transmitted to the Indians of the Colville Reservation adjacent to the project over the lines of a rural electric cooperative. President Roosevelt and Secretary Ickes sent eloquent messages contemplating the prospects that lay ahead, indicating once again that the most massive of New Deal undertakings would realize its potential and project the visions of its numerous promoters into reality during the critical war years when the capacity of power generated at Grand Coulee exceeded the total of the TVA dams.[27]

The final New Deal proposal to promote the planned promised land came to the fore in the spring of 1941. It aroused a tremendous controversy among New Dealers: Secretary Ickes, planners, and politicians in the region opposed the creation of an independent Columbia Valley Authority. Nevertheless, the proposal received serious consideration with the completion of Grand Coulee. To be sure, Ickes favored such a proposal provided he could select an administrator who would be directly responsible to him. Ickes was opposed to an independent TVA-like agency favored chiefly by Senator George W. Norris and other veterans of the power wars. Though the President thought it imperative that Congress quickly establish a permanent administration for the federally owned developments on the Columbia River, no decision was forthcoming. The Bonneville Power Authority, a temporary expedient, by default remains to this day the primary federal authority promoting regional interests.

From the outset planners in the region opposed a TVA-like agency. A 1936 report of the Pacific Northwest Regional Planning Commission concluded "an organizational framework equivalent to the TVA is not the best suited to the Columbia Basin. . . . the agency established for the transmission and sale of power should not be financially burdened with other types of service which were incapable of direct self support." These views were reflected in reports of the National Resources Committee chaired by Secretary Ickes who, in turn, continually reiterated them to the President. By 1941 Roosevelt publicly endorsed them.[28]

The President in writing to Senator Norris (whom he hoped to win over), expressed the hope that it would "be possible to set up a strong public power area in the Northwest so that local people will be distributing the power that is sold to them by the Federal authority. When this partnership has been firmly established," he concluded, "it will be impossible for any less progressive administration seriously to impair the work that we have done." But the veteran Nebraska Senator, the father of TVA, could not agree. Unless an independent agency was created, Norris said that it would become "a football of politics" and "degenerate into a political machine and will ultimately prove to be a stupendous failure." This battle coming late in the New Deal sharply divided public power proponents. It was part of a larger battle concerning the administration of various regional projects, both proposed and already functioning. The fight for a Columbia Valley Authority came to the forefront with the completion of Grand Coulee Dam in March 1941. It would continue on into the Truman Administration, when, despite presidential support, the proposal to establish a Columbia Valley Authority went down to defeat.[29]

If power was central to the impact of the New Deal in the Pacific Northwest, it was also an important aspect of the New Deal in the Southwest where conditions were vastly different and the impact of the New Deal was not nearly as significant. In fact, the impact there was less significant than in any other part of the West.

Chapter 11

California Is Different

ROBERT E. BURKE'S penetrating study, *Olson's New Deal for California* examines the administration of Culbert L. Olson (1938–42), the lone Democratic governor in the first half of the twentieth century. He concludes that it was basically a failure and comments continually on Olson's inability to secure the enactment of his reform program. If Olson's New Deal ended in failure, Franklin Roosevelt's New Deal enjoyed few successes in California. Many of its distinctive projects got under way too late to have much impact during the decade of depression and drought, while other programs became embedded in controversy that weakened their impact. Burke neatly summarized the impact of the New Deal when he wrote "California's role in this reform period was primarily passive, more so perhaps than that of any other major state."[1]

This is not to deny, of course, that California during the 1930s was one of the most tumultuous states, experiencing chaotic labor disturbances throughout its great agricultural heartland and on the San Francisco waterfront. The 1934 End Poverty in California (EPIC) gubernatorial campaign was one of the most exciting and viciously fought campaigns of the decade, while the plight of the "Okies" in the Golden State attracted national attention and projected the creative careers of two distinguished residents to national and even international recognition. Dorothea Lange and John Steinbeck, a talented photographer and a distinguished author, utilized the misery of migrants in California as the focus of their creative talents. And it was in California that Francis Everett Townsend, an obscure Long Beach medical official, launched his "Ham and Eggs" pension movement that spread like wildfire among senior citizens throughout the West with reverberations extending to the nation's capital. Yet despite chaotic conditions in California, often exacerbated by its racial and ethnic diversity, the impact of the New Deal in the state was considerably less than in any other part of the West.

Conditions in California certainly were as bad as elsewhere in the West. But opposition to aspects of the New Deal was perhaps stronger than in other states, and the Republican administration of Governor

Frank F. Merriam (1934–38) was singularly indifferent to the predicament of most people in the state. Moreover, several early New Deal programs suffered setbacks because of controversy among some administrators and indifference or hostility on the part of others. In addition, many unemployed Californians, insisting that "Self Help Beats Charity," organized cooperatives as one way of meeting their problems. Soon both skilled and unskilled workers were exchanging their services for food. The barter movement, occasionally assisted by a federal grant as in the case of a bankrupt sawmill operation near Oroville, allowed the workers to buy the mill and turn it into a cooperative producing unit. California had more self-help organizations than all the rest of the country, and barter had become for many an accepted way of life. In 1934 when Upton Sinclair, to the chagrin of New Dealers promoting and administering various programs, based his campaign on production for use he had no difficulty in relating to thousands upon thousands of Californians. By the summer of 1933, over 75,000 families in Los Angeles alone were involved with self-help cooperatives. And federal funds secured by unemployed workers through local Federal Emergency Relief Administration and Civil Works Administration operations assisted cooperative activities.[2]

One of the early scandals involving conflict between social workers and politicians occured in California and helped the New Deal get off on a poor footing in the state. In the summer of 1934 Ray Branion, head of CWA in California, and Pierce Williams, FERA western field representative, along with several other former CWA officials were indicted "for conspiracy to defraud the Government in allowing certain projects to have people put on the payroll without materials and equipment with which to work." Both men sought to follow Harry Hopkins's dictum to hire workers without regard for political affiliation; they ran into trouble with politicians who wished to provide jobs for deserving Democrats. Though the charges were dropped after the 1934 election, relations between New Dealers and California politicians were strained almost from the outset.[3]

While the state was buffeted with serious labor unrest, New Dealers played no significant role in any of these developments. Labor strife in San Francisco came to a head in 1934, first with a longshoremen's strike in the spring and summer, climaxed by a three-day general city strike in July. To be sure, while officials of the Department of Labor played a minor role in resolving differences that ended the strike, no New Deal policies or programs were involved directly, though section 7A of the National Industrial Recovery Act guaranteeing workers the right to organize played some role in stimulating the strike. And the National Longshoremen's Board, created by the President in June, made proposals in October that helped bring a measure of stability to Pacific Coast waterfronts.⁴ Nevertheless, the impact and influence of the New Deal in the labor disturbances was minimal.

On another level the New Deal helped ease tensions in the city and the Bay Area through Public Works Administration grants which provided jobs and helped speed the construction of San Francisco's mighty bridges. One, a combination double suspension and cantilever bridge cost almost $78 million and was the greatest double suspension bridge in the world, extending slightly over eight miles to Oakland and Berkeley on the east. The other, a record-breaking single suspension span, crossed the Golden Gate and joined San Francisco with Marin County on the north. Its cost was estimated at $35 million. Construction on both bridges, financed by bond issues, got under way before the New Deal was launched. PWA assistance speeded the work of the Bechtel and Kaiser organizations as members of Bridge Builders, Inc., the concern that built the Bay Bridge. It was opened in November 1936. The Golden Gate Bridge, constructed under the guidance of Joseph B. Strauss, a distinguished engineer who insisted that a bridge should be beautiful as well as useful, was completed in 1937.

On a more prosaic level, radical journalist Anna Louise Strong followed the advice of Mrs. Roosevelt that one could best understand the New Deal by examining its impact in a single county. She did not focus her attention on a major urban area. Instead she spent some time in Santa Clara County, some fifty miles south of San Francisco, chiefly because it provided her with an opportunity to visit with her sister. Strong noted that a Public Works Administration grant helped maintain and raise underground water levels, thereby relieving farmers of the annual cost of pumping water to the depleted wells in their orchards. She concluded that "the New Deal had fulfilled its typical function: to save the property owners from some of the ruin caused by their own mismanagement, and then to retire—without thanks."⁵

In San Jose, the county seat, she visited the new post office constructed with federal funds and tracked down the offices of several federal agencies scattered in buildings throughout the city. New Deal agencies, she perceptively remarked, had the term *administration* in their titles and granted funds under carefully prescribed guidelines. Pre-New Deal federal agencies usually were called associations; the Farm Loan Association and the Production Credit Association, for example, were cooperative organizations open to established farmers considered good business risks. These associations received federal funds which in turn were loaned to their members with a minimum of federal supervision. "The farther one goes down the economic scale," she concluded, "the more the people are compelled to submit to government." On the other hand "the further up the scale, the more they command."

Strong also visited a maternity ward and several tuberculosis cottages added to the county hospital by the Works Progress Administration. She was informed that the WPA also had improved the community's park system. Labor strife had considerably abated at the time of her visit. She noted without further comment that "workers in fruit packing sheds were organizing under shelter of the Wagner Act." In addition, bankrupt farmers were applying for rehabilitation loans at the local office of the Farm Security Administration, and at the National Youth Administration Office young people were receiving both guidance and financial assistance.

Strong said she intended to spend only three days listing the New Deal agencies. She finally turned the job over to others at the end of ten days, thereby noting the pervasiveness of the New Deal and the fact that it was affecting everyone's life, "serving some groups of people and dictating to others in various ways" and, she believed, "changing the whole organization of American life." The New Deal was engaging in these manifold activities, Strong wrote, because "the world smashed in 1929."[6]

What Anna Louise Strong saw and wrote about in San Jose and Santa Clara County was duplicated in one way or another in every community and county throughout the West and, taking into account regional variations, throughout the United States. The transformation of the landscape, the enrichment of public life, and "the relief of business" would be commented upon with variations of emphasis by other keen observers, such as Jonathan Daniels,[7] who, like Strong, prepared his accounts late in the 1930s. But it was not the New Deal in Santa Clara County that attracted outside attention to California during the 1930s. It was climate and the lure of opportunity in America's richest farming counties in the great Central Valley that eventually focused New Deal concern upon conditions in California in a most disparate way. Programs of the Department of Agriculture late in the New Deal sought to assist migratory workers, while projects falling within the ken of Harold Ickes directly assisted many Central Valley farmers in making their irrigated lands even more productive.

In 1933 and 1934 California was the most chaotic and tumultuous state in the Union. Besides labor disturbances in San Francisco and the EPIC campaign of Upton Sinclair, the state was plagued with a series of fiercely contested farm strikes. Overall, the New Deal played a minimal role, but it was in the latter area, affecting agricultural workers in the Central Valley, that the New Deal became directly involved in California affairs and made its small but significant contribution.

In the 1930s California and Iowa were the richest agricultural states. Several southern California counties consistently led the nation in the value of farm commodities produced. Many of the nation's fruits and vegetables were grown in California where ownership was often corporate and production was industrialized, involving a high degree of crop specialization as well as the use of expensive equipment and other facilities. The bulk of the crops were marketed outside the state, while the land was extensively cultivated on a large scale necessitating a heavy capital outlay and dependence upon seasonal and cheap labor. At the outset of the decade labor in the fields was largely ethnic: Hispanic (Mexican, Filipino, Chicano) and to a slight extent Hindu. However, as drought and depression engulfed the southern Great Plains and southern states west of the Mississippi River, individuals and families from these states drifted into California seeking new opportunities.

The history of California agriculture, the farm strikes led by radicals, and the extensive migration to California has already been detailed in an extensive literature and will be reiterated here only to the extent that it involved the New Deal.[8] Surprisingly, it was the National Recovery Administration and not a New Deal farm agency that was first involved, albeit briefly, in the wave of farm strikes.

Many of California's specialty farmers, faced with heavy fixed costs, abundant crops, and declining prices for their produce, sought to cut one of the fixed costs over which they had some control—wages paid to hired migratory workers. This endeavor led to the violent strikes and class conflict that aggravated conditions in the sunny fertile valleys of California. To ease their situation, producers took advantage of the marketing agreement provisions of the Agricultural Adjustment Act, but neither the legislation nor the contracts, designed to stabilize production by setting marketing quotas, concerned itself with wages paid to migratory workers. It was in the great upheaval involving over 10,000 pickers in the cotton-growing districts of the lower San Joaquin Valley in October 1933 that New Dealers, seeking to utilize section 7A of the National Industrial Labor Relations Act endorsing labor's right to organize, became briefly involved in farmer-labor relations in California.

The issue that quickly came to the fore was whether 7A could be applied to migratory farm workers. Could they be considered in the same category with workers in factories, shops, mines, and mills? The view of New Deal spokesmen was that the economic concerns of farm workers would be protected under the Agricultural Adjustment Act, but George Creel, Director of the Western District of the National Recovery Administration, ignored this view—as well as the fact that responsibility for settling industrial disputes had been transferred from the National Recovery Administration to the newly created National Labor Board. He sought to resolve the cotton strike by stating publicly that industrial disputes in agriculture came under the jurisdiction of the

National Labor Board and asserting that he was its representative in California. Both Creel's statement and assertion had no grounding in fact; nevertheless, he assumed responsibility of mediating the dispute "in a way fair to all," while letting the growers know that the government's sympathies were with them. He persuaded Governor James Rolph to appoint a fact-finding commission to review the strike situation and present a solution. He then suggested a wage of 75 cents per hundred pounds of cotton as a fair settlement, a suggestion the commission accepted and which Creel then sought to implement. Though both labor and growers denounced this suggestion, it became the basis for settling the cotton strike. Creel immediately sought to implement the labor policies he introduced in the name of the New Deal by contacting other growers to explain how they might curb union activities by working with government in equitably determining wages and working conditions. The solution to their labor troubles, Creel explained, consisted "in the promotion of some form of collective bargaining between employers and the workers, to the end that clear understandings may be reached and some sort of contractual relation promoted." Creel made it clear to employers that collective bargaining did not necessarily involve dealing with unions of their workers' choice and that they could make more effective use of California's criminal syndicalism law, instead of resorting to violence and lawlessness as in the cotton strike.

Creel resigned his position with the National Recovery Administration in 1934 to unsuccessfully challenge Upton Sinclair for the Democratic gubernatorial nomination. However, he deemed his high-handed role in the recovery program as preeminently successful and was proud of his contribution in promoting what he considered "a fundamental reorganization of our industrial structure along higher, finer lines. . . ." But once it became clear that Creel's role enjoyed no legal support and that government had no authority to intervene in agricultural labor disputes, farm employers felt free to contest all efforts to organize field workers and in March 1934 formed the Associated Farmers of California, Inc., to assist them. Creel's dubious intrusion marked the last effort of the New Deal to resolve labor relations in the agricultural regions of the Golden State. Late in the New Deal the Farm Security Administration played a role in meliorating living conditions of field workers. By that time California already had experienced a vast migration that made the plight of the "Anglo" newcomers as desperate as that of the strikers in the disorder and unrest accompanying the disturbances earlier in the New Deal.[9]

Migration westward of homeless people was keyed largely to the drought which in 1934 and again in 1936 and 1937 was particularly severe on the Great Plains, and the last four months of 1939 were drier over wider regions than any others in the decade. It was estimated that during the decade about 75,000 families had left the Great Plains drought area. That not all westward migrants came from critical drought areas on the Great Plains is indicated by the fact that during the 1930s about 110,000 families, largely from the southern Great Plains, migrated to California and about 43,000 families migrated to the Pacific Northwest states of Oregon, Washington, and Idaho. All were victims of the dislocating forces of depression, drought, and mechanization. Most of these families experienced difficulty in relocating themselves and most were victims of circumstances beyond their control. If their plight placed a responsibility upon their government, it was not fully evident in California until late in the New Deal.[10]

Since predominance of hired farm labor is found wherever intensification of agriculture requires a large amount of manual labor, gang labor for California's factories in the fields reached greater proportions than in any other state. The arrival of thousands of farm families exacerbated an already desperate situation for farm workers, and it threw large numbers of newly arrived "Anglo" farmers into competition with ethnic minority workers who previously were the vast majority. The groups provided pickers for California's specialized fruit, vegetable, and cotton crops. Tensions between these groups were heightened, but in several of the 1933 strikes various ethnic groups cooperated, and they would do so in other strikes during the decade. Nevertheless, the arrival of thousands of farm families from outside the state increased competition for jobs as well as ethnic tensions. It also increased class conflict. While these themes attracted a great deal of attention, both contemporary and historical, they did not immediately involve the New Deal.

From the beginning, the living conditions of migratory workers attracted attention. This theme was reiterated with variations in many reports: "filth, squalor, an entire absence of sanitation, and a crowding of human beings into totally inadequate tents or crude structures built of boards, weeds, and anything that was found at hand to give a pitiful semblance of a home at its worst." Early in the New Deal concerned citizens, such as photographer Dorothea Lange and her husband, Paul Taylor, a professor at the University of California at Berkeley, who at the time were employees of the Federal Emergency Relief Administration in its California Rural Rehabilitation Division, were calling for government camps where migrants could live decently with minimal, but adequate and sanitary, facilities. Lange with her penetrating photographs and Taylor with his accompanying remarks concentrated, albeit not exclusively, on the plight of newly arrived migrant families. As a result, largely because of the concern of aroused citizens, the Federal

Emergency Relief Administration allocated $20,000 in 1934 to construct two migrant labor camps, launching what Taylor called "the first federal public housing in the United States."[11]

But the idea of government camps aroused such opposition from growers and others—including the American Civil Liberties Union, which worried about the constitutional rights of migrants in these compounds—that proposals for the construction of additional camps were put aside for several years. Meanwhile migration into California continued and added conspicuously to the problems of relief, unemployment, housing, and health in the state, chiefly in the great agricultural counties of central and southern California. To many people in California the term *migrant* came to be synonymous with *indigent* and *migratory worker,* and popular attitudes toward newcomers became at best unfriendly and at worst actively hostile. Because of the large number of migrant families from Oklahoma, the term *Okie* assumed pejorative connotations and was applied to all newly arrived migrant families, even though as of 1930 only a little more than a third of the people in California (and in Washington and Oregon as well), were born in the state.[12]

Carey McWilliams, Chief of the Division of Immigration and Housing during the administration of California Governor Culbert L. Olson, estimated that 350,000 migrants in 1939 came across the Arizona border by automobile seeking employment. Since most of these people, like most of the migrants, were American citizens who moved as a family, their resettlement in California had far-reaching implications for the state. Unfortunately, as McWilliams candidly stated, "we have met this challenge by ignoring it." No plan or program was developed to assist the migrants, who fended for themselves, settling wherever and however they could. Social scientists and photographers in the employ of various bureaus or agencies, chiefly within the Department of Agriculture, prepared studies and photographs that explained and illuminated the nature and plight of the migrants. Aside from assistance on a limited scale by the Farm Security Administration late in the New Deal, the migrants essentially were on their own.

Carey McWilliams summed up this situation by quoting a phrase of British Prime Minister Neville Chamberlain, "We 'missed the bus.'" He illustrated it by noting the unplanned and undirected resettlement of migrants. Squatting or settling on the outskirts of existing communities; fleeing from submarginal lands they located on unoccupied marginal acres either doing without or receiving minimal community services and access to facilities. Tents and trailers were replaced by shacks and shanties, while the few who found jobs at the end of the decade were establishing themselves in small homes. The entire process was improvised and unplanned and could be observed throughout the San Joaquin Valley and in Los Angeles County as well. At every step along the way the migrants were taken advantage of by employers, realtors, local officials, and citizens who were not interested in having a "Little Oklahoma" in or near their established communities. Because of lack of planning on the part of the state, community lethargy or indifference, and political impotence on the part of the migrants, rural slums cluttered the California landscape, and those individuals who capitalized on resettling these migrants could be counted on to oppose any attempt by government to resolve this situation. This view was reiterated by many Californians who agreed that any meliorative actions would only encourage more Okies to cross into the state. To make this viewpoint self-evident, residence requirements for relief were increased and state officials sought to get out the message that there were no jobs in California. To ease the pressure for access to limited funds, local officials and others encouraged repatriation among Mexican groups, some of whom were willing to return because of expected reforms in the land situation there. Prior to 1935 migratory farm labor consisted largely of single men of Mexican or Filipino extraction who rode freight cars, hitch-hiked, or possibly trucked from harvest to harvest, lived in ranch bunkhouses when employed and in urban flophouses and cheap lodging between seasons. Thereafter, with the mass migration of farm families, migratory workers traveled with their families by automobile. When employed they lived with their families in camps provided by the growers or in improvised shelters; between seasons they often camped along the highway.[13]

What complicated the situation and made attempts to cope with it virtually impossible was the fact that migrants entering California collided and competed with the realities of industrial agriculture. Rather than meet head on the organized opposition of the Associated Farmers of California, state officials beat a hasty retreat after gathering the facts and offering suggestions because they lacked the political clout to implement their plans. If large-scale actions to cope with the deplorable situation affecting migrants in California were to be taken, it would have to be done by the federal government. When Washington got involved, its actions were too little and too late to affect the situation markedly.[14]

Two agencies were ideally equipped to assist in relocating farm families: the Bureau of Reclamation and the Farm Security Administration. The work of the bureau, to be examined in the following chapter, got under way too late in the New Deal to have any impact on the situation, while the Farm Security Administration had a choice to make. It could help settle migrants on large-scale cooperative farming projects comparable to those at Chandler and Casa Grande in Arizona,[15] or the agency could follow the more traditional pattern and scatter subsidized farmers in existing farm communities.

Here too the Farm Security Administration "missed the bus." Several model camps provided assistance to migrant families in the form of better living conditions and improved housing. There was little planning beyond this level that in any meaningful way affected their resettlement. The Farm Security Administration could not provide jobs. Its work took the form of rehabilitation, encountering the problem on the level of acute distress, meeting the emergency situation, and not considering the context in which this distress occurred: "the dictates of finance in a profit economy" predicated on an industrialized agricultural economy. The problem of stabilizing the migrant farm laborers of California became more acute during the 1930s but was not resolved by the New Deal. At best the problem gained widespread attention, and a deeper understanding of its dimensions was brought before interested citizens.

In Washington a Senate subcommittee chaired by Robert M. LaFollette, Jr., helped bring the problems of California agriculture to public attention. From 1936 to 1940 the Subcommittee on Education and Labor conducted "the most extensive investigation of civil liberties infractions ever undertaken by a Congressional committee." Its mandate was to investigate "violations of the rights of free speech and assembly and undue interference with the right of labor to organize and bargain collectively " It was not until 1939, however, that the committee took an interest in California and focused its attention on the impediments to farm labor organization. This was after the publication in the spring of John Steinbeck's angry novel, *The Grapes of Wrath,* and in July of Carey McWilliams's study, *Factories In the Field.* Also published in 1939 was the brilliant photographic essay, *An American Exodus: A Record of Human Erosion,* by Dorothea Lange and Paul S. Taylor, which helped to further arouse the attention of the New Deal.[16]

In the course of a year the committee heard many witnesses on various aspects of California's agricultural economy. It also received statistical tabulations and hitherto unpublished studies about California farming as it sought to investigate alleged violations of the rights of free speech and assembly and interference with the efforts of farm workers to organize and bargain collectively. Consequently the record of its hearings, the testimony of witnesses, and other materials provide a rich lode of information pertaining to conditions in a major sector of California agriculture during the New Deal.

However, the LaFollette committee's conclusions were clearly preempted several years earlier in the report of Pelham D. Glassford, who represented the National Labor Board and the Departments of Agriculture and Labor in the Imperial Valley during the strike by agricultural workers in 1934. Glassford stated:

> After more than two months of observation and investigation in Imperial Valley, it is my conviction that a group of growers have exploited a communist hysteria for the advancement of their own interests; that they have welcomed labor agitation, which they could brand as "red," as a means of sustaining supremacy by mob rule, thereby preserving what is essential to their profits, cheap labor; that they have succeeded in drawing into their conspiracy certain county officials who have become the principal tools of their machine.[17]

The LaFollette committee, concluding its investigation early in 1940, reviewed in a general way the scope and history of farm-labor problems and was told on several occasions by growers that they were losing money. One fruit grower said, "If it were not for Federal assistance, we'd all be bankrupt." One large ranch, generally considered among the most successful in the state, lost $450,000 in 1939. This type of data helped explain the violence and trampling of civil liberties involved in farmer-labor relations as well as the response of growers and their associates to the strikes and demands of migratory workers and others supporting their cause.[18]

The committee heard testimony reviewing conditions affecting the agricultural economy of a state dominated in all of its dimensions by large-scale industrialized operations: a state, for example, in which less than 10 percent of the cotton farmers controlled half of the cotton acreage; where 204 members of the Associated Farmers of California constituted only 2.34 percent of all cotton farmers and received 33 percent of all Agricultural Adjustment Administration cotton benefit payments in 1938 for California. And the situation for cotton was similar to that of practically every commercial crop raised in the state.

The committee, of course, focused attention on the labor situation and learned that large-scale mechanized farm operations resulted in a mechanization of the labor supply itself. It utilized workers, like farm machines, only when needed and discharged them once the particular operation was concluded. This type of specialized production tended to make large operators insensitive to the needs of workers, unconcerned about providing maximum employment or decent living conditions for their field workers. Because the labor force included large numbers of newly arrived migratory families, the committee was able to cite numerous infractions of civil liberties as these families sought to send their children to school, to have a home, to vote, to join a union and thereby seek to earn a living wage, to have access to services and rights available to other citizens. To secure these rights between 1933 and 1939 approximately 180 strikes occurred in 34 California counties, involving every major crop and at least 100,000 workers. Civil and criminal disturbances occurred in connection with 65 of the 180 strikes. Henry H. Fowler, chief counsel of the committee, commented that "California agriculture has and is suffering from employer-employee strife far out of proportion to the number of workers employed in comparison with the remainder of the country."

Since large-scale growers were effectively organized and met in advance of seasonal labor operations, they could agree among themselves on the wage scale and see that it was rigidly enforced. Once their workers sought to do the same thing, to organize and seek to improve the wage scale, tensions arose and erupted into conflicts pitting the growers against agricultural workers and others in the community, such as social workers, concerned with their plight. So well organized and so powerful were the Associated Farmers of California that they could muster support on all fronts from local officials and businessmen; in time of crisis they could deprive workers and their leaders of both their legal rights and access to credit. In turn the Associated Farmers had the backing of the great financial and industrial interests which controlled California agriculture.

As farmers who formerly enjoyed cheap and docile field labor found themselves dealing with increasingly belligerent migratory workers, vigilantism increased markedly, as the LaFollette committee noted. Fear of organization by field hands was intensified because the growers had a relatively short time to harvest their crops; a strike lasting two or more days in some instances could result in a lost crop. With local residents readily aroused by the presence of large numbers of strangers represented to be troublemakers, "reds," or "agitators," the step to vigilantism was made rather easy, especially because agricultural workers were exempt from the provisions of the National Labor Relations Act and thus were not guaranteed the right to participate in a supervised election and ballot in favor of a union of their own choice. Without that guarantee, union activities and strikes could come under the California Criminal Syndicalism Act. Growers fought all efforts to repeal this law and encouraged public authorities in refusing permits to assemble or to distribute leaflets. Moreover, since most migratory families had not established residency they had difficulty in gaining access to community welfare programs and did not qualify to participate in most New Deal programs.

Though the committee reports were not as widely read as the more popular studies that appeared in 1939, the work of the LaFollette subcommittee was more pervasive in its scope, more comprehensive in its findings, and more frightening in its conclusions. Paul S. Taylor, testifying before the subcommittee, suggested that California agriculture, with the largest rural wage-earning class in the country, provided a model of what agriculture might look like in other portions of the United States: diminishing income for farm workers, mounting rural poverty, displacement caused by mechanization,—all factors relating to agriculture increasingly geared to the arbitrary dictates of finance and a profit economy.[19]

The Federal Emergency Relief Administration constructed the first two migrant labor camps in California with funds appropriated in 1934, marking the initial participation of the New Deal in the melioration of labor conditions in California's agricultural regions. For more than two years thereafter, little was done either by employers, the state, or the New Deal. In 1936 the Resettlement Administration presented a program to break this impasse. Camps would be constructed to provide migratory families with minimum decencies: a healthful site, a pure water supply, sanitary facilities of all kinds, and other simple amenities. Ten to a dozen camps were planned; two were constructed by the Resettlement Administration before it was absorbed into the Farm Security Administration in 1937. One was at Marysville and the other near Weedpatch. Though these camps provided at best for only a small portion of the migrant families in California, they served as models that local communities and growers might emulate, and they emboldened state, county, and local officials to abolish squatters' camps and to force an improvement of facilities provided by farmers.

These camps, located in the harvest areas, made it easier for health and educational authorities to enforce the law and serve the needs of the migrants. They helped bring the problems of the migrants to the community and they allowed the migrants an opportunity to discuss their problems, including those pertaining to trade unionism and their right to organize and strike, in a reasonably calm and safe environment free from outside pressures. Moreover, contacts with the community were conducted on a friendlier basis than previously because families ensconced in a government camp no longer posed the same threat as a squalid Little Oklahoma. The government camps helped ease tensions exacerbated by the violent strikes in the summer and fall of 1936 that started in the lettuce sheds of Salinas when, early in September, 3,500 lettuce packers walked out to secure their demand for "preferential union hiring." These strikes, incidentally, marked a shift from the fields to the packing sheds and canneries and involved ethnic groups and local citizens more so than members of migratory families, though this distinction was not self-evident at the time.[20]

The availability of migratory farm labor at low wages assisted large growers in competing successfully during the depression years. At the same time, migratory farm families became victims of poverty, ill health, and miserable housing conditions in the great agricultural valleys where these Dust Bowl and Cotton Belt families became the victims of all the prejudices local inhabitants could manifest toward poverty-stricken outsiders. The great virtue of the government camps, constructed and operated after 1937 by the Farm Security Administration, was that they gave these migratory families an opportunity for an organized group life of their own. They helped make their emergence into the broader community, later facilitated by defense preparations and then by the war effort, less of an ordeal than their previous experiences in California.

Anna Louise Strong visited the camp at Visalia and found rows of tent platforms and one-room structures comparable to a military encampment designed to provide minimum space with maximum comfort. Community buildings with hot and cold water, showers, toilets, and laundry facilities were located in the middle of the camp. Nearby was a schoolhouse, playground, and a clinic. Strong found that recently planted trees were already providing enough shade for mothers with small babies to gather under them. At the time of her visit, 317 families lived there, and she remarked that "with all its crudeness the camp was almost the first place they had found in the fruitful valleys where they could be human beings, with human dignity and will."

Despite a constant change in campers, the camp retained a community atmosphere. Since it was administered by the campers themselves through elected councils, the sense of not belonging, of complete homelessness, was erased for the migrant families entering one or another of the government camps. Camp newspapers, for example, listed the names of incoming and outgoing families, presented the daily or weekly schedule of activities: dances, ballgames, suppers, meetings, and minutes of meetings, along with letters from former campers, and the camp manager. There were quotations from government reports, local newspapers, and articles by the camp nurse and others. There were also recipes, market lists, personals, a society column and, of course, births and deaths were duly noted.[21]

Near the Visalia camp was the Mineral King Ranch which the Resettlement Administration had purchased and, like Casa Grande in Arizona, started operating as a cooperative farm. The Farm Security Administration continued with the work of further equipping and leasing this 520-acre farm to a group of farm laborers for $3,500 a year, a sum covering taxes, interest, and amortization. The farm was operated by fifteen families who elected a board of directors. The Resettlement Administration appointed the farm manager and extended a $5,000 loan to launch the operation, which had been repaid by the time Strong visited the farm. She also learned that the board of directors ended the year with a surplus of $8,892 after all expenses, including rent and wages, had been met. Using the surplus to purchase a dairy herd, the board hoped to add more families to their group. But Mineral King, like Casa Grande, was an experiment. Its operation aroused community opposition and the cooperative approach caused internal tensions that prompted its demise during the war years when Mineral King was sold and the profits divided among the members.[22]

To establish the camp at Weedpatch, south of Bakersfield and surrounded by vast estates, federal officials agreed to forbid all union organization on the premises. This was the exception rather than the rule, though at the outset all the camps experienced hostile community pressures. In all the camps migratory families were charged ten cents a day for a camping site, the money being utilized for equipment to promote recreation and camp comfort. A form of self-government prevailed in all the camps and those who would not abide by the imposed rules and regulations were asked to leave. In the camps news spread about the need for workers in various localities, largely through the efforts of the Farm Placement Service in passing such information along to local Farm Security Administration officials. Unfortunately, the federal camps were the exception rather than the accepted pattern. They performed a valuable service on a limited scale shortly before the situation abated, owing to war in Europe and concerted efforts by Carey McWilliams and other California officials during the administration of Culbert L. Olson. Thereafter migratory workers disappeared into other sectors of California's expanding economy, induced by World War II.[23]

Though there were about 8,000 labor camps in California by 1940, only four were inspected and few could compare favorably with the sparse facilities, and opportunities provided by the Farm Security Administration. But by 1940 as migration into California slackened (having peaked in 1937–38), the state was beginning to play a meaningful role in working with migratory families to equalize educational opportunities in the agricultural districts, to prevent the spread of disease, and to cope with malnutrition in migratory families. The state also began to operate mobile birth clinics. In doing so it assumed responsibilities that the Farm Security Administration engaged in on a limited scale: assisting local authorities with problems affecting migrant families pertaining to relief, medical aid, housing, and helping a fortunate handful of migrant families in renting farms.[24]

There is no doubt that concentrations of migratory families put a tremendous added burden on county and community facilities. Kern County in the upper San Joaquin Valley (and the locale of the Farm Security Administration camp described in *The Grapes of Wrath*) for the fiscal year ending June 30, 1939, spent approximately $4,280,000 for various categories of relief, including federal, state, and local contributions. Kern County had a total fixed population of about 124,000 people. The 1939 cotton crop in the county was valued at about $5 million, indicating that the cost of relief almost equalled the total value of a major crop, one which required migrant workers. Though not all of Kern County's relief expenditures were made for migratory families, in the absence of a detailed analysis of the data, it can be assumed that such recipients constituted a heavy portion of the load. For example, of an estimated 727 babies born to migrants in Kern County, 544 were born in the county hospital, constituting 44 percent of all babies born in the hospital during the year.[25]

By the end of the decade the Farm Security Administration had ten permanent and at least five mobile camps in operation in California. Plans, never fully acted upon, called for from 20 to 48 small frame houses to be constructed at each location to be rented to select migrant families who could work for nearby growers and at the same time raise food for their own use on their home lots. Success in coping with the problems of migratory workers was accomplished at the end of the decade primarily because the Olson administration was sympathetic to the plight of migratory families and because the number of new arrivals was declining, owing in part to active federal programs by the Farm Security Administration and other New Deal agencies in the Dust Bowl and cotton-growing areas from whence came most of California's migrant families. But migratory workers were not eligible to benefit from a major New Deal program: Social Security. California Congressman Jerry Voorhis tried and failed to extend the medical and financial provisions of Social Security to migrants. In brief, the Farm Security Administration did more to lessen the distress of migrant families than any private, county, state or federal agency active in California during the New Deal. Funds for the migrant camps were derived from allocations made to the Farm Security Administration from annual relief emergency appropriations. Beginning in 1939 these funds were drastically curtailed as congressional critics sought to phase the agency and its several programs out of existence.[26]

In November 1941 the United States Supreme Court in *Edwards* v. *California* (314 US 160) set aside California's "Indigent Act," approved in 1933, which had made it a misdemeanor to bring into the state an "indigent person." Under guise of this law some local and county officials had sought to turn back migratory families crossing into California from Arizona, while others arrested, fined, and jailed migrant workers in their particular localities. Most of these incidents occurred in 1939 and 1940 but the law had served as an additional burden or threat hovering over migratory families. When it was set aside at the end of the New Deal, two weeks before Pearl Harbor, conditions for migratory families were easing and changing, in some instances for the better. But like almost everything else about the New Deal in California, it came too late and it did not immediately affect the magnitude of the farm crisis in the great agricultural valleys of the state.

War in Europe and America's defense efforts markedly shifted the disadvantaged position of migrant workers and led to an improvement in the economic and social position of migratory families in California. Assimilation became easier as jobs opened in industries centered in urban communities. Nevertheless, the plight of the migratory worker in industrialized agriculture in California and elsewhere throughout the nation continues unabated, with conditions in some parts of the country rivaling those which came to public attention in California during the New Deal. What news commentator Edward R. Murrow in 1960 called a "Harvest of Shame" periodically comes to national attention. In the postwar years the situation reverted to the condition prevailing in California prior to the New Deal. By then the vast majority of the migratory workers were of Hispanic origins; the ordeal of the Okies, migratory families from the Dust Bowl and the cotton fields of the Southwest, ended when New Deal concerns gave way to wartime demands.

Chapter 12

Interior's California

THE NEW DEAL IN California came too late and had a minimum impact upon those who should have benefited most from its programs and policies, the victims of the Great Depression—the migrants from man-made and natural disasters afflicting other parts of the West who poured into the Golden State. Their problems have already been discussed in examining the role of the Department of Agriculture. But Harold Ickes, the dominant figure of the New Deal in the West, was also involved with federal developments in California. Ironically, though the issues were not resolved during the New Deal years, the thrust of the programs endorsed by the Department of the Interior presaged assistance to California's large landowners and further consolidated and strengthened their position in the great interior valleys by assuring them an expanded and continual supply of water for the crops migratory workers picked. Ickes was aware of this possibility, stating in an address delivered after he left public office that "the future of this State of California possesses great potentialities. That very same future, as most Californians know, holds equally the germ of a disaster as great as ever confronted by this state."[1]

There was one notable exception, a new national park, one of two in the West that Ickes was instrumental in creating during the New Deal years. The territory extending from the Tehipite Valley to the Tule River is termed the Kings Canyon region because it contains the canyons of the south and middle forks of Kings River, whose walls rise on both sides from 3,000 to 5,000 feet above the valley floors. The area is a wild region of massive peaks, glacial cirques, and lake-dotted plateaus from 10,000 to 14,000 feet above sea level. In 1890 part of the region was set aside as Sequoia National Park, the second national park, to save its magnificent grove of sequoia trees. Nothing had been done, however—despite the efforts of John Muir, the Sierra Club, and others—to preserve the equally impressive wild scenery in its pristine state. As early as 1934 Ickes proposed to bring this area into the park system. Part of it, containing another grove of sequoias, was preserved as General Grant National Park, created in 1890, three weeks after Sequoia was established. In 1926 the size of Sequoia was more than doubled and thereafter the clamor to preserve the wild scenery increased. Ickes responded to it early in his tenure as secretary of the interior.

Like Olympic National Park, Ickes wished the proposed park to be treated as a primitive wilderness. Foot and horse trails to provide reasonable access would be encouraged, but roads would be held to an absolute minimum. While fishing would be encouraged, all other species of wildlife would be protected. Ickes knew exactly what kind of a park he wished to be created in this high mountain area. All that remained was for Congress to approve its creation.[2]

A bill (H.R. 10436) introduced in 1938 proposed to do just that by transferring from the Forest to the Park Service some 415,000 acres, including much of the finest High Sierra scenery. Ickes, of course, favored it. Henry Wallace, believing that the Kings River Canyon area should retain its national forest status, opposed it. Sportsmen, resenting Icke's opposition to hunting in the area, agreed with Wallace. While Ickes and Wallace feuded over the status of this magnificently forested and scenic area, the state of California was constructing a highway, clearing an area half a mile wide and 12 miles long, that would terminate in a canyon valley on the south fork of the Kings River, a site that compared favorably with the valley of the Yosemite. To provide himself with further information and to keep himself abreast of sentiment in the area, Ickes appointed Irving Brant and Horace Albright as special consultants and sent them off to California to investigate.[3]

The President reviewed the differences between his secretaries and then endorsed the park proposal. Early in the next Congress, the Seventy-Sixth, a new measure was introduced calling, as Ickes wished, for a "primeval" national park. The Sierra Club enthusiastically seconded the proposal and suggested that the park be named after John Muir. Like Ickes, the club was concerned that the primeval, roadless character of the region be guaranteed and that the state highway not be extended beyond the canyon floor.

Opposition came primarily from two groups: one group claimed that power resources would be locked up and another claimed that water for irrigation would be lost. Proponents, including the Sierra Club, the Commissioner of Reclamation, and the Chief of the Army Engineers, argued that satisfactory alternate reservoir sites for power and irrigation purposes were available outside the proposed park area. They agreed that the primeval status of the proposed park should not be impeded. An amendment adding such reservoirs to the bill (which also signified that the park be called Kings Canyon National Park) was voted down by a large majority in the House. Since the area contained little commercial timber, no mineral ores, and only a few small patches of grazing land, the measure faced minimum opposition on these grounds. At the House hearing it was endorsed by the Chief of the Forest Service. In the Senate it was unanimously approved by the Public Lands Committee. On the floor, however, Key Pittman objected to its prompt consideration, automatically dropping the bill from its priority place on the Senate calendar. Its chances for passage during the session would have been nil had not Senator Pittman withdrawn his objection; later other objections were raised and this meant that it would carry over to the third session of the Seventy-Sixth Congress scheduled to convene in January 1940.[4]

On February 19, 1940, the bill was brought up and passed the same day, despite speeches in opposition by Senators Pittman of Nevada and Henry F. Ashurst of Arizona. On March 4, 1940, it was approved by the President and Ickes had the satisfaction of playing a prominent role in helping establish a second primeval national park in the West during his tenure as secretary of the interior.

While all but 4,000 of the 454,000 acres in the High Sierras comprising the park were already owned by the United States, the land acquired by purchase included the famous Redwood Mountain and Redwood Canyon grove of giant sequoias, adjacent to General Grant National Park, now a grove within the new Kings Canyon National Park. Redwood Mountain, previously threatened by timbering operations, contained more than 7,000 large sequoias, including possibly the largest tree in the world, the Hart tree. This grove of sequoias is one of the largest and most diversified in existence.

Kings Canyon represented the preservationist aspect of Ickes's conservation views in California. Calling for its creation was a relatively easy decision for him to make. Water and lumber, essential to the well-being and happiness of people in the valleys and cities below, was or would be provided without desecrating this area. Prior administrations had not made commitments that he could ignore with impunity, and there were few contesting parties whose interests he had to consider seriously and balance before arriving at a decision. As an ardent conservationist and nature lover, the creation of Kings Canyon National Park provided Ickes with satisfactions that no other aspect of his role during the New Deal years offered.[5]

The other aspect of the Department of the Interior's programs affecting the New Deal in the Golden State focused on utilization and development of water and power resources which would directly benefit large farm operators, a group opposed to Kings Canyon and to New Deal programs designed to assist migratory families. If Ickes was aware of these ironies, he kept the matter to himself. There was no irony, however, about the problem of water in California. It was largely one of transportation: bringing water from either the Colorado River, forming the southeastern border of the state, or from the rich watershed in its northern mountains. Dams, reservoirs, canals, pipelines, pumping stations, and power plants were all integral parts of the water problem. It concerned both residents of San Francisco and Los Angeles as well as farmers throughout the vast arid reaches of the Sacramento and San Joaquin River valleys. By 1936, thanks to federal funds, water from Lake Mead behind Boulder Dam on the Colorado River was coursing 400 miles over a newly completed aqueduct to Los Angeles.

The Reconstruction Finance Corporation had supplied loans to the Metropolitan Water District for the completion of a 300-mile aqueduct tunneling mountains and stretching over valleys and deserts to provide greater Los Angeles with an abundant water supply. In addition, with federal funding the Bureau of Power and Light was completing a high-tension line from Boulder Dam to continue providing the Los Angeles area with ample and inexpensive electric power.

San Francisco, on the other hand, received much of its water from the Hetch Hetchy Valley in Yosemite National Park. This arrangement, calling for the construction of a dam in the park, was agreed upon only after a tremendous battle involving and dividing all the friends of conservation (along with many progressives) in the early years of the New Freedom. The battle's aftermath still concerned Harold Ickes, as Secretary of the Interior, during the New Deal.

What concerned Ickes was not the water flowing to San Francisco, but the power that the 1913 enabling act permitted the city to develop and use for the benefit of its citizens. It specifically forbade the sale of both water and power rights to private corporations for private gain. Under this law San Francisco constructed at a cost of about $50 million, dams, tunnels, and power plants. But the city supervisors failed to develop a municipal distribution system, leaving this necessary chore to the Pacific Gas and Electric Company which continued to service the city, purchasing part of its power from city-owned plants.

Ickes, as an old progressive and public power advocate, was outraged by these developments and as Secretary of the Interior sought to determine if the 1913 enabling measure, the Raker Act, was being violated. The 1913 law, he insisted, prohibited San Francisco "from selling or reselling power, except directly to its consumers." Pacific Gas and Electric therefore had no legal authority to distribute and sell electricity in the city. Discussing the matter with officials and others in San Francisco yielded no agreement with Ickes's view. Only two city commissioners supported him.[6]

As a result of Ickes's persistence several plans were presented to assure that San Francisco complied with the law. In April 1936 he held that one proposal when perfected would comply with the statute. The plan called for San Francisco to spend its funds for a distributing system. A year later nothing had changed and Ickes insisted that the U.S. Attorney General institute proceedings against the City and County of San Francisco. In 1938 Judge Michael E. Roche of the federal district court decided in the government's favor. But Ickes learned that the city, rather than start constructing a distributive system or seeking to purchase Pacific Gas and Electric's, proposed to appeal, if necessary, to the Supreme Court.

Mayor Angelo Rossi charged that Ickes intended to withhold approval of pending PWA projects because the city contemplated appealing Judge Roche's decision. Ickes admitted that Rossi's charge "was not entirely an unjustified one." While the President agreed with Ickes's position, San Francisco during the New Deal years never challenged Pacific Gas and Electric's right to deal directly with consumers. It constructed an addition to the Hetch Hetchy Dam in 1938 to increase its water supply, but despite a lower court decision and a 1940 Supreme Court ruling (310 US 16) upholding Judge Roche, the city to this day does not manage its own distribution system.[7]

San Francisco did not directly flout the Supreme Court. It called for a special election on a bond issue to raise funds for constructing a distributing system on November 4, 1941. Ickes delivered a strong address in San Francisco on October 28 reviewing the controversy, denouncing Pacific Gas and Electric, and calling upon the voters to fulfill the mandate of the Supreme Court by approving the bond issue. They did not. In 1945 Judge Roche denied San Francisco's request to suspend the court order that it directly service its residents with electric power. Ickes pursued the matter after he left public office suggesting that his successor also initiate legal action to devise a means of bringing about full compliance by the City and County of San Francisco with all the provisions of the 1913 law.[8]

Hetch Hetchy represented a serious setback for Ickes and the proponents of public power. In this sense it also represented a setback for the New Deal in California where its policies and programs were too little and too late or tended to serve the best interests of those who were usually opposed to the President and to the New Deal governor of California, Culbert L. Olson.[9]

In providing water for irrigation, the New Deal enjoyed its greatest success in California, much to the satisfaction of the large-scale farmers who usually opposed the New Deal. Ickes did not have to grapple fully during the New Deal years with the 160-acre principle embedded in the 1902 Reclamation Act. It would be challenged by "factory" farmers demanding more water for their vast acreages and prompt a titanic controversy involving the Corps of Engineers in the years immediately following the New Deal.

An All-American canal to provide Colorado River water to increase irrigation in the Imperial and Coachella Valleys was a dream that Boulder Dam made possible. Prior to the completion of this canal, farmers in these valleys received water from a canal that traversed Mexican territory. It irrigated numerous farms in Mexico, mostly owned by American citizens, before reaching the Imperial Valley where users had to pay high rates to maintain and improve the privately owned irrigation ditch. Owing to silt that accompanied the water into the canal, dredging costs by the early 1930s amounted to about $1 million a year. This meant that Imperial Valley farmers received less water at higher rates. When the Colorado River crested, it usually spilled over its banks and flood waters poured into the Imperial Valley, a large portion of which is below sea level. A dam that would keep these waters in check and then release them in volume to supply irrigation ditches was a plan behind the construction of the All-American Canal by the Bureau of Reclamation with additional support from Ickes in the form of PWA grants.[10]

An initial PWA allotment of $9 million launched the construction of 80 miles of the main canal extending from the Colorado River to the Imperial Valley and the 130-mile branch to the Coachella Valley. It was authorized initially as part of the Boulder Dam project in 1928. The water users in each of these valleys, through contracts with the Interior Department, agreed to pay a pro rata share of the cost of the canal, which was anticipated to irrigate approximately a million acres of rich desert lands in these two valleys, in addition to the 500,000 acres already irrigated in the Imperial Valley. What this development would mean was dramatically indicated in 1934 when the productive Imperial Valley suffered its most severe drought. The Colorado River virtually ran dry, resulting in crop losses approximating $10 million. The completion of Boulder Dam ended this menace, as well as the threat of floods.[11]

The world's largest dragline excavation, lifting 16 tons at a time, cleared the world's largest irrigation ditch to provide valley farmers with 25 times as much water as they had been getting. By the end of 1936, over half of the 80 miles of canal had been dug to prepare for a stream whose flow would equal that of the Potomac at Washington. Two years later, on October 18, 1938, at the new Imperial Diversion Dam, Ickes pressed a button opening the four All-American Canal headgates and the six influent channel gates into the desilting basins, and the Imperial Valley, a desert area at the outset of the century, now could fulfill its potential as an agricultural empire, the "Winter Garden of America," providing the nation with melons, dates, citrus fruits, peas, carrots, lettuce, and long-staple cotton.

By October 1938 when the All-American Canal was opened, federal expenditure totaled approximately $24 million. By the terms of the

December 31, 1932, contract between the United States and the Imperial Irrigation District (later joined by the Coachella Valley County Water District), these districts agreed to repay to the United States the total cost of the canal over a period of 40 years without interest. The contract also allowed the breaching of the 160-acre provision called for in the Reclamation Act. Assured of a steady and abundant supply of water, freed from concern about flooding or siltage, growers in both these districts had reason for satisfaction with the New Deal, mitigating their distaste for the role of the Farm Security Administration in its efforts to meliorate the plight of the stoop laborers picking the ever bountiful crops now assured to them.

To be sure, the water that Ickes turned into the canal merely marked the onset of a seasoning period during which particles of silt carried in the waters would seal the bottom and sides of the canal against seepage and loss. Farmers would not receive All-American Canal water for another two years, not until October 12, 1940. And yet to be constructed was the branch canal into the Coachella Valley. Coming late in the New Deal, the All-American Canal promised a prosperous future for those who could benefit directly from the activities of the Bureau of Reclamation in bringing water and electric power to various regions throughout the Inland Empire.[12]

A similar situation prevailed with regard to the most important venture that involved Ickes in California. The Central Valley Project got underway in earnest during the New Deal years. Its completion and the controversy it aroused came later. But here too a good portion of the benefits would accrue to the "factory" farmers of the Sacramento and San Joaquin River valleys, even though the President, Ickes, and the New Deal endorsed the concept of the family farm and the redistributive purpose embedded in the 1902 and later Reclamation Acts. Water from the Central Valley project would irrigate private lands and in most instances would supplement available waters, whereas in the Imperial Valley a public project replaced a private company providing water to irrigate private lands utilizing large numbers of migrant workers. In both instances public projects would be providing water to private lands in excess of 160 acres.

In August 1937 Congress approved the Central Valley Project Act, providing the Bureau of Reclamation with $12 million (nonreimbursable) toward project construction. The act stated that reclamation law was to govern other repayments and listed the dam and reservoir uses: first, river regulation, navigation, and flood control; second, irrigation and domestic uses; and third, power. The Central Valley Project, like others in the West, benefited from PWA grants and CCC labor during the New Deal years. It began operation in 1947, but construction was well under way by the time the United States entered

World War II. The project became the Bureau of Reclamation's greatest venture, irrigating 2 million acres and costing $2.3 billion, about half of which had been allocated to irrigation and would be returned to the U.S. Treasury.[13]

The Great Central Valley of California is surrounded by mountains: the Sierra Nevada on the east, the Coast Range on the west, the Siskiyous on the north, and the Tehachapi Range on the south. It is a 500-mile oblong watershed stretching through the interior of the state with an average width of 125 miles. The valley's floor consists of a 400-mile-long alluvial plain with an average width of 45 miles. Two river systems, the Sacramento in the northern portion and the San Joaquin in the southern portion, drain the valley. They meet, meander westward through the Delta, a low agricultural area, and on through the Carquinez Straits into San Francisco Bay. The valley was inhabited in 1937 by about 900,000 people.

Irrigation in one form or another had been conducted in the valley since the Gold Rush days. By 1939 about 2.75 million acres were irrigated, more than half of it from wells that pumped ground water to the surface. By the time the federal government became involved, ground water was being used faster than nature was restoring it. State officials long before the New Deal considered plans for developing the Central Valley, for bringing water from Sacramento Valley where most of the precipitation occurred to the more thirsty and irrigable lands in the larger, drier, and warmer San Joaquin Valley, for storing waters instead of allowing spring freshets to flow undisturbed to the sea. California state engineers coped with these problems and considered the generation of hydroelectric power, transmission lines, navigation, flood control, and incursions of salt water backing up from San Francisco Bay into the Delta as well. The last California plan, prior to the Bureau of Reclamation's involvement in August 1937, was presented by the state engineer in 1930. Both of these plans foresaw multiple benefits accruing chiefly to the agricultural interests throughout the valley who, according to a provision of the 1937 law, would be bound by the 160-acre water limitation first expressed in the 1902 Reclamation Act. Benefits of the Central Valley Project, as Ickes and other New Dealers wished, would be distributed widely and should not favor the large producers, the land monopolists so prevalent in many sections of the valley. The California legislature agreed. In 1936 both houses requested Congress, in a memorial citing the reclamation law, to approve and fund the Central Valley project. The assault on the 160-acre limitation as well as the preference clause in the power contracts got under way during the war years and continued hotly and somewhat successfully on into the Eisenhower presidency and beyond.[14]

As initially projected by the State of California and the Bureau of

Reclamation, the Central Valley Project contained four main components, all designed to bring water from the Sacramento to the San Joaquin Valley, from where there was too much to where there was too little. The components involved a series of dams, canals, power plants, and transmission lines. The coordinated canals, conveying water in some instances as far as 500 miles, provided the principal engineering feature of the project. Construction was well underway before World War II when the work was retarded. By that time the Bureau of Reclamation had already invested about $200 million in the project.[15]

In 1933 the California legislature sought to implement the 1930 plan of the state engineer but was unable to raise the $170 million needed to launch the project. In 1935 the New Deal came to the rescue with a $20 million allotment, approved by the President to the Bureau of Reclamation, to start the project. The federal government assumed financial responsibility in 1937 at the behest of the California legislature. During the New Deal years landowners throughout the Central Valley offered no objections to this project; they thought it would provide their salvation. Reclamation law forbade water to any one family beyond that needed to irrigate at most 320 acres, 160 acres per spouse. Large landowners could receive water only by agreeing to sell their excess lands within three years. In the midst of the depression and the euphoria of getting the project started, large landowners, absorbed in combatting the demands of migratory workers, found little time to concern themselves with the implications of a problem that was far from pressing and immediate. For a brief period under Ickes's tenure, resource planning in California was primarily a matter of engineering, during which time people in the Central Valley and elsewhere did not reckon their futures in terms of adjusting their property, institutions, and their individual wills to the engineering of collective action and responsibility.

This situation changed noticeably in 1940 at the end of the New Deal with the proposal of the Corps of Engineers for a "flood control" dam at Pine Flat on the Kings River, a tributary of the San Joaquin. Since the army does not charge citizens for its services, landowners could receive water provided from dams constructed by the Corps of Engineers without an acreage limitation and, equally important, without paying for it. In addition, Pacific Gas and Electric by requesting a power license at a dam constructed by the Corps of Engineers hoped to get around the preference clause. If the Corps of Engineers were to play a role in the Central Valley Project, many of the restrictions large landowners and the Pacific Gas and Electric Company would encounter under the aegis of the Bureau of Reclamation would evaporate.

Beginning with a feasibility report transmitted to Congress on February 10, 1940, Ickes of course insisted that development on the Kings River should be under the auspices of the Bureau of Reclamation, "and that the portion of the project cost to be charged to irrigation should be financed on the basis of the prevailing Federal policy of forty annual payments by irrigation beneficiaries." Franklin Roosevelt agreed that proposed developments on the Kings River and other tributary streams were predominantly irrigation projects that should be constructed "at the appropriate time" by the Bureau of Reclamation and not by the Corps of Engineers. That ended the controversy during what remained of the New Deal. But it reasserted itself late in the war years.[16]

While controversy surrounded and eventually engulfed the Central Valley Project, discussion of the specific details of construction did not get under way until the fall of 1935. In November the Department of the Interior presented a finding of feasibility that the project would be self-liquidating through the sale of electricity and water. The estimated cost, following the figure California authorities had developed, was $170 million. Elwood Mead, Commissioner of Reclamation, in September 1935 determined the order of construction to be followed after the approval of the $20 million allotment to launch the project. Mead said a dam at Friant on the San Joaquin River would be the principal work undertaken. Estimated to cost $14 million, the dam would be 250 feet high and would store approximately 400,000 acre feet of water to help irrigate 200,000 acres of highly developed agricultural land slowly reverting to desert because of the depleting supply of underground water. Two canals, the Madera and the Friant-Kern, would carry this water and were integral parts of the proposal.

Another major feature of the Central Valley Project, the Contra Costa Conduit, would provide fresh water to cities in the Delta whose supplies had been encroached by salt water infiltrating from San Francisco Bay. To complete this first phase of construction, Mead proposed a stand-by steam plant for generation of electric power and a distribution system in the Bay Area to make full use of the power that would be generated after the construction of a high dam on the Sacramento River. Total cost of these units, as estimated by Mead, was $12 million. With the construction of Friant Dam, there would remain $6 million from the allotment for expenditure on these units.[17]

Shortly after this allotment was announced it was modified. On December 10, Ickes announced that the President had approved a reallocation of $14 million of work relief funds for commencing work on the Central Valley Project. Instead of focusing exclusively on Friant Dam, initial work was started on the above-mentioned and other units on the Sacramento River utilizing Works Progress Administration laborers. As construction engineer in charge of the project, the Bureau of Reclamation brought in Walker R. Young, supervising engineer during the construction of Boulder Dam.[18]

Until October 1937 work was confined to extensive surveys, damsite exploration, and camp building. Much time also was devoted to right-of-way and water-right matters so that construction would not be delayed by involved court procedure. Actual construction began on October 14 on a four-mile section of the Contra Costa Canal. For construction purposes the vast multipurpose project was divided into three divisions. The Kennett Division in the north would include the giant Shasta Dam and Reservoir on the Sacramento River with a hydroelectric plant and a 200-unit transmission line. The Delta Division would include a Sacramento-San Joaquin Cross Channel, the Contra Costa Canal, and a pumping station in the northern San Joaquin Valley. The Friant Division in the south included the Friant Dam and Reservoir, plus the two canals designed to bring its water to areas both north and south of its location in the San Joaquin Valley.

The centerpiece of the entire project, the major construction effort, the second largest concrete dam in the world, exceeded in mass only by Grand Coulee and in height only by Boulder Dam, was Shasta Dam. Its site was finally chosen in January 1937 and construction began the following year. Its height was approximately 560 feet from its lowest foundation to the top, taller at the time than the tallest skyscrapers in the West. Its length of 3,400 feet on the crest was comparable to seven ordinary city blocks extending from end to end. The release of water at Shasta Dam, it was estimated in 1938 as construction was getting under way, would generate about 1.5 billion kilowatt hours of electricity annually for individual, agricultural, municipal, and project use. The reservoir was projected to have a gross storage capacity of 4.5 million acre feet.

Construction of Shasta Dam necessitated rerouting 37 miles of the Southern Pacific Railroad's main line to Portland, as well as rerouting 15 miles of the Golden State Highway located within the reservoir site. Estimated completion date of Shasta Dam was 1945; in 1940, as concern with national defense mounted and construction work was accelerated, the completion date was changed to 1943. The cost of the entire project, its proponents optimistically stated during these early years, would be self-liquidating, repaid by the sale of the water, the basis for the project, and power, an incidental but significant and lucrative by-product.

Construction of the Central Valley Project, besides the dams and canals, involved many auxiliary structures such as tunnels, bridges, culverts, inverted siphons, and wasteways. It also called for an infinite variety of heavy machinery and equipment. In addition, it absorbed raw materials and manufactured products on a grand scale and provided employment to several thousand persons. After Congress in August 1937 fully authorized the project, the Bureau of Reclamation was assured of legislative funding to complete the project.[19]

Ickes, as secretary of the interior, was enthusiastic and supportive of the Central Valley Project in every possible way. Privately, however, he had reservations, not about the project but rather about the opposition he encountered in California to his views on Hetch Hetchy and to the creation of Kings Canyon National Park. In February 1939 at a small conference with representatives of the project, Ickes said that he "was tired of handing things out to California" when the state showed "a reluctance to do anything" he asked of it. Shortly thereafter at dinner with Governor Culbert Olson at the Palace Hotel, Ickes assured the governor that he would do everything possible to expedite congressional funding for the project. In November Ickes delivered the major address as construction of Friant Dam got underway, proclaiming conservation as a national policy and lauding the work of the Bureau of Reclamation. He also noted that in his capacity as Public Works Administrator he had assisted numerous projects in California and the West; he promised that within a few years with the construction of Friant Dam "the 50,000 acres that today are desert because of the exhaustion of underground water will again be fruitful" and millions of acres similarly threatened would be saved.[20]

By the last years of the New Deal, 1940 and 1941, Ickes had further reason to be distressed with Californians opposed to his views. In December 1940 Governor Olson's private secretary in a radio broadcast complained that "the many problems and opportunities opened by the Central Valley Project are being worked out, not by one central public agency close to the people, but by many bureaus and agencies; some of them subject to remote control; some of them actually working at cross-purposes with others; all of them intent upon preservation and advancement of their own special interests and objectives." This barrage was followed by a call from Governor Olson for a regional federal authority to administer the Central Valley Project. Privately Olson told Ickes that the Central Valley Project under the Bureau of Reclamation was "getting nowhere fast" and that its actual benefits would go "to the big interests" and not to the people. Ickes responded to the effect that a regional agency was all right provided it was located in the Department of the Interior and he ran it. Olson also conferred with the President about his proposal. Roosevelt was sympathetic and authorized TVA Director David E. Lilienthal, who participated in the discussion, to work with the Department of the Interior, western congressional delegations, and Governor Olson in preparing a bill for consideration in the next Congress. Ickes did not publicly state his views about Olson's proposal and the President's seeming endorsement of it.[21]

In his correspondence, however, Ickes railed against any suggestion of removing the Central Valley Project from his jurisdiction. He wrote to the President, "protesting the impertinent interference of Lilienthal in the affairs of my Department" and was critical of Olson for not discussing the matter further with him after conferring in the White House. His campaign apparently enjoyed some success. Ickes asserted that Roosevelt, "without loss of time," sent word to Lilienthal that he should not interfere with the Bureau of Reclamation; it was to remain in the Department of the Interior. Olson, too, apparently relented, indicating no objections to an authority administered from headquarters at Sacramento but responsible directly to Ickes. Olson was more concerned about public ownership of the power distribution facilities and the operation of the project "for the economic welfare of the people and not for the enrichment of special interests" than he was bothered by who or what federal agency would have jurisdiction over the Central Valley Project.[22]

By the end of the New Deal troublesome clouds were threatening stormy weather ahead for the Central Valley Project. Jurisdictional disputes were already evident in the Kings River controversy between the Army Corps of Engineers and the Bureau of Reclamation. The Pacific Gas and Electric Company, enjoying a virtual monopoly in central and western California, opposed the preference clause in Bureau of Reclamation power contracts and lobbied in 1941 against funds for the construction of the stand-by steam plant to convert secondary power from Shasta and the projected Keswick Dam to firm power. If constructed, bureau officials claimed, the plant would increase the gross revenue of the Central Valley Project by many millions of dollars. And Governor Olson was calling for a broad regional authority headquartered in Sacramento to administer the project and to prevent special interests, large-scale farmers, and utility companies from thwarting or gaining undue influence in securing benefits from the project.[23]

Meanwhile, construction continued unabated on various units of the project despite serious setbacks incurred by winter storms and flooding on the Sacramento River. By the spring of 1941 it was estimated that Shasta Dam, which would be the second largest concrete structure ever built by man, was about one-sixth completed. Work had been under way on Shasta Dam for more than two and a half years; the first concrete was poured on July 8, 1940. The expected completion of the dam was now set in 1943 or early in 1944. And near the southern end of the Central Valley, construction work on Friant Dam was rapidly catching up with Shasta Dam, already the two largest masonry structures in California. Friant's completion was now optimistically anticipated at the end of 1942.

As the New Deal came to an end with the nation's entrance into World War II, the vast and complex multipurpose Central Valley Project, like the work on Grand Coulee, was not yet completed. The promise of future benefits was yet to be realized. Completion of the project, as originally conceived by California engineers, would be carried through by private contractors carefully supervised and directed by Bureau of Reclamation engineers and other qualified personnel. While future benefits beckoned, there were serious problems indicating that the postwar struggle over the disposition of these benefits would be long and acrimonious. The outline of these problems was evident by the end of the New Deal. In addition, there were two developments during these years that would affect water programs in the West in the postwar period. Evident, with the completion of the All-American Canal, was the servicing by the Bureau of Reclamation of public water onto privately owned "factory" farms. Heretofore the Bureau had provided water to farmers under the terms of reclamation legislation which limited the amount of water a farmer, homesteading on public land, could receive to what was required to irrigate 160 or in some instances 320 acres. Both principles were breached in California during the New Deal and this breach would provide the basis for controversy in California and the West for decades following the tenure of Harold Ickes.

Chapter 13

Roosevelts in the West

THE WEST AND THINGS "western" lay close to the heart of Franklin D. Roosevelt during the New Deal years. And to a lesser degree the same could be said for his wife, Eleanor, who in her "My Day" columns commented on her western trips. The President's concerns were a combination of politics, conservation interests, and a genuine regard for regional developments, many of which involved the federal government. During the New Deal years Roosevelt traveled widely in the West, campaigning and visiting in the years 1934 through 1938. The last years of the New Deal found him concerned more and more with defense efforts and the war in Europe and unable to go West. The outbreak of war in Europe, much to his chagrin, forced him to cancel a long-planned western trip in 1939. But his interest in the region never flagged, the western states constituting what he called "a great area . . . of incalculable importance to the prosperity of the United States." Roosevelt uttered these remarks in 1939 and noted further that "the vigor and boldness of these states—a direct inheritance from pathfinding forbears—are equally helpful in the social pioneering that has been commanded by today's necessities."[1]

Roosevelt's first great support before the 1932 Democratic Convention came from leaders in the West, and western delegations played a prominent role in securing his nomination and election in 1932. The New Deal thereafter devoted much attention to the West and its problems, and Roosevelt paid close attention to events and developments throughout the region. In the summer of 1934, returning from Hawaii, he disembarked from the *U.S.S. Houston* in Portland, Oregon, and slowly made his way across the northern tier of western states back to Washington, D.C. He inspected both Bonneville and Grand Coulee. To the delight of citizens throughout the Northwest, he prophesied that "we are going to see . . . with our own eyes electricity and power made so cheap that they will become a standard article of use, not only for agriculture and manufacturing, but also for every home within reach of an electric light line."

Then on Sunday, August 5, Roosevelt discussed the national park system in a radio address from Glacier National Park: "We have won the fight to obtain and to retain these great public park properties for the benefit of the public." Thereafter, as his train moved onto the drought-devastated northern plains, his remarks focused on agricultural programs and water diversion projects. Local politicians, flocking aboard the train at every stop, indicated that the political situation was warming up and that the 1934 election would reveal whether or not the New Deal had slipped politically.

Most of the President's remarks were extemporaneous. At Fort Peck he viewed construction on what would become the largest earthwork dam in the world, and at Devils Lake, North Dakota, on August 7, he remarked that he had now seen "some of the things that I have been reading and hearing about for a year and more." Noting a sign that said "You gave us beer, now give us water," the President quipped, "Well, the beer part was easy." Prior to his appearances, he was briefed by various federal officials on North Dakota's water problems, but he was not warned in advance of the "deplorable working and living conditions" at the Fort Peck Dam site. The place was "dressed up and work suspended" while the President visited.[2]

The President spent less than a week in the West in 1934, but he kept abreast of the various state-wide political campaigns, chiefly through Postmaster General James A. Farley, chairman of the Democratic National Committee. While in a personal letter he wished Key Pittman well in his primary race, Roosevelt added "an imposed silence in things like primaries is one of the many penalties of my job." But Farley went West and did his best to smooth over internecine squabbles affecting Democratic politics. "You did more to get the Democratic Party together on your trip to Santa Fe and Albuquerque than has ever been accomplished before," wrote the Mayor of Albuquerque to Farley. Senator P. James Pope wrote, "You made a fine impression and were of great assistance to the party," adding "Idaho's now definitely in the Democratic column. . . ." From Fargo the Roman Catholic Bishop wrote Farley, "Just now there is no opposition [that] could stand before the National Government in North Dakota." And Farley on his part made sure that officials in Washington quickly responded to the complaints he heard during his travels, such as the one concerning the progress of the Corn-Hog program in Oregon.[3]

Both Farley and Roosevelt were concerned about the West in 1934 because of crucial senatorial races involving Democratic incumbents in Utah, Arizona, Montana, and in other states where they hoped to gain a seat: Nebraska, Wyoming, New Mexico, Washington, and California, where Hiram W. Johnson had New Deal backing. In addition, both men hoped the launching of the New Deal would reverse the usual midterm trend toward a decline in the number of congressional seats held by the dominant party. On election eve in a letter to the President,

Farley predicted the election of Joseph C. O'Mahoney to the Senate from Wyoming and the return of Key Pittman from Nevada. He thought that in New Mexico Dennis Chavez had a "better than even chance" of defeating the incumbent Republican senator, Bronson Cutting. He also correctly predicted the Senate victory of Lewis Schwellenbach in Washington over the Republican incumbent, Clarence C. Dill, and that James E. Murray would hold on to the Senate seat from Montana which he filled in a special election. He added, "neither have we anything to worry about" with regard to the reelection of the other Montana senator, Burton K. Wheeler. He refused to predict the outcome of the complex situation in California, noting only "the slump in the [Upton] Sinclair vote is likely to affect some of our Congressional nominees."

In all, the New Deal came through the campaign better than most observers expected. Several successful Democratic governors wrote Farley after the election expressing their states' support. "I am very glad to report to you," wrote the newly elected governor of Idaho, "that we went almost one hundred percent for the New Deal." His counterpart in North Dakota wrote, "The New Deal and its thinking and administration has been a tremendous inspiration to North Dakota." Moreover, Farley knew that more Senate seats were contested in the West than in other sections of the nation. Judging from the election results of 1934, the New Deal in the West was a successful operation. It would continue so for several more years.[4]

Roosevelt's interest in things western did not abate following the 1934 elections. In January 1935 in a message to Congress transmitting reports by the National Resources Board and the Mississippi Valley Committee, the President summarized what he envisioned as the fulfillment of the New Deal in the West. And to a remarkable degree the vision and the reality were not far apart. In several instances, however, such as petroleum and silver policy, there was a marked discrepancy between the two.

Roosevelt noted that "Men and Nature must walk hand in hand. The throwing out of balance of the resources of nature throws out of balance the lives of men." And he added, "We think of our land and water and human resources not as a static and sterile possession but as life giving assets to be directed by wise provision for future days. We seek to use our natural resources not as a thing apart but as something that is interwoven with industry, labor, finance, taxation, agriculture, homes, recreation, good citizenship." The goal or the results of this process, Roosevelt concluded, "will have a greater influence on the future American standard of living than all the rest of our economics put together."[5]

In his western trip beginning in late September 1935 the President had a chance to elaborate further on this message. Late in the morning of September 28, the President and his party boarded a Union Pacific train in Council Bluffs that would take him to Los Angeles and then to San Diego to help open the Exposition in that city. At whistle stops along the way he spoke briefly to assembled crowds. At Fremont, Nebraska, he discussed accomplishments and future aims for agriculture under the New Deal, noting that the government had supplied the unifying element essential to success in agriculture. The fullest elaboration of the message was symbolized by his presence at the dedication of Boulder Dam and by the construction of the Colorado River Aqueduct. Roosevelt received a tremendous reception. Boulder Dam meant more than 8,000 jobs for people in the Los Angeles area, the approximate number of men employed on the aqueduct that autumn. Harold Ickes noted that "there were upward of seventy-five thousand people in the Coliseum" to see and hear the President and that enroute "he was greeted by pretty close to a million people." Concluding the trip in San Diego on October 2, the President swiftly defended the principles and measures of his administration. Thereafter he boarded the *U.S.S. Houston* for a cruise through the Panama Canal back to the East Coast.[6]

If the people of Los Angeles were enthused about seeing and hearing their President, Roosevelt was equally enthused, informing the Mayor of Los Angeles that "it was the greatest reception he had ever received." So impressed was Farley, chairman of the Democratic National Committee, with the success of the President's western trip, that several weeks later in contemplating the 1936 presidential campaign, he wrote, "We will have no trouble at all . . . in all the states West of the Mississippi."[7]

Roosevelt either was unaware of Farley's optimism or did not take it seriously. In the 1936 campaign he did not take the West for granted. And neither did other political observers. Francis J. Heney, a longtime California progressive, wrote the President early in 1936 that he was worried about the West and explained, "I am strongly of the opinion that the only issue upon which you can carry these western states . . . is expressed by the slogan: 'Shall this country be governed openly by a majority of the people or invisibly by a few tremendously wealthy Wall Street bankers?' " While Roosevelt did not take Heney's advice that seriously, he did make three western trips during this election year.[8]

The first trip, in June, was brief. Roosevelt went to participate in the Texas Centennial, giving speeches at the San Jacinto battleground, at the Alamo, and at the Centennial Exposition in Dallas. Besides whistle-stop remarks from the rear platform of the presidential train, Roosevelt also found time to speak at the unveiling of a memorial statue of Robert E. Lee in Dallas. The response was overwhelming during Roosevelt's two or three days in Texas. Driving between Fort Worth and Dallas, the highway was lined with hundreds of young men, NYA boys, saluting with their shovels. Lyndon Johnson, state NYA director, arranged this tribute and was among the group thus welcoming the President. The City Council of Austin, for another example, approved a resolution noting that "Prosperity's Rose Blooms Again With Roosevelt"; it applauded the "great good" that had been accomplished by the New Deal.[9]

While Texans celebrated, elsewhere in the West the situation was far from pleasant. Drought, dust, high winds, grasshoppers, intense heat, all helped to make this summer almost as bad as 1934, which was the worst on record. Lorena Hickok reported overhearing a young man reciting a poem that ended "Come to South Dakota and starve." She also noted that not even Russian thistles were growing; the country was "all burnt up" and that small wild animals, "panting for breath," were too utterly miserable to scatter when a car approached. Hickok made these and similar comments in her reports to Mrs. Roosevelt, Harry Hopkins, and other New Deal officials. The conditions they reflected aroused grave concerns. As their intensity increased, Hickok noted that wells in some small communities were going dry, that towns were bankrupt, and that some farmers "haven't had a crop since 1932." Though the situation was bleak, Hickok insisted that the New Deal had accomplished some significant things during these dry and dusty years: 580 small earthen dams in South Dakota alone still contained some water, though wells had gone dry and rivers and spring-fed lakes had dried up. These dams, constructed by "so-called 'relief labor,'" directly benefitted livestock men and farmers, many of whom had been hired by the government to help construct them. In short, though criticism of New Deal programs was mounting in some quarters, Hickok also reported satisfaction with what the New Deal was doing to assist drought- and depression-weary people on the Great Plains.[10]

At the end of July, Farley carefully assessed the situation in the West, just before the campaign moved into its final frantic phase. He felt confident, "definitely sure," of the Pacific Coast states as well as all of the states in the Inland Empire. He envisioned difficulty in the Dakotas, not because of drought conditions but because Representative William Lemke, presidential candidate on the Union Party ticket, was from North Dakota. There was also a possibility of defeat in Nebraska, where Senator George W. Norris, running as an independent, was seeking a fifth term. Norris, a strong supporter of the New Deal, would have a difficult campaign because both he and the New Deal did "not have much newspaper support." The President would have to depend, Farley said, upon his own popularity "and the influence of

Senator Norris." Though leading Kansas Democrats told Farley the party could carry the state, he was not optimistic that Alfred M. Landon, the Republican candidate, would lose in his home state. Farley considered Oklahoma and Texas as Southern states and they were "of course all right."[11]

States on the northern and central Great Plains, suffering severely from drought, were a cause of concern. The President, before starting a tour of these areas, kept abreast of conditions through reports forwarded to him from the National Emergency Council. By September all of the counties in the Dakotas, Kansas, and Oklahoma were listed as emergency drought counties. All but four or five Nebraska counties were also cited, as were a majority in Wyoming and Montana. The 1936 drought area did not include any portion of the states of Arizona, California, Idaho, Nevada, New Mexico, Oregon, and Utah—and only a handful of Texas counties. These facts help explain Farley's optimism about Roosevelt carrying the Inland Empire and the Pacific Coast states in 1936.

About midnight on Tuesday, August 25, the President departed, accompanied by Secretary of Agriculture Henry A. Wallace, WPA Administrator Harry Hopkins, and a host of Secret Service men for a personal inspection of the drought areas, to see at first hand its effects, to discuss with local officials and farmers the best means of providing them with further assistance, and to consider ways and means for the alleviation of future droughts. The presidential train headed for Bismarck where Roosevelt was scheduled to confer with state officials and United States senators from both Montana and North Dakota. A similar conference was scheduled for Pierre with the governors, United States senators and other officials from South Dakota and Wyoming. Roosevelt also delivered rear-platform extemporaneous speeches in several Dakota, Wyoming, Colorado, and Nebraska communities. In addition, he conducted smaller conferences at Sidney, Nebraska, and at Rapid City, South Dakota. At the conference in Bismarck the President presented a summary of the Great Plains Drought Area Committee's preliminary findings, a report he presented in final form to Congress early in 1937. At some stops Roosevelt motored into the country to talk with farmers and to inspect some of the small, WPA-constructed earthen dams that Hickok wrote about in her reports from South Dakota. The fact-finding trip, which extended as far west as Salt Lake City, served Roosevelt well in this election year. He spent about a week in the West and conducted similar conferences in the drought-devastated areas of the midwest as well.[12]

With Roosevelt off on his fact-finding trip, Farley in Washington found no reason to change his optimistic views about the political situation in the West. The only state he was "a little bit disturbed" about—because of the local situation—was Nebraska where George W. Norris had cast aside his Republican label and was seeking a fifth term in the United States Senate as an Independent. Farley refused to be budged in his views, despite concern expressed to him by Henry A. Wallace, who explained that "the farm people aside from the Catholics are Republican by ancestors and they feel it is not quite respectable to be Democrats." This historic inertia in the direction of Republicanism, Wallace concluded, would be hard to overcome "except when the farmers are scared or excited." Apparently Farley concluded that farmers in the West were either scared or excited; he refused to modify his premise that "the situation in the Western part of the country is apparently all right."[13]

Roosevelt, back in the White House after his inspection trip, continued to maintain an active interest in the campaign as it affected the West. For example, in a memorandum for Farley and Texas Congressman Sam Rayburn, who was directing the campaign in the West, he urged that they "beg Senator [Burton K.] Wheeler [Montana] to start speeches [in] key places at once." He also took time to thank Senator Norris for his remarks broadcast on a national hook-up urging Roosevelt's reelection. Roosevelt would reciprocate in a major speech in Omaha on October 14, endorsing Norris as "one of the major prophets of America." And, fully aware of the effectiveness of WPA work in constructing small earthen dams, he urged that an effective slogan for the agency in drought-devastated Oklahoma might be "A Pond For Every Farmer."[14]

In October Roosevelt was again in the West, this time on a tour that took him through Nebraska into Wyoming and then on to Denver. His special train then headed east through Kansas. In all, the President spent four days on the campaign trail, delivering major addresses in Omaha, Denver, Wichita, and Kansas City, as well as rear-platform extemporaneous remarks in almost every community his train passed through. In Cheyenne and Lincoln he toured the community, speaking at the State Capitol in Lincoln and at Fort Warren in Cheyenne.[15]

On election eve, November 2, 1936, Farley sent by special messenger, a report to the President in which he reaffirmed that Roosevelt would carry every state but Maine and Vermont. His optimism about the West remained firm. He stated that all the Democratic "nominees for Governor in the Western States should win without any difficulty." He was wrong in only one instance, South Dakota, where the Democratic candidate lost by 9,000 votes. With regard to congressional races he thought, mistakenly, that the Democrats might elect a Congressman in North Dakota and correctly that party candidates would gain Senate seats in Wyoming, Montana, and New Mexico and that Hiram Johnson would be reelected in California. He also noted that Republican

Senator Charles L. McNary in Oregon would have a tough race. He did, winning by about 5,000 votes. When the results were tallied, California had given the President the biggest majority of any state, a plurality over Landon of 930,405 votes. It remained, however, for William Allen White in an editorial for his *Emporia Gazette* to sum up the significance of the election, not only in the West but for the nation as well. "It was," White wrote, "not a Roosevelt victory. It was not a Landon defeat. It was a revelation of a changed attitude toward government by a vast majority of the American people." That changed attitude, White explained, was "a firm desire on the part of the American people to use government as an agency for human welfare." The nation, in effect, had taken a turn at a crossroads and White concluded with the words of an old hymn, "it is a grand and awful time."[16]

Overwhelming victory and a host of new problems, beginning with the Supreme Court fight, did not lead Roosevelt to ignore the West during his second term. Moreover, Eleanor Roosevelt, launching her career as a columnist, commented on things western beginning in 1936 in the course of her peregrinations. The President did not visit the West again until September 1937, but his wife was in the West in the spring of the year. In one of her early columns she commented favorably on a New Mexico malaria control project conducted in cooperation with the WPA and the United States Public Health Service. This project, she wrote, besides controlling the disease, was providing employment, reclaiming land, improving highways, conserving water, and also educating people about malaria and its prevention. In the spring of 1937 she visited Texas and Oklahoma and expressed surprise "that the wife of the President rates any particular attention." She toured primarily WPA and National Youth Administration (NYA) projects, speaking and meeting people wherever she went in both states.[17]

In September she accompanied the President on a tour that took them through the Northwest to Seattle. On the trip the President proposed to stop at Yellowstone National Park and to inspect a number of the larger government projects, including Fort Peck, Grand Coulee, and Bonneville, and in general to obtain first-hand information about conditions in the West. While in Seattle, the Roosevelts intended to enjoy a brief visit with their daughter, Mrs. John Boettiger. Once it was announced that the President would go West, he was innundated with requests to visit and to speak before various groups. These requests and the trip itself gave Roosevelt the opportunity to evaluate the support the New Deal had in the West, despite the battering it was receiving as a result of his losing battle to enlarge the Supreme Court. As usual he delivered a large number of informal extemporaneous remarks from the rear platform of the presidential train, beginning on September 24 in Cheyenne and continuing at whistle-stops throughout Wyoming, Montana, Idaho, Oregon, Washington, and on the return trip in North Dakota as well. He also found time to visit Victoria, British Columbia. He delivered more formal addresses at Bonneville Dam, at Timberline Lodge on Mt. Hood, and at Grand Forks, North Dakota, as he was concluding the western portion of the trip. He spent eleven days in the West on this trip and in the course of it managed to visit with the governors and other officials of several western states.[18]

Mrs. Roosevelt, who initially wondered what one could see and learn about conditions from the windows of a train, soon began to analyze what she was viewing. One thing she noticed was that "the grass is better this year . . . there has been a little more rain." In consequence she noted, "the cattle and the sheep look better and the people themselves look more cheerful" and she concluded that in this "hard hit" part of the country, confidence was returning as people responded to the President's rear-platform queries about crops and general conditions; in turn they asked him questions. Anna Boettiger, her husband, and children joined the presidential party at the entrance to Yellowstone Park. In the park a bear became a bit too friendly and put his paws on the side of the open car where the President was seated.[19]

In visiting a reclamation project in Oregon with the President, Mrs. Roosevelt remarked, "If some one said to me that I would see a desert one minute with sage brush the only visible vegetation, and the next minute some of the best farming land that I have seen anywhere, I would have thought they were telling me a talc!" She was interested in water rates and the fact that on one Oregon project "the original outlay for providing water had all been paid." At Bonneville Dam the thing that most interested her were the runways enabling the fish to get upriver past the dam. And at Mt. Hood in the Forest Reserve she was as much interested in the "giants of the forest" as in the lodge the President dedicated, built exclusively of native products by WPA labor.[20]

While the President spoke about the New Deal and the progress of its programs and Mrs. Roosevelt commented on what she saw, Marvin McIntyre, one of the the President's secretaries, received comments on the press coverage the trip was receiving. Most eastern newspapers played up the political implications of the trip: that Senator Joseph C. O'Mahoney, though not invited, boarded the presidential train and received a chilly reception in Cheyenne, and that Senator Burton K. Wheeler was nowhere to be seen while the President was in Montana. Both Senators had opposed his court plan. But Senator William E. Borah, who also opposed the President in the court fight, welcomed him in Boise as "our great President." In turn, as the press noted, he was warmly commended.[21]

In Washington, a summary of the editorial reactions to the President's trip was compiled. If not overwhelmingly favorable, it was more positive than negative. The more critical comments were usually tied into national politics, referring, for example, to the court fight or to the nomination of Senator Hugo L. Black to the Supreme Court. Ickes noted, however, that Roosevelt "was plainly elated" about the trip, believing that the throngs greeting him were larger than those he saw during his campaign tour in the West the previous year. Ickes also insisted that the people did not understand and were not much interested in the court issue. And Ickes added: "That they are interested in the President and believe in him even the correspondents of the opposition newspapers all unanimously attest."[22]

This western trip gave Roosevelt a personal opportunity to view conditions and New Deal projects in the West, while escaping for a while from mounting political opposition in Congress and in the editorial columns of many prominent newspapers. It also helped drive home a point he had forcefully made in a Constitution Day address delivered in Washington on September 17, a week before he departed. Roosevelt said, "In our generation a new idea has come to dominate thought about government—the idea that the resources of the Nation can be made to produce a far higher standard of living for the masses, if only government is intelligent and energetic enough in giving the right direction to economic life." This western trip indicated that, among the people, he was as popular as ever.[23]

If the 1937 trip gave the President much satisfaction, his travels in the West in 1938 were highly political. In the primaries Roosevelt hoped to purge several highly critical and increasingly hostile members of his own party and to endorse those who supported the New Deal. In July he departed on a long trip which again took him across the continent to the Pacific Coast, this time via Texas to San Diego, where he boarded the U.S.S. Houston for a leisurely return trip through the Panama Canal.

As soon as the news of the impending trip became known, invitations to visit a particular city or view a specific project inundated the White House mail room. Before the presidential train headed for Texas, Sam Rayburn pointed to a more serious concern. In 1938 there were fourteen primary candidates for governor. Since it would be impossible to welcome all fourteen aboard the presidential train, Rayburn suggested that none be invited or asked to ride in a car with Roosevelt. All along the way it required skilled political maneuvering to determine who should be invited aboard the train, where in the various states the President should speak, and how state officials and other noncongressional candidates should be treated.[24]

While political concerns were paramount in the preparations and plans for the President's trip, in March Mrs. Roosevelt was on a more personal western trip. In Amarillo at least 100,000 people lined the streets for a parade led by three governors attired in cowboy costume. Along with representatives from New Mexico, Colorado, Oklahoma, and Kansas, Mrs. Roosevelt helped Texans celebrate Mother-in-Law's Day. She also found time to visit a government homestead at Popesville, to view various NYA and WPA projects, to speak on college campuses in Texas, New Mexico, and Arizona where buildings and other improvements were provided by WPA workers, and to meet people, young and old, in all walks of life. Outside Amarillo she was impressed with a tuberculosis "preventorium" constructed by WPA workers and operated by a group of active and concerned women. In El Paso she viewed a police project in which WPA workers were helping to check and fingerprint immigrants about to be deported.

In both New Mexico and El Paso Mrs. Roosevelt observed Mexican American customs and styles, including the making of adobe bricks. At Fort Bliss she inspected buildings constructed by WPA workers, toured a government hospital for veterans improved by WPA projects. She was impressed in most public buildings with the murals done by WPA artists. It gave her some satisfaction "to realize that in spite of the fact that the depression forced upon us the necessity for giving people work through WPA, we have managed to make that work so useful that much of it will be enjoyed long after the depression is forgotten."[25]

At the end of the month she was in the Northwest continuing her tour, speaking on college campuses, visiting WPA and NYA projects, concerned about children and people in hospitals, touring land utilization projects, and seeing the rolling wheat fields of the Palouse country in southwestern Washington where the government was working with farmers to curb developing soil erosion. On the campus of the University of Idaho in Moscow she planted "a little native tree" nearby a strong and straight one planted by her uncle, Theodore Roosevelt. She then returned to Spokane, caught a "sleeper plane" to Chicago with a brief stopover in Salt Lake City, and noted that a fellow passenger was the movie star, Errol Flynn.[26]

When the President visited Texas in July, the hospitality and welcome afforded his wife was also extended to him. In Amarillo he was greeted by a 2,500-piece band. As he started speaking the heavens yielded torrents of water, a commodity in short supply in the baked Texas panhandle. Roosevelt, realizing his good fortune, continued with his remarks endorsing congressional candidates and reviewing New Deal programs pertaining to land and water resources, a theme he reiterated throughout the trip. Everywhere he spoke—in Oklahoma City, in several Oklahoma and North Texas communities; in Colorado and Nevada; and then finally in San Francisco, Los Angeles, and San Diego—he was surrounded by local candidates and prominent officials. Ostensibly he discussed the New Deal and its relationship to local or regional problems and issues. But he was also seeking the return or election of New Deal supporters to Congress so that he could further the domestic reform program that had bogged down when he ran into controversy over the Supreme Court. The President spent a week in the West in the summer of 1938.[27]

Though Roosevelt's train did not stop in Utah, the Democratic National Committeeman wrote to the President that James Farley, also traveling in the West, had informed him "that Utah's quota for November 1938 is one United States Senator and two Congressmen." He then added, "I give you my pledge we will reach our quota." Since Utah's candidates were New Dealers and since most Democrats in the state, as the chairman noted, "are enthusiastic in their approval of your administration," Roosevelt undoubtedly felt he could spend his time more effectively elsewhere in the West. And he was correct. Utah returned its Democratic incumbents in the November election.[28]

Indeed, most of what Roosevelt learned as he toured the West pleased him. In Nevada, for example, the governor, the lone congressman, and Senator Patrick A. McCarran, seeking a second term, all boarded the presidential train. Roosevelt reported to Key Pittman, the senior United States senator from the state, that "things on the whole are going pretty well in Nevada." And again he was correct, though he would have preferred another candidate than McCarran, a conservative anti-New Deal Democrat, whom he pointedly treated with "due courtesy." His disappointment about McCarran was perhaps offset by a wire he received while in Nevada informing him that New Deal Senator Elmer Thomas was leading in the senatorial primary in Oklahoma, while "Alfalfa Bill" Murray, a New Deal critic, was losing his bid for a second nomination as the gubernatorial candidate. In the Texas primaries one of the candidates Roosevelt specifically endorsed, Maury Maverick, was defeated. But Lyndon Johnson and Marvin Jones, who also received presidential endorsement, were renominated. Though enormous crowds had turned out to greet the President in Texas, John Nance Garner, his vice-president and a fellow Texan, was nowhere to be seen. He was supposedly busy "fishing" on his ranch.[29]

On this trip the President treated anti-New Deal Democratic incumbents with silence or "due courtesy." When a New Deal candidate was opposing a conservative, he advocated the nomination of the New Dealer. In Colorado where there was no real choice, and where Senator Alva B. Adams was so far ahead that there was no chance of defeating him, Roosevelt simply kept quiet.[30]

In California Senator William Gibbs McAdoo was being heavily pressed by Sheridan Downey, Upton Sinclair's running mate in 1934 and now a close associate of Francis Everett Townsend and his "Ham and Eggs" pension plan. Roosevelt gave McAdoo, who tied himself to the President's coattails, a tepid endorsement. During the three days he spent in California, Roosevelt was greeted by large and friendly crowds. He visited the Golden Gate International Exposition, reviewed the United States fleet, saw Yosemite National Park for the first time, dedicated the new San Diego Civic Center building (erected in part with federal funds), and in general, enjoyed himself.

Throughout the remainder of this election year, Roosevelt kept abreast of the campaign in the western states. In Idaho, for example, he was distressed to learn of the primary defeat of Senator John P. Pope, whom he had earlier endorsed, and whose defeat was hailed as a slap at the President. In Nebraska the situation, Farley learned, was "bad," that "it would be easy for the Republicans to knock us off in a clean sweep," in good part owing to the niggardly PWA funds allocated to Nebraska projects compared to that received by neighboring states. Reports from Oregon were equally discouraging. The New Deal suffered reverses in all these states in the November elections, though the New Deal governor of Nebraska was reelected in a tight race.[31]

Elsewhere in the West the results were equally bleak, though the Democrats elected a New Deal governor in North Dakota. Otherwise in the Dakotas, New Deal candidates were defeated. In Oregon internal feuding brought about the defeat of Democratic candidates, causing the loss of a House seat and the failure to gain a Senate seat which Farley thought the Democratic candidate "would win easily." California was a bright spot. An ardent New Dealer was elected governor; Farley exclaimed, "The state stood up in a year when things were going against us." Democrats were elected to all major offices in Colorado except that of governor but their election provided little solace to the President. In Kansas a New Deal Senator was defeated. To Farley it was expected "due to the falling off all through the farm belt area" because of dissatisfaction with low farm prices and AAA controls. In Kansas, Colorado, Wyoming, Idaho, and Oregon, Republicans gained control of the State House by ousting Democratic occupants. In short, aside from the Southwest, California, and Washington State where a strong New Deal delegation had been elected to Congress, the President could take little solace from the 1938 election results in the West.[32]

Rebuffed in the West and elsewhere in the 1938 elections, Roosevelt planned an extensive trip in 1939 that would take him to San Francisco through the central states, on into the Pacific Northwest, and then eastward by way of the northern route. Ostensibly his purpose was to speak at the Golden Gate International Exposition. It also would provide him another opportunity to feel the political pulse of the region and determine whether he still enjoyed tremendous popularity. As in the previous year, Eleanor Roosevelt preceded him.

Certainly she enjoyed popularity in Texas, which she had visited in March. In her travels she continued to inspect WPA and NYA projects, to comment on the work of women, to speak on college campuses, including Prairie View College, the only state-supported black college in Texas, all the while expressing the social concerns of the New Deal. She experienced a dust storm in Sherman and "began to taste the earth." Residents told her "it was the worst they had seen in a long time." Elsewhere people said the rains north Texans enjoyed in late 1937 and the programs sponsored by the Soil Conservation Service greatly assisted those areas afflicted by drought and dust. Mrs. Roosevelt was convinced "that much of the country which has been put under cultivation should go back into grass and be used as range for cattle." San Antonio was her last stop in Texas before departing for California and the Pacific Northwest where, as in Texas, she visited with her children and their families. Her Texas hosts, Mr. and Mrs. Maury Maverick took her to see various needlework shops as well as places of historical interest. She was distressed to learn that San Antonio had the highest tuberculosis rate in the country and was not far behind in "social disease."[33]

Late in the year she visited the West again, very briefly. This time she took a three-hour trip to examine the shelterbelt in Kansas. Her first stop was at some planting which had been done four years previously. Mrs. Roosevelt noted the fences strung on either side of the shelterbelt to keep cattle out and that weeds had to be kept down to permit the trees to gain their maximum growth. "To achieve the best results in breaking the wind velocity" she reported, "each shelterbelt should be half a mile long." She also chatted with "old time farm people" who, though skeptical at the outset, were now staunch supporters of shelterbelt plantings. She also made a revealing comment in her column about this visit that "those farms where oil had been found, and a few other farms, looked prosperous and well kept." Elsewhere it was evident that most farms had not yet recovered from the effects of drought and depression.[34]

The President, much to his regret, was unable to visit and travel in the West. The congressional battle over neutrality legislation and the outbreak of war in Europe in September 1939 forced Roosevelt to cancel his long-planned western trip. Indeed, following his 1938 trip, he never set foot in the West again, though he did cross the country in 1944 en route to Hawaii for a meeting with his military commanders. Moreover, the pressure of foreign affairs meant that he was forced to curb his interest and enthusiasm for developments affecting the region; by 1940 the New Deal in the West came to an end. A new focus was evident, too, in Eleanor Roosevelt's "My Day" columns. No longer was she commenting on NYA and WPA projects, visiting people involved with New Deal projects, when she visited Texas in December 1940. She still followed an exhausting schedule but the New Deal was no longer prominently discussed in her columns after her April 1940 visit to migrant camps in California.

In 1940 as the primary season approached, politicians in the West and elsewhere debated whether or not Roosevelt would seek a third term. Late in 1939, Farley sensed that Burton K. Wheeler might be interested in the nomination. In April a fight broke out in Texas between politicians seeking to endorse native son John Nance Garner, the vice president, and supporters of the President, led by Representative Lyndon B. Johnson, "a 100 percent New Dealer and third term advocate." With Roosevelt's sanction a compromise was worked out between the two factions, allowing delegates to vote for Garner as a favorite-son candidate and at the same time acclaiming the administration record and refraining from participation in any "stop Roosevelt" movement. Roosevelt, in short, was keeping his options open and had not alienated politicians in the western state that played a major role in securing his nomination in 1932.[35]

It was in the midst of the political maneuverings leading to the Chicago convention, which nominated Roosevelt for a third term, that the New Deal in the West, symbolically if not officially, came to an end. The exact date can be pinpointed. It was May 20, 1940. Roosevelt sent the following memorandum to Harold Ickes:

> I yield to your importuning. I will go, if it is at all possible, to Grand Coulee IF I go West.
> The rub is that I think my Western trip is definitely off—at least until the volcano in Europe ceases erupting—a matter of a month, a year, five years or a century. In the latter case you and I will be tottering old men and the Coulee Dam, in spite of the merits of the Reclamation Service, may have disintegrated into dust!
> I like the observation balcony and the pedestal which will contain both our names![36]

The last sentence, probably added to assuage Ickes's easily ruffled sensibilities, indicated that the names of the dominant figures of the New Deal in the West would be cast in concrete until the day one of its noblest edifices disintegrated into dust.

Chapter 14

From Pioneering to Planning

THE NEW DEAL OFFERED the West an opportunity to transform itself. The Great Depression with its accompaniment of drought and dust brought disaster to the arid regions of the nation. This formidable trio helped to break down America's earlier version of the agrarian ideal based on the individual self-reliant citizen-farmer. Throughout the rural regions, soil erosion had its counterpart in an eroding social order. In the South the social order, though seriously impaired, held on tenaciously to be challenged in different ways in subsequent decades. But in the West the vast federal presence caused significant changes to occur, some of which were permanent in their impact. Those that were not permanent nevertheless could serve future generations as a reminder that their errant ways, like those of their parents before them, would lead eventually to the same result in a West where water and its most effective utilization were matters of prime concern.

What became crystal clear in the 1930s to most residents of the region was that western concerns and problems could not be resolved through state or regional action alone. Depression, drought, and dust undermined dependence on the marketplace as an arbiter of economic activities. Westerners accepted, sometimes begrudgingly, federal aid and support during the New Deal. Federal largesse, more so than in the past, became an increasingly important—indeed, an integral—component of western life during the New Deal, more so than elsewhere in the United States. Moreover, the New Deal in the West indicated the necessity for government action to lead the economy back to prosperity. It had to cope with massive soil erosion and water problems through more centralized control over resource use and management of river basins as the key to regional development and stimulation of employment. Government assistance subsidized "free enterprise" in the West on a grand scale.

Animating the New Deal in the West was concern for rational planning of resource use. Reports of the National Resources Planning

Board, several presidential committees, various regional, state and local boards, all provided guidelines designed to encourage more meaningful regional economic development. In some instances development meant encouraging nature's healing powers. This was the case in matters affecting soil erosion, range management, and (in some instances) water management as well. It involved efforts to control the environment by harnessing rivers and managing forest lands to promote sound productivity upon which economic prosperity could firmly rest. Growth and expansion were envisioned by most New Dealers in the West, though some, particularly those associated with agricultural programs on the Great Plains, recognized that this would be at best a long-term process involving lowered expectations and a shift in priorities before people could enjoy a measure of prosperity by living in harmony with their harsh environment. There also was a preservationist side to the New Deal in the West manifested in the establishment of two new national parks, concern for wildlife, and the encouragement of Native American cultures, customs, and crafts. To be sure, preservation was not a dominant theme of the New Deal in the West, but it had its ardent advocates and it did reflect a growing national concern for learning about and preserving America's manifold heritage in an increasingly unstable world. Planning for future growth and development, however, was the more dominant theme encompassing the New Deal in the West.

The West by the 1930s was for all intents and purposes not far removed from a pioneering stage of development in the way it utilized its grass, its soil, its timber, and its watersheds. All were exploited; some were seriously deteriorated. Bernard De Voto called the West a plundered province, and people debated the historic question of just who exploited the region: eastern corporations, local residents, or both? The New Deal, avoiding the question, through planning made strenuous efforts to manage the arid environment so that people could live utilizing nature's treasures without substantially depleting them from one generation to the next. Planning efforts, which to succeed had to be based upon the confidence and consent of the people, were accepted during the New Deal largely because of the afflictions experienced by people in the West. The ordeal experienced by most western residents made them more susceptible to proposals presented by New Deal planners than they had been to the pleas of agricultural experiment stations and cooperatives. The soil could not change unless the farmer changed it; sustained-yield forestry could not occur until lumbermen agreed to diminish the destruction by bringing into balance annual production with annual harvest. During the New Deal planning became an acceptable method of resolving public problems by defining goals and objectives and arranging efficient ways and means of attaining them with federal assistance. In the West planning for natural resource use was probably more pronounced than other approaches because it encompassed most of them. Public works planning, city, state, and regional planning, planning with regard to social and economic concerns—though all types occurred in the West, almost all were also related to natural resource planning.

During the New Deal national planning could very well be pictured as a mighty river in which regional plans were the major tributaries, in turn fed by state plans which found their sustenance in local thinking. No matter how small the immediate objective of a plan might be, its fulfillment added, like the ripples of a pebble dropped in a still pond, to the well-being of people beyond its immediate range. At the same time local groups and organizations involved in these activities became integrated into an expanding network of similar and related groups and organizations that further projected the West into the orbit of a modernizing mass society.

East of the Rockies, the Department of Agriculture played the leading role in resource planning; west of the Rockies, the Department of the Interior predominated. Neither department, from the secretaries on down, had much confidence in the other. But, since the Department of the Interior under Harold Ickes dominated the New Deal in the West, complaints by agricultural officials were more numerous because they were excluded by the nature of their responsibilities and programs from much of the West, and because Harold Ickes, assisted with Public Works Administration funds, had at his disposal many more millions to allocate than Henry Wallace, whose programs on the Great Plains were largely designed to withdraw acreage from crop use and to reduce the production of crops in commercial surplus. In the area under Wallace's hegemony, New Deal planning called for lowering horizons: reducing the number of farms and the number of people living on those farms. Beyond the Rockies, largely under Ickes's hegemony, hundreds of millions of dollars were available for new projects, some of which might add to the agricultural surplus Wallace and his associates were utilizing federal funds to curb or eliminate. In the West Wallace could not compete with Ickes, the Department of Agriculture could not compete with the Department of the Interior, yet the programs each were espousing were meaningful for their respective portions of the West. Though there was overlapping of responsibility, the Rockies were not an arbitrary dividing line; cooperation between the two secretaries, their departments, and officials in the bureaus or agencies administering their programs throughout the West was minimal.

In the 1930s then, people in the West and elsewhere in the nation were ready to accept government as an agency for human welfare. The general welfare clause of the preamble to the American Constitution pointed the way for the course the New Deal chose to follow in the West. It was conclusively ratified in the 1934 and 1936 elections and less so when factors other than planning and regional programs interfered in 1938 and 1940. Nevertheless, the New Deal remained popular in the West and most people accepted without serious debate government's new direction and their own shift in attitude toward the role of government. The New Deal was not successful, primarily for political reasons, in curbing major oil producers, some mining interests, and "factory" farmers in California. Otherwise the New Deal made strenuous efforts to resolve the problems of people in the region whose income was tragically out of line with the returns of capital and who by themselves could not bargain or plan collectively.

In July 1933 President Roosevelt appointed a National Planning Board as an arm of the Public Works Administration. Through its several name changes, the reports of its various committees considering settlement patterns and land use on the Great Plains were essentially similar, as were those of presidential committees and others examining the situation. All concluded in one way or another, with the Land Planning Committee of the National Planning Board in December 1934, that "extensive areas of the Great Plains . . . must be classed as unsuited to sustain cultivated crops and should therefore never have been plowed, but retained in grass for stock raising." It further observed that there were no "extensive unsettled areas suitable for full-time commercial farming" remaining under prevailing conditions on the Great Plains.[1]

Solutions suggested throughout the New Deal included reducing and replacing wheat farming by extensive grazing, increasing the size of farms in more arable areas to achieve viable economic units, and providing for the extension of pasture. Implicit in these suggestions was the premise that the small subsistence farm was no longer an answer for displaced farmers, many of whom migrated westward. To ease the harshness of the environment, the Forest Service, assisted by the Civilian Conservation Corps and by the Works Progress Administration, launched a massive shelterbelt program extending from the Dakotas to Texas. Since suffering was more severe on the plains than elsewhere in the nation, much attention was given to its problems. The report of the Great Plains Drought Area Committee presented in 1936 noted that "fifty or more important Federal agencies, in addition to State, county and municipal governments and numerous types of districts" were at work calling for and promoting readjustments in agricultural production.

Late in the New Deal, Congress went one step further and provided funding that brought the Bureau of Reclamation onto the plains to support construction and maintenance of small earthen water projects:

ponds, reservoirs, wells, pumping installations, and similar facilities, all designed to provide more effective utilization of localized water supplies. These projects, along with recommendations of local Soil Conservation Service agents and with support and assistance from the Resettlement Administration and its successor, the Farm Security Administration, provided for fragmentary land-use reform and improvement by offering farmers new opportunities. Basically, however, the essence of New Deal suggestions called for a shift from one-crop production to a greater emphasis on grazing. But as conditions improved, as the drought and dust abated with a change for the better in the weather cycle, and as the demand for grain increased markedly with the outbreak of war in Europe, the plea of New Dealers for more sensible land-use patterns was first ignored and then forgotten. Farmers in the breadbasket of America resumed full production, with the encouragement of federal agencies moving to a wartime footing, and began to enjoy prosperity. The reports, the advice, the suggestions, the pleas of the New Dealers would be exhumed in later decades when conditions experienced in the 1930s reasserted themselves. Sensible land use to curb erosion's loss of topsoil on the Great Plains, despite heroic efforts during the New Deal, is yet to be achieved. Planning, however, did make headway among rural residents, especially as it allowed them by the late 1930s to improve their economic well-being and further consolidate their operations. Wheat farmers on the Great Plains recognized by the end of the decade that only with federal assistance might planning be effective in meeting many of the problems and conditions they experienced. They also knew that, if they could secure three annual crops out of five, they could prosper. They could live on two crops out of five. To the extent that government might help improve their chances of prospering, they would listen to and accept advice. But there was reluctance to consider fundamental land-use changes.[2]

Adjustment of land and population required more than a physical rearrangement of farms, trees, and range lands. A new attitude toward land had to be developed, one in which, as Rex Tugwell observed, "permanence will replace speculation, conservation will replace waste and wise use will replace exploitation." There can be no doubt that New Dealers, working primarily through agencies in the Department of Agriculture, sought valiantly to inculcate such views among residents of the plains states; that they enjoyed a measure of success can be noted. How lasting or deep an impression they made is open to debate and discussion.[3]

An indication was provided by a speaker at the initial meeting of the Missouri Valley Regional Planning Commission in Omaha in September 1941. He remarked that he was greatly encouraged, "even inspired," by the general improved conditions apparent everywhere: "The fine, green, well-stocked pastures of the Dakotas," the tall corn of Nebraska, "and the evidence everywhere of heavy small grain crops." All was very heartening. Yet the speaker was also "depressed by evidences of faulty land use," all of which indicated that "we have a long way to go before all the resources of the region are adequately planned and utilized most effectively."[4]

In the Inland Empire, the domain of Harold Ickes, where the open range was located, the impact of the New Deal was more marked and lasting. The Taylor Grazing Act represented a termination of the long process of surrendering the nation's land resources to private control. The 110 million acres of public domain would now be managed and protected. Erosion would be controlled through the reduction of overgrazing, conducted under a coordinated rehabilitation program that provided for improved forage facilities, rodent control, and the construction of roads, trails, fences, corrals, and watering places. Programs under Ickes's supervision called for livestock production as the primary focus of land utilization in areas for which irrigation was not suitable.

Throughout his tenure Ickes stressed conservation as a matter of paramount concern. Though he did not ignore the preservation aspect, as was evident in the creation of two new national parks in the West, in his concern for preserving the life cycle of the salmon in the Northwest and maintaining wildlife in wilderness areas, Ickes devoted most of his attention to the prudent use of natural resources. In 1941 he remarked "we must use what is needful but we must not waste; we must learn to know what we have to extract from our stocks to find new uses for those which are plentiful so as to husband those with which we are less adequately supplied."[5] During the New Deal years Ickes tried valiantly to follow this prescription. But he was not always successful, as in his disagreements with major oil producers interested in production control and restraining trade to fix prices, all in the name of stabilization. In the case of silver operators and their powerful allies, the Senate Silver Bloc, Ickes could do nothing because stabilization was achieved through federal subsidization.

In the areas where he was not so hindered, Ickes was able to use Public Works Administration funds to assist in western development. It was the control he exercised over these funds that helped make Ickes the dominant figure of the New Deal in the West. In the states west of the Mississippi River, Public Works Administration funds alone helped finance projects costing $2 billion during the decade from 1933 to 1943. Nearly $500 million alone was spent in the three Pacific Coast states. And in all areas the figures indicating growth and development, thanks in large part to the injection of these monies, were stupendous compared to previous data. Power installations, primarily in the West, in terms of kilowatt hours increased twenty-fold since 1933, from less than 150,000 kilowatts to nearly 3 million by 1940, and over 21 million by 1943. The number of irrigated acres increased from less than 3 million to 4 million acres by 1943. By 1940 the irrigation, power, and municipal water plants built with the aid of federal funds were serving about 5 million people in the West compared to less than a million people in 1933. In that year there were only 28 Bureau of Reclamation projects in operation and but one authorized. In 1943 the figure had doubled; there were 56 projects in operation and 26 more had been authorized but held in abeyance because of wartime shortages.[6]

Where PWA funds could not do the job, Ickes was able to utilize Civilian Conservation Corps workers in renovating and improving the national parks, the Oregon and California Railroad and Coos Bay Wagon Road grant lands, and Indian lands under his jurisdiction. Similarly the Forest Service was able to use such labor in promoting better management and conservation on their vast tracts throughout the Inland Empire, just as various agricultural agencies applied their services in pursuing programs on the Great Plains.

The broad program of conservation of the nation's natural resources pursued by agencies under the aegis of Harold Ickes and Henry Wallace involved modernization, laying the foundations for a more stable economy in the West that would expand enormously and bring in its wake a rising standard of living, increased population, and a greater measure of equality with other sections of the country. In addition, an effort was made through the Indian New Deal to advance the well-being and further the education of Native Americans. Through the Indian Reorganization Act they were granted an opportunity for self-government, an opportunity which by the end of the New Deal more than 80 tribes had accepted. While Indian-owned lands increased by approximately 279,000 acres, the results were not always what New Dealers anticipated. The plight of the Indians, if anything, would become more difficult in the years immediately following the New Deal. Nevertheless, a groundwork and a vision for self-determination and equality was presented during the New Deal that would provide at least a launching pad for Indian leaders in the following decades.

Basic to the modernization of the West and to the welfare of its people was effective use of water resources. Here the New Deal, largely through the Bureau of Reclamation, made its greatest contribution, while at the same time manifesting a concern, seriously challenged after Ickes's tenure, against monopolization of these resources for the benefit of large landowners, private utilities, and powerful corporate interests. The New Deal in the West, with some notable exceptions, manifested a traditional concern through its various programs for individual producers and operators. The federal government in the twentieth century launched the process of supporting irrigation development as a recognition of its importance to the western economy. It also insisted on providing water to only 160 acres of each farmer's land, thereby reaffirming the premise of the 1862 Homestead Act "that our land shall be farmed by working owners." Originally intended for only public lands, the Reclamation Act was modified to include private lands and to allow spouses to claim an additional 160 acres for irrigation. The principle remained intact through the New Deal. Exceptions were made in approving two or three projects completed after the New Deal because of the topography of the lands to be irrigated. The Hoover Administration in the case of Imperial Valley farmers provided another notable exception. The fight, however, got under way during the 1930s, once construction of the Central Valley Project in California was launched. Ickes held firm on the 160-acre principle, but the issue became complicated as California producers sought and received support for their challenge from the Corps of Engineers, Pacific Gas and Electric, the leading private utility corporation in the state, and from members of the California congressional delegation. The lines were formed late in the New Deal for a battle of major proportions in the postwar years.

Water for irrigation was necessary to "prime the pump" of regional development. As the Bureau of Reclamation shifted to multipurpose projects (beginning with Boulder Dam) and generated prodigious quantities of electricity, industrial development in the Pacific Coast states received an impetus that changed the balance of their economic base. The West became less dependent upon the industrial East as a source or market for goods and services. Moreover, industrial development helped change and increase the volume of agricultural production to better serve expanding urban-industrial areas. In brief, through the various programs and projects it launched, the New Deal was largely responsible for the development of a great industrial and agricultural empire in the West in the post-war years. Thus the Bureau of Reclamation, in shifting from an agency concerned with irrigation and reclaiming arid lands to one involved with both agricultural and industrial development, was the primary instrument in the modernization of the West. Prior to the 1930s water development in the West was promoted mainly by private developers; thereafter the federal government took the lead.

Along with the expanded role of the Bureau of Reclamation came a disturbing tendency also evident in many other New Deal agencies furthering resource development in the West. It involved a serious weakening of the original concern of the progressive movement for efficiency and prudent management characteristic of the Forest Service and Bureau of Reclamation created during the presidency of Theodore Roosevelt. During the New Deal the various agencies in the West developed organized constituencies in their grazing and soil conservation districts, in the National Reclamation Association, among the California fruit growers championing the Corps of Engineers, among lumbermen and others. As these groups became better organized, and as the various New Deal agencies in the West sought to enhance their own operations, they became more susceptible to the pleas, pressures, and demands of their constituencies, who in many instances also secured the support of legislators and other officials. Jurisdictional disputes came to the fore and pressure politics became increasingly evident in the sparsely populated western states. To the extent that bureaucrats at all levels became susceptible to such pressures, to that extent was the progressive impulse that centered around efficiency and scientific management vitiated. Though both Ickes and Wallace were proud of their progressive heritage and they certainly did not condone this process, it became more pronounced during their tenure. And it could be argued that pressure politics in the West in the post-New Deal years rivaled party politics as a method of resolving issues of public concern affecting resource development.

The Bureau of Reclamation was responsible for another significant development greatly accelerating the economy of the West. The huge multipurpose projects constructd under its direction provided for large-scale employment as well as heavy expenditures for materials, equipment, and supplies, providing thereby a substantial stimulus to a depressed western economy. Unlike the Tennessee Valley Authority, which chose to construct dams with its own work force, the Bureau of Reclamation, beginning with Boulder Dam, provided for private construction. The Six Companies, all western firms, that built Boulder, Grand Coulee, and Shasta dams got started with government contracts on careers that made them and their executives some of the most prominent firms and corporate leaders in the West and the nation. The Six Companies was a joint corporation involving Bechtel & Kaiser and MacDonald & Kahn, construction companies based in San Francisco, Morrison-Knudson Corporation in Boise, the Utah Construction Company of Salt Lake City, and Portland's J. F. Shea Corporation and the Pacific Bridge Company. These companies went on to construct shipyards, bridges, military installations, steel mills, and other industrial plants in the West. They usually operated with lucrative government contracts and in the postwar years extended their activities to countries in the Third World. The New Deal effectively launched these companies, which played a prominent role in modernizing the West.

The planning ethic was furthered by the massive multipurpose dams, some of which, like Boulder and Grand Coulee, provided big blocks of cheap power and irrigated acreage. Most of these benefits would be achieved after 1940, as only a handful of the larger projects were completed and fully functioning by the end of the New Deal. Their construction merely amplified and accelerated the chaos of capitalism's lack of planning throughout the West in the 1930s. And they illustrated, too, the principle espoused by the President and New Dealers in general that the resources of the nation, through intelligent and energetic government assistance, could produce a higher standard of living in the western regions of the United States.

This approach to planning achieved its greatest success during the New Deal in the Pacific Northwest where three programs administered by the federal government formed an integral part of the development of the area. The Bonneville and Columbia Basin (Grand Coulee) projects and the revested Oregon and California Railroad lands dealt respectively but not exclusively with electric power, agriculture, and stabilization of the lumber industry. Together they helped provide a broad concourse of economic and social benefits of local and regional importance. Together they helped provide for industrial expansion in the Northwest within a balanced economy.

The basic change that occurred in the West revolved around power development, which in turn stimulated and promoted industrialization. Power development also played a significant role in stabilizing local and regional economies. Electricity, for example, increased regional processing of raw materials and developed local industries for the manufacture of consumer goods, thus saving transportation and distribution costs. In addition, widespread use of electricity on the farm, in the home, and in the community helped improve the quality of life throughout the West.

Electricity helped break the dependence of the West upon an economy derived primarily from agricultural and mining pursuits, from producing raw materials that were either largely consumed or fabricated into finished products in other parts of the country, and where the population compared to other sections of the country had a low per capita income. Electricity, in short, allowed the western economy to "take off" with results that would have distressed many New Dealers, who, with their concern for planning, sought a harmonious and balanced ecological system along with an economy not dominated by corporate interests. A conservation ethic went hand in hand with Harold Ickes's concern for multipurpose development. Henry Wallace understood that the Great Plains could become a vast alkaline desert unless carefully nurtured. Wallace understood that land could not be permanently abused, that meaningful land use necessitated careful planning. Both men recognized that government had to play a significant role in posting guidelines and otherwise assisting as the

West underwent a vast transformation and entered the mainstream of American life.

In extricating the West from the depths of the depression, the New Deal also lifted it to a new and higher plateau. In doing so it left a legacy of constructive government accomplishments in conservation, public power, and natural resource use, a legacy not always lived up to during the New Deal and increasingly ignored by future administrations. While different historical times call for different styles and approaches to problems, the concern of the New Deal in the West for conservation, energy, and natural resources, while seeking to relieve human misery and preserve individual self-respect, has not disappeared. Its goal of mature economic development balanced by local ownership and control was not achieved, but thus far no administration, past or present, has done better. The model of its accomplishments in the West can still bear careful scrutiny. The vision that the New Deal projected of an economy predicated on the prudent use of natural resources remains a vision that has become increasingly blurred in recent years.

Notes

Chapter 1

1. James A. Farley, *Behind the Ballots: The Personal History of a Politician* (New York: Harcourt, Brace & Co., 1938), p. 83.
2. Ibid., p. 87; Arthur F. Mullen, *Western Democrat* (New York: Wilfred Funk, Inc., 1940), p. 260.
3. Elliott A. Rosen, in *Hoover, Roosevelt and the Brains Trust* (New York: Columbia University Press, 1977), fully discusses western opposition to Roosevelt's nomination. Chapters 9 and 10, passim.
4. Farley, p. 132. Hearst, Farley later learned, could exert no influence. Under California law, committee delegates could not shift unless released by the candidate or until it was conclusively shown he could not secure the nomination.
5. Fred L. Israel, *Nevada's Key Pittman* (Lincoln: University of Nebraska Press, 1963), pp. 97–98.
6. Farley, p. 138; Mullen, pp. 274–75.
7. Farley, p. 148. Elliott Rosen argues that McAdoo, not Garner, held the key to the convention's outcome and that winning him to the Roosevelt cause was finally achieved by an old Wilsonian, Daniel C. Roper. See Rosen, pp. 259–61. Arthur F. Mullen, Roosevelt's floor manager and hostile to McAdoo, claims California was not necessary for the nomination, that "Virginia would be ours for the asking." See Mullen, p. 278.
8. Richard Oulahan, *The Man Who . . . The Story of the 1932 Democratic National Convention* (New York: Dial Press, 1971), p. 117. The quote is from the telegram Hearst sent Brown.
9. Ibid., pp. 43–44.
10. Frank Freidel, in *Franklin D. Roosevelt, The Triumph* (Boston: Little, Brown & Co., 1956), discusses the Commonwealth Club address and "The Big Trip to the Coast" in chapter 23, pp. 338–59.
11. Richard Lowitt, *George W. Norris: The Persistence of a Progressive, 1913–1933* (Urbana: University of Illinois Press, 1971), pp. 557–62. Also Israel, p. 99. Republican Senator Bronson Cutting of New Mexico in October also endorsed Roosevelt.
12. Raymond Money, *After Seven Years* (New York: Harper & Bros., 1939), pp. 49–50.
13. For an example of efforts by those who wanted Roosevelt to "do something for silver," see Moley, p. 57.

Chapter 2

1. Lorena A. Hickok Papers, Introductory Chapter Draft, n.d. [1937], Box 12, Franklin D. Roosevelt Library, Hyde Park, N.Y. All Hickok letters, unless otherwise noted, are from this source. Most are now conveniently available in Richard Lowitt and Maurine Beasley, ed., *One Third of a Nation: Lorena Hickok Reports on the Great Depression,* (Urbana: University of Illinois Press, 1981).
2. Lorena A. Hickok to Harry L. Hopkins, September 3, 1934, Box 11. All items are from Box 11 unless otherwise noted.

3. Hickok to Hopkins, October 30, 1933.

4. Ibid. Later, in South Dakota, she learned of people eating Russian thistle soup. See Hickok to Hopkins, November 18, 1933.

5. Hickok to Hopkins, October 30, 1933, and November 1, 1933.

6. Hickok to Hopkins, November 1, 1933.

7. Hickok to Hopkins, November 3, 1933.

8. Hickok to Hopkins, November 6, 1933. For a discussion of North Dakota during the decade focusing on political reverberations revolving around William Langer, see Elwyn B. Robinson, *History of North Dakota,* (Lincoln: University of Nebraska Press, 1933), chapter 18, "The Thirties: Drought and Depression."

9. Hickok to Hopkins, November 7 and 10, 1933.

10. Hickok to Hopkins, November 7, 9, 10, and 18, 1933. Hickok also reported that railroads, so desperate was their situation, were asking for freight payments in advance, thereby compounding the plight of most South Dakota ranchers. See Hickok to Hopkins, November 10, 1933.

11. Hickok to Hopkins, November 9 and 18, 1933.

12. Hickok to Hopkins, November 9, 1933.

13. Hickok to Eleanor Roosevelt, November 11 and 12, 1933, Box 12. See too Hickok to Hopkins, November 18, 1933, wherein she discusses the same conditions she wrote Mrs. Roosevelt about. The letters to Mrs. Roosevelt were cast in more human terms; those to Hopkins were interspersed with comments about politics and programs.

14. Hickok to Hopkins, November 20, 1933.

15. Ibid. For a discussion of the remarkable PWA program of irrigation, flood control and public power multipurpose projects in Nebraska, see Richard Lowitt, *George W. Norris: The Triumph of a Progressive, 1933-1944,* (Urbana: University of Illinois Press, 1978), passim.

16. Hickok to Eleanor Roosevelt, November 21, 1933. Box 12.

17. Ibid. And Hickok to Hopkins, November 23, 1933. Bryan spoke for an hour "in a weak, rather high voice"; his delivery was "atrocious" and he kept repeating himself so much that Hickok had trouble believing that his brother made the "Cross of Gold" speech.

18. Hickok to Hopkins, November 23, 1933. Incidentally, Hickok believed that Communist agitation against relief workers in Nebraska and Iowa was part of a broader party endeavor. Literature distributed at the South Sioux City demonstration were "regular propaganda sheets" emanating from Omaha and Kansas City.

19. Ibid.

20. Hickok to Hopkins, April 11, 1934.

21. Hickok to Hopkins, April 17 and 25, 1934.

22. Ibid.

23. Hickok to Hopkins, April 17, 1934.

24. Hickok to Hopkins, April 17 and 25, 1934.

25. Hickok to Hopkins, April 17, 1934.

26. Ibid. In El Paso, which was economically depressed, the situation was made worse by a heavy case load of alien Mexicans, "all of whom came in before the present immigration restrictions were imposed and are not deportable." For a discussion of this situation which was arousing Anglo resentment in El Paso, see Hickok to Hopkins, April 25, 1934.

27. Hickok to Hopkins, April 17 and 25, 1934. She reiterated the entire situation in a less distressed tone though arriving at the same conclusions in her

April 25 letter written in Albuquerque wherein she summed up her views on Texas. In this letter she noted too that in the oil refineries there was no place "for the man over 45 or 35;" they were hiring only younger men.

28. Hickok to Hopkins, April 17, 1934.
29. Hickok to Hopkins, April 27, 1934.
30. Hickok to Hopkins, April 27, May 4 and 8, 1934.
31. Hickok to Hopkins, May 4, 1934.
32. Ibid.
33. Ibid.
34. Hickok to Hopkins, May 6, 1934.
35. Ibid.
36. Hickok to Hopkins, May 8, 1934.
37. Ibid.
38. Ibid.
39. Hickok to Hopkins, June 17, 1934.
40. Ibid.
41. Ibid.
42. Hickok to Hopkins, June 17 and 23, 1934. The Mexican-American worker signed a contract to tend and harvest a specific acreage. He was paid by the acre. To make "the barest sort of living," he had to work his entire family.
43. Hickok to Hopkins, June 17, 1934.
44. Hickok to Hopkins, June 17 and 23, 1934.
45. Hickok to Hopkins, June 23, 1934.
46. Hickok to Hopkins, June 24, 1934.
47. Ibid.
48. Hickok to Hopkins, June 25, 1934.
49. Hickok to Hopkins, June 27, 1934. For the way in which Los Angeles handled its problems as they pertained to Mexicans, see Abraham Hoffman, *Unwanted Mexican Americans in the Great Depression: Repatriation Pressures, 1929-1939,* (Tucson: University of Arizona Press, 1974). Over 400,000 Mexican aliens were repatriated during the early 1930s.
50. Hickok to Hopkins, June 27, 1934.
51. Hickok to Hopkins, July 1, 1934.
52. Ibid.
53. Hickok to Aubrey Williams, August 15, 1934.
54. Ibid.
55. Ibid.
56. Ibid.
57. Hickok to Williams, August 17, 1934.
58. Hickok to Williams, August 20, 1934.
59. Ibid.
60. Ibid.
61. Hickok to Williams, August 23, 1934.
62. Hickok to Williams, August 24, 1934.
63. Hickok to Williams, September 2, 1934.
64. Hickok to Hopkins, September 2, 1934.
65. Hickok to Hopkins, September 1 and 3, 1934.
66. Hickok to Hopkins, September 1, 1934.
67. Hickok to Hopkins, September 3, 1934.
68. Hickok to Hopkins, September 9, 1934.
69. Ibid.
70. Ibid.

71. Ibid.
72. Ibid.
73. Hickok to Hopkins, September 15, 1934.
74. Ibid.
75. Ibid.
76. Ibid.
77. Ibid.
78. Ibid.

Chapter 3

1. Samuel I. Rosenman, ed., *The Public Papers and Addresses of Franklin D. Roosevelt,* 9 vols. (New York: Random House, 1938; Macmillan Co., 1941), vol. 1: *The Genesis of the New Deal, 1928–1932,* p. 3

2. Ibid., pp. 477–95. See too Edgar B. Nixon, ed., *Franklin D. Roosevelt and Conservation, 1911–1945,* 2 vols. (Hyde Park, N.Y.: Franklin D. Roosevelt Library, 1957), 1:77–81, 109–10. I am in no way implying that these views were unique to Roosevelt alone, merely that some New Deal programs operative in the West reflected them. M. L. Wilson at Montana State College in March 1932 requested 40 copies of the speech for distribution to a land economics seminar.

3. Calvin Hoover, "The New Deal in the United States," *The Economic Journal* 44 (1934):581–83. See also two articles by C. Roger Lambert, "The Drought Cattle Purchase, 1934–1935: Problems and Complaints," *Agricultural History* 45 (1971):85–93 and "Drought Relief for Cattlemen; The Emergency Purchase Program of 1934–35," *Panhandle-Plains Historical Review* 45 (1972): 21–35.

4. Jay N. Darling, "Wildlife Areas and National Land Planning," in Harlean James, ed., *American Planning and Civic Annual* (Washington, D.C.: American Planning and Civic Association, 1935), p. 37. The notion of the Great Plains as a potential desert attracted widespread attention. It was evident in the remarkable success of a technical university press book, Paul Sears, *Deserts on the March* (Norman: University of Oklahoma Press, 1935). Two recent studies examine the Dust Bowl from markedly different perspectives, but both are critical of the New Deal. Paul Bonnifield in his study (Albuquerque: University of New Mexico Press, 1979) argues that New Deal programs went too far and were really not needed, while Donald Worster in his volume (New York: Oxford University Press, 1979) claims that the New Deal did not go far enough. Both volumes focus on the Southern Plains and are entitled *Dust Bowl.* The best, most balanced and most comprehensive study is by R. Douglas Hurt (Chicago: Nelson Hall, 1981). It too is entitled *Dust Bowl.* The heart of the Dust Bowl included eastern Colorado, western Kansas, the Panhandle of Oklahoma and Texas, and northeastern New Mexico. By April 1935, all the winter wheat in this area was dead and, owing to lack of rain, very little grass had started to grow.

5. Drought and dust storms in 1934 affected Canada as well. In Manitoba roads were reportedly "drifted over with dust piles almost as big as winter snowdrifts." See *The Literary Digest* 117 (May 19, 1934):50.

6. Carl C. Taylor et al., *Disadvantaged Classes in American Agriculture,* Social Research Report No. 8 (Washington, D.C.: Government Printing Office, 1938), pp. 68–69.

7. *The Literary Digest* 118 (August 18, 1934):5.

8. See H. H. Castle, "Summary of Drought Relief," *Monthly Report of the Federal Emergency Relief Administration*, November 1935, pp. 11–23.

9. "Fighting the Grasshopper," *U.S.D.A. Extension Service Review* 5 (1934): 110–11.

10. Wilmon H. Droze, *Trees, Prairies and People: A History of Tree Planting in the Plains States* (Denton: Texas Woman's University Press, 1977) is a definitive study of the shelterbelt, known as the Prairie States Forestry Project.

11. "Farm Practices that Helped in an Emergency," *U.S.D.A. Extension Service Review* 5 (1934): 152–54, 159.

12. See, for example, the discussion of a 1938 WPA bulletin by R. S. Kifer and H. L. Stewart, "Farming Hazards in the Drought Area" in *Rural Sociology* 4 (1939): 359–60.

13. WPA monthly reports on the progress of the works program for the last half of 1936 contain sections discussing "Emergency Drought Relief Measures." During the eight years from 1933 to 1941, the WPA and its predecessors spent more than a billion dollars in six Great Plains states: North and South Dakota, Kansas, Nebraska, Oklahoma and Texas. See John C. Page, "Don't Forget The Drought," *The Reclamation Era* 38, no. 11 (November 1941): 282.

14. Nixon, 1:367–68; Lawrence Svobida, *An Empire of Dust* (Caldwell, Idaho: Caxton Printers, 1940) details with remarkable poignancy how a farmer in western Kansas battled to save his lands from wind erosion—and lost.

15. Nixon, 1:541–42. Roosevelt wrote to Cooke on July 18, 1936.

16. Kenneth E. Trombley, *The Life and Times of a Happy Liberal: A Biography of Morris Llewellyn Cooke* (New York: Harper & Bros., 1954), pp. 112–24 for a discussion of the Mississippi Valley Committee.

17. *Report of the Mississippi Valley Committee of the Public Works Administration: October 1, 1934* (Washington, D.C.: Government Printing Office, 1934), passim. See, too, Harold L. Ickes, "Saving the Good Earth: The Mississippi Valley Committee and its Plan," *Survey Graphic* 23 (February 1934): 53–59, 91–93. The Morris L. Cooke Papers on deposit in the Franklin D. Roosevelt Library (Containers 263 and 264) contain Cooke's files on the Mississippi Valley Committee.

18. Henry A. Wallace to Franklin D. Roosevelt, August 5, 1936, in Nixon, 1:544–45; H. H. Adams, *Harry Hopkins,* (New York: G. P. Putnam's Sons, 1977), p. 102.

19. Rosenman, vol. 5: *The People Approve, 1936* (New York, Random House, 1938), 293–95, 299–301.

20. Nixon, 1:557–59; Rosenman, 5:301–5.

21. Nixon, 1:568–71; Rosenman, 5:331–39. Rosenman printed the entire fireside chat; Nixon excerpted the remarks that focus on the drought situation.

22. Nixon, 1:575–76, 583–84; Rosenman, 5:369–70. Nixon cites the date of the President's letter to Cooke as September 17, 1936. Rosenman prints the letter with September 19, 1936, as the date.

23. Nixon, 1:608–609 and 2:3–5. In the summary of the final report that was presented to Congress, the recommendations were increased and more specifically stated than in Cooke's December 29, 1936, covering letter to the President. The report was transmitted to the Congress on February 10, 1937, just as the Supreme Court controversy was getting under way.

24. Nixon, 2:19–20 for Roosevelt's message transmitting the report to Congress. It also appears in "The Future of the Great Plains," 75th Congress, 1st Session, House Document No. 144.

25. For a discussion of *The Plow that Broke the Plains*, see Robert L.

Snyder, *Pare Lorentz and the Documentary Film* (Norman: University of
Oklahoma Press, 1968), pp. 27–49, 75–76.

26. Richard Dyer MacCann, *The People's Films* (New York: Hastings
House, 1973), pp. 65–66.

27. This outline of suggested outlays is located in Container 324, Great
Plains, of the Morris L. Cooke Papers, Franklin D. Roosevelt Library, Hyde
Park, N.Y.

SUMMARY OUTLINE OF SUGGESTED GREAT PLAINS OUTLAYS
for Fiscal Years 1937, '38, and '39 and for 20-year period.

	Deficiency 1937, for immediate action	*1938*	*1939*	*20 years*
1. Land planning	84,000	1,400,000	1,500,000	7,000,000
2. Other planning, such as underground water supply and mineral resource surveys	50,000	700,000	750,000	5,000,000
3. Land purchase, sub-marginal (24 million acres)	1,000,000	2,500,000	4,000,000	90,000,000
4. Land purchase, for revision of holdings (14,400,000 acres)	1,000,000	5,000,000	10,000,000	75,000,000
5. Development of purchased lands				8,500,000
6. Resettlement of families	100,000	3,000,000	5,000,000	60,000,000
7. Conservation work: soil and water including flood irrigation	250,000	4,500,000	5,000,000	80,000,000
8. Irrigation, small projects	100,000	300,000	500,000	6,500,000
9. Irrigation, large projects	250,000	2,500,000	3,000,000	50,000,000
10. Education and extension		300,000	500,000	5,000,000
11. Miscellaneous Development, as control of grasshoppers, farm credit, tree planting for farm shelters, etc.	100,000	750,000	1,000,000	20,000,000
12. Administration	313,400	2,245,000	3,325,000	65,000,000
Totals	3,247,400	23,195,000	34,575,000	472,000,000

The land purchased acreage for revision of holdings includes about $200,000,000 to be obtained through County tax delinquents. Both land purchase items will probably be reduced over the 20-year period through lease offsets and lower purchase prices than estimated. Over a longer period they might be amortized.

15,000 stock ponds at an average price of $2,000 (total $30,000,000) should be built but it seems inadvisable to suggest that these be paid for by the Federal Government except as they are worked into the AAA or work relief program. No mention is made in this Summary of applications for AAA, CCC, relief or major structures for flood control.

Chapter 4

1. Francis D. Cronin and Howard W. Beers, "Areas of Intense Distress, 1930–1936," series 5, no. 1, Division of Social Research, Works Progress Administration (Washington, D.C.: Government Printing Office, January 1937).

2. In 1938 the Division of Social Research published a comprehensive monograph bringing together their findings about the relief needs of farm families in 13 selected areas of the Great Plains. See R. S. Kifer and H. L. Steward, "Farming Hazards in the Drought Areas," Research Monograph 16, Division of Social Research, Works Progress Administration (Washington, D.C.: Government Printing Office, 1938).

3. See Edgar B. Nixon, ed., *Franklin D. Roosevelt and Conservation, 1911–1945,* 2 vols. (Hyde Park, N.Y.: Franklin D. Roosevelt Library, 1957), 2:74–75, for a June 19, 1937, letter from the President to Representative James F. O'Connor of Montana discussing drought programs in eastern Montana and elsewhere on the Great Plains.

4. Nixon, 2:184–85. A committee chosen by the National Resources Committee prepared a special review of conditions in the northern Great Plains which, in accord with New Deal gospel, concluded that "rehabilitation and stabilization can come only through fundamental readjustments in land utilization." The Northern Great Plains Committee was appointed to suggest measures, including changes in procedure and policy, affecting land and water conservation. Congressional action was de-emphasized and constructive steps by state and local agencies were stressed. See White House press release, October 7, 1938, and the October 19 memorandum and letter by Roosevelt in Nixon, 2:258, 263–64. In addition, Roosevelt asked Congress for $5 million in the Department of the Interior appropriation for the Great Plains so that federal agencies could more effectively assist individuals and communities in becoming self-sustaining.

5. Samuel I. Rosenman, ed., *The Public Papers and Addresses of Franklin D. Roosevelt,* 9 vols. (New York: Random House, 1938; Macmillan Co., 1941), vol. 8: *War and Neutrality, 1939,* pp. 574–76 for a November 15, 1939, letter from the President to Edwin A. Hall discussing the drought situation. See also Roosevelt to Burton K. Wheeler, June 8, 1939; to Harold Ickes, June 14, 1939; and to M. O. Ryan, June 19, 1939—all in Nixon, 2:347–48, 351—for a more specific discussion of how the $5 million item included in the Interior Appropriation Act for the Great Plains would be allocated. The money for labor costs eventually came from the $1.425 billion made available to the Works Progress Administration.

6. *The Literary Digest* 123, no. 16 (April 17, 1937):27–28 for a discussion of the "Pest Menace." Grasshoppers were a problem on the Great Plains in the

summer of 1936 thereby arousing anxieties that 1937 would be worse. It was. Between 1929 and 1938 crop loss to grasshoppers amounted to $52.5 million in South Dakota. Only North Dakota suffered more extensive losses.

7. *The Literary Digest* 122, no. 4 (July 25, 1936):4–5 for the data on soil erosion. Bennett estimated that over a million acres in the Great Plains had been essentially ruined for further cultivation; over 4 million acres had been seriously affected by wind erosion, and an aggregate of 56 million acres, including 25 percent of the farm land, were seriously affected. See Hugh Hammond Bennett, "Soil Erosion and its Preservation," in A. E. Parkins and J. R. Whitaker, eds., *Our Natural Resources and Their Conservation* (New York: J. Wiley & Sons, 1936), p. 76.

8. Lawrence Svobida, *An Empire of Dust* (Caldwell, Idaho: Caxton Printers, 1940), p. 192.

9. The Wheeler-Case Act of August 1939 slightly modified the Water Facilities Act of 1937 but Harold Ickes wanted it further amended so that the Department of Agriculture would not duplicate activities of a kind usually administered by the Bureau of Reclamation. Agriculture did not agree with his proposal. See Harold D. Smith to Roosevelt, June 1, 1940, in Nixon, 2:451–52. It was only after 1940 that the Department of the Interior played a role in the administration of a Great Plains water conservation program. Armed with a $5 million allocation, the Bureau of Reclamation with WPA labor would be the chief construction agency. The first project, the Buford-Trenton irrigation project at the confluence of the Yellowstone and Missouri Rivers in North Dakota, was started on May 6, 1940. While the Bureau of Reclamation would be the construction agency, the Farm Security Administration would purchase and clear the land, recruit farm families for resettlement and administer the completed project. The National Resources Planning Board assisted in the planning and the project was initially approved by the Northern Great Plains Committee created by the President in 1938. See also footnotes 4 and 5.

10. By September 1940 enabling legislation for the establishment of soil conservation districts had been adopted by 38 states; 375 districts were operative involving approximately 233 million acres. By March 1942 there were more than 700 districts in operation representing a total acreage of over 413 million.

11. In 1936 Congress enacted the Soil Conservation and Domestic Allotment Act, replacing the Agricultural Adjustment Act which was declared unconstitutional in 1935. This legislation enhanced the role of the Soil Conservation Service, though it did create the Agricultural Stabilization and Conservation Service (ASCS) as the successor agency to the Agricultural Adjustment Administration (AAA).

12. For a discussion of the 1934 survey see R. Burnell Held and Marion Clawson, *Soil Conservation in Perspective* (Baltimore: Johns Hopkins University Press, 1965), pp. 157–66.

13. Department of the Interior: Memorandum for the Press, November 19, 1933, titled "Soil Erosion Program Gets Under Way." Copy in Morris L. Cooke Papers, Box 265, Soil Erosion, Franklin D. Roosevelt Library, Hyde Park, N.Y.

14. D. A. Dobkins and Virgil S. Beck, "Stabilizing the Dust Bowl," *Soil Conservation* 2, no. 6 (December 1937):158, 167.

15. See, for example, Edd R. Roberts, "Soil Conservation Districts Make Progress," *Extension Service Review* 10, no. 2 (February 1939):23, 31. Also

Hugh Hammond Bennett, "Sunshine and Shadow," *Soil Conservation* 3, no. 2 (August 1937):30–33. Bennett discusses a recent trip to the Pacific Northwest devoting much attention to South Dakota and the talk he gave about soil and water conservation in Rapid City before the annual meeting of the South Dakota Bankers Association.

16. L. C. Gray, "Federal Purchase and Administration of Submarginal Land in the Great Plains," *Journal of Farm Economics* 21, no. 1 (February 1939): 123–31. Gray argued that the objective of the purchase program was not to withdraw land from agriculture but "to make possible a change in the type of agriculture."

17. For an excellent detailed discussion of the functioning of one Soil Conservation District, the Cedar District in North Dakota, see Glenn K. Rule, *Soil Conservation in Action on the Land*, United States Department of Agriculture, Miscellaneous Publication No. 448, July 1941, pp. 2–14.

18. See the article by Peter Nelson titled "Tenancy—a Major Factor in Soil Conservation" in *Journal of Land and Public Utility Economics* 14, no. 1 (February 1938):88–91.

19. See, for example, M. L. Wilson, "Economic Democracy in Soil Conservation," *The Agricultural Situation* 21, no. 9 (September 1937): 9–10, and the following articles by Hugh Hammond Bennett, who published extensively about his work: "Soil Conservation," *The Agricultural Situation* 25, no. 12 (December 1941):13–15, and "Our Soil Can Be Saved," in the 1940 yearbook of agriculture titled *Farmers in a Changing World* (Washington, D.C.: Government Printing Office, 1940), pp. 429–40. For an overall survey see Theodore Saloutos, "The New Deal and Farm Policy in the Great Plains," *Agricultural History* 43 (1969):345–55. Most New Dealers also recognized that the Homestead Acts, supposedly the basis of a democratic land policy, encouraged the settlement of land on the Great Plains unsuited to crop farming and that a new program based on adequate research was needed. For a succinct statement of this premise, see Sherman E. Johnson, "Land Use Readjustments in the Northern Great Plains," *Journal of Land and Public Utility Economics* 13, no. 2 (May 1937):153–62 and Roy I. Kimmel, "Unit Reorganization Program for the Southern Great Plains," *Journal of Farm Economics* 22, no. 1 (February 1940):264–69. See too a provocative article by Carl F. Kraenzel, "New Frontiers on the Great Plains: A Cultural Approach to the Study of Man-Land Problems," in *Proceedings of the Western Farm Economic Association*, July 1940, published by State College of Washington (Pullman) and University of Idaho (Moscow).

20. *Extension Service Review* 11, no. 12 (December 1940):163.

21. An analysis of the results of a survey made by the Soil Conservation Service of farmer evaluation and criticism of conservation practices in the southern Great Plains indicated overwhelming approval. Both farm value and farm income increased as a result of installing a conservation program. Questionnaires were mailed to 4,200 farmers and ranchers; over 2,200 replied. See H. H. Finnell and Theodore A. Neubauer, "Farmer Evaluation of Conservation Practices in Southern Plains," *Soil Conservation* 2, no. 7 (January 1941):172–73 and Harry L. Carr, *War Time Farming on the Northern Great Plains*, United States Department of Agriculture, Soil Conservation Service, Miscellaneous Publication No. 497, June 1942. Carr suggests that conservation farming was paying extra dividends in good years and that farmers and ranchers were benefiting through this understanding.

Chapter 5

1. E. Louise Peffer, *The Closing of the Public Domain: Disposal and Reservation Policies, 1900–1950* (Stanford, Calif.: Stanford University Press, 1951).

2. *The Western Range,* 74th Congress, 2d Session; Senate Document No. 199.

3. For a discussion of the bias written into *The Western Range* see William Voigt, Jr., *Public Grazing Lands* (New Brunswick, N.J.: Rutgers University Press, 1976), pp. 67–70.

4. By 1939 income from grazing fees amounted to roughly $1 million annually.

5. Since the national forests were under the jurisdiction of the Department of Agriculture, this provision of the Taylor Grazing Act was a coup for Ickes.

6. My discussion of the Taylor Grazing Act is based largely on two articles by Virgil Hurlburt, "The Taylor Grazing Act" and "The Taylor Grazing Act Amendments," which appeared in *Journal of Land and Public Utility Economics* 2, no. 2 (May 1935):203–6, and ibid. 2, no. 4 (November 1935):410–11; and one by Andrew R. Cordova, "The Taylor Grazing Act," *New Mexico Business Review* 4, no. 4 (October 1935):193–201. I have also relied on Phillip O. Foss, *Politics and Grass* (Seattle: University of Washington Press, 1960). Foss focuses on the administration of the Taylor Grazing Act and carries his discussion into the 1950s.

7. All fell within or included territory within the Great Basin, including the mountain ranges bordering it on the east and west: Utah, California and Nevada, Oregon, Idaho, Montana, New Mexico, Colorado, Arizona and Wyoming. Within these regions at the end of 1940 there were 56 grazing districts.

8. See *The Grazing Bulletin* 2, no. 3 (April 1939):3 for Ickes's views. Portions of the range provided forage for a considerable portion of the nation's elk, antelope, deer, and other wildlife.

9. In September 1940 both Ickes and R. H. Rutledge, director of grazing, were pleased to announce effective cooperation between stockmen and the Grazing Service. See *The Grazing Bulletin* 3, no. 4 (September 1940):3–4, 21–22. Incidentally, the total area of Department of Interior lands in the western states was approximately 280 million acres, about half of which was within established grazing districts under Grazing Service supervision. For an example of a request for federal assistance in range rehabilitation see Elbert D. Thomas to Franklin D. Roosevelt, October 30, 1934, in Edgar B. Nixon ed., *Franklin D. Roosevelt and Conservation, 1911–1945,* 2 vols. (Hyde Park, NY.: Franklin D. Roosevelt Library, 1957), 1:330–32.

10. See *The Grazing Bulletin* 4 (October 1941), p. 3, for comments regarding Edward T. Taylor, and pp. 33–35, for approving letters from stockmen. For further evidence of stockmen support see Harold L. Ickes, *The Secret Diary of Harold L. Ickes,* vol. 3: *The Lowering Clouds, 1939–1941* (New York: Simon & Schuster, 1954), pp. 337–38. For differing views see "Dependency Relationships between Public Range and Private Lands," *Proceedings of the Western Farm Economics Association,* Fourteenth Annual Meeting (Salt Lake City, Utah, June 25–27, 1941), pp. 131–37. Page 137 notes that many range areas had too many small units "not capable of providing the operator's family with the minimum requirements for wholesome living." See also, William E. Borah to Harold L. Ickes, April 11, 1938, Box 491, William E. Borah Papers, Library of Congress, for complaints by small ranchers. For a suggestion of what happened to these lands by the end of the 1940s, see DeVoto to Harold Stassen,

June 10, 1948, in Wallace Stegner, ed., *The Letters of Bernard DeVoto* (Garden City, N.Y.: Doubleday & Co., 1975), pp. 351–57, and Charles McKinley, *Uncle Sam in the Pacific Northwest* (Berkeley and Los Angeles: University of California Press, 1952), pp. 265–66. For a positive assessment of what had been accomplished, see Bernard Frank and Arthur Netboy, *Water, Land and People* (New York: Alfred A. Knopf, 1950), pp. 188–89. The authors also agreed that much remained to be done.

11. See Mont H. Saunderson, "Economic Relationships of Public Lands and Privately Owned Grazing Lands in the Western States," *Journal of Farm Economics* 20, no. 4 (November 1938):841–53 and Francesca M. Blackmer, "The West, Water and the Grazing Laws," *Survey Graphic* 26 (July 1937):387. For Ickes's views see Ickes to Roosevelt, August 26, 1935, in Nixon, 1:421–26, wherein Ickes recommends that the President veto H.R. 3019, a measure amending the Taylor Grazing Act. Much of the difficulty arising among stockmen was based upon using the 1929–34 period to determine who among them could use the range and how many animals they could pasture on it. See also J. L. Driscoll to N. F. Waddell, April 20, 1938, Box 491, William E. Borah Papers, for an extended critique of the Taylor Grazing Act as it applied to small stockmen in Idaho. Driscoll was a Boise banker and Waddell a special investigator for the Department of the Interior.

12. For an indication of tensions and difficulties with regard to grazing between the Forest Service and the Grazing Service, see Roosevelt to Key Pittman, March 25, 1939, in Nixon, 2:311; and Henry A. Wallace to Roosevelt, March 2, 1940, and Ickes to Roosevelt, March 7, 1940, in Nixon, 2:425–27 and 429–32. In New Mexico, for example, "free-users" and "wild-life" men were included on the advisory boards.

13. A 1936 amendment to the Taylor Grazing Act stipulated that all high-level administrative officers, including district graziers, must have been residents of a western public land state for at least a year prior to appointment. In addition, the Civil Service Commission was directed to consider practical range experience in determining eligibility for appointment.

14. Quote appears in T. H. Watkins and Charles S. Watson, Jr., *The Land No One Knows: America and the Public Domain* (San Francisco: Sierra Club, 1975), p. 115.

15. Harold L. Ickes, "The National Domain and the New Deal," *Saturday Evening Post*, December 23, 1933, p. 10.

16. Wesley Carr Calef, *Private Grazing and Public Lands* (Chicago: University of Chicago Press, 1960), p. 59.

17. M. L. Wilson, "A Land Use Program for the Federal Government," *Journal of Farm Economics* 15 (April 1935):217–35.

18. See the discussions by Mont H. Saunderson, "Some Economic Aspects of the Upland Watershed Lands of the Western United States," *Journal of Land and Public Utility Economics* 15, no. 4 (November 1939):480–82, and by C. F. Clayton, "Program of the Federal Government for the Purchase and Use of Submarginal Lands," *Journal of Farm Economics* 17, no. 1 (February 1935):55–63. Roland R. Renne noted in 1934 that "most of the lands of the western states, with the possible exception of California, are still to be classified by a detailed soil reconnaissance." See his remarks in *Proceedings of the Western Farm Economics Association*, Seventh Annual Meeting, June 21–22, 1934, at the University of California at Berkeley, p. 90.

19. L. C. Gray, "National Policies Affecting Land Use," *Rural America* 11, no. 8 (October 1935):10–11.

20. Richard L. Neuberger, "Public Domain," *Survey Graphic* 20, no. 2 (February 1941):75; Robert Y. Stuart, "Emergency Work in the National Forests," in Harlean James, ed., *American Civic Annual* (Washington, D.C.: American Civic Annual Press, 1934), p. 57.

21. Stephen N. Wycoff, "The Use of Uncultivated Lands in Western States," *Proceedings of the Western Farm Economics Association,* Fifteenth Annual Meeting, June 24–26, 1942 at Stanford University, pp. 43–45. Western forests in 1940 produced 13 billion board feet of lumber out of a national production of 29 billion.

22. See F. A. Silcox, "A Forest Program and a Plan of Action," *Extension Service Review* 10, no. 7 (July 1939):102. The Forest Service, under legislation dating back to the Taft Administration, was adding to its domain additional federally purchased forest lands. For a discussion of the functioning of a western national forest, see J. C. Witham, "Land Use Administrative Problems on the Gallatin National Forest," *Proceedings of the Western Farm Economics Association,* Eleventh Annual Meeting, July 6–8, 1938, at Montana State College at Bozeman, pp. 136–42.

23. *Proceedings of the Third Pacific Northwest Regional Planning Conference* at Spokane, Washington, February 13–15, 1936, p. 34; Works Progress Administration *Report on Progress of Works Program,* June 15, 1936, pp. 36–41. Congress on June 15, 1936, authorized the establishment of a Great Plains Forest Experiment Station. On June 30, 1942, the Prairie States Forestry Project was terminated as an emergency activity and transferred from the Forest Service to the Soil Conservation Service.

24. Prior to 1933, federal acquisition of forest lands was provided for in the Weeks Act (1911), allowing purchase for the forest fire protection of the headwaters of navigable streams, and the Clarke-McNary Act (1924), broadening the original authority to include purchase of land for timber production as well as for stream-flow protection. The McNary-Woodruff Act and the McSweeney-McNary Act, both approved in 1928, further strengthened the programs for the acquisition of national forests and for cooperation with the states. In addition, CCC funds were used during the New Deal to purchase forest lands. Much of this acreage was added to eastern national forests. Henry Wallace was convinced that most of the major problems of American forestry stemmed from private ownership and that the first steps in rectifying the damage done to forest lands necessitated a large extension of public ownership and more intensive management of publicly owned lands. See Robert Y. Stuart to Henry A. Wallace, April 18, 1933, in Nixon, 1:153–54; Roosevelt to Miller Fallman, September 19, 1940, in Nixon, 2:474–75, provides data on the acquisition of additional forest lands. Wallace was merely reflecting the major findings of the 1,650-page report he transmitted to the Senate on March 27, 1933, "A National Plan for American Forestry." It quickly became known as the Copeland Report, after Senator Royal S. Copeland, who in 1932 introduced the resolution calling for such a report.

25. The lumber code established in 1934 under the National Industrial Recovery Act provided Wallace, the President, and other New Dealers an opportunity to call for conservation and sustained-yield production of forest resources from the lumber industry. With the approval of the lumber code came the first organized effort of the American forest industry to apply on a national scale the principles of conservation to the management of privately owned timber lands. For examples of Roosevelt's interest in forestry, see Roosevelt to the State Governors, January 2, 1935, and Roosevelt to (Oregon Governor) Charles H. Martin, August 12, 1935. Both items are published in

Nixon, 1:339 and 410–11, as is his March 14, 1938, message to the Congress, pp. 190–97. For a discussion of the lumber code see Rodney C. Loehr, ed., *Forests for the Future: The Story of Sustained Yield as Told in the Diaries and Papers of David T. Mason, 1907–1950* (St. Paul: Minnesota Historical Society, 1952), pp. 99–106, 127–28, 149–63. For an indication of the favorable response of lumbermen, notably those on the west coast, to the lumber code, see David Cushman Coyle, *Conservation* (New Brunswick, N.J.: Rutgers University Press, 1957), pp. 104–5. Senator Charles L. McNary in April 1936 introduced "a sustained-yield forest management bill" (S4507) calling for a ten-year program of national forest acquisition on the basis of $30 million per year. The bill never got out of committee. See Charles H. Martin to Roosevelt, May 27, 1936, Box 39, Charles L. McNary Papers, Library of Congress. Martin, Governor of Oregon, in endorsing S4507 discussed the lumber situation in Oregon and how McNary's bill would meliorate it.

26. 77th Congress, 1st Session: Senate Document No. 32, entitled "Forest Lands of the United States," presented March 24, 1941, p. 20. For the views of a progressive group of lumbermen willing to cooperate with the Forest Service, see "Resolutions Adopted by Western Forestry and Conservation Association: December 10–12, 1936." Copy in William E. Borah Papers, Box 468.

27. The annual reports of the National Forest Reservation Commission during the New Deal years were published as Senate Documents. Prior to fiscal 1936 there were no western land purchases.

28. See the discussion in Charles McKinley, *Uncle Sam in the Pacific Northwest* (Berkeley and Los Angeles: University of California Press, 1952), pp. 296–99. In 1935 a series of infestations of the Douglas fir beetle followed the Tillamook burn, destroying 200 million board feet and another 100,000,000 in 1938. For an insight into the forest fire devastation on the Pacific Coast, see *The Literary Digest* 22, no. 25 (December 19, 1936):13–14. Between November 1, 1936, and the end of the decade, a total of 2,500 acres of national forest in three Pacific Coast states had been fired. In three southwestern Washington counties 20,000 acres of farm and timber land were destroyed and 5,000 acres blackened in western Oregon in one week. In 1936, according to the Forest Service, 439,632 acres of national forest had been burned in these three states, a sizable increase over 1935, when 178,133 acres were fired. The jump was attributed to extensive drought conditions. For a contemporary insight into the problems of small lumbermen in the West and of relations with the Forest Service, see Anna Louise Strong, *My Native Land* (New York: Viking Press, 1940), pp. 135–38 and Harold L. Ickes, *The Secret Diary of Harold L. Ickes: The Inside Struggle, 1936–1939* (New York: Simon & Schuster, 1953), pp. 453–54. For a brief perceptive discussion of the industry, see "Technology, Productivity, and Employment in the Lumber Industry," *Monthly Labor Review* 51 (July 1940):53–61. The quote is in Ovid Butler, ed., *American Conservation* (Washington, D.C.: American Forestry Association, 1941), p. 45. See too Thornton T. Munger, "Problems of Forest Land Ownership and Use," *Proceedings of the First Pacific Northwest Regional Planning Conference,* (Portland, Ore., March 5–7, 1934), pp. 66–69.

29. Irving Brant to Roosevelt, March 6, 1940. Box 19, Irving Brant Papers, Library of Congress. For an indication of the feuding between Interior and Agriculture, see Harold K. Steen, *The U.S. Forest Service: A History* (Seattle: University of Washington Press, 1976), pp. 206–9.

30. The Timber Products Bureau of the Spokane Chamber of Commerce meeting on July 7, 1937, "strongly opposed" moving the Forest Service into the Department of the Interior. Since Spokane is located in an area close to several

national forests and near a highly developed agricultural section, the members of its Chamber of Commerce were impressed by "the successful application of the department (USDA) of the principles basic to the conservation of these two types of renewable resources and have become convinced that any system of government reorganization which involves separation of these two closely allied federal functions into two executive departments could only be conducive of confusion and unfortunate results." Copy in William E. Borah Papers, Box 468. In 1940, Wallace said that summer grazing in national forests furnished a means of livelihood to "small home-owners" and that there were about 25,000 permittees on the national forests. See Wallace to Roosevelt, March 2, 1940 in Nixon, 2:425–26. These permittees yielded the Forest Service in fiscal 1940 grazing receipts of $1,457,120. Alan Macdonald, "Forests for Conservation and Use," *The Agricultural Situation* 25, no. 2 (February 1941):20.

31. Harold L. Ickes, *The New Democracy* (New York: W. W. Norton & Co., 1934), pp. 85, 119–21; Jean Christie, "New Deal Resources Planning: The Proposals of Morris L. Cooke" *Agricultural History* 53, no. 3 (July 1979):598–602. This article discusses the work of Cooke on the Mississippi Valley Committee (1934) and the Great Plains Committee (1936). While Cooke's reports have been discussed in the previous chapter, the point to note here is that several committee and staff members were recruited from the National Resources Committee. In addition, for example, the National Resources Planning Board conducted major investigations of problem areas and policy issues in the Northern Great Plains, the Upper Rio Grande Valley and the Pacific Northwest and initiated joint field action with agencies in the Departments of Interior and Agriculture. See Charles E. Merriam, "Planning in a Democracy," in Harlean James, ed., *American Planning and Civic Annual* (Washington, D.C.: American Planning and Civic Annual Press, 1940), p. 9. Merriam was vice chairman of the National Resources Planning Board. A 1936 government publication by Harlow S. Person titled *Little Waters* attracted widespread attention to the problems of erosion along the headwaters of streams. At the time Person was chairman of the Water Planning Committee of the National Resources Committee. For Roosevelt's remarks, see Nixon, 1:341–344.

32. Frederic A. Delano to Ickes, November 23, 1935; Roosevelt to Delano, September 9, 1936. Nixon, 1:450–52, 571 and 2:442–43. Delano in responding to the President's inquiry commented upon his conversations with Idaho Congressman Compton I. White who was seeking mine-to-market roads in the national forests and on the public domain in Idaho. The Forest Service, the Bureau of Public Roads, and the Bureau of Mines were already "conversant with the problem" and were working with the Idaho State Planning Board. While the Forest Service already had a program for forest roads and trails in Idaho there was some concern about constructing roads "which tend primarily to develop private property" and which would encourage "promiscuous and uncontrolled mineral resource exploitation" running counter to any plan for natural resource utilization. See Delano to Roosevelt, September 17, 1936, in Nixon, 1:576–77.

Chapter 6

1. John C. Page, "Water Conservation and Control" *The Reclamation Era* 27, no. 3 (March 1937):48. For a general statement about the Bureau of Reclamation and its multipurpose approach see Harold L. Ickes, "Though for the Morrow," *Collier's,* December 8, 1934. Copy in Box 103, Harold L. Ickes Papers, Library of Congress. For an excellent concise overview see Donald C.

Swain, "The Bureau of Reclamation and the New Deal, 1933–1940," *Pacific Northwest Quarterly* 61 (1970):137–46.

2. Beverly Bowen Moeller, *Phil Swing and Boulder Dam* (Berkeley and Los Angeles: University of California Press, 1971) and Norris Hundley, *Water and The West: The Colorado River Compact and The Politics of Water in the American West* (Berkeley and Los Angeles: University of California Press, 1975) discuss the developments leading to Boulder Dam. See too the unsigned article in *Fortune* 8, no. 3 (September 1933) titled "The Dam" on pp. 74–88. The best and most comprehensive analysis is provided by Linda J. Lear, "The Boulder Canyon Project: a Reexamination of Federal Resource Management," *Northwest Quarterly,* in press.

3. "The Dam," p. 82. See too Wallace Stegner, *The Sound of Mountain Water* (Garden City, N.Y.: Doubleday & Co., 1969), pp. 61–62, for his 1946 diary comments. Stegner in 1946 became a booster after spending two days on Lake Mead and going through the dam and powerhouses.

4. Box 133 of the Key Pittman Papers in the Library of Congress contains much material pertaining to the construction and operation of Boulder Dam. For example, J. L. Leonard to George Creel, December 26, 1933, discusses working conditions and notes that in September, eight IWW organizers attempted to organize the employees, 32 of whom went out on strike. At the time there were 3,200 men employed, 42 percent of whom were veterans, at a minimum wage of $4.00 per day for seven days a week. The Six Companies created Boulder City by constructing more than 600 houses, nine large dormitories, a mess hall, recreation hall, department store, hospital and other buildings. For a survey of the community at the end of the New Deal, see Rupert B. Spearman, "Boulder City is a Growing Community," *The Reclamation Era* 31, no. 3 (March 1941):72–73, and S. R. DeBoer, "The Plan of Boulder City, Nevada," in Harlean James, ed., *American Civic Annual* (Washington, D.C.: American Civic Association, 1934), pp. 210–11. See too the articles by Elwood Mead in *The Literary Digest* 116, no. 19 (November 4, 1933):15 and ibid. 122, no. 16 (October 17, 1936):19–20. This later article is titled "Boulder Dam: Engineering Triumph."

5. The full speech, the second half of which was a defense of public works as a means of providing employment and enhancing national wealth, can be found in Samuel Rosenman, ed., *The Public Papers and Addresses of Franklin D. Roosevelt,* 9 vols. (New York: Random House, 1938; Macmillan Co., 1941), vol. 4: *The Court Disapproves, 1937,* pp. 397–402.

6. Harold L. Ickes, *The Secret Diary of Harold L. Ickes: The Inside Struggle, 1936–39* (New York: Simon & Schuster, 1953), pp. 580–81 (for his views on Las Vegas, p. 693); Edgar B. Nixon, *Franklin D. Roosevelt and Conservation, 1911–1945,* 2 vols. (Hyde Park, N.Y.: Franklin D. Roosevelt Library, 1957), 2:367–69, 384–88, 395; Key Pittman to William E. Borah, February 8, 1939; Pittman to Ickes, November 28, 1938; and Harry Slattery to Pittman, December 22, 1938. All in Box 521, William E. Borah Papers, Library of Congress. The files in Box 133 of the Key Pittman Papers indicate his longstanding Nevada interest in Boulder Dam.

7. *Civil Engineering* 2, no. 5 (May 1941):293.

8. *The Reclamation Era* 29, no. 3 (March 1939):61, 64. By 1948, 260 miles of transmission lines were supplying electricity to the Gila and Salt River irrigation projects in central Arizona. Transmission lines from Boulder Dam utilized copper rather than aluminum, thereby benefiting Nevada copper producers who hoped similar provisions would be included in contracts for Parker

Dam transmission lines. See Henry M. Rives to Key Pittman, August 24, 1935, Box 133, Key Pittman Papers.

9. See the protests in Box 133 of the Key Pittman Papers, and Norris Hundley, Jr., *Water and the West,* passim.

10. Key Pittman to Harold Ickes, November 12, 1937, Box 133; [James A.] White to *Nevada State Journal,* June 21, 1940 (telegram), Box 134; S. B. Robinson et al. to Committee of Sixteen, July 26, 1939, copy in Box 135. All in the Key Pittman Papers. The last item in particular gives some of the background leading to the 1940 enactment.

11. E. M. Debler, "The Colorado River Basin," an address to the Conference of Colorado River Basin States, Phoenix, Arizona, December 14, 1938. Copy in Box 134, Key Pittman Papers.

12. James F. Wickens, *Colorado in the Great Depression* (New York: Garland Publishing, Inc., 1979), pp. 203–4. Wickens in chapter 7 presents an excellent discussion of the PWA in Colorado. Oliver Knight, "Correcting Nature's Error: The Colorado-Big Thompson Project," *The Reclamation Era* 30, no. 9 (September 1949):267–69, reviews the project as it stood at the end of the New Deal; Donald B. Cole, "Transmountain Water Diversion in Colorado," *The Colorado Magazine* 25, no. 2 (March 1948):49–64, and ibid. 25, no. 3 (May 1948):118–35, places transmountain water diversion, including the Big Thompson project, in historical perspective. See too Ickes to Roosevelt, December 20, 1937, in Nixon, 2:157–58.

13. Thomas H. Langevin, "Development of Multiple-Purpose Water Planning by the Federal Government in the Missouri Basin," *Nebraska History* 34 (1935):7–19. Samuel Rosenman, vol. 3: *The Advance of Recovery and Reform,* pp. 363–65. Roosevelt reiterated the multipurpose approach when he spoke again at Fort Peck on October 3, 1937; see Rosenman, vol. 6: *The Constitution Prevails, 1937,* pp. 397–99. In 1941 Bureau of Reclamation engineers were discussing the possibilities of diverting water and power from Fort Peck to the Red River country of North Dakota to reclaim about 1.5 million acres.

14. For a critical appraisal of the model town of Fort Peck see James Rorty, *Where Life is Better: An Unsentimental American Journey* (New York: Reynal & Hitchcock, 1936), chapter 21 titled "The Exiles of Fort Peck."

15. Elwood Mead, "Making the North Platte River Do More Work," *The Literary Digest* 116, no. 22 (November 25, 1933):15; H. W. Bashore, "Progress at Casper-Alcova," *The Reclamation Era* 26, no. 2 (February 1936):53. See too Harold L. Ickes to Charles H. Dennis, November 25, 1933, Box 258, Harold L. Ickes Papers, Library of Congress. Ickes assured Dennis, an editorial writer for the *Chicago Daily News,* that the project would not be adding to the agricultural surplus because most of the crops would be either used as cattle feed and consumed in the vicinity or would replace crops from depleted lands taken out of production elsewhere.

16. T. A. Larson, *History of Wyoming* (Lincoln: University of Nebraska Press, 1978), pp. 420–23. Wyoming was favored with projects because its federal oil reserves by 1940 provided more than half the funds received by the Reclamation Fund from this source. By the end of 1940 Wyoming had three projects in operation (Riverton, Hart Mountain-Shoshone, and Kendrick) and another (Eden) recently approved.

17. For a discussion of the Nebraska projects see Richard Lowitt, *George W. Norris: The Triumph of a Progressive, 1933–1944* (Urbana: University of Illinois Press, 1978), particularly the chapters focusing on Nebraska. The congressional files of Lyndon Baines Johnson in the presidential library at

Austin contain much material on the Colorado River Development, largely located in Johnson's (Tenth) Congressional District. See too the discussion of the 1937 flood in John C. Page, "The Multiple Purpose Project," *The Reclamation Era* 29, no. 5 (May 1939):94. These dams were constructed for the Lower Colorado River Authority by the Bureau of Reclamation assisted with PWA funds. Reimbursement arrangements for this funding were concluded in 1948. Harold L. Ickes, "Our Right to Power," *Colliers,* November 12, 1938. Draft copy in Box 104, Harold L. Ickes Papers, Library of Congress, contains an excellent brief discussion of the project on the Colorado River in Texas.

18. Leonard J. Arrington and Lowell Dittmer, "Reclamation in Three Layers: The Ogden River Project, 1934–1965," *Pacific Historical Review* 35 (1966):20–27. See too Kenneth W. Baldridge, "Reclamation Work of the Civilian Conservation Corps, 1933–1942," *Utah Historical Quarterly* 39 (1971):265–85 for a discussion that focuses exclusively on CCC work in Utah, including the Pine View Dam project.

19. The Wheeler-Case Act, which originally applied only to the northern Great Plains, was subsequently amended to include water projects in all of the arid and semiarid states of the West.

20. John C. Page, "Water Conservation and Control," *The Reclamation Era* 27, no. 3 (March 1937):48; and "Don't Forget the Drought," *The Reclamation Era* 28, no. 11 (November 1941):282.

21. See Page, "Don't Forget the Drought," p. 282, for relief expenditures in the West.

22. For Ickes's views see Nixon, 2:334–35, 375. See also Ickes to Roosevelt, July 13, 1935, Box 258, Harold L. Ickes Papers. Ickes argued that "the Bureau of Reclamation ought to be made the agent of the Resettlement Administration for the purchase of lands in connection with reclamation projects."

23. Works Financing Act of 1939: (S2759) Hearing Before the Committee on Banking and Currency. U.S. Senate: 76th Congress, 1st Session, pp. 110–12. Bureau spokesmen claimed 100 percent repayment was not achieved because many of its earlier projects were rescue missions where original developers failed to provide an adequate and stable water supply.

24. Works Financing Act of 1939 (S2759): Hearings Before the Committee on Banking and Currency. U.S. Senate: 76th Congress, 1st Session, pp. 112–17. The quote is from a 1935 "Report on Survey of Federal Reclamation in the West" by F. E. Schmitt and John W. Haws, as presented in *The Reclamation Era* 25, no. 2 (February 1935):29. Schmitt was editor of *Engineering News-Record* and Haws was director of agricultural development for the Northern Pacific Railroad.

25. Editorial, "Thirty-five Years of Reclamation," *The Reclamation Era* 27, no. 6 (June 1937):123 for the data in the paragraph. See too "Purchasing Power of Federal Reclamation Projects," ibid. 29, no. 5 (May 1939):114–15 and "Reclamation Contracts Create Industrial Activity," ibid. no. 9 (September 1939):240–41. See also G. W. Grebe to William E. Borah, May 16, 1935, Box 431; and Borah to Grebe, March 27, 1936, Box 455, William E. Borah Papers. Grebe, president of the Federal Irrigation Congress, was seeking an extension of the moratorium on construction charges. The congress was organized to promote the welfare of water users on federal irrigation projects.

26. 75th Congress, 3rd Session: Senate Report No. 1544 (to accompany S3681) presents the outlines of the 1938 legislation with a letter from Ickes to Alva B. Adams on March 23, 1938, endorsing the measure. The National

Reclamation Association, the Federal Irrigation Congress, and individual water users' associations supported both the 1938 and 1939 laws.

27. "The Place of Hydroelectric Power in Reclamation," *The Reclamation Era* 30, no. 6 (June 1940):157–58; Harry W. Bashore, "A Multiple-Purpose Program to Meet Defense Needs," *The Reclamation Era* 31, no. 9 (September 1941):248–51.

28. "Value of Reclamation to the United States." Copy of a paper submitted to the Conference of Colorado River Basin States held at Phoenix, Arizona, December 14, 1938, Box 134, Key Pittman Papers. To be sure, cotton was grown on four southwestern federal reclamation projects but it was long-staple cotton and was practically the only domestic source for this variety. Acreage devoted to cotton was one half of 1 percent of the total national value. See Karl Harris, "The Irrigation of Cotton," *The Reclamation Era* 31, no. 10 (October 1941):266.

29. Sugar legislation was tied in with tariff schedules affecting cane sugar producers in American dependencies as well as domestic sugar refiners who exercised considerable clout in Washington. Material in this paragraph is derived from Rosenman, vol. 2: *The Year of Crisis, 1933* (New York: Random House, 1938), pp. 86–90, 219–21. For the impact of this legislation on Texas cane sugar refiners, see statement titled "Existing and Proposed Sugar Legislation as it Affects the Cane Sugar Refining Industry," n.d., Box 202, Jesse Jones Papers, Library of Congress. For an overall discussion of "The Sugar Programs of the Roosevelt Administration," see chapters under this heading in Joshua Bernhardt, *The Sugar Industry and the Federal Government* (Washington, D.C.: Sugar Statistics Service, 1948). During the New Deal Bernhardt was chief of the sugar section in the AAA and successor organizations in the Department of Agriculture.

30. Rosenman, vol. 6: *The Constitution Prevails*, pp. 107–11, and Elizabeth S. Johnson, "Wages, Employment Conditions and Welfare of Sugar-Beet Laborers," *Monthly Labor Review* 46 (February 1938):323–24.

31. Rosenmen, vol. 8: *War and Neutrality, 1939*, pp. 507–9, 611–12; and vol. 9: *War—and Aid to Democracies, 1940* (New York: Macmillan Co., 1941), pp. 134–38. See too Ickes, *The Secret Diary of Harold L. Ickes: The Lowering Clouds, 1939–41* (New York: Simon and Schuster, 1954), pp. 269, 482. In 1940 Colorado and Nebraska, both states in which beet sugar was a factor in the economy, were among the ten states voting against Roosevelt.

32. See the excellent article by Johnson, "Wages, Employment Conditions, and Welfare of Sugar Beet Laborers," pp. 322–40, and the discussion in chapter 2. An average of $222 earned per family in 1935 was reported for a group of beet workers on relief in Weld County, Colorado. For a discussion of the minimum wage rates which varied between the beet sugar producing areas, see "Minimum Wages for Sugar Beets and Sugar Cane Labor," *Monthly Labor Review* 53 (July 1941):167–68 and William T. Ham, "Sugar Beet Field Labor Under the AAA," *Journal of Farm Economics* 19 (May 1937):643–47. See too Joshua Bernhardt to William E. Borah, February 23, 1938, Box 486, William E. Borah Papers. For a comprehensive analysis see Kent Hendrickson, "The Sugar-Beet Laborer and the Federal Government: An Episode in the History of the Great Plains in the 1930s," *Great Plains Journal* 3, no. 2 (Spring 1964):44–59.

33. James F. O'Connor, "Sugar Beet Acreage on Reclamation Projects," *The Reclamation Era* 30, no. 1 (January 1940):3. O'Connor was a member of

Congress from Montana. See John E. Dalton, *Sugar: A Case Study of Governmental Control* (New York: Macmillan Co., 1937). In chapter 10 he argued that the western beet sugar industry came into being, developed, and existed in its current state because of government assistance which was responsible for molding the economic life of areas in the West into "specialized one-crop islands" insuring, despite recession elsewhere, general prosperity for beet sugar factories.

34. Richard Lowitt, *George W. Norris: The Triumph of a Progressive, 1933–1944* (Urbana: University of Illinois, 1978), pp. 232, 266–67, 307–8. William E. Borah to the President, October 15, 1934; Oswald Wilson to Henry A. Wallace, October 31, 1934; Wallace to Borah, November 14, 1934, all in Box 402; C. Ben Ross to Wallace, December 3, 1935, Box 433. All correspondence from William E. Borah Papers. For an indication of the antipathy of irrigation farmers to the Department of Agriculture and Henry A. Wallace for their assignments of acreage allotments, see the 1938 petition of the Idaho State Beet Growers Association in Box 505 of the William E. Borah papers.

35. Marshall N. Dana, "Reclamation as a National Policy," *The Reclamation Era* 25, no. 3 (March 1935):48. The address of President O. S. Warden to the 1937 annual convention of the National Reclamation Association discusses its lobbying efforts. See *The Reclamation Era* 27, no. 11 (November 1937):268–71. Remarks comparable to those cited in this paragraph abound in almost every discussion of reclamation during the 1930s.

36. The Ickes quote is cited in Page, "A Sector for the Future," *The Reclamation Era* 29, no. 12 (December 1939):328. See also "Highlights of the Address of John C. Page," *The Reclamation Era* 30, no. 10 (October 1940):278.

Chapter 7

1. Linda J. Lear, in "Harold L. Ickes and the Oil Crisis of the First Hundred Days," *Mid-America* 63, no. 1 (January 1981):3–13, presents a comprehensive analysis upon which I have relied heavily. Equally important as a base for the discussion in this chapter is a paper presented at a session of the 1980 meeting of the American Historical Association by the same author, "The Politics of Oil: Harold L. Ickes and the Struggle for Federal Regulation, 1933–1935."

2. Harold L. Ickes: Memorandum, April 10, 1936, Box 155, Harold L. Ickes Papers, Library of Congress. Governors of the major oil-producing states also recognized that Federal action was necessary. See, too, Samuel I. Rosenman, ed., *The Public Papers and Addresses of Franklin D. Roosevelt*, 9 vols. (New York: Random House, 1938; Macmillan, 1941), vol. 2: *The Year of Crisis, 1933*, pp. 103–6 and 208–209 for documents and notes reviewing the situation at the outset of the New Deal prior to the approval of the National Industrial Recovery Act on June 16, 1933.

3. "Hot oil" was a problem primarily in the East Texas oil field where it was estimated that 60,000 to 75,000 barrels per day were being shipped. It was this concern that led the President to call for legislation that resulted in the Connally Act. See Rosenman, vol. 3: *The Advance of Recovery and Reform, 1934*, pp. 256–58.

4. For an overall discussion see Joe S. Bain, *The Economics of The Pacific Coast Petroleum Industry: Part II* (Berkeley and Los Angeles: University of California Press, 1945), especially Chapters 4 and 5. See also Oscar Sutro to Harold L. Ickes, January 22, 1935, Box 218, Harold L. Ickes Papers; and

William Scully to Charles Fahy, July 17, 1935, Box 14, Charles Fahy Papers, Franklin D. Roosevelt Library, Hyde Park, N.Y.

5. The following year in Los Angeles at its annual meeting, Axtell J. Byles, President of the American Petroleum Institute, stated "on this question of Federal control, the industry is united against it almost to a man." See *The Literary Digest* 120, no. 21 (November 23, 1935):38.

6. The Interstate Compact to Conserve Oil and Gas was renewed in 1937 and again in 1939. The Connally Act and the Interstate Compact in effect made it a federal crime to violate a state law.

7. My discussion follows Ickes's account as related in his book, *The New Democracy* (New York: W. W. Norton & Co., 1934), pp. 27–28. See too *The Literary Digest* 115, no. 22 (June 3, 1933):6, for the press quote. Others expressing similar views are included in the story.

8. In the first six months of 1934 retail prices in 50 representative cities averaged 13.90 cents per gallon compared with 12.76 cents per gallon in 1933. From 1924 to 1930, retail prices averaged in excess of 16.33 cents per gallon. These figures are from Ickes, *The New Democracy,* p. 109.

9. One thing Ickes would not do in his capacity as Petroleum Administrator, though he was under "tremendous pressure from the oil people," was to fix prices except as a last resort. See Harold L. Ickes, *The Secret Diary of Harold L. Ickes: The First Thousand Days, 1933–1936* (New York: Simon & Schuster, 1953), pp. 95, 102.

10. In his diary, Ickes records a meeting in April 1934 with Walter C. Teagle, president of the Standard Oil Company of New Jersey, in which Teagle proposed the government "make an oil reserve out of the East Texas oil field" to curb the production of hot oil. Teagle, whose company was the largest producer in the field, thought the government should determine how much oil it wanted to produce, and then allocate quotas in "the proportion represented by the respective ownerships of the properties at the time they were taken over." Moreover, Teagle thought other large producers would fall in with his suggestion. Ickes, who no doubt agreed with Teagle's suggestion, recorded in his diary only that it was " a rather startling proposition to come from the president of the Standard Oil Company of New Jersey." See Ickes, *Secret Diary: The First Thousand Days,*pp. 158–59.

11. That some oilmen were grateful for what Ickes had done in saving the industry from collapse and then in stabilizing it, so that "oil could be produced, processed and sold at a profit," was noted by Ickes in his diary entry for January 3, 1937. See Ickes, *Secret Diary: The Inside Struggle, 1936–1939* (New York: Simon & Schuster, 1953), p. 27.

12. See H. O. Rogers, "Employment Prospects in the Petroleum and Natural Gas Industry," *Monthly Labor Review* 50 (June 1940):1295–96 for a discussion of petroleum reserves. It was estimated in 1939 that for every barrel used, five were left wasted and were unrecoverable. Moreover, by 1937 Americans used in one year more oil than was produced during the industry's first fifty years.

13. Statement by Senator Elmer Thomas: February 26, 1935. Copy in Raymond Clapper Papers, Reference File, Box 190, Library of Congress. The Thomas-Disney bill, though favored by Ickes, gave way to the measure sponsored by Senator Tom Connally. The unpublished paper by Linda J. Lear cited in footnote 1 provides a guide to the struggle for federal regulation.

14. The archives of Notre Dame University contain a small collection of letters by Charles Fahy to his wife from Tyler, Texas, written in 1934 as the

Tender Board was being established. Fahy became chairman of the Petroleum Administrative Board in the Department of the Interior and in this capacity was responsible for supervising the activities of the Federal Tender Board. I have also relied upon James Presley, *A Saga of Wealth: The Rise of the Texas Oilmen* (New York: G. P. Putnam's Sons, 1978) particularly Chapter 7, "The Hot Oil War." Incidentally, Presley notes that a leading hot oil producer was Clint Murchison.

15. *Panama Refining Co. et al.* v. *Ryan, et al. and Amazon Petroleum Corp. et al.* (293 US 388). Chief Justice Charles Evans Hughes wrote the opinion of the court with Justice Benjamin Cardozo dissenting.

16. For example, see Petroleum Administration Board, *Cost of Production of Crude Petroleum* (Washington, D.C.: Government Printing Office, 1936). This 137-page report provides a storehouse of information and data.

17. Samuel B. Pettengill, *Hot Oil* (New York: Economic Forum Co., 1936) reviews the work of the Cole committee including a discussion of Margold's measure (pp. 118–33) and excerpts from Ickes's testimony (pp. 117–18). Pettengill, a Republican Congressman from Indiana, was a member of the subcommittee.

18. The National Resources Board was one of the few public agencies to agree with Ickes. It called for a Federal Oil Conservation Board to regulate the production and commerce in crude petroleum. In addition it would insure that oil and gas were extracted by methods that would avoid waste and protect the interests of producers drawing from a common reservoir. The board would provide safeguards and assistance to enable the industry to avoid the wastes of destructive competition.

19. "Hearings Before Subcommittee of the Committee on Mines and Mining," United States Senate: 73rd Congress, 2d Session on S. 3495. "A Bill To Regulate Commerce in Petroleum And For Other Purposes," May 21–22, 1934, p. 9.

20. Ickes was educated in part to the realities of oil conservation by two young lawyers in the Department of the Interior: Norman L. Meyers and J. Howard Marshall. See, for example, their "Memorandum to the Secretary," July 26, 1933, Box 217, Harold L. Ickes Papers. Meyers became Secretary of the Petroleum Administrative Board in the Department of the Interior with the task of forwarding all communications from the industry or from the public to proper groups or individuals for action. In 1934 he became chairman of the Federal Tender Board, which worked with the Texas Railroad Commission in issuing certificates for petroleum cleared for shipment in interstate commerce.

21. "Silver, Just Silver," *Fortune* 8, no. 1 (July 1933):56–63, 98–106, provides an excellent introduction to the problems of silver. John A. Brennan, *Silver And The First New Deal* (Reno: University of Nevada Press, 1969) is the basic study concerned more with national policy than with conditions in the West.

22. For an excellent discussion of the Thomas Amendment, see the essay by David D. Webb, "The Thomas Amendment: A Rural Oklahoma Response To The Great Depression," in Donald E. Green, ed., *Rural Oklahoma* (Oklahoma City: Oklahoma Historical Society, 1977), pp. 105–112.

23. For a discussion of "The Silver Lining of the London Conference," see *The Literary Digest* 116, no. 6 (August 5, 1933):7.

24. For an indication of the differences among silver proponents see letter of ex-Senator C. S. Thomas to Editor of *Rocky Mountain News*, June 23, 1933, and stories in the *Washington Herald* and *Washington Star* on June 25, 1933,

by Senator Wheeler criticizing the views of Senator Pittman. Copies are available in the Key Pittman Papers, Box 140, Library of Congress. See also, Pittman to W. Mont Ferry, October 13, 1933, Box 143, Key Pittman Papers. For Borah's views see William E. Borah to W. Mont Ferry, December 30, 1933, Box 401, William E. Borah Papers, Library of Congress.

25. C. H. McIntosh to Pittman, December 26, 1933, Box 141, Key Pittman Papers.

26. Pittman to George W. Snyder and W. Mont Ferry, July 14, 1934, Box 143, Key Pittman Papers. Elliott V. Bell, "The Silver Fiasco," *Current History,* February 1936, pp. 473–78. Critics focused on the international ramifications of the legislation and castigated "the fourteen Senators comprising the Silver Bloc and their inflationist confederates in Congress." They noted how the world market for silver had become demoralized as a result of U.S. Treasury purchases which prompted drastic fluctuations in the market price of silver.

27. Memo: The Silver Purchase Act. . . , Box 218, Henry L. Morgenthau, Jr., Papers, Franklin D. Roosevelt Library, Hyde Park, N.Y. *Las Vegas* (Nev.) *Evening Review-Journal,* May 8, 1934.

28. Rosenman, vol. 3: *Advance of Recovery and Reform,* Note, p. 381. See also *The Literary Digest* 118, no. 7 (August 18, 1934):7, 38, for story titled "What The Nationalization of Silver Means."

29. For an incisive discussion of silver policy for the three years following the approval of the Silver Purchase Act, see John M. Blum, *From The Morgenthau Diaries: Years of Crisis, 1928–1938* (Boston: Houghton Mifflin Co., 1959), pp. 188–99.

30. Edwin C. Johnson to Franklin D. Roosevelt, September 19, 1935. Official File 200L, Box 18, Franklin D. Roosevelt Papers, Hyde Park, N.Y. A. L. Fish to Raymond Clapper, October 25, 1935, Reference File, Box 222, Raymond Clapper Papers.

31. D. W. Bell to L. W. Knoke, August 27, 1935, Box 227, Henry L. Morgenthau, Jr., Papers. A. G. Mackenzie to Elbert D. Thomas, October 14, 1935, Box 18, Elbert D. Thomas Papers. Both collections are in the Franklin D. Roosevelt Library.

32. Senator Elbert D. Thomas: speech draft, February 14, 1936, Box 3, Elbert D. Thomas Papers. A. L. Fish to Clapper, October 25, 1934, Reference File, Box 222, Raymond Clapper Papers. Fish was general manager of the *Salt Lake Tribune* and the *Salt Lake Telegram.* For examples of Morgenthau satisfying members of the Silver Bloc see Henry L. Morgenthau, Jr., Diary, vol. 14, p. 36 (December 16, 1935, entry) and vol. 18, p. 120 (February 27, 1936, entry) in the Henry L. Morgenthau, Jr., Papers. A radio address by Thomas examined "newly mined domestic silver and its relation to agriculture" on November 26, 1937. See *Congressional Record:* 75th Congress, 2d Session, Appendix 205–6.

33. James F. McCarthy to Borah, November 19, 1936, Box 457, William E. Borah Papers. See Henry L. Morgenthau, Jr., Diary, Box 99, pp. 126–30 (November 24, 1937 entry) for a telephone conversation with Key Pittman on silver matters. Silver had not equaled one-fourth of the money stock because of the influx of gold into U.S. Treasury vaults owing to the devaluation of the dollar.

34. Pittman to Morgenthau, December 4, 1937, and December 19, 1937; Box 227, Henry L. Morgenthau, Jr., Papers. J. W. Gwinn to Borah, December 7, 1937, Box 483, William E. Borah Papers.

35. Barzilla W. Clark to The President, December 11, 1937. Copy in Box 314, Henry L. Morgenthau, Jr., Papers. Roosevelt felt justified in reducing the domestic purchase price because the world or market price for silver had drastically declined to the depressed 45-cent-level that prevailed in 1934.

36. A. S. Brown to My Dear Mr.———, December 8, 1938, a form letter. Copy in Box 7, Elbert D. Thomas Papers. Pittman to Morgenthau, December 2, 1938, Box 227, Henry L. Morgenthau, Jr., Papers.

37. Pittman to Borah, April 24, 1939, Box 525, William E. Borah Papers. Pittman to Morgenthau, June 11, 1939, Henry L. Morgenthau, Jr., Diary, Book 195.

38. Borah to Irvin E. Rockwell, June 23, 1939, Box 525, William E. Borah Papers.

39. For an indication of conditions in the mining industry in 1939 see Ezra R. Whitla to Borah, July 6, 1939, Box 525, William E. Borah Papers. For Roosevelt's views, see Roosevelt to Pittman, June 27, 1939, in Elliott Roosevelt, ed., *F.D.R.: His Personal Letters: 1928–1945*, 2 vols. (New York: Duell, Sloan and Pearce, 1950), 2:898. While farmers were subsidized, paid not to produce, there was a demand for crops and none for silver. For an indication of the Silver Senators' lack of interest in foreign purchases of silver see Memorandum For The Record: Conference in Senator Barkley's Office, March 13, 1940, Henry L. Morgenthau, Jr., Diary, Book 247, and the remarks of Elbert D. Thomas favoring prohibition of foreign silver purchases in the *Congressional Record:* 76th Congress, 3d Session, May 1, 1940, pp. 5526–34.

Chapter 8

1. Kenneth R. Philp, *John Collier's Crusade for Indian Reform, 1920–1954* (Tucson: University of Arizona Press, 1977) is a basic book. John S. Painter's paper, "Congressional Conservatism and Federal Indian Policy, 1928–1950," presented at the 1981 Annual Meeting of the Organization of American Historians in Detroit, carefully delineates the major handicap under which the Indian New Deal functioned; namely, declining Congressional support, especially funding. In addition, I have relied heavily upon essays in the *Social Work Year Books* (New York: Russell Sage Foundation, 1935–41) published during the New Deal years (numbers 3 through 6) for factual data and general information on the American Indians.

2. "A New Deal for the American Indian," *The Literary Digest* 117, no. 14 (April 7, 1934):21, for the quotes and figures provided in this and the preceding paragraph. Margaret Connell Szasz, *Education and the American Indian: The Road to Self Determination Since 1928* (Albuquerque: University of New Mexico Press, 1974) in chapters 5 through 8 examines the New Deal years most competently.

3. See, for example, Donald L. Parman, "The Indian and the Civilian Conservation Corps," *Pacific Historical Review* 40 (1971):39–56.

4. Samuel Gerson, "Federal and State Relations in Indian Relief," *Proceedings of the National Conference of Social Work* (Chicago: University of Chicago Press, 1935), pp. 589–97. Gerson was Director of Social Service for the Montana Emergency Relief Administration.

5. The *Monthly Reports* of the Federal Emergency Relief Administration for July 1933 (p. 9) and December 1933 (p. 42), for example, comment on authorization to extend federal relief to Indians by the state emergency relief administrations and by the Federal Surplus Relief Administration, at the re-

quest of the Secretary of the Interior, agreeing to purchase 100,000 sheep from the Navajos in Arizona and New Mexico. When processed the mutton was taken by the Indian Service for distribution to distressed Indians in Wyoming during the winter months.

6. Peter M. Wright, "John Collier and the Oklahoma Indian Welfare Act of 1936," *Chronicles of Oklahoma* 50 (1972):347–71, provides a thorough study of the situation in Oklahoma resulting in this special piece of legislation. B. T. Quinten, "Oklahoma Tribes, the Great Depression and the Indian Bureau," *Mid-America* 49 (1967):29–43, presents background material on the desperate situation of most Oklahoma Indians during the Hoover Administration. For the response of another Oklahoma tribe opposed to the Indian New Deal, see the commentary by W. David Baird in Jane F. Smith and Robert M. Kvasnica, eds., *Indian-White Relations: A Persistent Paradox* (Washington, D.C.: Howard University Press, 1976), pp. 216–20. Baird examines the response of the Quapaw tribe, some of whose members received royalties from valuable lead and zinc deposits. The 1936 measure was redrafted in part so as to exclude the Osage tribe, the wealthiest tribe in the United States, which in that year drew an income of about $5 million from their oil and gas leases.

7. Hugh G. Calkins and D. S. Hubbell, "A Range Conservation Demonstration in The Land of the Navajos," *Soil Conservation* 6, no. 3 (September 1940):64–67, examines the conservation research and demonstration projects undertaken by the Navajo Experiment Station at Mexican Springs, New Mexico. The article notes the connection between the station and Boulder Dam. A large portion of the silt pouring in behind the dam structure was traced to the drainage of the San Juan River, much of which is located within the Navajo Reservation. When this situation, together with the rapid rate at which erosion was destroying Navajo ranges, was brought to Collier's attention early in 1933, he requested an investigation of erosion conditions on the reservation. This request led to the creation of the station at Mexican Springs with the permission of the Navajo Tribal Council. It was staffed first by the Soil Erosion Service, which in 1935 was succeeded by the Soil Conservation Service.

8. Representatives of the Navajo People . . . to Franklin D. Roosevelt, April 19, 1935, in Edgar B. Nixon, ed. *Franklin D. Roosevelt and Conservation, 1911–1945,* 2 vols. (Hyde Park, N.Y.: Franklin D. Roosevelt Library, 1957), 1:369–70, provides a succinct statement of most aspects of the Navajo situation. See too Walter E. Woelke, "The Economic Rehabilitation of the Navajos," in *Proceedings of The National Conference of Social Work* (Chicago: University of Chicago Press, 1934), pp. 548–56. For an indication of agricultural diversification on Navajo lands by the end of the New Deal see L. L. Harrold, "Floods in Navajo Country," *Soil Conservation* 7, no. 7 (January 1942):172–73. Peter Iverson, *The Navajo Nation* (Westport, Conn.: Greenwood Press, 1981), Chapter 2 titled "The Stock Reduction Era" succinctly views various programs from the Navajo perspective and explains Indian dissatisfaction with Collier and much of the Indian New Deal. But the definitive study is by Donald L. Parman, *The Navajos and The New Deal* (New Haven, Conn.: Yale University Press, 1976). George Boyce, *When Navajos Had Too Many Sheep: the 1940's* (San Francisco: The Indian Historian Press, 1974) is a personal reminiscence. Boyce was an official in the Indian Service who began his career in the late 1930s. A critical account of the Navajo Soil Conservation Program under Collier's aegis is presented in an unpublished paper by Jack August, "The Progressive Impulse and the Navajo Soil Conser-

vation Program, 1930–1935." For a precise statement of the Department of the Interior's position in the Navajo crisis, see "Memorandum for the Press: August 14, 1937," Box 247, Harold L. Ickes Papers, Library of Congress. See also Franklin D. Roosevelt To The Navajo People, June 19, 1941, in Nixon, 2:516–17, in which Roosevelt in "these days of world crisis" further encouraged the Navajo to protect their lands from erosion by reducing their livestock.

9. Dewey Dismuke, "Acoma and Laguna Indians Adjust Their Livestock to Their Range," *Soil Conservation* 6, no. 5 (November 1940):130–31, indicates that these pueblos in western central New Mexico made a series of livestock reductions and successfully brought their 388,000 acres of overgrazed and eroded reservation ranges to grazing capacity.

10. John Collier, "The Owners of a Golden Land," *Rural America* 14, no. 1 (January 1936):8–9; Thomas E. Daughty and Kenneth Fiers, "Range Conservation on Big Horn Draw," *Soil Conservation* 4, no. 3 (September 1938):62–64, examines a cooperative Soil Conservation Indian Service project on a segment of the Shoshone Reservation.

11. C. C. Sikes, "Conserving Key Areas in Southwest Range Lands," *Soil Conservation* 5, no. 11 (May 1940):261–63, 282.

12. See discussion, "Development of American Indian Arts and Crafts," *Monthly Labor Review* 46 (1938):655–57.

13. Quote is from a speech by John Collier in 1938, as noted in a commentary by D'Arcy McNickle in Smith and Kvasnika, eds., *Indian-White Relations: A Persistent Paradox*, p. 256.

14. Graham D. Taylor, in *The New Deal and American Indian Tribalism: The Administration of the Indian Reorganization Act, 1934–45* (Lincoln: University of Nebraska Press, 1980) utilizes a case-study approach to indicate recurring tensions between bureaucrats and tribal members in pursuing tribal reorganization. Taylor concludes that tribal reorganization failed because the new tribal governments won little support among the people they were supposed to represent. Opposition on another level is presented in an unpublished paper by Benay Blend titled "The American Indian Federation and the Indian New Deal," presented at a session of the Southwestern Social Science Association meeting in Fort Worth in March 1979. The Federation, a pressure group of assimilationist-oriented Indians, largely from Oklahoma and led by Joseph Bruner, a full-blooded Creek, lobbied against the Wheeler-Howard bill and other Collier-endorsed measures. The organization gained support from fascist organizations and from several western Congressmen who became disillusioned with what they considered the increasing paternalism and communal approach of the Indian New Deal.

15. Conflicts arose at times when the Indian Service recommended purchase of additional grazing lands that local officials claimed had been used by settlers "from time immemorial" as a range, or which they hoped to utilize for other purposes, such as an irrigation project. For an example of this situation, see A. G. Sandoval, an official of the New Mexico Relief Administration serving in Taos County, to Bronson Cutting, April 9, 1935, Box 28, Bronson Cutting Papers, Library of Congress.

16. For a brief overview of Indian irrigation projects, see Albert L. Wathen, "Indian Irrigation," *The Reclamation Era* 31, no. 12 (December 1941):322–23.

17. Parman, "The Indian and the Civilian Conservation Corps," *Pacific Historical Review* 40 (1971):39–56, provides a critical and comprehensive re-

view. See too *Monthly Labor Review* 46 (1938):363 for a discussion titled "Placement of American Indians, 1936–37" and *Monthly Labor Review* 52 (1940):872–74 for a report titled "Employment Conditions Among Indians."

18. K. Ross Toole, *The Rape of the Great Plains* (Boston: Little, Brown & Co., 1976), p. 42.

19. Norris Hundley, Jr., "The Dark and Bloody Ground of Indian Water Rights: Confusion Elevated to Principle," *Western Historical Quarterly* 9 (1978):474–75.

20. Scudder McKeel, "An Appraisal of the Indian Reorganization Act," *American Anthropologist* 46 (1944):209–17; Graham D. Taylor, "Anthropologists, Reformers and the Indian New Deal," *Prologue* 7 (1975):156–62.

21. Statement by Harold L. Ickes: May 9, 1935. Indians: p. 1, Box 168, Harold L. Ickes Papers; Ickes, *The Secret Diary of Harold L. Ickes: The First Thousand Days, 1933–1936* (New York: Simon & Schuster, 1953), p. 443.

22. For example, an experimental sheep breeding laboratory on the Navajo reservation sought to develop a breed of sheep of good commercial quality, suited to the arid region. Navajo sheep, long-legged with carcasses of poor meat quality, were well adapted to their environment. Their long-staple, coarse wool was ideal for hand spinning and weaving but had minimal commercial value.

23. John R. Nichols to William E. Borah, March 20, 1937, Box 470, William E. Borah Papers, Library of Congress. Nichols mentioned several bills designed to curb or abolish the Indian Reorganization Act. For a discussion of an effort by Congressman Martin Dies in 1938 to denounce Ickes, Collier, and others in the Indian Office for communistic sympathies and connections, see Ickes, *Secret Diary: The Inside Struggle, 1936–1939* (New York: Simon & Schuster, 1953), pp. 506–7.

Chapter 9

1. The Pacific Northwest Regional Planning Commission, chaired by Marshall N. Dana, was set up at the suggestion of the National Planning Board as part of the program of the Federal Emergency Administration of Public Works (the Public Works Administration).

2. Marshall N. Dana, "Regional Planning in the Pacific Northwest," in Harlean James, ed., *American Civic Annual* (Washington, D.C.: American Civic Association, 1934), pp. 118–20. Held in Portland March 5–7, 1934, this was the first regional conference in the United States under the planning program of the President and the Administration of Public Works.

3. Dana, "The Planning Achievements of the Pacific Northwest," in Harlean James, ed., *American Planning and Civic Annual* (Washington, D.C.: American Planning and Civic Association, 1935), pp. 130–34. See too R. F. Bessey, "The Pacific Northwest," in James, ed., *American Planning and Civic Annual* (1937), pp. 152–59, and P. Hetherton, "The Pacific Northwest Regional Planning Commission," *Plan Age* 2, no. 6 (June–July 1936):2–5.

4. For a comprehensive general discussion see Charles McKinley, *Uncle Sam In The Pacific Northwest: Federal Management of Natural Resources in the Columbia River Valley* (Berkeley and Los Angeles: University of California Press, 1952), pp. 459–67. In addition, the annual proceedings of the Pacific Northwest Regional Planning Conference have been published.

5. Eugene A. Cox, "Let's Look At The Landscape," *Proceedings of the First Pacific Northwest Regional Planning Conference* (Portland, Ore., March 5–7, 1934), pp. 109–12.

6. Joseph S. Davis, *Wheat and the AAA* (Washington, D.C.: Brookings Institution, 1935), chapter 9 titled "The Pacific Northwest Export Arrangement," pp. 264–302; Don F. Hadwiger, *Federal Wheat Commodity Programs* (Ames: Iowa State University Press, 1970), p. 154. See too Henry A. Wallace, *New Frontiers* (New York: Reynal & Hitchcock, 1934), pp. 184–85, and the article by Frank A. Theis in the *Yearbook of Agriculture for 1935* (Washington, D.C.: Government Printing Office, 1935), pp. 339–41.

7. For careful studies of migration into Oregon, see the article by Charles S. Hoffman, "Drought and Depression Migration Into Oregon, 1930–1936," *Monthly Labor Review* 46 (January–June 1938):27–35, and V. B. Stanbery, "Migration Into Oregon, 1930–1937," *Monthly Labor Review* 49 (July–December 1939):1106–8. Migrants into Oregon first came from the adjacent mountain and Pacific states but their proportion declined as settlers from the Midwest increased. Kansas, Colorado, and Nebraska contributed nearly a fifth of the migrants into Oregon by 1935. By 1937, 84 percent of the recent migrants came from 14 states: 3 adjoining, 7 northern Great Plains states, and 4 north central states, the same states from which most of the 1920–30 migration came.

8. John Blanchard, *Caravans To The Northwest* (Boston: Houghton Mifflin Co., 1940), pp. 25, 32, and passim. This volume was prepared under the direction of the Northwest Regional Council. See too *The Reclamation Era* 27, no. 12 (December 1937):283 for an excerpted report on migration to the Pacific Northwest.

9. Blanchard, p. 53.

10. The quote by Ovid Butler was utilized by Gifford Pinchot in a May 31, 1937, address to the American Forestry Association. Copy in Harold L. Ickes Papers, Box 155, Library of Congress. Pinchot in this address blasted Ickes for neglecting the O & C lands, for exercising no control over cutting and never maintaining "an adequate force to protect the lands and timber from fire." Pinchot did not state that under the 1916 Revestment Act returning these lands, no degree of forest management was possible. See Charles W. Eliot to Charles L. McNary, January 4, 1935, Box 42, Charles L. McNary Papers, Library of Congress. Eliot was executive officer of the National Resources Board. See too Department of the Interior Memorandum: June 29, 1936, wherein Ickes had to revoke an order suspending timber sales because of the initial failure of Congress to approve the O & C sustained-yield legislation. Copy in Box 42, Charles L. McNary Papers.

11. For a comprehensive discussion focusing on the 1938 legislation affecting the O & C lands, see the important study by Elmo Richardson, *BLM's Billion-Dollar Checkerboard: Managing the O & C Lands* (Washington, D.C.: Government Printing Office, 1980). Chapters 2 and 3 cover the years 1931–44. In 1939 the law was modified to bring under the jurisdiction of the Oregon and California Revested Land Grant Administration the Coos Bay Wagon Road lands. See also Rodney C. Loehr, ed., *Forests For the Future: The Story of Sustained Yield As Told in the Diaries and Papers of David T. Mason, 1907–1950* (St. Paul: Minnesota Historical Society, 1952), pp. 195–97.

12. Richardson, p. 74. Walter Horning wrote the remarks quoted ca. 1942.

13. Harry G. Ade, "Objectives and Types of Development on Submarginal Lands," *Proceedings of the Western Farm Economics Association* (Corvallis, Oregon, August 12, 1935), pp. 88–92. For concern about further utilization of submarginal lands in Oregon by the Resettlement Administration, see Charles H. Martin to Franklin D. Roosevelt, September 13, 1935, in Edgar B. Nixon, *Franklin D. Roosevelt and Conservation, 1911–1945*, 2 vols. (Hyde

Park, N.Y.: Franklin D. Roosevelt Library, 1957), 1:428–29. Martin was governor of Oregon. Roosevelt responded on October 14, 1935, delineating the status of the five Resettlement Administration projects under way in Oregon. See pp. 442–43.

14. See the discussion of the Longview Homesteads in *Monthly Labor Review* 44 (January–June 1937):1393–35, 1399.

15. See the discussion of reclamation in the Yakima Valley in the December 1936 Land Policy Circular, pp. 7–8. The circular was a publication of the Resettlement Administration.

16. "Storage Reservoirs On Snake River," *The Reclamation Era* 29, no. 4 (April 1939): 90–91; "Thousand Persons Celebrate Delivery of First Water To Payette Division," ibid. 29, no. 6 (June 1939):144–46; "Reclamation Progress in Idaho," ibid. 31, no. 8 (August 1941):212–14.

17. In 1941 about 27,000 acres of the Owyhee project west of the Snake River was in Idaho.

18. Carl P. Heisig and Marion Clawson, "New Farms On New Land," a mimeographed article published by the Bureau of Agricultural Economics in cooperation with the Oregon Agricultural Experiment Station and the Farm Security Administration in January 1941. Walter K. M. Slavik, "The Human Side of the Owyhee Development," *The Reclamation Era* 29, no. 5 (May 1939):96–98.

19. McKinley, p. 370. See also Irving Brant to Franklin D. Roosevelt, November 19, 1937, in Nixon, 2:141–43, wherein Brant critically reviews Forest Service and business objections to the proposed park while arguing for keeping the area clear of commercial interests. Brant argued that the forests on the Olympic peninsula were not needed for the economic life of the area because "sawmills are doomed anyway and pulpwood is growing four times as fast as it is being cut." For further indication of Forest Service opposition to the proposed park see Harold L. Ickes, *The Secret Diary of Harold L. Ickes: The First Thousand Days* (New York: Simon & Schuster, 1953), pp. 374, 383–84.

20. Harold L. Ickes to John Boettiger, April 30, 1938, Box 222, Harold L. Ickes Papers, Library of Congress. See too Ebert K. Burlew to Franklin D. Roosevelt, June 29, 1938, in Nixon, 2:241–42, for an explanation of the acreage figures and pp. 274–75 for a December 10, 1938, memo from Roosevelt to Ickes indicating the President's acute interest in the Olympic National Park. Anna Louise Strong, in *My Native Land* (New York: Viking Press, 1940), pp. 142–43, claims that in the fight for the Olympic National Park the New Deal encouraged the people of Washington to battle "for their woods" against the lumber interests and Governor Clarence D. Martin.

21. See the 1939 series of memoranda and letters pertaining to expanding the park area in Nixon, 2:396–404, and Ickes, *Secret Diary: The Lowering Clouds, 1939–41,* (New York: Simon & Schuster, 1954), pp. 86, 94. For the best available study see Richardson, "Olympic National Park: Twenty Years of Controversy," *Forest History* 12 (April 1968):6–15.

22. Irving Brant to Harold L. Ickes: December 1939 memorandum regarding Additions To Olympic National Park, Box 19, Irving Brant Papers, Library of Congress. Brant in this item delineates the opposition of planning groups and notes their ties to the lumber industry.

23. The Pittman-Robertson Act of 1937 provided federal aid to wildlife in those states contributing some matching funds. Federal funds came from an excise tax on sporting arms and ammunition. Projects proposed by the states

required approval of the Fish and Wildlife Service before funds could be forwarded.

24. Theodore W. Cart, " 'New Deal' for Wildlife: A Perspective on Federal Conservation Policy, 1933–1940," *Pacific Northwest Quarterly* 63 (1972):113–20. The most important piece of legislation was the Pittman-Robertson law enacted in 1937. It applied the 10 percent federal arms and ammunition tax monies to state wildlife conservation projects. For "Ding" Darling's brief career as Chief of the Biological Survey see David Lendt, *Ding: The Life of Jay Norwood Darling* (Ames: Iowa State University Press, 1979), pp. 76–85. At the outset of the New Deal there were 109 game and bird refuges in the United States, mostly in the West. On July 1, 1937, this number had increased to 245 refuges with the acreage more than doubling from about 5,639,000 acres to approximately 11,379,000.

25. J. N. Darling to Irving Brant, June 20, 1935, Box 18, Irving Brant Papers. See too Franklin D. Roosevelt to Harold L. Ickes, January 28, 1935, in Nixon, 1:344–45. A copy of the agreement between the Bureau of Reclamation and the Biological Survey can be found in Box 258 of the Harold L. Ickes papers.

26. Ira N. Gabrielson, *Wildlife Conservation* (New York: Macmillan Co., 1959), passim, and "Land Use Considers Wildlife," *Extension Service Review* 10, no. 11 (November 1939):163. The Conservation of Fish Act of 1934 directed the secretary of the interior to cooperate with fish and game management units so as not to adversely affect the propagation of native species.

27. My discussion relies on the general remarks of G. W. Grebe, "Recreational Problems In A Regional Land Program," *Proceedings of the Fourth Pacific Northwest Regional Planning Conference* (Boise, Idaho, April 1937), pp. 55–58, and also Kathrine Glover, *America Begins Again* (New York: McGraw-Hill Book Co., 1939), pp. 219–29.

28. Elbert D. Thomas to Franklin D. Roosevelt, January 29, 1937, and Thomas to W. W. Seegmiller, April 8, 1937. Box 18, Elbert D. Thomas Papers, Franklin D. Roosevelt Library.

29. A listing can be found in *The Grazing Bulletin* 3, no. 4 (September 1940):19–20.

Chapter 10

1. *America Builds: The Record of PWA* (Washington, D.C: Government Printing Office, 1939), pp. 116–118. By September 1941 five generators were in operation bringing installed capacity at Bonneville to 248,000 kilowatts.

2. Charles E. Jackson to Charles L. McNary, November 9, 1933, Box 33, Charles L. McNary Papers, Library of Congress.

3. Neuberger is quoted in Anthony Netboy, *Salmon of the Pacific Northwest* (Portland: Binfords & Mort, 1958), p. 43. For a discussion of the role of the Bureau of Fisheries in protecting salmon, see *Twenty-Fourth Annual Report of the Secretary of Commerce* (Washington, D.C.: Government Printing Office, 1938):82–83. See too Ivan Bloch, "The Columbia River Salmon Industry," *The Reclamation Era* 28, no. 2 (February 1938):26–27.

4. Edgar B. Nixon, ed., *Franklin D. Roosevelt and Conservation, 1911–1945*, 2 vols. (Hyde Park, N.Y.: Franklin D. Roosevelt Library, 1957), 1:383.

5. For a discussion of the Grand Coulee salvage operations see Netboy, pp. 46–49, and Sterling B. Hill, "Transplanting the Migratory Salmon and Steelhead of The Upper Columbia River," *The Reclamation Era* 30, no. 6 (June

1940):175–78. For the quote by Elwood Mead see "Is $15,000,000 Salmon Industry Facing Doom?" *The Literary Digest,* August 3, 1935, p. 16.

6. Federal Emergency Administration of Public Works: Release No. 835, n.d. (1934). Copy in Reference File, Box 115, Raymond Clapper Papers, Library of Congress.

7. *Denver Post,* August 26, 1934, story by Chesley Manly. Harold L. Ickes, *The Secret Diary of Harold L. Ickes: The First Thousand Days, 1933–1936* (New York: Simon & Schuster, 1953), p. 183.

8. Charles H. Martin to Franklin D. Roosevelt, April 29, 1935, Box 33, Charles L. McNary Papers. For an indication of the work done by the Oregon State Planning Board pertaining to possible uses of Bonneville power, see Charles H. Martin to Charles L. McNary, August 9, 1936, Box 34, Charles L. McNary Papers.

9. See, for example, Philip J. Funigiello, *Toward a National Power Policy: The New Deal and the Electric Utility Industry, 1933–1941* (Pittsburgh: University of Pittsburgh Press, 1974) and William E. Leuchtenburg, "Roosevelt, Norris and the 'Seven Little TVAs,'" *Journal of Politics* 14 (1952):418–41. See too the Statement by Secretary of the Interior Harold L. Ickes: May 10, 1937, in Box 37 of the Charles L. McNary Papers for an indication of the various views regarding the operation of the Bonneville project. For an excellent discussion of the Bonneville Power Administration, one upon which I have relied, see Charles McKinley, *Uncle Sam In The Pacific Northwest* (Berkeley and Los Angeles: University of California Press, 1952), pp. 157–228. See too the discussion in Samuel I. Rosenman, ed., *The Public Papers and Addresses of Franklin D. Roosevelt,* 9 vols. (New York: Random House, 1938; Macmillan Co., 1941), vol. 6: *The Constitution Prevails, 1937,* pp. 93–98. For a further indication of Roosevelt's interest in the Bonneville project and public power see Franklin D. Roosevelt to Morris L. Cooke, January 16, 1937, Box 415, Morris L. Cooke Papers, Franklin D. Roosevelt Library, Hyde Park, N.Y.

10. For an indication of how Ross sought public input to assist in determining rates, see his Memorandum of Public Rate Hearings: March 26, 1938, Box 35, Charles L. McNary Papers. Ross conducted a series of eight hearings in three states of the Northwest.

11. McKinley, p. 227. See too The Bonneville Project: Speical Bulletin No. 12, May 15, 1938. Copy in Box 35, Charles L. McNary Papers.

12. For a discussion of Bohn's proposal, see the story by Herbert S. Lampman in *The Oregonian,* August 1, 1935. Only one concern, the Chipman Chemical Company of Philadelphia, went beyond the talking stage. It purchased land at Cascade Locks, not far from the dam, and planned to produce sodium chlorate. Cascade Locks was the first community to buy power from Bonneville Dam.

13. Rosenman, *The Constitution Prevails,* pp. 387–92.

14. Bayard O. Wheeler, "The Production and Distribution of Bonneville Power," *The Journal of Land and Public Utility Economics* 14, no. 4 (November 1938):359–69. I have relied heavily on Wheeler's article. In 1940 public electric systems utilizing Bonneville power reduced their rates, further enhancing the use of electricity throughout the region. For an overall discussion placing the BPA within a national perspective, see Philip J. Funigiello, "The Bonneville Power Administration and the New Deal," *Prologue* 5 (Summer 1973):89–97. Funigiello also discusses the confusion and controversy that occurred following the death of J. D. Ross.

15. Rosenman, vol. 9: *War—And Aid to Democracies, 1940* (New York: Macmillan Co., 1941), pp. 341–46.

16. Grand Coulee would not be fully operational, ready to generate power and, through earthen dams at both ends, ready to pump water from the Columbia into a huge artificial lake to be utilized in irrigating the vast stretch of level land in the basin to the south until after World War II.

17. For a good general discussion see McKinley, pp. 138–45. For a tourist's description see Nancy Wilson Ross, *Farthest Reach: Oregon and Washington* (New York: Alfred A. Knopf, 1941), pp. 157–66.

18. Ickes, *Secret Diary: The First Thousand Days*, pp. 183–84; Rosenman, vol. 3: *The Advance of Recovery and Reform, 1934* (New York: Random House, 1938), pp. 355–58. Clarence C. Dill, "Introduction Of The President," August 4, 1934. Copy in Reference File, Box 115, Raymond Clapper Papers, Library of Congress.

19. Franklin D. Roosevelt to the Secretary of the Interior, Memorandum: December 28, 1934, Box 258, Harold L. Ickes Papers, Library of Congress. Rexford Guy Tugwell, *The Battle For Democracy* (New York: Columbia University Press, 1935), pp. 38–42.

20. Roy E. Huffman, *Irrigation Development and Public Water Policy* (New York: Ronald Press Co., 1953), p. 63. The first action to withdraw a water right under terms of the act occurred in 1949.

21. James Rorty, "Grand Coulee," *The Nation*, March 20, 1935, pp. 329–31.

22. See, for example, Katherine Glover, "Planning For Power," *Survey Graphic* 25, no. 10 (October 1936):568–72, 582–83; John Blanchard, *Caravans to the Northwest* (Boston: Houghton Mifflin Co., 1940), passim. *The Spokesman-Review* for November 26, 1936, for example, carried a story about the special fund-raising drive of the Spokane Chamber of Commerce to lobby for a continuance of appropriations for the construction of Grand Coulee Dam. One of the better articles examining the spectacular dimensions of the project, "Grand Coulee," appeared in *Fortune* 16, no. 1 (July 1937). The most exuberant article and one of the most balanced about the potential expressed in Grand Coulee was undoubtedly the one written by Richard Neuberger, "The Biggest Thing On Earth," *Harpers* 174 (February 1937). Neuberger repeated himself two years later in an undated progress report, "The Columbia Flows to the Land," *Survey Graphic* 28, no. 7 (July 1939):440–45, 461–64. See also the informal extemporaneous remarks by the President at Grand Coulee on October 2, 1937, in Rosenman, *The Constitution Prevails*, pp. 395–97, and the exuberant comments of Anna Louise Strong in *My Native Land* (New York: Viking Press, 1940), pp. 144–48.

23. During the New Deal years the Bureau of Reclamation constructed in the West the five largest concrete dams in the world. In rank order after Grand Coulee they were: Shasta Dam in California; Boulder Dam, the highest dam in the world (Grand Coulee is the most massive); Friant Dam in California; and Marshall Ford Dam on the Colorado River in Texas.

24. Ickes, "Grand Coulee Dam, A National Development," *The Reclamation Era* 28, no. 1 (January 1938):1. See also pp. 4–5 for a story discussing Commissioner Page's recommendations, and ibid. 28, no. 3 (March 1939):48 for a story noting the approval of "Coulee Irrigation District." For carefully reasoned discussions of what might be anticipated upon the completion of Grand Coulee, see R. K. Tiffany, "The Columbia River as a Key To Pacific

Northwest Regional Development;" Charles E. Carey, "The Place of Power In The Development of Pacific Northwest Industries;" and Walter W. R. May, "Power In This Situation" in *Proceedings of the Fifth Pacific Northwest Regional Planning Conference* (Seattle, April 27–29, 1939), pp. 104–11, 121–25. Barrows soon had more than 100 specialists at work developing an outline that involved 32 federal, state, and local agencies in the vast undertaking of surveying and mapping the land to be irrigated.

25. Franklin D. Roosevelt to Harold L. Ickes, Memorandum: December 21, 1939, in Nixon, 2:405–7. See too his comments at the January 19, 1940, press conference on pp. 415–16. For Ickes's comments further elaborating on the President's proposal, see Ickes, *Secret Diary: The Lowering Clouds, 1939–1941* (New York: Simon and Schuster, 1954), pp. 100–101.

26. See story titled, "Joint Investigations, Columbia Basin Project," *The Reclamation Era* 30, no. 8 (August 1940):219–20, for a discussion of the various studies undertaken under Barrow's initiative. See too Ben H. Pubols, "The Columbia Basin Irrigation Project," in *Proceedings of The Western Farm Economics Association* (Salt Lake City, June 25–27, 1941), pp. 159–64, and Edward N. Torbert, "The Columbia Basin: Studies in Progress," *Land Policy Review* 4, no. 10 (October 1951):3–9.

27. By late 1941 the Pacific Northwest was beginning to be called an American Ruhr as metal reducing and other plants, chiefly related to defense industries, moved into the region seeking abundant and inexpensive electric power.

28. National Resources Committee: Release No. 8, February 19, 1936. Copy in Val Kuska Papers, Box 172, Nebraska State Historical Society, Lincoln, for a discussion of the Regional Planning Commission Report.

29. See Nixon, 2:510–16, for correspondence between the President and Senators Howard T. Bone and George W. Norris concerning legislation for administering the federal projects on the Columbia River. See too the discussion in Richard Lowitt, *George W. Norris: The Triumph of a Progressive, 1933–1944* (Urbana: University of Illinois Press, 1978), pp. 399–401. For Ickes's views see Ickes, *Secret Diary: The Lowering Clouds*, pp. 478–79, 501–2, 524. For an overall balanced account and a reasoned explanation why a TVA-like agency would have difficulty in the Northwest, see B. H. Kizer, "The Columbia Power Authority," in Harlean James, ed., *American Planning and Civic Annual* (Washington, D.C.: American Planning and Civic Association, 1941), pp. 109–14. The best overall discussion is Herman C. Voeltz, "Genesis and Development of a Regional Power Agency in the Pacific Northwest, 1933–1943," *Pacific Northwest Quarterly* 53 (1962):65–76.

Chapter 11

1. Robert E. Burke, *Olson's New Deal for California* (Berkeley and Los Angeles: University of California Press, 1953), p. 230.

2. Paul S. Taylor and Clark Kerr, "Whither Self-Help?" *Survey Graphic* 23, no. 7 (July 1934):328–31. The Wagner-Lewis Act of June 1933, in creating the Federal Emergency Relief Administration, provided a means for assisting cooperatives.

3. In "Social Workers and New Deal Politicians in Conflict: California's Branion-Williams Case, 1933–1934," *Pacific Historical Review* 42 (1973):53–73, Bonnie Fox Schwartz provides a definitive account of the controversy and an interesting discussion of CWA operations in California. See too Lillian Symes, "Politics vs. Relief," *Survey Graphic* 24, no. 1 (January 1935):8–10, 46.

4. See *Monthly Labor Review* 39 (July–December 1934):1437–38. The

maritime strike lasted from May 9 to July 31, 1934. The general strike started on July 16. The longshoremen who went back to work on July 31 agreed to have the strike issues settled by arbitration.

5. Anna Louise Strong, *My Native Land* (New York: Viking Press, 1940), pp. 38–39.

6. Ibid., pp. 40–48.

7. Jonathan Daniels wrote two perceptive travel accounts, *A Southerner Discovers the South* (New York: Macmillan Co., 1938), and *A Southerner Discovers New England* (New York: Macmillan Co., 1940). See too Jay Franklin, *Remaking America* (Boston: Houghton Mifflin Co., 1942).

8. Among the better studies are Carey McWilliams, *Factories in the Field* (Boston: Little, Brown & Co., 1939): Clarke Chambers, *California Farm Organizations* (Berkeley and Los Angeles: University of California Press, 1952); Walter J. Stein, *California and the Dust Bowl Migration* (Westport, Conn.: Greenwood Press, 1973); and the best single volume, Cletus E. Daniel, *Bitter Harvest: A History of California Farm Workers, 1870–1941* (Ithaca, N.Y.: Cornell University Press, 1981).

9. See Daniels, pp. 167–221, for a discussion of the cotton strike and the role of George Creel. I have relied on Daniel's well written and carefully researched account. George Creel, *Rebel At Large* (New York: G. P. Putnam's Sons, 1947), pp. 274–79 briefly discusses his role in administering the National Recovery Act on the Pacific coast. Incidentally, California cotton pickers, approximately 15,000 of them, again went out in early October 1939 to raise the wage rate from 80¢ per hundred pounds to $1.25. The strike was terminated at the end of the following month with the United Cannery, Agricultural, Packing and Allied Workers of America (UCAPAWA) claiming that a rate of $1.00 was widely established as the accepted wage rate.

10. Harold L. Ickes to Carl Hayden, January 18, 1940, published on the inside front cover of *The Reclamation Era* 30, no. 2 (February 1940). Another estimate states that there were in California in the spring of 1939 approximately 139,000 families, over 1 million people, who had entered the state after 1929. See Seymour J. Janow and Davis McEntire, "Migration to California," *Land Policy Review* 3, no. 4 (July–August 1940):25–26 and Seymour J. Janow and William Gilmartin, "Labor and Agricultural Migration To California, 1935–40," *Monthly Labor Review* 53 (July–December 1951):18–33 for a comprehensive discussion by two economists.

11. Milton Meltzer, *Dorothea Lange* (New York: Farar, Straus & Giroux, 1978), 99, 101.

12. As of 1940 the proportion of farmers and farm laborers from Oklahoma in California was somewhat greater than the proportion of the working population of Oklahoma in 1930. See Janow and McEntire, p. 32.

13. Abraham Hoffman, *Unwanted Mexican Americans in the Great Depression* (Tucson: University of Arizona Press, 1974) spotlights the procedures, local and federal, by which more than 400,000 people were returned to Mexico from 1933 to 1939. Hoffman's focus is chiefly on Los Angeles and southern California. See too D. H. Dinwoodie, "Deportation: The Immigration Service And The Chicano Labor Movement In The 1930s," *New Mexico Historical Review* 52 (1977):193–206.

14. Carey McWilliams, "Migration and Resettlement of the People," in Harlean James, ed., *American Planning and Civic Annual* (Washington, D.C.: American Planning and Civic Association, 1940), pp. 21–28. I have relied on McWilliams's discussion of the California response to the influx of migrants.

For an account of a "Little Oklahoma," see Stuart M. Jamieson, "A Settlement of Rural Migrant Families in the Sacramento Valley, California," *Rural Sociology* 7 (1942):49–61.

15. For a detailed discussion of the Casa Grande Farm see Edward C. Banfield, *Government Project* (Glencoe, Ill.: Free Press, 1951).

16. Jerold S. Auerbach, *Labor And Liberty: The LaFollette Committee and the New Deal* (Indianapolis, Bobbs-Merrill Co., 1966), pp. 1, 180. Chapter 7 examines the committee's work in California. Lange and Taylor devote the latter portion of their book to the "Last West" wherein they examine the "modern emigrants" in California. Lange in her work as a Farm Security Administration photographer helped bring to national attention the plight of migrant families. For a brief account of this phase of her career, focusing on California, see Meltzer, pp. 188–91. By 1940 a Select Committee Investigating the Interstate Migration of Destitute Citizens, a House committee chaired by California Congressman John H. Tolan, continued where the LaFollette committee left off in investigating conditions pertaining to California agriculture. Like the LaFollette committee, its investigation did not focus exclusively on migration to California and its emphasis quickly shifted from destitute migration to defense migration. See John H. Tolan, "Our Migrant Defenders" *Survey Graphic* 30, no. 11 (November 1941):615–18, 657–60.

17. Quote was utilized by Paul S. Taylor, "The Place of Agricultural Labor in Society," in *Proceedings of the Western Farm Economics Association: Twelfth Annual Meeting* (1939), p. 86. See too Robert M. LaFollette, Jr., to Alfred W. Eames, March 1, 1940, Series C, Box 35A, LaFollette Family Collections, Library of Congress. A draft letter responding to the charge that LaFollette and the investigating committee in its California hearings was soft on Communism, giving aid and comfort to Communist labor leaders, and hard on the Associated Farmers.

18. See the story by Byron Darnton in *The New York Times,* March 4, 1940. For a list of witnesses and the topics they discussed, see *Land Policy Review* 4, no. 2 (February 1941):27–31.

19. Carey McWilliams cites Paul S. Taylor's testimony in "Rural Dependency in California," *Proceedings of the National Conference of Social Work: 1940* (New York: Columbia University Press, 1940), pp. 330–31. I have made extensive use of McWilliams's account in my remarks. See too Richard L. Neuberger, "Who Are the Associated Farmers?" *Survey Graphic* 28, no. 9 (September 1939):517–21, 555–57. Though Neuberger devotes most of his attention to the Associated Farmers of California, he also discusses the Oregon organization. Both were hostile to any form of labor unionism among their field hands. For an outline of the LaFollette Committee Report on its California hearings, see the copy dated March 16, 1940, in Series C, Box 35A, LaFollette Family Collections. For a survey of its findings see Katharine Douglas, "West Coast Inquiry," *Survey Graphic* 29, no. 4 (April 1940):227–31, 259–61. The report asserted that the record of the Associated Farmers presented "a challenge to democratic government in California and the nation."

20. For an indication of how bitter the Salinas lettuce strike was, see *The Literary Digest* 122, no. 18 (October 31, 1936):8–9. For an insight into the living conditions of migratory families, see Carleton Beals, *American Earth* (Philadelphia: J. B. Lippincott Co., 1939), pp. 393–98.

21. Clarence J. Glacken, "Tents, Trailers, and Culture in Migratory Camps," *Labor Information Bulletin* 7, no. 8 (August 1940):1–3.

22. Strong, pp. 102–7. For a more detailed and prosaic account of "Govern-

ment Camps for Agricultural Workers," see *Monthly Labor Review* 50 (January–June 1940):625–27.

23. Beals, p. 405, presents a brief description of the camp at Weedpatch. See too Laurence Hewes, *Boxcar In The Sand* (New York: Alfred A. Knopf, 1957), pp. 110–50. Hewes was Farm Security Administrator for Region 9 comprising California, Arizona, Nevada, and Utah beginning in 1939. Byron Darnton in *The New York Times,* March 6, 1940, interviewed a camp family.

24. See the comments of Samuel May and Paul S. Taylor in the *Proceedings of the Fifth Pacific Northwest Regional Planning Conference* (Seattle, 1939), pp. 69–70. It should be noted that California required a year's residence in a county and three in the state before a person could qualify for relief. For a discussion of the Farm Security Administration work in California other than operating camps for migratory families, its distinct contribution, see Mary G. Luck and Agnes B. Cummings, *Standards of Relief in California* (Berkeley and Los Angeles: University of California Press, 1945), pp. 56–67. See too the discussion of medical care for migratory workers in *Monthly Labor Review* 51 (July–December 1940):333–37.

25. Murray R. Benedict, "Economic Aspects of Remedial Measures Designed to Meet the Problems of Displaced Farm Laborers," *Rural Sociology* 5 (1940):169, footnote 5. See too Tyr. V. Johnson and Frederick Arpke, *Interstate Migration and County Finance in California,* Report No. 10, Bureau of Agricultural Economics, United States Department of Agriculture (July 1942) Berkeley, California.

26. For excellent general accounts of migratory labor with special emphasis on the California situation, see "Migratory Labor: A Social Problem," *Fortune* 19, no. 4 (April 1939):91–94, 112–20, and Paul S. Taylor, *Adrift On the Land,* Public Affairs Pamphlet No. 42 (New York: Public Affairs Committee, 1940). The best account, one that focuses exclusively on California, is by John Steinbeck, "Their Blood is Strong," published as a pamphlet in 1938 and reprinted in Warren French, ed., *A Companion to "The Grapes of Wrath"* (New York: Viking Press, 1963), pp. 53–92.

Chapter 12

1. Draft of a Radio Talk, February 15, 1946, Box 403, Harold L. Ickes Papers, Library of Congress.

2. Harold L. Ickes to Director, National Park Service, September 20, 1935, reprinted in *Sierra Club Bulletin* 20, no. 4 (August 1935).

3. Daniel W. Bell to Franklin D. Roosevelt, July 8, 1938, in Edgar B. Nixon, ed., *Franklin D. Roosevelt and Conservation, 1911–1945,* 2 vols. (Hyde Park, N.Y.: Franklin D. Roosevelt Library, 1957), 2:244–45; Arno B. Cammerer to Frank A. Kittredge, July 14, 1938, copy in Box 18, Irving Brant Papers, Library of Congress; Harold L. Ickes, *The Secret Diary of Harold L. Ickes: The Inside Struggle, 1936–1939* (New York: Simon & Schuster, 1953), p. 584.

4. *Sierra Club Bulletin* 24, no. 1 (February 1939):1–8; ibid., no. 2 (April 1939):13–22; ibid., no. 4 (August 1939):29–30. See too Ickes, p. 378, and Harold L. Ickes to Franklin D. Roosevelt, April 28, 1939, in Nixon, 2:325–26. Both Henry A. Wallace and Chief Forester F. A. Silicox publicly endorsed the proposed park. The chairman of the Federal Power Commission, Clyde L. Seavey, favored power development in the park but the President, endorsing Ickes's views, insisted that power development would diminish the recreational value of the proposed park. See Nixon, 2:337–39.

5. See the article by Irving Brant in the 1940 *Yearbook of the National Park Service* (Washington, D.C.: Government Printing Office, 1939), pp. 19–21. For an excellent outline see Francis P. Farquhar, "Legislative History of Sequoia and Kings Canyon National Park," *Sierra Club Bulletin* 26, no. 1 (February 1941):42–58.

6. Harold L. Ickes, *Secret Diary: The First Thousand Days, 1933–1936* (New York: Simon & Schuster, 1953), p. 357.

7. Ibid., p. 563, and Ickes, *Secret Diary: The Inside Struggle*, pp. 124–25, 422, 426–27. Justice Hugo L. Black, speaking for the Supreme Court in an 8-to-1 decision reversing the judgment of the Circuit Court, affirmed that of the District Court and remanded the case to it. For an insight into the opposition to public distribution in San Francisco, see Frank R. Havenner to Victor Harding, July 1, 1938, OF 200 CCC, Box 79, Franklin D. Roosevelt Papers, Hyde Park, N.Y.

8. Speech by Harold L. Ickes, October 29, 1941, Box 6, Michael W. Straus Papers, Library of Congress; Oscar L. Chapman to Harold L. Ickes, September 1, 1950, Box 82, Harold L. Ickes Papers.

9. For an excellent study of Olson's administration, see Robert E. Burke, *Olson's New Deal for California* (Berkeley and Los Angeles: University of California Press, 1953).

10. For a brief discussion of the situation affecting agriculture in the Imperial Valley during the 1920s, see Richard Lowitt, *George W. Norris, The Persistence of a Progressive, 1913–1933* (Urbana: University of Illinois Press, 1971), pp. 265–67. It was estimated in 1935 that $38.5 million in federal funds, exclusive of interest charges, would be expended by 1938 on the All-American Canal. See Arthur D. Gayer, *Public Works in Prosperity and Depression* (New York: National Bureau of Economic Research, 1935), pp. 163–64.

11. Elwood Mead to Harold L. Ickes, July 6, 1935, Box 258; Statement by Ickes, April 10, 1936, Box 155, Harold L. Ickes Papers; *The Reclamation Era* 29, no. 9 (September 1939):241.

12. *The Reclamation Era* 28, no. 11 (November 1938):217–18, for Ickes's address at Imperial Dam on October 18, 1938; and ibid. 30, no. 1 (November 1940):314–15, noting the opening of the canal; Harold Lavine and Violet Edwards, "All American Canal," *Current History* 28, no. 4 (April 1938):25–27, for a discussion of the construction of the canal. See too Alfred Friendly, "Carrots from California," *Survey Graphic* 28, no. 7 (July 1939):460–61, for an account of the workers who picked the 1939 crops in Imperial Valley. Water diverted from the Imperial Dam also serviced the Gila Reclamation Project in Arizona.

13. Clayton R. Koppes, "Public Water, Private Land: Origins of the Acreage Limitation Controversy, 1933–1953," *Pacific Historical Review* 47 (1978):614. Though Koppes's article examines the Central Valley Project, its emphasis is on the years beyond the scope of this study. It is basic to an understanding of the controversy that engulfed the project.

14. Paul S. Taylor, "Central Valley Project: Water and Land," *Western Political Quarterly* 2 (1949):228–53. My brief discussion has benefited greatly from Taylor's careful analysis. See too Robert de Roos, *The Thirsty Land: The Story of the Central Valley Project* (Stanford, Calif.: Stanford University Press, 1948), pp. 3–14. The preference clause, challenged by the Pacific Gas and Electric Company which serviced most of northern California and the Central Valley, stated that power generated at various dams should be sold first to municipalities, cooperatives, and other public groups before sale to private companies.

15. de Roos, p. 7.
16. Franklin D. Roosevelt to Harold L. Ickes, May 29, 1940; Roosevelt to Henry L. Stimson, May 5, 1941. Both items are published in Nixon, 2:450–51, 503. Copies in Box 258, Harold L. Ickes Papers. See also the report in *The Reclamation Era* 30, no. 3 (March 1940):91.
17. "Central Valley Project Approved," *The Reclamation Era* 25, no. 10 (October 1935):201–2. Bureau of Reclamation: Division of Applications and Information Press Release, September 12, 1935. Copy in Val Kuska Papers, Box 64, Nebraska State Historical Society, Lincoln.
18. "Work to Start on Several Phases of Central Valley Project," *The Reclamation Era* 26, no. 1 (January 1936):11. See also "Central Valley," ibid. 27, no. 4 (April 1937):80–81.
19. See the articles by Walker R. Young on the Central Valley Project in *The Reclamation Era* 28, no. 2 (February 1938):22–25; ibid., no. 5 (May 1938):80–82; and ibid. 30, no. 12 (December 1940):325–27.
20. Ickes, *Secret Diary: The Inside Struggle,* pp. 578–79; Ickes's address at Friant Dam celebration, November 5, 1939, published in *The Reclamation Era* 29, no. 11 (November 1939):289–90, 305. Estimated completion date for Friant Dam was 1943.
21. *Pittsburgh Post Gazette,* December 13, 1940, and December 19, 1940, wire service dispatch. For copies of both items see Box 258, Harold L. Ickes Papers. "Conference with the President," December 19, 1940, Box 193, David E. Lilienthal Papers, Princeton University, Princeton, N.J. Lilienthal had the impression the President wished to revive the 1937 regional authority bill calling for seven Little TVAs. See also Ickes, *Secret Diary: The Lowering Clouds, 1939–1941* (New York: Simon & Schuster, 1954), pp. 391–92.
22. Harold L. Ickes to Charles Kramer, January 21, 1941, and Culbert L. Olson to Frank W. Clark, February 6, 1941, telegram. Box 258, Harold L. Ickes Papers for both items.
23. For the opposition of Pacific Gas and Electric Company to the standby steam plant, see the statement of May 21, 1941, in Box 258, Harold Ickes Papers. The statement was prepared for delivery to the Senate Appropriations Committee. See too Abe Fortas, "Relationship of Power to Reclamation," *The Reclamation Era* 31, no. 12 (December 1941):312.

Chapter 13

1. Samuel I. Rosenman, ed., *The Public Papers and Addresses of Franklin D. Roosevelt,* 9 vols. (New York: Random House, 1938; Macmillan Co., 1941), vol. 8: *War and Neutrality, 1939,* pp. 141–42. The quotes are from remarks by the President on February 18, 1939, as he opened the Golden Gate Exposition from Key West, Florida, prior to boarding the cruiser *U.S.S. Houston* to fish and view naval war games in the Caribbean.
2. For Roosevelt's remarks, see Rosenman, vol. 3: *The Advance of Recovery and Reform, 1934* (New York: Random House, 1938), pp. 352–67. See too Stephen Early to Emil Hurja, August 5, 1934, OF 200F, Box 5; and Turner W. Battle to Marvin H. McIntyre, August 3, 1934, OF 200F, Box 6, Franklin D. Roosevelt Papers, Franklin D. Roosevelt Library, Hyde Park, N.Y.
3. Franklin D. Roosevelt to Key Pittman, August 25, 1934, in Elliott Roosevelt, ed., *F.D.R.: His Personal Letters, 1928–1945,* 2 vols. (New York: Duell, Sloan & Pearce, 1950), 1:416. See too William H. Murray to James A.

Farley, August 10, 1934; Clyde Tingley to Farley, August 20 and September 17, 1934; James P. Pope to Farley, August 29, 1934; Henry A. Wallace to Charles H. Martin, September 27, 1934; James Reilly to Farley, October, 1934. All items are in Box 2, James A. Farley Papers, Library of Congress.

4. James A. Farley to Franklin D. Roosevelt, November 3, 1934; C. Ben Ross to Farley, November 9, 1934; and Thomas H. Moodie to Farley, November 10, 1934. All in Box 2, James A. Farley Papers.

5. *Congressional Record:* 74th Congress, 1st Session, January 24, 1935, pp. 865–66 for the complete message.

6. Franklin Thomas to Franklin D. Roosevelt, September 17, 1935, OF 200L, Box 18, Franklin D. Roosevelt Papers; Harold L. Ickes, *The Secret Diary of Harold Ickes: The First Thousand Days, 1933–1936* (New York: Simon & Schuster, 1953), p. 446.

7. Alfred A. Cohn to James A. Farley, October 4, 1935; James A. Farley to Claude Bowers, October 14, 1935; Box 3 for both items, James A. Farley Papers.

8. Francis J. Heney to Franklin D. Roosevelt, February 24, 1936, Box 3, James A. Farley Papers.

9. The resolution dated June 11, 1936, can be found in OF 200V, Box 34, Franklin D. Roosevelt Papers. For the main address delivered in Texas, see Rosenman, vol. 5: *The People Approve: 1936* (New York: Random House, 1938), pp. 203–16. Alfred Steinberg, *Sam Johnson's Boy* (New York: Macmillan Co., 1968), p. 98.

10. Lorena Hickok to Eleanor Roosevelt, July 1936 (excerpts); to Howard Hunter, August 1, 1936; to Harry Hopkins, August 9, 1936; Box 12, Lorena Hickok Papers, Franklin D. Roosevelt Library.

11. James A. Farley to Mrs. Franklin D. Roosevelt, July 25, 1936, Box 3, James A. Farley Papers.

12. For a sampling of Roosevelt's remarks see Rosenman, *The People Approve*, pp. 293–95, 299–316. For his itinerary see Press Release of August 21, 1936, in OF 200EE, Box 42, Franklin D. Roosevelt Papers. See too *The Literary Digest* 122, no. 10 (September 5, 1936):9.

13. James A. Farley to Claude Bowers, September 3, 1936; Henry A. Wallace to James A. Farley, September 15, 1936; both items in Box 4, James A. Farley Papers. Wallace's comments were expressed in a holograph postscript. Farley, however, was quite disturbed about speeches made earlier by Harry Hopkins about relief programs in the West. For a discussion of Hopkins's trip and both his and Farley's views about its impact, see H. H. Adams, *Harry Hopkins* (New York: G. P. Putnam's Sons, 1977), pp. 105–8.

14. Franklin D. Roosevelt to James A. Farley and Sam Rayburn, September 17, 1936; Franklin D. Roosevelt to George W. Norris, September 19, 1936. Both items appear in Elliott Roosevelt, 1:616,618. Franklin D. Roosevelt to Aubrey Williams, September 21, 1936, in Edgar B. Nixon, ed., *Franklin D. Roosevelt and Conservation, 1911–1945,* 2 vols. (Hyde Park, N.Y.: Franklin D. Roosevelt Library, 1957), 1:578.

15. Rosenman, *The People Approve*, pp. 427–73, for a sampling of the President's speeches from October 10 through October 13.

16. James A. Farley to Franklin D. Roosevelt, November 2, 1936, Box 4, James A. Farley Papers; William G. McAdoo Press Release: December 30, 1936, Box 565, William G. McAdoo Papers, Library of Congress; Draft Editorial, "The National Election" Series E, Box 25, William Allen White Papers, Library of Congress.

17. *My Day:* Columns for March 24, 1936, Box 3067, Eleanor Roosevelt Papers, Franklin D. Roosevelt Library.

18. Rosenman, vol. 6: *The Constitution Prevails: 1937* (New York: Macmillan Co., 1941), pp. 379–403, for a sampling of the President's remarks.

19. *My Day:* Columns for September 24 and 26, 1937, Box 3070, Eleanor Roosevelt Papers.

20. *My Day:* Columns for September 28 and 29, 1937, Box 3070, Eleanor Roosevelt Papers.

21. M. C. Latta to Marvin McIntyre, September 25 and 26, 1937, OF 200SS, Box 65, Franklin D. Roosevelt Papers: *The [Literary] Digest* 124, no. 13 (October 9, 1937):5.

22. Summary of Editorial Reaction to President Roosevelt's Recent Tour Through Northwestern States, October 12, 1937, OF 200SS, Box 65, Franklin D. Roosevelt Papers; Ickes, *Secret Diary: The Inside Struggle, 1936–1939* (New York: Simon & Schuster, 1953), pp. 222–23. See too James A. Farley to Claude Bowers, October 9, 1937, Box 5, James A. Farley Papers.

23. For an excellent discussion of Roosevelt's western trip that contrasts political setbacks in Congress with personal popularity, see Richard L. Neuberger, "Roosevelt Rides Again," *Current History* 47 (November 1937):42–47.

24. Sam Rayburn to Marvin McIntyre [n.d.] 1938; Josh Lee to Franklin D. Roosevelt, June 28, 1938. For both items, OF 200CCC, Box 81, Franklin D. Roosevelt Papers.

25. *My Day:* Columns for March 9, 10, 11, and 13, 1938; Box 3071, Eleanor Roosevelt Papers.

26. *My Day:* Columns for March 25 and 28, 1938; Box 3071, Eleanor Roosevelt Papers.

27. Rosenman, vol. 7: *The Continuing Struggle for Liberalism, 1938* (New York: Macmillan Co., 1941), pp. 44?–58, for a sampling of Roosevelt's remarks.

28. A. S. Brown to Franklin D. Roosevelt, July 12, 1938, OF 200CCC, Box 81, Franklin D. Roosevelt Papers.

29. Franklin D. Roosevelt to Key Pittman, July 13, 1938; to Elliott Roosevelt, July 13, 1938; to James Roosevelt, July 15, 1938—all in Elliott Roosevelt, 2:796–98.

30. Ickes, *Secret Diary: The Inside Struggle*, p. 421.

31. Walter F. Dillon to James A. Farley, August 17, 1938, Box 6; James E. Lawrence to James A. Farley, October 11, 1938, Box 7; Charles H. Martin to James A. Farley, October 14, 1938, Box 7, James A. Farley Papers.

32. Roi L. Morin to James A. Farley, November 10, 1938; James A. Farley to Claude Bowers, November 11, 1938, Box 7 for both items, James A. Farley Papers; Franklin D. Roosevelt to John Boettiger, December 3, 1938, in Elliott Roosevelt, 2:835.

33. *My Day:* Columns for March 10, 15, and 18, 1939, Box 3145, Eleanor Roosevelt Papers.

34. *My Day:* Column for November 4, 1938, Box 3145, Eleanor Roosevelt Papers.

35. James A. Farley to William Phillips, December 29, 1939, Box 8, James A. Farley Papers; Sam Rayburn and Lyndon B. Johnson to A. V. Wirtz, n.d. (telegram) Box 5, House of Representatives files, Lyndon B. Johnson Library, Austin, Texas. *Washington Post*, April 30, 1940, story by Robert C. Albright.

36. Franklin D. Roosevelt to Harold L. Ickes, May 20, 1940, OF 200RRR, Box 94, Franklin D. Roosevelt Library. Roosevelt did not campaign in the West in 1940.

Chapter 14

1. Mary W. M. Hargreaves, "Land Use Planning in Response to Drought:The Experience of the Thirties," *Agricultural History* 50 (1976):566.
2. William Allen White, *The Changing West* (New York, Macmillan Co., 1939), p. 70, for the odds upon which wheat producers operated.
3. Rexford Guy Tugwell, "Changing Acres," *Current History* 44, no. 6 (September 1936):57.
4. *Proceedings:* First Meeting, Missouri Valley Planning Commission (Omaha, Nebraska, September 4–5, 1941), p. 6 (mimeographed pamphlet.)
5. Harold L. Ickes, "The Preservation of our Natural Assets," *The Reclamation Era* 31, no. 4 (April 1941), inside front cover.
6. Harold L. Ickes statement, n.d. (1943?) re Public Works Administration, Box 380, Harold L. Ickes Papers, Library of Congress:

COSTS OF ALL PUBLIC WORKS ADMINISTRATION PROJECTS IN THE WESTERN STATES

	Number of Projects	*Total PWA Allotment*	*Estimated Total Cost*
Arizona	538	$ 57,604,066	$ 63,000,684
California	1,622	194,961,837	316,490,969
Colorado	513	45,465,014	72,111,406
Idaho	337	20,453,085	25,404,838
Kansas	790	46,850,874	74,299,575
Montana	561	91,712,905	99,766,400
Nebraska	554	97,297,931	109,509,623
Nevada	189	32,040,285	33,779,983
New Mexico	413	28,449,831	32,692,152
North Dakota	625	15,157,250	21,611,140
Oklahoma	704	65,062,377	78,447,574
Oregon	617	67,377,869	80,763,535
South Dakota	524	17,535,204	22,153,773
Texas	1,750	177,449,828	232,008,094
Utah	420	27,139,138	35,797,993
Washington	922	112,699,334	160,593,889
Wyoming	373	25,123,288	28,361,561

A distinguished student of the West has noted in analyzing New Deal expenditures that "the top fourteen states in benefits received were all in the West." See Leonard Arrington, "The New Deal in the West: A Preliminary Statistical Inquiry," *Pacific Historical Review* 38 (1969): 311.

A Bibliographical Note

Sources for a study of the New Deal in the West are almost boundless; besides the federal government, every western state generated a host of documentary material. Since my manuscript is at best suggestive and interpretative and since my focus is on New Deal programs and their impact in the West, I have been selective in using source materials and have not hesitated whenever possible to utilize available secondary materials. The bulk of the research is based, however, upon two general sources: the vast periodical literature generated by public agencies and professional organizations of all kinds during the 1930s, and manuscript collections available in the Franklin D. Roosevelt Library at Hyde Park and in the Manuscript Division of the Library of Congress. Since I have extensively documented all the preceding chapters, I will comment here in a general way on the sources and not precisely note all the items cited in the footnotes.

First as to manuscript materials. Obviously the most important collection is that of the dominant figure in the New Deal, President Franklin D. Roosevelt. It is a voluminous collection and I dipped into it at many points for material on political developments in the western states, for information about the several western trips the President made, and for details about various programs under way in the West. A good portion of the material in the last category, however, is easily available in published form in an invaluable two-volume collection compiled and edited by Edgar B. Nixon, titled *Franklin D. Roosevelt and Conservation 1911–1945* (Hyde Park, N.Y.: Franklin D. Roosevelt Library, 1957). Other published sources that eased my way through the Roosevelt material are Samuel I. Rosenman, ed., *The Public Papers and Addresses of Franklin D. Roosevelt*, volumes 2 through 9 (New York: Random House, 1938, and Macmillan Co., 1941) and the two volumes edited by Elliott Roosevelt, *F.D.R.: His Personal Letters, 1928–1945* (New York: Duell, Sloan & Pearce, 1950). In addition, at the Franklin D. Roosevelt Library I dipped into the papers of Eleanor Roosevelt to read files of her daily newspaper column, "My Day." I also examined the Lorena Hickok papers; supplemented with those also available in the Harry Hopkins papers, her 1933–34 reports of her travels in the West commented on conditions pertaining primarily to relief and unemployment. These reports comprise the material presented in chapter 2. They are now available in Richard Lowitt and Maurine Beasley, eds., *One Third of a Nation: Lorena Hickok Reports on the Great Depression* (Urbana: University of Illinois Press, 1981).

At Hyde Park I also found valuable material in the papers (including his famous diary) of Henry L. Morgenthau, Jr., and in those of Elbert D. Thomas, United States Senator from Utah. Both collections yielded significant information pertaining to silver policy. John M. Blum, *From The Morgenthau Diaries: Years of Crisis, 1928–1938* (Boston: Houghton Mifflin, 1959) is far more than a selective editing of portions of the diary. Blum's discussion of silver policy is most perceptive. His concern, however, is with its broad ramifications; mine was with its western impact. The Morris L. Cooke papers contain Cooke's files on "The Mississippi Valley Committee" and other materials about conditions prevailing on the Great Plains. The biography by Kenneth E. Trombley, *The*

Life and Times of a Happy Liberal (New York: Harper & Bros., 1954) contains supplementary information about Cooke's role.

In the Manuscript Division of the Library of Congress I made extensive use of the papers of Harold L. Ickes. Along with the Franklin Roosevelt papers, it was the most important collection I consulted containing materials pertaining to most of the themes examined in this volume: land use, water resources, petroleum policy, forestry and national parks as well as Indian affairs. Though they were heavily abridged, I made extensive use of all three volumes of the published version of his diary, Harold L. Ickes, ed., *The Secret Diary of Harold L. Ickes* (New York: Simon & Schuster, 1953–54). The papers of Michael W. Straus, who later became Commissioner of Reclamation, were helpful for the New Deal years. Straus was close to Ickes and drafted some of his speeches. The Raymond Clapper papers yielded interesting bits of information. Clapper collected all sorts of clippings and press releases for possible use in his widely syndicated newspaper column. Equally valuable were the Irving Brant papers. Brant was most interested in conservation and played a significant role in the establishment of the two national parks created in the West during the New Deal.

In addition, the James A. Farley papers contained penetrating insights into politics in the West during his tenure as chairman of the Democratic National Committee. The papers of Charles L. McNary, Bronson Cutting, William G. McAdoo, and Robert M. LaFollette, Jr., provided some information about forest management, water power, Indian affairs, as well as politics and labor policies in the 1930s; those of William E. Borah and Key Pittman were more valuable in providing information on numerous western themes pertaining to reclamation projects, including Boulder Dam, agriculture, silver policy and Indian affairs, among others.

During a hurried visit to the Nebraska State Historical Society in Lincoln, by accident I discovered a surprising source: the Val Kuska Papers. Kuska was the chief agent of the Chicago, Burlington and Quincy Railroad in Nebraska. Over the years he collected an enormous amount of documentary and other materials pertaining to the West in the late nineteenth and twentieth centuries. With the aid of a guide prepared by Douglas Bakken in 1966, I was able to extract from the massive collection significant random items cited in this study.

Several contemporary periodicals and proceedings of scholarly organizations yielded valuable information on different topics pertaining to the New Deal in the West. While the specific articles and papers are cited in the footnotes, I mention the periodicals and proceedings in this essay because they could be of great value on a variety of topics and themes to readers researching in the New Deal period.

Cited in the footnotes of one or several chapters are articles from mass circulation periodicals: *Survey Graphic, The Literary Digest, Fortune, Current History;* from professional or more specialized journals: *Rural Sociology, Journal of Farm Economics, Journal of Land and Public Utility Economics, Plan Age, Sierra Club Bulletin;* from magazines published by bureaus or agencies housed primarily in either the Department of Agriculture or the Department of the Interior: *The Reclamation Era, Soil Conservation, Extension Service Review, The Agricultural Situation, The Grazing Bulletin, Monthly Labor Review, Land Policy Review.*

Also cited with a degree of frequency are government documents, most notably pamphlet publications of the United States Department of Agriculture and less frequently from *The Congressional Record,* committee hearings, and yearbooks of the National Park Service and the Department of Agriculture. Some of the research monographs prepared for the Works Progress Administration contain material pertaining to conditions in the West and were quite useful. Specific reports of various committees such as the *Mississippi Valley Committee* and those pertaining to conditions on the Great Plains and the famous 1936 report on *The Western Range* are discussed in the text and cited in the footnotes.

In addition, the annual proceedings of several organizations contained papers, reports, or articles that touched upon various aspects of the New Deal in the West and are cited with some frequency in the footnotes of various chapters. Harlean James edited the *American Civic Annual* which in 1935 became the *American Planning and Civic Annual*. *The Proceedings of the Pacific Northwest Regional Planning Conference* contained a wealth of information. The first conference was held in Portland in 1934. Thereafter the conference was held in different cities throughout the region. Of equal value on a larger scale were the *Proceedings of the Western Farm Economic Association* which met annually on a different campus throughout the decade of the 1930s. *The Proceedings of the National Council of Social Work* and *Social Work Year Books* occasionally contained remarks on western topics, such as Indian affairs and migratory labor.

Another primary source of keen insights and useful information was travel literature. Most valuable was the account by Anna Louise Strong, *My Native Land* (New York: Viking Press, 1940). She traveled in the West and was particularly interested in New Deal activities. James Rorty, *Where Life is Better: An Unsentimental American Journey* (New York: Reynal & Hitchcock, 1936) was more critical in his evaluations than Strong though his comments on developments in the West are limited. Carleton Beals, *American Earth* (Philadelphia. J. B. Lippincott Co., 1939) contains interesting material on the living conditions of migratory families in California.

Not quite a travel account, Katherine Glover, *America Begins Again* (New York: McGraw-Hill, 1939) is a study based primarily on government documents; it surveys conservation work throughout the nation. Jay Franklin, *Remaking America* (Boston: Houghton Mifflin, 1942) based largely on interviews with government officials in effect does the same thing. Both volumes discuss developments in the West.

In considering published books and articles comprising chiefly but not exclusively secondary sources, the third prop upon which this study is based—the other two being manuscript materials and contemporary periodical literature—I need mention here only items that are cited usually more than once.

In examining the role of Western politicians in helping secure the nomination and subsequent election of Roosevelt in 1932, I relied primarily upon standard, easily available, books. James A. Farley, *Behind the Ballots: The Personal History of a Politician* (New York: Harcourt, Brace & Co., 1938) and Arthur F. Mullen, *Western Democrat* (New York: Wilfred Funk, Inc., 1940) are accounts by Roosevelt's campaign manager and floor leader at the Chicago Convention. Equally useful were Elliot A. Rosen, *Hoover, Roosevelt and the Brains Trust* (New York: Columbia University Press, 1977) and Fred L. Israel, *Nevada's Key Pittman* (Lincoln: University of Nebraska Press, 1963). Richard Oulahan, *The Man Who . . . The Story of the 1932 Democratic National Convention* (New York: Dial Press, 1971) is a carefully researched secondary account, while Raymond Moley, *After Seven Years* (New York: Harper &

Bros., 1939) presents the views of a disillusioned member of the Brains Trust. For the 1932 campaign in the West my chief sources were Frank Freidel, *Franklin D. Roosevelt, The Triumph* (Boston: Little, Brown & Co., 1956) and Richard Lowitt, *George W. Norris: The Persistance of a Progressive 1913–1933* (Urbana: University of Illinois Press, 1971).

Literature on the Dust Bowl is already extensive and growing. Initial interest was evident in the contemporary account by Paul Sears, *Deserts on the March* (Norman: University of Oklahoma Press, 1935). Recent studies with different viewpoints that are elaborated upon in the footnotes to Chapter 3 are Paul Bonnifield, *The Dust Bowl* (Albuquerque: University of New Mexico Press, 1979), Donald Worster, *Dust Bowl* (New York: Oxford University Press, 1979) and R. Douglas Hurt, *The Dust Bowl* (Chicago: Nelson Hall, 1981).

A dramatic response of the New Deal to the situation on the Great Plains is definitively examined in Wilmon H. Droze, *Trees, Prairies and People: A History of Tree Planting in the Plains States.* (Denton: Texas Woman's University Press, 1977). Roger Lambert examined another response in "The Drought Cattle Purchase, 1934–1935; Problems and Complaints," *Agricultural History,* 45 (1971) and "Drought Relief for Cattlemen: The Emergency Purchase Program of 1934–35," *Panhandle-Plains Historical Review,* 45 (1972). An account of how one farmer coped in the 1930s is provided in Lawrence Svobida, *An Empire of Dust* (Caldwell, Ida.: Caxton Printers, 1940).

Creative responses by film makers and photographers to conditions on the Great Plains in particular and to the West in general can be found in Robert L. Snyder, *Pare Lorentz and the Documentary Film* (Norman: University of Oklahoma Press, 1968); Richard Dyer MacCann, *The People's Films* (New York: Hastings House, 1973); Milton Meltzer, *Dorothea Lange* (New York: Farar, Straus & Giroux, 1978); and a contemporary account by Paul S. Taylor and Dorothea Lange, *An American Exodus* (New York: Reynal & Hitchcock, 1939).

R. Burnell Held and Marion Clawson, *Soil Conservation in Perspective* (Baltimore: Johns Hopkins University Press, 1965) provides a good general introduction. A contemporary account by Hugh Hammond Bennett, "Soil Erosion and its Preservation," is available in A. E. Parkins and J. R. Whitaker, eds., *Our Natural Resources and Their Conservation* (New York: J. Wiley & Sons, 1936). Jean Christie, "New Deal Resources Planning: The Proposals of Morris L. Cooke," *Agricultural History* 53 (1979) examines the views of another leading conservationist, while Mary W. M. Hargreaves, "Land Use Planning in Response to Drought: The Experience of the Thirties," *Agricultural History* 50 (1976) focuses on the Great Plains and the concerns of planners.

E. Louise Peffer, *The Closing of the Public Domain: Disposal and Reservation Policies, 1900–1950* (Stanford, Calif.: Stanford University Press, 1951) is the standard account. Wesley Carr Calef, *Private Grazing and Public Lands* (Chicago: University of Chicago Press, 1960) and William Voigt, Jr., *Public Grazing Lands* (New Brunswick, N.J.: Rutgers University Press, 1976) provide more recent surveys, while Phillip O. Foss in a classic study, *Politics and Grass* (Seattle: University of Washington Press, 1960) examines the administration of the Taylor Grazing Act, approved in 1934 and amended the following year on into the 1950s.

Forestry conditions, most notably in the West, are discussed in Rodney C. Loehr, ed., *Forest for the Future: The Story of Sustained Yield as Told in the*

Diaries and Papers of David T. Mason, 1907–1950 (St. Paul: Minnesota Historical Society, 1952), more generally in David Cushman Coyle, *Conservation* (New Brunswick, N.J.: Rutgers University Press, 1957) and Harold K. Steen, *The U.S. Forest Service: A History* (Seattle: University of Washington Press, 1976). Conditions in the Pacific Northwest pertaining to forestry and other public concerns during the New Deal and most particularly in the 1940s are amply discussed in Charles McKinley's indispensable study, *Uncle Sam in the Pacific Northwest* (Berkeley and Los Angeles: University of California Press, 1952). Forestry in the Northwest is also examined in Elmo Richardson, *BLM's Billion Dollar Checkerboard: Managing the O & C Lands* (Washington, D.C.: Government Printing Office, 1980).

There are several important secondary studies examining the problem of water in the West. An overview is provided by Donald C. Swain, "The Bureau of Reclamation and the New Deal, 1933–1940," *Pacific Northwest Quarterly* 61 (1970). Beverly Bowen Moeller, *Phil Swing and Boulder Dam* (Berkeley and Los Angeles: University of California Press, 1971) provides an excellent account of the Boulder Dam controversy which was largely resolved before the advent of the New Deal. Norris Hundley, *Water and the West: The Colorado River Compact and the Politics of Water in the American West* (Berkeley and Los Angeles: University of California Press, 1975) discusses the same theme within a much broader context.

An excellent state study, one of the best for any western state, that touches among other things on water development is James F. Wickens, *Colorado in the Great Depression* (New York: Garland Publishing, Inc., 1979), while Oliver Knight and Donald B. Cole specifically examine transmountain water diversion: Oliver Knight, "Correcting Nature's Error: The Colorado Big Thompson Project," *Agricultural History* 30 (1956) and Donald B. Cole, "Transmountain Water Diversion in Colorado," *The Colorado Magazine* 25 (1948). Cole places the project within a historical context extending back into the nineteenth century.

Other projects in western states are examined in Richard Lowitt, *George W. Norris: The Triumph of a Progressive, 1933–1944* (Urbana: University of Illinois Press, 1978). In the chapters on Nebraska, the WPA-funded Tri-county and other water-power projects are discussed. For Utah projects see Leonard J. Arrington and Lowell Ditmer, "Reclamation in Three Layers: The Ogden River Project, 1934–1965," *Pacific Historical Review* 35 (1966) and Kenneth W. Baldridge, "Reclamation Work of the Civilian Conservation Corps, 1933–1942," *Utah Historical Quarterly* 39 (1971). Roy E. Huffman, *Irrigation Development and Public Water Policy* (New York: Ronald Press Co., 1953) covers developments throughout the West and does not specifically concern itself with the New Deal years.

Beet sugar was a crop raised on lands irrigated by several western water projects. Joshua Bernhardt, *The Sugar Industry and the Federal Government* (Washington, D.C.: Sugar Statistics Service, 1948) is a basic study by the chief of the sugar section of the Agricultural Adjustment Administration and successor organizations. Part III examines "The Sugar Programs of The Roosevelt Administration." John E. Dalton's *Sugar: A Case Study of Governmental Control* (New York: Macmillan Co., 1937) argues that the industry was prospering primarily because of government assistance. Kent Hendrickson, "The Sugar-Beet Laborer and the Federal Government: An Episode in the History of the Great Plains in the 1930s," *Great Plains Journal* 3 (1964) examines the same theme from a different perspective.

James Presley, *A Saga of Wealth: The Rise of the Texas Oilmen* (New York: G. P. Putnam's Sons, 1978) is a good introductory volume which also was of value in its discussion of "Hot Oil." Basic to my understanding of the petroleum industry during the New Deal are two essays by Linda J. Lear, "Harold Ickes and the Oil Crisis of the First Hundred Days," *Mid-America* 63 (1981) and "The Politics of Oil: Harold L. Ickes and the Struggle for Federal Regulation, 1933–1935," a paper presented at a session of the 1980 meeting of the American Historical Association. Joe S. Bain, *The Economics of The Pacific Coast Petroleum Industry: Part II* (Berkeley and Los Angeles: University of California Press, 1945) clarified the differences between the situation in California and elsewhere in the West during the New Deal. Samuel B. Pettingill, *Hot Oil* (New York: Economic Forum Co., 1936) is a primary documentary source by an Indiana Congressman intimately involved with legislative matters affecting the petroleum industry.

John A. Brennan, *Silver and The First New Deal* (Reno: University of Nevada Press, 1969), focuses more on national policy than with conditions in the West. An essay that does is David D. Webb, "The Thomas Amendment: A Rural Oklahoma Response To The Great Depression," in Donald E. Green, ed., *Rural Oklahoma* (Oklahoma City: Oklahoma Historical Society, 1977).

The literature on the Indian New Deal is vast and growing rapidly. I found the following of help in my examination of Indian affairs: Kenneth R. Philp, *John Collier's Crusade for Indian Reform, 1920–1954* (Tucson: University of Arizona Press, 1977); John S. Painter, "Congressional Conservatism and Federal Indian Policy, 1928–50," a paper presented at the 1981 meeting of the Organization of American Historians; Margaret Connell Szasz, *Education and the American Indian: The Road to Self-Determination Since 1928* (Albuquerque: University of New Mexico Press, 1974) and Donald L. Parman, "The Indian and the Civilian Conservation Corps," *Pacific Historical Review* 40 (1971).

The situation among Oklahoma Indians is examined in Peter M. Wright, "John Collier and the Oklahoma Indian Welfare Act of 1936," *Chronicles of Oklahoma* 50 (1972) and B. T. Quinten, "Oklahoma Tribes, the Great Depression and the Indian Bureau," *Mid-America* 49 (1967). For the situation among the Navajo, the largest tribe in the nation, the basic study is Donald L. Parman, *The Navajos and the New Deal* (New Haven, Conn.: Yale University Press, 1976). I gained further insights from George Boyce, *When Navajos Had Too Many Sheep: the 1940's* (San Francisco: Indian Historical Press, 1974), Peter Iverson, *The Navajo Nation* (Westport, Conn.: Greenwood Press, 1981), and from an unpublished paper by Jack August, "The Progressive Impulse and the Navajo Soil Conservation Service."

Graham D. Taylor, *The New Deal and American Indian Tribalism: The Administration of the Indian Reorganization Act, 1934–45* (Lincoln: University of Nebraska Press, 1980) is an important monograph utilizing a case-study approach. Taylor concludes that tribal organization was largely a failure. A similar conclusion from another perspective is provided by Benay Blend, "The American Indian Federation and the Indian New Deal," an unpublished paper presented at a session of the Southwestern Social Science Association meeting in 1979.

The role of anthropologists is examined by Scudder McKeel, "An Appraisal of the Indian Reorganization Act," *American Anthropologist* 46 (1944). McKeel, a distinguished anthropologist served in the Indian New Deal. A more detached view is provided by Graham D. Taylor, "Anthropologists, Reformers and the Indian New Deal," *Prologue* 7 (1975).

Shifting to the Pacific Northwest, the emergency wheat program affecting the region is examined in Joseph S. Davis, *Wheat and the AAA* (Washington, D.C.: The Brookings Institution, 1935) and briefly explained by Henry A. Wallace in *New Frontiers* (New York: Reynal & Hitchcock, 1934). Migration into the region is discussed in John Blanchard, *Caravans To The Northwest* (Boston: Houghton Mifflin, 1940), a volume prepared under the auspices of the Northwest Regional Council and designed to explain the virtues of the region to prospective settlers. The fight for a national park in the Northwest is carefully examined in Elmo R. Richardson, "Olympic National Park: Twenty Years of Controversy," *Forest History* 12 (1968), while Theodore W. Cart, " 'New Deal' for Wildlife: A Perspective on Federal Conservation Policy, 1933–1940," *Pacific Northwest Quarterly* 63 (1972) examines an interesting and neglected aspect of the New Deal. David Lendt, *Ding: The Life of Jay Norwood Darling* (Ames: Iowa State University Press, 1979) devotes attention to Darling's brief career as Chief of the Biological Survey during the New Deal. Ira N. Gabrielson, Darling's successor surveyed the problem within the context of his own experience in *Wildlife Conservation* (New York: Macmillan Co., 1959).

Developments on the Columbia River concerning fishermen are discussed in Anthony Netboy, *Salmon of the Pacific Northwest* (Portland, Ore.: Binfords & Mort, 1958). Power politics affecting the river basin are examined in Philip J. Funigiello, *Toward A National Power Policy: The New Deal and the Electric Utility Industry, 1933–1941* (Pittsburgh: University of Pittsburgh Press, 1974) and more directly in "The Bonneville Power Administration and the New Deal," *Prologue* 5 (1973). William E. Leuchtenburg, "Roosevelt, Norris and the 'Seven Little TVA's'," *Journal of Politics* 14 (1952) examines a national proposal that directly concerned developments on the Columbia River. Focusing on the region is Herman C. Voeltz, "Genesis and Development of a Regional Power Agency in the Pacific Northwest, 1933–1943," *Pacific Northwest Quarterly* 53 (1962).

Of all the western states, California (with the possible exception of Texas) has generated a tremendous historical literature. When confined to the twentieth century, California surpasses Texas. Volumes examining the decade of the 1930s, while abundant, do not always examine in a direct and extended way the impact of the New Deal on the Golden State. Robert E. Burke, *Olson's New Deal for California* (Berkeley and Los Angeles: University of California Press, 1953) was particularly helpful because it helped reaffirm my insight that the New Deal, if not a failure, was largely ineffective in California. Another indication was provided by Bonnie Fox Schwartz, "Social Workers and New Deal Politicians in Conflict: California's Branion-Williams Case, 1933–1934," *Pacific Historical Review* 42 (1953).

The plight of agricultural workers has been examined in numerous volumes. Among the better studies which discuss the tense situations that developed in the 1930s are Cary McWilliams, *Factories in the Field* (Boston: Little, Brown & Co., 1939) a contemporary account; Clarke Chambers, *California Farm Organizations* (Berkeley and Los Angeles: University of California Press, 1952); Walter J. Stein, *California and the Dust Bowl Migration* (Westport, Conn.: Greenwood Press, 1973); and Cletus E. Daniel, *Bitter Harvest: A History of California Farm Workers, 1870–1941* (Ithaca, N.Y.: Cornell University Press, 1981). Abraham Hoffman, *Unwanted Mexican Americans in the Great*

Depression (Tucson: University of Arizona Press, 1974) explores the plight of over 400,000 people who were deported from Southern California as their labor was no longer needed owing to the arrival of migratory families from the Dust Bowl and other depressed agricultural areas. D. H. Dinwoodie, "Deportation: The Immigration Service and The Chicano Labor Movement in The 1930's," *New Mexico Historical Review* 52 (1977) complements Hoffman's study. Jerold S. Auerbach, *Labor and Liberty: The LaFollette Committee and the New Deal* (Indianapolis: Bobbs-Merrill Co., 1966) reviews the committee's examination late in the New Deal of the farm labor situation in California, while Laurence Hewes, *Boxcar In The Sand* (New York: Alfred A. Knopf, 1957) reflects a different perspective. Hewes was Farm Security Administrator for Region 9, including California, beginning in 1939, the year the LaFollette Committee began its work in the state. John Steinbeck, "Their Blood is Strong," published as a pamphlet in 1938 and reprinted in Warren French, ed., *A Companion to "The Grapes of Wrath"* (New York: Viking Press, 1963) is an excellent incisive essay on migratory labor that appeared a year before the author's famous novel.

Published accounts of water developments in California in the 1930s usually focus on the Central Valley Project which got underway during the New Deal years. Clayton R. Koppes, "Public Water, Private Land: Origins of the Acreage Limitation Controversy, 1933–1953," *Pacific Historical Review* 47 (1978) and Paul S. Taylor, "Central Valley Project: Water and Land," *Western Political Quarterly* 2 (1949) are excellent studies, basic to an understanding of the controversies that engulfed this remarkable project. Most of their emphasis is on the years beyond the New Deal. Robert de Roos, *The Thirsty Land: The Story of the Central Valley Project* (Stanford, Calif.: Stanford University Press, 1948) is a more general account, one that provides a basic introduction to the project and its problems.

Index